SPEECH AND PERFORMANCE IN SHAKESPEARE'S SONNETS AND PLAYS

David Schalkwyk offers a sustained reading of Shakespeare's sonnets in relation to his plays. He argues that the language of the sonnets is primarily performative rather than descriptive, and bases this distinction on the philosophy of Ludwig Wittgenstein and J. L. Austin. In a wide-ranging analysis of both the 1609 quarto of Shakespeare's sonnets and the Petrarchan discourses in a selection of plays, Schalkwyk addresses such issues as embodiment and silencing, interiority and theatricality, inequalities of power, status, gender and desire, both in the published poems and on the stage and in the context of the early modern period. In a provocative discussion of the question of proper names and naming events in the sonnets and plays, the book seeks to reopen the question of the autobiographical nature of Shakespeare's sonnets.

DAVID SCHALKWYK is Associate Professor and Head of the Department of English Language and Literature at the University of Cape Town. He has published on Shakespeare, literary theory, philosophy and South African literature in *Shakespeare Quarterly, English Literary Renaissance,* the *Journal of Aesthetics and Art Criticism, Pretexts, Linguistic Sciences, Textus* and the *Journal of Literary Studies.*

D1427314

SPEECH AND PERFORMANCE IN SHAKESPEARE'S SONNETS AND PLAYS

DAVID SCHALKWYK

CAMBRIDGE
UNIVERSITY PRESS

CAMBRIDGE UNIVERSITY PRESS
Cambridge, New York, Melbourne, Madrid, Cape Town, Singapore, São Paulo

Cambridge University Press
The Edinburgh Building, Cambridge CB2 8RU, UK

Published in the United States of America by Cambridge University Press, New York

www.cambridge.org
Information on this title: www.cambridge.org/9780521811156

First published 2002
This digitally printed version 2007

A catalogue record for this publication is available from the British Library

ISBN 978-0-521-81115-6 hardback
ISBN 978-0-521-03633-7 paperback

To Christina, Andrew and James

Contents

Acknowledgements   *page* viii

Introduction: the sonnets   1

1   Performatives: the sonnets, *Antony and Cleopatra* and
    As You Like It   29

2   Embodiment: the sonnets, *Love's Labour's Lost*, *Romeo and
    Juliet* and *Twelfth Night*   59

3   Interiority: the sonnets, *Hamlet* and *King Lear*   102

4   Names: the sonnets, *Romeo and Juliet*, *Troilus and
    Cressida* and *Othello*   150

5   Transformations: the sonnets and *All's Well that Ends Well*   198

    Conclusion   238

Bibliography   243
Index   253

Acknowledgements

This book began as an idea sparked by a paper given by John Roe. The germ of that idea was nurtured in the seminars on Shakespeare's sonnets at the meetings of the Shakespeare Association of America in Albuquerque in 1994 and the World Shakespeare Congress in Los Angeles in 1996, and took root during my tenure as a Solmsen Research Fellow at the Humanities Institute of the University of Wisconsin in Madison, in 1999. I owe more than I can express to Lars Engle and Heather Dubrow, who ran the respective seminars, for their help, encouragement and acute criticism throughout the project. Lars got me to take the sonnets seriously; Heather enabled me to pursue that seriousness in the ideal collegial environment of the Humanities Institute in Madison. Both have been exceptionally generous colleagues and friends.

More generally, I wish to thank Jacques Berthoud, under whose guidance I first began to explore the relevance of Wittgenstein to literature. I have benefited in equal measure from his boundless generosity and toughness of mind over the past twenty years. I owe a great deal of personal and intellectual debt for their selfless engagement and readiness to read parts of the manuscript to Jacques Lezra, Lesley Marx, Tony Parr and Susanne Wofford. Anston Bosman, Jonathan Crewe, John Higgins, Stephen Greenblatt, Randy McCloud, the late Nick Visser and Robert Weimann all contributed to the formation of this project through their conversation and comments. Sarah Stanton of Cambridge University Press has offered patient guidance and advice, and I owe the two Press readers a great deal of thanks for their acute and helpful comments on the original typescript.

An earlier version of chapter 1 appeared in *Shakespeare Quarterly* (1998), a version of chapter 2 in *Shakespeare Quarterly* (1994), and some paragraphs from the introduction in *Shakespeare Quarterly* (1999).

The research for this book was generously supported by a grant from the National Research Foundation of South Africa. I also wish to thank the University of Cape Town and my colleagues in the English Department for providing the collegial support that made this project possible. Most important is the generosity, friendship and encouragement that I received from the members of the Institute for Research in the Humanities at the University of Wisconsin, in Madison. My special thanks go to the director, Paul Boyer, who made our trip to Madison a voyage of discovery and delight. Christina, Andrew and James know, I hope, how much of this book is theirs.

Note

The text of Shakespeare's sonnets used in this book is the facsimile of the 1609 Quarto reproduced in *Shakespeare's Sonnets*, ed. Stephen Booth (New Haven, CT and London: Yale University Press, 1978). Quotations from the plays are from *The Oxford Shakespeare*, ed. Stanley Wells and Gary Taylor (Oxford: Oxford University Press, 1987).

Introduction: the sonnets

Why are there proper names in Shakespeare's dramatic works, but none in Shakespeare's sonnets? What roles do proper names (or the absence of proper names) play in these poems, and how are such roles related to the varieties of language used in the sonnets and Shakespeare's plays? Are the sonnets primarily concerned with description, or is their language chiefly performative? And how are these questions about language, proper names and genre conceptually related to the life of the author and the historical conditions under which the texts were produced?

These questions provide a framework for the analysis of Shakespeare's sonnets in this book, which takes as the central condition of the sonnets the fact that their author was also the period's foremost dramatist.[1] The sonnets are deeply informed by the player-poet's peculiar self-consciousness about his lowly social status. Despite the added sense of personal inadequacy and social taint that such self-consciousness about his profession brings to the poet's Petrarchan moments, as player-dramatist he is, nevertheless, able to bring to the poet's task an extraordinarily developed sense of language as a *performative* force. By focusing on such performative dimensions I seek to take forward an approach to language that began in the philosophical writings of Ludwig Wittgenstein and John Austin. It enjoyed some status within literary criticism and theory in the 1970s and 1980s, but has lately received less attention in the era of high historicism.[2] Austin's status within literary theory never recovered

---

[1] This is not to claim that there were no other dramatists who were also substantial poets. Marston, Chapman and, especially, Jonson, were both poets and dramatists, but none of them wrote substantial sonnet sequences, nor is their poetry informed by a self-consciousness of the common player's lowly social position.

[2] See Mary Louise Pratt, *Towards a Speech-Act Theory of Literary Discourse* (Bloomington, IN: Indiana University Press, 1977). For a pioneering application of these two philosophers' work to Shakespeare, see Keir Elam, *Shakespeare's Universe of Discourse: Language Games in the Comedies* (Cambridge: Cambridge University Press, 1984). A very fine, recent post-speech-act study of the rhetoric of social exchange in early modern England is Lynne Magnusson's *Shakespeare and Social*

from the polemic between Jacques Derrida and John Searle,[3] and the apparently formalist focus of speech-act theory has been overlooked by Cultural Materialist and New Historicist concerns with Foucauldian notions of discourse and power. But Wittgenstein and Austin offer a powerful picture of the multifarious ways in which language works as a form of action in the world: negotiating, constituting and informing social and personal relationships in the situations of its actual use.[4] Until Lynne Magnusson's path-breaking book, *Shakespeare and Social Dialogue*, little close attention had been paid to the intricate relationship between dialogical interaction and social context. In place of the current bifurcation of criticism into 'formalist' analysis of language on the one hand, and 'historicist' or 'materialist' interest in culture and politics on the other, Magnusson shows that we need a philosophical framework that is alive to the *utterance* in all its situated richness, rather than the sentence or the sign or the code as product of an overarching system of language, discourse or ideology. Such a framework will enable the fullest investigation of both the linguistic textures and forces of literary texts and the actions upon and within them of society, politics and history.

The aim of this book is thus to link close linguistic analysis with questions of power and society. By treating Shakespeare's sonnets as the product of a dramatist who was himself embroiled in a social struggle for acceptance and status, I hope to make palpable their shape and force as situated forms of social action. Plainly, Shakespeare's dramatic art made possible the extraordinary uses of language in the sonnets. But the plays themselves also render more palpable circumstances of address that escape inclusion within the restricted body of the sonnet. The concrete situation of address that is the condition of the Petrarchan sonnet is clearest in the plays in which sonnets are represented, not as disembodied texts, but as a performative discourse in which embodied characters seek to transform their circumstances and relationships. Each of the plays through which the sonnets are discussed in the following pages – *As You Like It, Antony and Cleopatra, Love's Labour's Lost, Twelfth Night, Hamlet, King*

Dialogue: Dramatic Language and Elizabethan Letters (Cambridge: Cambridge University Press, 1999). Magnusson's book appeared after I had completed most of the present work, so I have been unable to incorporate its many insights into the body of my text. My book is much the poorer for this omission.

3 See Jacques Derrida, *Limited Inc*, ed. Gerald Graff (Evanston: IL: Northwestern University Press, 1988) and John R. Searle, 'Reiterating the Differences: A Reply to Derrida', *Glyph* 2 (1977), 198–208 (201).

4 Ludwig Wittgenstein, *Philosophical Investigations*, trans. G. E. M. Anscombe (Oxford: Blackwell, 1953) and J. L. Austin, *How To Do Things With Words* (Oxford and New York: Oxford University Press, 1975).

Lear, *Romeo and Juliet*, *Troilus and Cressida*, *Othello* and *All's Well that Ends Well* – either represents the sonnet as a form of social action or embodies forms of verbal practice that approximate key moments in the 1609 Quarto. The sonnets as 'embodied texts' are thus closely imbricated, in both sociological and aesthetic terms, with their poet's work in the newly commodified space of the theatre.

The notion of an embodied text has recently been used by Douglas Bruster to argue that the period during which the sonnets were written, and in which Shakespeare became increasingly well known through his appearance in the new, professionalised theatre, saw a dramatic increase in the connections between author and text.[5] Shakespeare's sonnets display a consistent awareness of the ways in which 'every word doth almost tell my name' (sonnet 76), not merely in stylistic but also in social terms. His presence, even attenuated through writing, is thought to disgrace the young man of birth. The very 'public space' in which 'writers publicized hitherto private bodies and identities, including their own' (Bruster, 'Structural Transformation', 65) contaminates those of high birth who are brought into its ambit as more than aloof spectators, at the same time as it transforms the very conditions of traditional authority.[6] Some have argued that the familiarity of the sonnets precludes the possibility of an aristocratic addressee or lover.[7] But this overlooks the way in which familiarity alternates with extreme abjection and the power of the new public space, which was both shaped by and in turn shaped Shakespeare's 'publick manners' (sonnet 111), to transfigure relationships of authority and subjection.

If Shakespeare's sonnets may be said to be 'embodied' in Bruster's sense by the presence of their public poet in their 'every word', they are also embodied through the representation of similar sonnets in the plays themselves. Approaching Shakespeare's sonnets through the staged worlds of his plays enables one to interrogate two sets of critical assumptions. The embodiment of addressee, the sonneteer and the sonnet itself through the plays counters the recent tendency to dissolve

---

[5] Douglas Bruster, 'The Structural Transformation of Print in Late Elizabethan England', in *Print, Manuscript, & Performance: The Changing Relations of the Media in Early Modern England*, ed. Arthur F. Marotti and Michael D. Bristol (Columbus: Ohio State University Press, 2000), 49–89.

[6] See Robert Weimann, *Authority and Representation in Early Modern Discourse*, ed. David Hilman (Baltimore, MD: Johns Hopkins University Press, 1996) and *Author's Pen and Actor's Voice: Playing and Writing in Shakespeare's Theatre* (Cambridge: Cambridge University Press, 2000), for an extensive account of the transformation of authority through the dynamics of representation in both its political and mimetic senses.

[7] See especially, Joseph Pequigney, *Such Is My Love: A Study of Shakespeare's Sonnets* (Chicago: University of Chicago Press, 1985).

the corporeality of the referent in a solution of textuality and subjectivity, either through a formalist concentration on their verbal or lyrical complexity, or through a more theoretical interest in their forging a new poetic subjectivity.[8] Such embodiment also questions the assumption that the primary work of the sonnet in general, and Shakespeare's sonnets in particular, is to praise their subjects through description. I shall focus on the performative, rather than the descriptive, nature of their language; that is to say, on the ways in which they seek to be transformative rather than merely denotative. This will mean reopening the question of the 'dramatic' nature of the sonnets: taking seriously the fact that the 1609 Quarto is the only major body of sonnets in early Modern England written by a dramatist, and exploring the interaction of the sonnet and the theatre on a variety of sociological and aesthetic levels.[9]

To take into account the fact that the 1609 Quarto was the only body of sonnets written by a dramatist opens a wider passage between the poems and the plays via the rootedness of their common author in a particular community at a particular time. Such a passage will naturally reveal their differences, among the most obvious being the fact that the sonnets, unlike the plays, are written in an autobiographical mode. This raises the question of names and pronouns, and the logical role that they play in the two genres. I will argue that the grammatical or logical

---

[8] These two critical positions are exemplified by two of the most influential recent critics of the sonnets: Stephen Booth and Joel Fineman. That they continue to exert an inordinate degree of influence is shown by the fact that they continue to be the two most frequently cited critics in the most recent collection of essays on the sonnets. See James Schiffer (ed.), *Shakespeare's Sonnets: Critical Essays* (New York: Garland, 1999), 52.

[9] For early interest in their dramatic nature see G. K. Hunter, 'The Dramatic Technique of Shakespeare's Sonnets', *Essays in Criticism*, 3 (1953), 152–64 (161); Giorgio Melchiori, *Shakespeare's Dramatic Meditations: An Experiment in Criticism* (Oxford: Clarendon Press, 1976), 15. See also, Anton M. Pirkhoffer, 'The Beauty of Truth: The Dramatic Character of Shakespeare's Sonnets', in *New Essays on Shakespeare's Sonnets*, ed. Hilton Landry (New York: AMS Press, 1976), 109–28; and David Parker, 'Verbal Moods in Shakespeare's Sonnets', *Modern Language Quarterly*, 30.3 (September 1969), 331–9. Such criticism has been superseded by investigations of their 'inner language' (Ann Ferry, *The 'Inward' Language: Sonnets of Wyatt, Sidney, Shakespeare, and Donne* (Chicago: University of Chicago Press, 1983)); the exploration of their 'speaker's psyche' (Heather Dubrow, *Captive Victors: Shakespeare's Narrative Poems and Sonnets* (Ithaca, NY and London: Cornell University Press, 1987), 212); their novel construction of poetic subjectivity (Joel Fineman, *Shakespeare's Perjured Eye: The Invention of Poetic Subjectivity in the Sonnets* (Berkeley, Los Angeles and London: University of California Press, 1986)); their formal, essentially *poetic* structure and richness (Stephen Booth, *An Essay on Shakespeare's Sonnets* (New Haven, CT and London: Yale University Press, 1969) and *Shakespeare's Sonnets*, ed. Stephen Booth (New Haven, CT: Yale University Press, 1978); and Helen Vendler, *The Art of Shakespeare's Sonnets* (Cambridge, MA: Harvard University Press, 1997)); or the social, sexual or ideological 'scandal' that they represent (Margareta de Grazia, 'The Scandal of Shakespeare's Sonnets', in *Shakespeare's Sonnets: Critical Essays*, ed. Schiffer, 89–112; Peter Stallybrass, 'Editing as Cultural Formation: The Sexing of Shakespeare's Sonnets', in *Shakespeare's Sonnets: Critical Essays*, ed. Schiffer 75–88, and Joseph Pequigney, *Such Is My Love*).

questions of proper names and pronouns, and the sociological condition of the player-poet in his relation to a well-born addressee, are closely related. Can the modes and conditions of address indicated by the preponderance of the second-person pronoun in Shakespeare's sonnets (by comparison with Sidney, Spenser, Daniel and Drayton)[10] be related to the peculiar interdependence of player and audience that informs Shakespeare's work in both genres? And how is this relationship complicated or illuminated when a sonnet's situation of address is represented on stage? How is the sense of the textual or 'inward' nature of the poems as lyrics complicated by reading them through the historical embodiment of sonnets in theatrical representations? C. L. Barber's suggestion that in Shakespeare's sonnets 'poetry is, in a special way, an action, something done for and to the beloved'[11] brings the poems closest to the primary means of Shakespeare's livelihood. It emphasises their concern with what Jacques Berthoud has explored as the 'dialogical interaction' of the plays.[12] The sonnets' performative language encompasses much more than the solitary mind of their lyric speaker or isolated reader: it arises out of the triangular relationship of addresser, addressee and the context or event of such action that is not merely a grammatical effect of language. It is a relationship embodied in particular lived circumstances, which Shakespeare's dramatic works frequently re-present in that fullness on the public stage.

However Shakespeare's plays and sonnets may be united or differentiated in poetic terms, they share a mutual investment in *interaction*: in provoking a response, and themselves responding to provocation, through the negotiation of relationships that are erotic, political, filial and ideological. They seek self-authorisation, justifying themselves in the 'eies of men' (sonnet 16). Whether we approach them sociologically or internally via the fiction of a poetic 'persona', the poet of the sonnets is clearly a *player*-poet. He suffers from the social and personal vulnerability of someone whose role as a poet is always informed by his position as actor and

---

[10] See Melchiori, *Shakespeare's Dramatic Meditations*, 15:

> The most notable variation in respect of the other collections remains...Shakespeare's use of the second person, which is almost as frequent as that of the first: 37.2 percent as against 40.3 percent, while in the other poems under consideration the highest percentage reached is 20 percent... This balance between *I* and *thou*, this direct exchange, this dialogue, is also an obvious demonstration of the dramatic and theatrical character of his [Shakespeare's] poetic genius, even when using the lyrical form.

[11] C. L. Barber, 'An Essay on the Sonnets', in *Elizabethan Poetry: Modern Essays in Criticism*, ed. Paul J. Alpers (New York: Oxford University Press, 1967), 299–320 (303).

[12] Jacques Berthoud, Introduction to *Titus Andronicus*, The New Penguin Shakespeare (Harmondsworth: Penguin, 2001).

playwright. At the same time, the sureness of his poetic art arises out of the practice of the theatre. He might consequently be said to be playing at being a poet proper in purely sociological, though not aesthetic, terms, pretending through the writing to the superior poetic and social status of a Sidney, a Greville or a Surrey.[13] That we now consider him the greatest poet of the age does not change the ways in which his poetry is informed by a sense of his own inferior social station – as indelible, by his own admission, as the stain upon the dyer's hand. Shakespeare's role as a man of the theatre thus conditions his sonnets in both a sociological and an aesthetic sense. They are the products of a powerful hand steeped in the aesthetic practice of the stage, but they are also marked by the perceived social inferiority of that practice.

Although it might seem obvious that Shakespeare's plays represent to the highest degree the 'interactive dialogue' by which 'individuals may be imagined to exist in society', the sonnets are no less embroiled in such forms of social interaction and dialogue (Berthoud, Introduction, *Titus Andronicus*, 22). Such dialogue represents the singularity of each speaking position and its place in a wider social context; but it does not reduce the one to the other. 'Insofar as they are the centre of their own lives,' Berthoud remarks, 'individuals belong to themselves; but insofar as they are members of a community, with its history, its institutions, and its social and cultural divisions, they belong to others' (22). Viewing these intensely individual poems through the glass of the plays enables us to see how the sonnets *enact*, 'at the moment of its operation' (22), the degree to which people belong both to themselves and to others. The voice that speaks in the sonnets is neither wholly 'solitary' nor entirely public. It is both the centre of a *singular* manifold of feelings, attitudes and passions, and at the same time continually displaced by its necessary acknowledgement of a world of others.

Reading Shakespeare's sonnets in the context of his plays renders more visible the circumstances that make speech acts intelligible and make possible the language of interiority. Such contexts of embodiment and address, often obscured in the case of the lyric, are inescapable on the stage. In chapter 2 I ask what happens to our reading of the sonnets when we take such embodiment seriously as the very condition, not only of the theatre, but also of the sonnet's address. To ask such a

---

[13] Paul Ramsey, *The Fickle Glass: A Study of Shakespeare's Sonnets* (New York: AMS Press, 1979), 33, reminds us of the actor-poet of the sonnets' intense feeling of insecurity and vulnerability before a greater poet's verse: 'the rival poet's sonnets are at once laudatory, even a little awe-struck, and satiric: a little mocking, but also more than a little frightened'.

question is to complicate the signified with the referent – in the form of embodied addressee and addresser and the actual circumstances of the address, including unequal social relations – and to leaven the concept of subjectivity with the public reality of an audience. It also reopens questions regarding the disembodying force of Petrarchism itself, and the asymmetrical nature of the voiced and the silenced in the poems.

In chapter 1 I explore most fully what it means to read the sonnets as a primarily performative art, using 'performative' in the technical sense instantiated by the philosophy of speech acts. In developing my argument I use as my foil the critical text that has had an unsurpassed impact in the field: Joel Fineman's *Shakespeare's Perjured Eye: The Invention of Poetic Subjectivity in the Sonnets.*[14] Channelled through the work of Lacan and Derrida, Fineman's thesis is deeply informed by a contrary, Saussurean picture of language. It depends upon the assumption that the tradition of sonnet writing, of which Shakespeare's sonnets are a belated and transformative part, is primarily concerned with description, with matching what the pen writes to what the eye sees through an 'idealizing language' that is essentially 'visionary' (*Shakespeare's Perjured Eye*, 11). To praise someone in this tradition is essentially to try to describe them. Thus Shakespeare's poems to the 'dark lady' are said to transform the specular descriptiveness of epideixis by discovering, before the fact, the neo-Saussurean principle that there is an essential and unbridgeable disjunction between language and the world: 'because they are a discourse of the tongue rather than of the eye, because they are "linguistic", Shakespeare's verbal words are, in comparison to the *imago*, essentially or ontologically at odds with what they speak about' (15). The self-reflexive recognition of this ontological disjunction constitutes the decisively modern poetic subjectivity that Fineman attributes to Shakespeare's sonnets. They invent a modern subjectivity by recognising what has always been ontologically true about language and its relation to (or rather disjunction from) any object in the world. My major argument against the Fineman thesis is that Shakespeare's sonnets offer very little description at all. They are not primarily concerned with presenting what Fineman calls the *imago*. It is natural to assume that the sonnets make good their promise to the young man to make him live in their lines by making his image outlast the hardiest of human monuments. How else, we may ask, can this promise

---

[14] Fineman's book remains the most referred-to text in a collection of mostly new essays published as late as 1997. See *Shakespeare's Sonnets: Critical Essays*, ed. Schiffer.

be made good, especially in the absence of the beloved's name? Without either name or image, what can survive?

A close examination of the first 126 sonnets, traditionally assumed to be addresses to the 'fair friend', reveals very little by way of portraiture. Do we know what the friend looked like? Well, we like to think we know: blond hair, blue eyes, young, beautiful. Rather than being a product of anything that Shakespeare actually *tells* us about him (see sonnet 144), such a portrait is the negative image of the 'women colloured il' (sonnet 144). We are certain that he is blond; but that is because the poems call him 'fair'. The two words are not synonymous. Rosaline, in *Love's Labour's Lost* is called 'fair', yet her eyes and hair are as 'raven black' as the dark beauty of the sonnets. Beatrice (*Much Ado About Nothing*), Cressida (*Troilus and Cressida*), Julia (*The Two Gentlemen of Verona*) and Hermia (*A Midsummer Night's Dream*) are also called 'fair', sometimes repeatedly and obsessively, and yet they variously fall short of the blonde ideal.[15] It is one of the well-known paradoxes of the sonnets that there is no natural synonymy between colouring and beauty or between physical fairness and spiritual light. So why do we assume that the 'fair friend' has blond hair? Do the poems tell us this; do they describe him as having blond hair? We assume too hastily that, because he is twinned with a woman 'colloured il', the young man cannot have dark hair. There is *literally* very little explicit portraiture in the sonnets to support this assumption.

The 1609 Quarto is curiously reticent about indulging in the Petrarchan blazon, despite its repeated invocation of the image of the beloved. Apart from the counter-discursive sonnet 130 ('My mistres eyes are nothing like the sun') – an anti-blazon – the only poem that comes close to such anatomy is the playful sonnet 99:[16]

> THe forward violet thus did I chide,
> Sweet theefe whence didst thou steale thy sweet that smels
> If not from my loues breath,the purple pride,
> Which on thy soft cheeke for complexion dwells?
> In my loues veines thou hast too grosely died,
> The Lillie I condemned for thy hand,
> And buds of marierom had stolne thy haire,
> The Roses fearefully on thornes did stand,
> Our blushing shame,an other white dispaire:
> A third nor red,nor white,had stolne of both,

---

[15] Lysander addresses Hermia as 'fair love' (2.2.41), yet she is enough of a brunette for him later to call her an 'Ethiope' and a 'tawny tartar' (3.2.258 and 265).

[16] All quotations from the sonnets are taken from the reproduction of the 1609 Quarto *Shakespeare's Sonnets*, ed. Stephen Booth, with the necessary transcriptions.

And to his robbry had annext thy breath,
But for his theft in pride of all his growth
A vengfull canker eate him vp to death.
>More flowers I noted,yet I none could see,
>But sweet,or culler it had stolne from thee.

Quirky in tone and attitude as much as for its extra line, this poem gestures towards the ideals of colouring traditionally expected of (or projected on to) an English, Petrarchan beloved. But such gestures are teasingly grotesque. 'Roses damaskt, red and white' (sonnet 130) are fair enough; 'purple pride' 'too grosely died' upon the beloved's cheek (even if we read 'purple' as 'red'), a little over the top. The roses 'blush shame' and stand in 'white dispaire', not because they reflect his colouring, but because they have been caught red-handed, stealing the beloved's beauty. That is to say, their colouring is presented as the temporary result of the player-poet's censure; they are not the eternal mirrors of his features. Such epithets are, however, readily transferable to the beloved himself by anyone who is determined to see him as an instance of 'roses damaskt'. Although John Kerrigan quotes John Gerard's *The Herbal* (1597) to the effect that marjoram was a whitish herb, G. Blakemore Evans notes that it remains unclear whether the comparison is meant to invoke the colour, texture or fragrance of the young man's hair.[17] The poem as a whole is less concerned with a description of the beloved than in elaborating a series of mischievous reprimands, whereby the player-poet is able to project the beloved as the source of all beauty through speech acts that are not primarily descriptions. Although not as blatant as sonnet 130, this poem is as much a parody of hyperbolic description, and its place within a cluster of poems centrally concerned with imaginative projection further calls into question any status we might be tempted to give it as an exercise in presenting an *imago*.

Even if we grant, on the strength of one sense of the word 'fair' and the supposed whiteness of the herb to which his hair is compared in sonnet 99, that the young man is blond, the other sonnets offer scant information on which to base an identikit. If anything, they coyly play with the idea of his picture without offering anything concrete. In fact the image of the beloved is invoked variously as the object of contention between the player-poet's eye and heart (sonnets 24, 47, 47), or as the haunting 'shadow' of his absent dreams (sonnets 27, 37, 42, 53, 61, 98),

---

[17] John Kerrigan (ed.), *The Sonnets and A Lover's Complaint*, The New Penguin Shakespeare (Harmondsworth: Penguin, 1986); G. Blakemore Evans (ed.), *The Sonnets*, The New Cambridge Shakespeare (Cambridge and New York: Cambridge University Press, 1996), 208.

or as something quite beyond description (sonnets 17, 18, 21, 79, 82, 83, 84, 85). Sonnet 17, for example, speaks conditionally of its own poetic power, suggesting that even if it could offer an accurate image of the beloved, it would be scorned as the invention of a 'poet's rage / And stretched miter of an Antique song'. And the cluster of poems responding to the rival poet famously (and strategically) claim that any attempt to describe the youth that goes further than tautology ('you are you') insults him. The only image that is invoked as a true and possible reflection of the beloved is that of his own imagined offspring, and he is himself considered to be an exact reflection of his mother, but the poems offer descriptions of neither. The sonnets speak of offering images, of drawing pictures, of making the beloved live on in their own 'black lines'. But to speak of pictures is not to draw them, to use the word 'images', even repeatedly, is not to present one. The gestures of description or portraiture throughout the 1609 Quarto are a series of elaborate feints; there is no shadow so shadowy in their lines as the figure to which they promise eternal life.

Without the grounding presupposition that it is the fundamental aim of these poems to render in words what the eye sees, Fineman's claim – that Shakespeare's sonnets make the revolutionary discovery that words can *never* match the world – is empty. If the sonnets were trying to do something other than describe, then their supposed failure to match insufficient word to ineffable, ideal object would be less momentous, indeed it would not matter at all. The poems are performative rather than constative. This is internally apparent from their speech acts. But the pre-eminence of rhetoric in the early modern period also shows that language was principally appreciated as a *force* working in the world rather than as a (always-already failed) reflection of it. Thomas Wilson, for example, opens the dedication of his *Art of Rhetoric* (1560) with a tale about the power of words to achieve what weapons could not.[18] George Puttenham's *The Arte of English Poesie* (1589) is informed throughout by an awareness of poetic language as a power that imprints itself upon the receiving consciousness: it 'carieth his opinion this way and that, whether soever the heart by impression of the eare shalbe most affectionately bent and directed'.[19] The sonnet tradition of the period forms part of a general interest in language as a form of action. David Parker recognises this

---

[18] Thomas Wilson, *The Art of Rhetoric (1560)*, ed. Peter E. Medine (University Park, PA: Pennsylvania State University Press, 1994), 35.

[19] George Puttenham, *The Arte of English Poesie* (London: 1589), Scholar Press Facsimile (Menston, England: The Scholar Press, 1968), c iiij.

when he reads the sonnets as examples of a particularly well-controlled and directed persuasive rhetoric, arguing that the apparently indicative mood of many of the sonnets obscures more dynamic, complex and interactive uses of language. 'The heart of eloquence', he writes, 'is not assertion, the expression of fact, but demand, the expression of will in such a way that the person addressed responds, or at least feels guilty about not responding.'[20] What appears at first glance to be a series of indicative moods in Shakespeare's sonnets are in fact 'elaborate disguises of the imperative mood' (Parker, 'Verbal Moods', 332) and many other modes of the performative.

Taking Parker's specific observations to a more general, philosophical level, we note Wittgenstein and Austin's challenge to the view that the indicative is the primary model of language. Wittgenstein based his revolutionary critique on painstaking reminders of the myriad of language games in which people engage in the speech that actually constitutes their lives, rather than the arcane archetypes of philosophical enquiry. Austin takes this re-evaluation further with his trenchant questions concerning how we *do* things with words. Both philosophers refined the ancient notion that language can be used to effect and affect things in the world by differentiating the kinds of logic that inform the same formal structures across different instances of use. Parker treats the complex play of 'moods' in the sonnets in purely affective terms – that is to say, as purely rhetorical procedures that attempt to work on the feelings and attitudes of their addressees. Austin's analysis of the ways in which an utterance that looks as if it is merely stating something is actually performing something (and is thus a 'performative'), draws a crucial and productive distinction between different kinds of performative, namely, between 'perlocutionary' and 'illocutionary' force. The former is rhetorical in the traditional sense of the word, while the latter is transformative by an internal convention. I discuss this distinction more fully in chapter 1. It renders more precise and concrete the otherwise rather vague notion of the 'power of language to make and unmake the world'[21] and it enables us to see that power operating, not in a contingent way upon an external addressee who may or may not be moved in a variety of ways by a sonnet's rhetorical force, but internally, in terms of the socially underwritten logic of particular language games or speech acts.

---

[20] Parker, 'Verbal Moods in Shakespeare's Sonnets', 331–9.

[21] Stephen Greenblatt, Introduction to *Romeo and Juliet*, The Norton Shakespeare, ed. Stephen Greenblatt, Walter Cohen, Jean E. Howard and Katherine Eisaman Maus (London and New York: W. W. Norton, 1997), 865.

Many of Shakespeare's sonnets to the young man attempt to negotiate the unequal political and social relationship between actor-poet and
aristocratic patron via such performative uses of language, by which the
actor-poet seeks, sometimes in vain, less to persuade careless nobility than
to transform the terms of the relationship or situation *in* the performance
of the speech act. Negotiations between power and weakness, authority and subordination in the sonnets are bound up with performative
or illocutionary rather than descriptive or even rhetorical or perlocutionary uses of language, and the player-poet uses such performatives
to negotiate a politics of self-authorisation. The illocutionary force of
the performative constitutes a major part of that 'dynamic, unending
slippage between power and powerlessness and between their principal
sources, success and failure' that Heather Dubrow has characterised as
being typically Petrarchan.[22] Even if Shakespeare was not acquainted
with Austin, his poetic practice reveals a subtle understanding of the
ways in which the necessary logic of the illocutionary act, as opposed
to the merely contingent force of a perlocutionary or rhetorical utterance, may transform the relationship between addresser and addressee.
In Shakespeare's sonnets, language is mobilised not merely to say that
things are so, or to move an audience through rhetorical skill, but to
transform a situation, to make something so merely *in* saying something.
This is a political process. It attempts to rewrite the already scripted
social relations of power and inequality through a force that lies not so
much in the rhetorical rules of effective persuasion as the publicly available logic of the performative. This logic operates as a transformative
power within certain utterances or speech acts: in the force of promising,
blaming, swearing, commanding, pleading, upbraiding, questioning, re-
pudiating or foreswearing. While such a force is not as uncertain in its
operation as its perlocutionary cousin, it does not act independently of
how things are in the world, especially the world of social relations. There
may be circumstances in which particular speech acts such as commanding or even blaming someone fail, because the relationship between the
people involved in the speech act is inappropriate by social convention.
A poet cannot command a queen, for example, although whether he or
she can blame her is a more complex matter. Shakespeare's sonnets, with
their situations of deep inequality, offer equally complex negotiations of
such discursive and social intricacies via illocutionary uses of language.

---

[22] Heather Dubrow, *Echoes of Desire: English Petrarchism and its Counterdiscourses* (Ithaca, NY and London:
Cornell University Press, 1995), 10.

They do so by deliberately exploiting the formal ambiguities of language which have flummoxed philosophers for so long: that what looks like a statement may in fact be doing something other than stating. Equally, what looks like a merely rhetorical appeal may transform a relationship *in* its very utterance.

The public quality of this process is especially important, for it operates in the 'eies of men'. That is to say, being independent of any contingently personal affect, unlike rhetorical or perlocutionary force, the illocutionary force of an utterance is essentially public: it is shared and, given the appropriate constitutive circumstances, it takes effect at once, independently of the 'private' states of mind of the participants. It is, in this broadest sense, interactive. This fact transforms another debate that has been raging recently: the vexed question of privacy or interiority. The issue has many tangled strands. Two will concern me here: the question of whether Shakespeare's sonnets, as lyrics, are essentially, by virtue of the 'normativity' of their genre, solitary or private in the sense that they eschew all social determinations; and the historical debate about whether Elizabethans had access to a concept of interiority at all. I deal with these issues more fully in chapter 3.

For the moment, I remark on the tendency to strip from Shakespeare's sonnets their character as public documents, circulated, perhaps on paper, but also perhaps through recital, within a specific social world.[23] Helen Vendler's magisterial *The Art of Shakespeare's Sonnets* argues that the lyric is intrinsically asocial:

> Contemporary emphasis on the participation of literature in a social matrix balks at acknowledging how lyric, though it may *refer* to the social, remains the genre that directs its *mimesis* toward the performance of the mind in *solitary* speech. Because lyric is intended to be voicable by anyone reading it, in its normative form it deliberately strips away most social specification (age, regional location, sex, class, even race). A social reading is better directed at a novel or a play; the abstraction desired by the writer of, and the willing reader of, normative lyric frustrates the mind that wants social fictions or biographical revelations.[24]

Vendler claims an essential *generic* difference between the lyric and other supposedly more socially directed genres, such as the novel and drama. These genres, by implication, *do* participate in the 'social matrix'.

---

[23] See William Nelson, 'From "Listen Lordings" to "Dear Reader"', *UTQ*, 46 (1976–7), 110–24; Roger Chartier, 'Leisure and Sociability: Reading Aloud in Modern Europe', trans. Carol Mossman, in *Urban Life in the Renaissance*, ed. Susan Zimmerman and Robert E. Weissman (Newark: University of Delaware Press, 1989), 103–20.

[24] Vendler, *The Art of Shakespeare's Sonnets*, 1–2.

Lyric does not. Therefore, to apply the methods of reading the former to the latter is to make a category mistake that misrepresents the nature of lyric poetry.

Taken as a strictly phenomenological project, Vendler's reduction of the 'voice' of the lyric by stripping away all the empirical qualities of its historical moment makes sense. If the 'voice' with which each reader reads a lyric is always his or her own, then the 'social specification' of the poem will indeed suffer a phenomenological reduction, leaving the solitary reading consciousness – completely removed from the originating social matrix – as its only intentional object. The 'abstraction' that Vendler questionably attributes to the normatively transhistorical intentionality of all poets, however, produces, not an enriched lyrical voice, untrammelled by the extraneous dross of social specification, but rather a solipsistic shadow of whoever happens to be reading the poem at any time. That voice, rather than being an unbiased glass in which the 'performance of the mind in solitary speech' is faithfully reflected, willy-nilly carries its own 'social specifications' into the poem, charging it arbitrarily with its own socially shaped consciousness. This devouring self-centredness may well be the function of Vendler's own belief that, despite their appropriations by thousands of others, the sonnets are in fact virginal critical territory, and that no voice captures their tone and direction so well as her own.[25] It cannot, however, be legitimately projected as a law inscribed in the genre. Equally questionable is the impersonal intentionality that Vendler attributes to the genre as such. She needs to offer a historical argument to locate and justify such 'normativity'. I suspect that, given such historical consideration, Shakespeare's sonnets may turn out not to be lyrics in Vendler's sense at all. Or rather, their attempts to move from public declaration to the solitary reading that she regards as the essence of the lyric end in failure. When the player-poet cries, at the end of sonnet 23, 'O learne to read what silent loue hath writ', he is indeed trying to reduce a trammelling, embodied, social context exemplified by public speech to the privacy of the written page. But this is a particular, historically conditioned strategy, not a universal truth about the lyric. Historicising criticism shows that the normativity that she asserts as intrinsic to the genre is not transcendental but produced historically, and that 'solitary speech' is as marked by social specification as any other.

---

[25] See Helen Vendler, 'Reading, Stage by Stage: Shakespeare's Sonnets', in *Shakespeare Reread: The Texts in New Contexts*, ed. Russ McDonald (Ithaca, NY: Cornell University Press, 1994), 23–41.

That is not to say that Vendler's aversion to a certain kind of historicising criticism is groundless. 'Theory', which all too often ignores the syntactical play of language games and speech acts in particular poems in favour of broad, theoretically driven or historically derived abstractions, has in many cases had a debilitating effect on our sense of the poems precisely as historically specific artefacts. This is a paradox, considering historicism's desire to restore to these texts the sense of 'social specification' that Vendler eschews. One of the major drawbacks of a certain style of historicism is its tendency to treat concepts as signs: as place markers in a code, ignoring the way in which they are engendered in the meeting place of syntax and social practice. Such signs are treated as already having a meaning before the syntactical movements of utterance and speech act. They are ossified as ideological 'structures' or products of historical 'discourses' which are then projected into the text regardless of their particular uses in the text.[26] If Wittgenstein is right that the meanings of words lies in their use, then this poetics, which maintains a debilitating link to structuralism no matter how far it thinks it transcended that doctrine, cannot hope to cast more than an obfuscating shadow over the texts that it pretends to illuminate.

Vendler's reading of Shakespeare's sonnets as speech acts rather than as descriptions thus marks an affinity with my own project, however much we disagree about the social nature of the lyric. To see the language of the sonnets as 'situationally motivated speech-acts' (Vendler, *The Art of Shakespeare's Sonnets*, 492) – forms of linguistic action, performative or illocutionary force – rather than merely a collection of metaphors, images, propositions or a collection of rhetorical devices, is to recognise the dynamic quality of interaction and response in the poems. They do not merely describe or state; they enquire, respond, boast, deny, beg, apologise, promise, complain, scorn, decry, argue and insult. In fact, the most productive analytical and philosophical insights of Vendler's approach to the sonnets as speech acts contradict her dogmatic eschewal of the social and the contextual. Wittgenstein and Austin demonstrate that analysis must occur at the level of the *utterance*, with all its irreducible references to 'social specification' and circumstance, rather than at the

---

[26] For an expansion of my argument, see David Schalkwyk, 'The Chronicles of Wasted Time'? Shakespeare's Sonnets Revisited', *The English Academy Review*, 16 (2000), 121–44. A similar tendency to impose preordained ideological notions derived from theory mars Paul Innes's *Shakespeare and the English Renaissance Sonnet: Verses of Feigning Love* (New York: St. Martin's Press and London: Macmillan, 1997), otherwise the most sustained attempt to offer a materialist reading of the sonnets.

grammatical abstraction of the sentence.[27] By cutting the lyric off from its reference to the surrounding social circumstances – society, history, class, gender, age, regional location and race – Vendler vitiates the philosophical power of the speech act. Her claim that the sonnets' status as lyrics necessarily exclude the 'social' arises from a failure to see that the social does not lie *outside* their discourse, in the way that the referent differs from its sign, but *inhabits* them through their very singularity. Even the most private or interior of discourses – when each of us feels most securely at the centre of our own lives – is informed by the social world, which is in turn central to each of us. The 'performance of the mind in solitary speech' requires the setting of a 'public' stage. The stripping away of 'most social specifications' from such a performance leaves, not a leaner, deeper or more essential representation, but one that has been divested of the very means of performance itself.

The modern formalist disembodiment of poetry from its context of original readers and social action, in which it was a 'kind of social currency', was, however, already occurring in the early modern dissemination of sonnets in printed anthologies. There they were set adrift from their original context 'in a system of transactions within polite or educated circles'.[28] Their disembodied appearance in print leaves little or no trace of their original contexts – social, political or erotic. But marks of such interactional contexts *do* remain in the representations of the sonnet in Shakespeare's plays, especially in the form of embodied readings or recitals. I explore the different effects of decontextualisation and embodiment in chapter 1, but for the moment I wish merely to register a more general point. My concern is theoretical and interpretative rather than empirical or scholarly. Even Arthur Marotti's subsequent booklength study of the manuscript circulation of early modern poetry has maddeningly little to say about Shakespeare's sonnets. Stephen May's extensive treatment of courtier poets excludes the common player-poet by definition, while Marotti and Michael Bristol's recent collection, *Print, Manuscript and Performance*, includes Shakespeare the playwright but ignores the sonneteer.[29] I have no further evidence to offer concerning the actual bodies or relationships that subtended the sequence of sonnets that Thorpe published in 1609, nor have I been able to find any empirical documentation to expand on Meres's insinuation about Shakespeare's

---

[27] This concern with the active, social nature of the utterance also marks M. M. Bakhtin's work.
[28] Arthur Marotti, *John Donne: Coterie Poet* (Madison: University of Wisconsin Press, 1986), 12–13.
[29] Stephen May, *The Elizabethan Courtier Poets: The Poems and their Contexts* (Columbia and London: University of Missouri Press, 1991).

'sugred Sonnets among his private friends' (Meres, *Palladis Tamia*, quoted in *The Sonnets*, ed. Katherine Duncan-Jones, 1). There are, of course, differences between the representation of a sonnet's forms of reception in a play and the more complex relations of dissemination through print. I want to argue that the necessary embodiment that is inescapable in the theatre may recall the similarly embodied original contexts of the sonnets. Whatever 'inner voice', 'silent speech' or 'performance of the mind in solitary speech' Shakespeare's sonnets enact, such interiority arises out of an acutely felt engagement in a public world which touches the 'private' world of the poem in every way. The sonnets give us access to the ways in which each individual is the centre of his or her own life. But that very access reveals the constitutive ties of that self to others in embodied situations.

The subject whose life is at the centre of the sonnets has elicited more controversy than any other in these much-disputed poems. After a period in which biographical quests overshadowed all others, there has for some time now been a decisive turning away from biography in any form. Part of this reaction stemmed from a formalist turn in literary studies. This turn was followed by an interest in the political, cultural or ideological life of texts that – under the continued influence of anti-humanist theory – has been more interested in subject positions than in individual subjects, conditions of representation rather than the condition of the representer.[30] If Peter Stallybrass's claim is correct that the scholar who restored the integrity of the 1609 Quarto was also responsible for the modern 'construction of a unified character attributed to Shakespeare' ('Editing as Cultural Formation', 86), then that 'character' has continued to exercise a strangely powerful sway even with the repeated proclamation of the 'death of the author'.

The widespread polemical impact of Roland Barthes's 1968 essay has tended to obscure Michel Foucault's almost contemporaneous and similar-sounding 'What Is an Author?',[31] which nevertheless deals with the issue differently, not least because Foucault poses it as a question. In its Wittgenstein-like examination of the use of the term 'author' and the

---

[30] See for example, Innes, whose aversion to formalism is nevertheless matched by an eschewal of anything that smacks of biographical criticism.

[31] Roland Barthes, 'The Death of the Author', in *The Rustle of Language*, trans. Richard Howard (Oxford: Blackwell, 1986), 49–55; Michel Foucault, 'What Is an Author?', in *Language–Countermemory–Practice*, ed. Donald F. Bouchard, trans. Donald F. Bouchard and Sheery Simon (Oxford: Blackwell, 1977).

language games in which it is used, Foucault's essay may be seen as a response to Barthes's more dogmatic polemic:

> It is obviously insufficient to repeat empty slogans: the author has disappeared; God and man died a common death. Rather, we should reexamine the empty space left by the author's disappearance . . . we can briefly consider the problems that arise in the use of an author's name. What is the name of an author? How does it function? Far from offering a solution, I will attempt to indicate some of the difficulties related to these questions.
>
> The name of an author poses all the problems related to the category of the proper name. (Foucault, 'What Is an Author?', 121)

With the last statement, Foucault indicates that his interest lies in the grammatical and logical roles of proper names, and more specifically, with the actual use of the peculiar species of proper name that we call the 'author', not with a *theory* of the author. It is therefore not surprising that he should use John Searle's work on proper names as his starting point.[32]

Foucault highlights in Searle's work precisely what Saul Kripke was subsequently to subject to the severest criticism: the idea that a proper name is an abbreviated set of descriptions. According to the 'description theory', 'Shakespeare' (for example) stands for a conglomeration of propositions: 'The man born in Stratford in 1564', 'The author of Shakespeare's sonnets', 'A shareholder in a major theatre company in London', 'The husband of Anne Hathaway', and so on. One or more of these may turn out, on further research, to be wrong. But Searle maintains that some of them would have to be true of their object in order to secure the sameness of identity without which a proper name would cease to pick out any unique object at all. Now it is precisely on this point that Foucault indicates an important logical difference between the functioning of the proper name as the name of an author and that of anyone else. A name continues to designate a particular human being (say Elizabeth Tudor) in the same way even if we should discover that many – or, as Kripke will argue, *all* – of the descriptions usually thought to be true of that person were false. This is also true of William Shakespeare. It would make no difference to the designation of the name to discover that he was not in fact born in Stratford. But, as Foucault appositely points out, if we were to find out that he was not the author of the sonnets then the name as author would function in a significantly different way ('What Is an Author?', 122). That is to say, the name of an author is tied

---

[32] John R. Searle, *Speech Acts: An Essay in the Philosophy of Language* (Cambridge: Cambridge University Press, 1969), 162ff.

to a network of written texts in ways in which non-authorial names are not. This is precisely what makes it the name of an *author*: 'the name of an author is not precisely a proper name among others' (122).

The logical difference that Foucault indicates between the two kinds of proper name may be taken in two directions. One, exemplified by the anti-humanist stance of the critical theory of the past three decades, would divorce the two functions of the proper name. It would abandon the name as it designates a person with a particular personal history and experience in favour of the name as a designating point that merely ties certain written texts together. The other approach holds that whereas the proper name 'William Shakespeare' does indeed function differently with regard to the historical human being and the author of that name, this logical difference cannot be raised to an absolute opposition. Would it really make no difference to the function of the author's name if we were to discover that William Shakespeare was not born in Stratford, or that he was not a member of the King's Men, or that he had no connection whatsoever with the London playhouses? The discovery of these facts about the man would in various ways affect the way in which the name of the author functions 'at the contours of texts', as Foucault puts it ('What Is an Author?', 123). The challenge is to acknowledge the logical differences between the two uses of the proper name while recognising that even if the author's name is indeed 'not the function of a man's civil status', that 'civil status' must be taken into account if we are to comprehend the 'status of the discourse within a society and culture' along the contours of which the author's name moves (123). Shakespeare's sonnets exemplify the complex relationship between the two functions of the name of the author and the name of the man. Attention to their criticism will show that despite the current revulsion from biography they continue to invite the most powerful of biographical interests, even among critics who would usually eschew such questions altogether.

Tracing the interplay of pronouns in the sonnets, Bruce R. Smith warns against the common identification of readers with the central 'I' in the sequence, since such an identification is liable to overwhelm the singularity of the historical persona and its relationships to the 'you/thou', 'she', 'they' and 'we' of the poems with the preoccupations of a different time and place.[33] Smith argues that if readers feel able, in a 'liberal' age, to concede that the plays express homoerotic desire, that is only

---

[33] Bruce R. Smith, 'I, You, He, She, and We: On the Sexual Politics of Shakespeare's Sonnets', in *Shakespeare's Sonnets: Critical Essays*, ed. Schiffer, 411–29.

because they can distance themselves from the characters in the plays as removed, third-person entities. They refuse the possibility of such desire in the sonnets, however, because they too readily identify and hazard their own identities in the name, as it were, of the central 'I' of the poems. In this tendency are combined the worst aspects of biographical criticism and formalism: the 'I' who is so powerfully at the centre of the life of the sonnets takes up residence at the centre of the reader's life. But it is then overwhelmed by the average reader's historically conditioned notions of 'normality'. Smith's analysis is related to Peter Stallybrass's historical argument that the character of 'Shakespeare' has, since the Malone/Steevens debate, been a retroactive creation from the prior charge of sodomy levelled at the writer of the sonnets by readers such as Steevens. The person 'Shakespeare' as the essence of 'normality' in Western culture thus arises from the sonnets rather than the plays. But this creature is also dependent upon the *denial* of the 'abnormality' found in the poems in the first place, which is tied, not to a poetic persona, but to the man, William Shakespeare, as he is mediated through powerful cultural representations and desires.

Stallybrass's and Smith's arguments implicitly attest to a widespread reading of the sonnets as autobiography, even though they may evaluate that reading differently. In *Such Is My Love*, a forceful argument for the bisexual character of the sonnets, Joseph Pequigney takes care to separate the question of the sexuality of the sonnets, or their personae from that of Shakespeare himself, precisely because the denial of their 'questionable' sexuality has been predicated upon the identification of their sexuality and that of their author. Separate the author from the persona, and perhaps readers will more readily acknowledge their possible homo- or bisexuality as a fictional exploration of the *meaning* of sexuality more generally.[34] That Pequigney has been so systematically and unjustly accused of returning to autobiography shows how prevalent the identification continues to be. In a later essay, however, after reiterating and defending his earlier distinction between poet and persona, he returns to the question of autobiography, and especially to the question of the proper name.[35] He claims that the poems themselves and the layout of the 1609 Quarto strongly suggest an identification between the 'Will' that is their speaker and the name that figures so

---

[34] This is strikingly like Astrophil's plea to Stella to treat him as a fictional entity: 'I am not I: pitie the tale of me' (sonnet 45).

[35] Joseph Pequigney, 'Sonnets 71–74: Texts and Contexts', in *Shakespeare's Sonnets: Critical Essays*, ed. Schiffer, 284–301.

prominently and repeatedly in their title: 'SHAKE-SPEARES SONNETS'. Both Pequigney and Katherine Duncan-Jones argue that this title, highly unusual in its explicit identification of the sonnets with their author, at the very least suggests that the poems were not only written by Shakespeare, but that they are also *about* him. The title may signal an unusually close relationship between the name of the author and the name of the man, especially considering the rise of the 'embodied text' that Bruster traces ('Structural Transformation').[36]

The answer to the question of whether Shakespeare's sonnets are or are not autobiographical has been consistently elusive when approached empirically. It may, however, be approached (if it can be answered at all) by looking at internal, logical evidence. Being a question about a *name*, it may be negotiated along the paths offered by the presence (or absence) of names in the sonnets. (The absence of names, like the dog that did not bark in the Sherlock Holmes story, is as important, as I shall show, as their presence.) By drawing our attention to the role that the title, with its ambiguous signification of the possessive, plays *in* the Quarto itself, Pequigney turns the title into a part of the text, drawing it into the body of Shakespeare's sonnets. 'Whoever reads the Sonnets "Never before Imprinted" – as it says on Q's title page' he reminds us, 'will see the author's name in block capitals on each and every left-hand page' ('Sonnets 71–74', 300). This *presence* of Shakespeare's name 'on each and every left-hand page' is balanced by the *absence* of his name in the poems themselves. Yet in the sonnets the 'I' who speaks refers to 'my name' six times, including the intriguing claim that the poems themselves constitute the author's signature: 'That euery word doth almost tel my name/ Shewing their birth, and where they did proceed' (Sonnet 76). Pequigney points out that the allusions to 'my name' in the sonnets need a point of reference to make sense. To whom do they refer? Anyone pursuing a strictly anti-autobiographical line would have to exclude anything that could not strictly be gleaned from the persona alone. That is to say, no evidence from beyond the words on the page would be allowed. But doing that would render these references wholly opaque. Whose 'name' do the verses 'tell'? Well, the persona's? And what is that? Don't know, we aren't told . . . Replace 'the persona's name' with 'William Shakespeare', however, and a whole history of criticism is both foretold and vindicated. Pequigney furthermore reminds us that the other references, in which 'my name' is said to receive 'a brand', or the beloved is told to 'let my

---

[36] Bruster, 'The Structural Transformation of Print in Late Elizabethan England'.

name be buried where my body is' (sonnet 72), because of the social disgrace that that name represents, are intelligible only if we bring to them the biographical context of William Shakespeare as what I have called player-poet. They remain opaque if we restrict them to the persona of the text alone. The problem with the persona as he is usually projected into Shakespeare's sonnets is that it is too thin a designation to sustain a fictional narrative. Anyone who wishes to make sense of these poems together rather than singly needs to go beyond their text to a world that is indicated by the historical reality of William Shakespeare, man of the theatre. Commentators on the sonnets do this all the time, even the most anti-autobiographical of them, stealing information about William Shakespeare while pretending to restrict themselves to the mere persona in order to flesh out their critical narratives. The question is thus not whether we should succumb to the temptations of biography, but whether we can ever foreswear them altogether. Here the absence of names – other than that of the author – from the text of the sonnets is as decisive as it is unusual.

What's in a name? Each of the following titles contains questions about the nature of the name, especially the 'proper' name: *Romeo and Juliet*, *Troilus and Cressida*, 'SHAKE-SPEARES SONNETS'. But the works for which these titles stand themselves also subject the problem of names to scrutiny in a peculiarly self-conscious way. The two plays announce the insepara-bility of both their existence and their nomination from the eponymous characters that allow them to bear their names. In other words, the plays depend, in the most inescapable way, upon proper names. With-out names they could not exist. Pope believed differently. In the Preface to his 1723 edition of Shakespeare's *Works*, he claims that 'had all the speeches been printed without the very names of the Persons, I believe one might have apply'd them with certainty to every speaker'. Such confidence arises from an extreme belief in the individuality of each of Shakespeare's characters. Each of their names is assumed to be inscribed in the singularity of their speech: it is as if Shakespeare's sentiment about his sonnets expressed in sonnet 76 were applicable to every word in the plays. For Pope the actual names are superfluous because the speeches themselves act as names, as tags of identification.[37] Sceptical of Pope's confidence, which does not in fact contradict my central point that a

---

[37] Random Cloud, ' "The very names of persons": Editing and the Invention of Dramatic Char-acter', in *Staging the Renaissance: Reinterpretations of Elizabethan and Jacobean Drama*, ed. David Scott Kastan and Peter Stallybrass (London and New York: Routledge, 1991), 88–96 (91).

Shakespeare play requires speeches to be individuated by something that acts as a name, I now ask why a text like the 1609 Quarto of the Sonnets can do without such tags.

To claim that proper names are indispensable for Shakespeare's dramatic texts is not to say that these names are not, in the usual sense, arbitrary. *Romeo and Juliet* might have been called *A Pair of Star-Crossed Lovers* or *Tragedy in Verona; Troilus and Cressida* could have been *The Trojan War* or *Love Betrayed*. That they bear the names of their protagonists is wholly conventional but not logically inevitable. What is logically necessary is that their texts should be woven out of names: Romeo and Juliet, but also Escalus, Montague, Friar John, Peter, Nurse and so on; not merely Troilus and Cressida, but also Helen, Hector, Achilles, Ajax and Thersites. Fictional texts are tissues of proper names. Or rather, names are the indispensable loom around which fictional narrative or speech acts are woven. Proper names are, as Saul Kripke puts it, 'rigid designators'. They are the still, logical points that allow for a manifold of contingent description and designation.[38] In fictional texts they are the tags out of which what we call 'characters' are constructed. Without proper names these texts would be a loose bundle of unconnected speech acts.[39]

Both *Troilus and Cressida* and *Romeo and Juliet* submit to the necessity of the proper name. But at the same time they subject that necessity to critical analysis. Chapter 4 examines their analysis of this necessity and their subjection to it. Juliet's solitary rumination on the burden of the proper name ('Romeo, Romeo! Wherefore art thou Romeo?/ Deny thy father and refuse thy name!' (2.1. 74–6)) is matched by the more public declaration by Troilus, Cressida and Pandarus of the historical definition of paradigmatic behaviour *through* the name ('If ever you prove false to one another ... let all pitiful goers-between be called ... after my name; call them all panders. Let all constant men be Troiluses, all false women Cressids, and all brokers-between panders. Say, "Amen" ' (3.2. 195–200)). They therefore seem to differ from a text that announces that difference in its own name: 'SHAKE-SPEARES SONNETS'. Its proper name is different not merely for generic reasons. Other sonnet sequences bear names that are closer to the plays, such as *Astrophil and Stella*, or *Delia*, or *Pamphilia to Amphilanthus*. Katherine Duncan-Jones reminds us that the generic (in the grammatical sense) form of Shakespeare's title is, with

[38] Saul Kripke, *Naming and Necessity* (Cambridge, MA: Harvard University Press, 1980).
[39] Jean-François Lyotard, *The Differend: Phrases in Dispute*, trans. Georges van Den Abbeele (Minneapolis: University of Minnesota Press, 1988).

one exception, unique in Elizabethan sonnet sequences.[40] Is this title a proper name or a description? Is it both at once? As a description, the phrase picks out poems of a certain kind as being merely written by an author called Shakespeare. As a name it designates the poems as being much more closely bound to whoever it is that 'Shakespeare' designates: as if 'Shakespeare', like 'Romeo' or 'Juliet' or 'Hamlet', were the chief protagonist of these poems. In this sense the sonnets are textual embodiments of Shakespeare the man.[41]

The collection of poems originally entitled 'SHAKE-SPEARES SONNETS' contains no proper names. One might quibble about 'Will', but that name is hardly a designator like 'Romeo' and 'Cressida'. If anything, it underlines the generic coupling of the author's name to the sequence itself, though not before punningly opening the proper name – which, Kripke insists, has no signified, sense, connotation or meaning – to a variety of semantic fields, thereby rendering it 'improper' or 'common'. Why do Shakespeare's sonnets contain no proper names? More important, how is it that they can contain no proper names other than the direct reference to their author in the title and the oblique references to his (shortened) first name in the poems themselves, especially if, as I have just claimed, plays such as *Romeo and Juliet* and *Troilus and Cressida* depend on proper names for their coherence as dramatic texts?

Shakespeare's sonnets can do without proper names because, in a delimited sense, the text designated by this name is *not* fictional. It can get away with almost pure deixis, indicating person, place, event or time entirely through the use of 'shifters': 'this', 'there', 'that', 'now', 'then', 'before', 'after', 'later'; 'you', 'he', 'she', 'they', 'I'. It can do so because of its original rootedness in space, time, event and social purview. This means that it assumes a contemporary, shared knowledge of its physical, historical and human referents. It does not have to name names, certainly not in the way in which a fictional world has to call itself into being *through* nomination and denomination. The (inevitable) loss of its original, shared purview, which made the systematic recourse to the deixis possible, is precisely what has made Shakespeare's sonnets so frustratingly opaque. Reading the sonnets is like trying to make sense of a play such as *Romeo and Juliet* from which the speech tags have been removed and in which all references to other characters are entirely pronominal.

---

[40] Katherine Duncan-Jones (ed.), *Shakespeare's Sonnets*, The New Arden Shakespeare (London and New York: Routledge, 1997), 85.
[41] Katherine Duncan-Jones, in *ibid.*, makes a similar point.

The search for proper names in the sonnets (which is traditionally conceived biographical scholarship by another name), is thus entirely understandable, but it is also curiously misguided. Biographical criticism has been disparaged by a form of criticism that wishes to insist upon the literary or fictional nature of the sonnets. Paradoxically, attempts to replace their pronouns with proper names, their purely deictic indications of time with dates and their gestures towards events that existed in a shared purview between addresser and addressee with happenings marked on an historiographical grid, fail to acknowledge the rootedness of these writings in an actual place and time. They seek to impose upon the sonnets a matrix of denomination that belongs to Shakespeare's fictional texts. They look for the precisely plotted co-ordinates of proper names in fiction where there are only deictic, autobiographical references to the here and now. It is thus precisely the maddening casualness with which Shakespeare's sonnets can dispense with proper names that marks their difference from pure fiction: it marks their status as 'pure' autobiography.

The narrative that Malone imposed upon the 1609 sonnets has proved to be so enduring because it solves in part the problem of their aphoristic nature. They are discrete texts held together only loosely by their order and unsystematic deictic references to people and events. They lack the rigid designation of proper names, times or places that mark Shakespeare's fictional work. In his 1640 edition, Benson confirmed that aphoristic status by rearranging them to form different narrative patterns: he changed the odd pronoun, disregarded the discreteness of the quatorzain by running a number of sonnets together and provided titles which suggested narrative situations. Why Benson should have been so vilified in an age that is properly sceptical of the self-integrity of form, the naturalness of certain kinds of interpretation and the holiness and authority of the literary text, is puzzling. Benson's arrangements do graphically what most critics do interpretatively. In questioning the interests that are served by the Malone narrative, Heather Dubrow reminds us of the tension between narrative and lyric.[42] She claims that the narrative impulse to see linear orders in the sonnets is misplaced. Reading the sonnets is like finding a collection of sketches or snapshots rather than watching a movie. They are the disparate records of repeated traversals of the same terrain, often approached from different angles. The figures in them can

[42] Heather Dubrow, ' "Incertainties now crown themselves assured" ', in *Shakespeare's Sonnets: Critical Essays*, ed. Schiffer, 113–34.

often be discerned but not identified. Sometimes we think we recognise them from previous photographs. Sometimes the terrain and the people seem familiar to us. But at other times they are wholly strange. This is a function of their performative nature, of the fact that it is not their primary business either to offer pictures or descriptions or to fail to offer such pictures, but rather to engage in day-to-day interaction with others. We do not know if the order in which we found them is the order in which they were taken. We can try to find some sense in the given order, or we can rearrange them, looking for other possible connections and differences. The order in which they were taken is moreover not their only or natural order. Arranging their syntax in different ways, as in a collage, brings out different aspects, some of them more or less striking, puzzling or satisfying.

Since we are not the people in the snapshots, or the person who took them, we have no broader context in which they would make sense as a total narrative or set of experiences. We do not even know for certain that the same person took them, although this seems likely. Because they are discrete aphorisms rather than paragraphs in a novel, the sonnets can be put together differently under headings and circulated, as Benson did. They can be kept in the order in which they were found and a reasonably coherent story offered about the events and the characters that they seem to depict. That order can be changed in order to try to find the 'real' form of composition that will fit some other narrative gleaned partly from their discrete shards and partly from our own interests. Or, we can rearrange them according to interpretative schemata, connecting the ones that seem to belong together in terms of theme, imagery, situation, character or attitude. Nor is there anything to stop us from abandoning the mode of autobiographical or single poetic persona altogether and seeing them as the expressions of different voices. The 'young man' and the 'dark lady' might 'write back' as it were, as Stella does in the songs of *Astrophil and Stella* or, if we follow Jonathan Crewe's reading, in sonnet 83 of that sequence.[43] Is it unimaginable that sonnet 109, for example, might be written in the voice of either their dark lord or woman?

The very lack of internal coherence, of denomination and context, speaks very strongly for the idea that the 1609 sonnets are not works of fiction in the usual sense of the word. Like a series of snapshots, they arise from, respond and refer to a world that they make no attempt to recover,

[43] Jonathan Crew, *Hidden Designs: The Critical Profession and Renaissance Literature* (New York and London: Methuen, 1986), 87ff.

because that world was self-evident to the people who appear in the photographs and to the person who took them. It can only be glimpsed in the discrete shards of the poems. By an ironic paradox, then, the rootedness of the sonnets in real experiences and relationships leaves them especially abstracted and open to subsequent appropriation and projection: to precisely the 'death of the author' that is the consequence of 'the birth of the reader' as Barthes celebrates it. This fact is exemplified grammatically by the referential emptiness of their pronouns, which can be filled (as Smith laments) by various readers in whichever ways they wish.

In drawing attention to the sonnets' status as collage or aphorism, I am not rejecting the imposition of a narrative structure upon them. If we are to treat them as a body of poems rather than singly, then such an imposition in some form or other is inevitable. The same sonnets from the 1609 Quarto tend to be anthologised over and over again. This is not merely because, since 1780, we have gradually reached a consensus about those of outstanding aesthetic merit. It is because the majority of them make little sense outside a narrative that gives them a living context. Most of them defy the very idea of the anthology. It was possibly their contextual inscrutability – in contrast with more highly fictionalised sequences such as *Astrophil and Stella* or the narrative unity of Shakespeare's longer poems – that prevented them from being reprinted, until Benson was bold enough to fashion a fictional framework for them. Benson was responding as deeply as anyone to the *problem* of the sonnets, namely their non-fictional mode. That problem has been addressed in a variety of ways since Benson, but it has always involved attempts to supplement the fundamental lack that they display as autobiographical works. By surrounding them with different kinds of critical fictions critics hoped to get them to make coherent sense. Repeated attempts to fix the Quarto order by arguing that it was indeed authorised by its author (albeit in some haste to escape the plague, we are told) offer no new factual evidence, but merely rearrange old fictions in predictable ways. Such scholarship is furthermore pressed into the service of prior commitments to particular narratives that hold the poems together, in an attempt to fill in the gaps that are the marks of their autobiographical origin. The claim that Shakespeare authorised their order appears to forestall arguments such as Dubrow's by endorsing the Malone narrative as authorial rather than externally imposed. But even if the order as we have it were Shakespeare's, that would not override the aphoristic or snapshot character of the poems in relation to each other. Nor could we rely on such imputed authorial intentionality, however attenuated, as if the philosophical complication of the very notion of authorisation over the past four decades had not occurred. Other attempts to fill the gaps that they necessarily contain as non-fiction with historical fact have failed notoriously: these were desperate and comical attempts, from forgery to wish-fulfilment, to supply the missing proper names, dates and events in an effort to solve their scandalous 'problem' once and for all. The unnoticed scandal of the 1609 sonnets lies in their refusal to behave in the way in which realist fiction behaves, with its ordering characters and dates, events and relationships, beginnings, developments and denouements, whether cosy or cathartic. Everything hangs on this refusal. It can, paradoxically, be negotiated not through fact but through further fiction.

This book attempts to make sense of these sonnets' remarkable engagement with a world that is now irrecoverable by surrounding them with a different kind of fiction: Shakespeare's own – his plays. This move remains true to their historical context because it uses their author's own work to illuminate them. Furthermore, while pressing the demands of a certain, inescapable kind of biographical criticism, it eschews the biographical wild-goose chase by sticking to fictional relationships within the plays, rather than trying to indulge in tenuous speculation. Finally, it preserves historical integrity by using as its explanatory framework texts from the same period and by the same author as the sonnets. This approach, I will claim, allows us to appreciate the poems as they were originally conceived, performed and read: as forms of social action and interaction, as the theatre in which individual subject and society engage.

CHAPTER I

Performatives: the sonnets, Antony and Cleopatra *and* As You Like It

In the Introduction I argued that it is not fruitful to assume that the rhetorical aims of Shakespeare's sonnets in particular, and early modern Petrarchan poetry in general, are primarily epistemological. Commentators' assumptions about what the language of the sonnets is doing lead them to overlook the ways in which the conditions of address of the sonnet are embodied in particular social and political contexts of performance. I now develop this argument by shifting attention from the generally theatrical notion of performance to the more philosophically technical concept of the performative as a particular trans-generic use of language. Shakespeare's sonnets use language as forms of social action, in a series of performatives through which the power relations between 'you' and 'I' are negotiated. The Cratylitic identity of word and object (encompassed by the poetics of 'true vision'), which Joel Fineman sees as the historical essence of *epideixis*, is neither the central concern of Shakespeare's sonnets nor a dominant view of language in the early modern period.[1] Both the sonnets to the young man (which, in Fineman's view, strive to achieve an epistemological correspondence between word and object) and those to the dark woman (in which he sees the enactment of a Saussurean difference between tongue and sight) are concerned with the exigencies of performance and the performative, rather than the formal and theoretical semiotics of difference.

'Ornament' as Fineman explains it is a 'discourse of special vividness', which nonetheless remains subservient to the ideal of similitude:

praise is conventionally understood to be a referential discourse that amplifies its referent by means of ornamental trope ... traditional poetic and epideictic theory tend regularly to describe both mimesis and metaphor in terms of the

[1] Joel Fineman, *Shakespeare's Perjured Eye: The Invention of Poetic Subjectivity in the Sonnets* (Berkeley, Los Angeles and London: University of California Press, 1986), 15.

29

same notion of likeness: verisimilar likeness or resemblance in the first case, the likeness of figural comparison and similitude in the second. (*Shakespeare's Perjured Eye*, 3)

His thesis depends upon this 'traditional' poetics, for it allows him to argue for Shakespeare's breakthrough into a new dimension of the (post)modern deconstruction of both the speaking self and the relationship between words and their objects via the essential discrepancy between language and sight: 'Shakespeare's sonnets "give the lie to my true sight" because they truly speak against a strong tradition, not only poetic, of linguistic idealization for which words in some sense *are* the things of which they speak' (Fineman, *Shakespeare's Perjured Eye*, 15). But the inescapability of difference will give rise to anguish over the division of subject from object and word from reality only if a Cratylitic match between word and object is the overriding aim of all kinds of praise. C. L. Barber claims that in Shakespeare's sonnets 'poetry is, in a special way, an action, something done for and to the beloved'.[2] Viewing them as different sorts of materially and socially situated linguistic performance – always, as Lars Engle puts it, 'participating in a covert struggle for the vocabulary in which social values are negotiated'[3] – may enable us to avoid an overly theoretical characterisation of their differences.

George Puttenham's vernacular translations of classical terms of rhetoric convey the activity of language in use rather than the stasis of language as image. He writes of poetry as force and action rather than picture and truth.[4] Specifically, 'ornament' is not a mere decorative supplement to something that is already essentially complete, or even a 'heightening' of a given object, but rather a condition of being: the function of time, social place and action. The 'great Madames of honour' who are Puttenham's exemplars of ornament do not obscure their 'true' selves beneath their 'silkes or tyssewes & costly embroideries' but rather act out a role that 'custome and civilitie have [properly] ordained'.[5] When he speaks of figure as the ornament of poetic language he does so in terms of the force or power of language to move or persuade,

---

[2] C. L. Barber, 'An Essay on the Sonnets', in *Elizabethan Poetry: Modern Essays in Criticism*, ed. Paul J. Alpers (New York: Oxford University Press, 1967), 299–320 (303).

[3] Lars Engle, *Shakespearean Pragmatism: Market of His Time* (Chicago and London: University of Chicago Press, 1993), 39.

[4] See especially Heather Dubrow, *Captive Victors: Shakespeare's Narrative Poems and Sonnets* (Ithaca, NY and London: Cornell University Press, 1987) for an account of the sonnets in terms of Puttenham's rhetorical categories.

[5] George Puttenham, *The Arte of English Poesie*, ed. G. D. Willcock and A. Walker (Cambridge: Cambridge University Press, 1936; reprinted 1970), 137.

not the correspondence between word and object. Poetry is, like all language for Puttenham, a form of social action; ornament is necessary, both to maintain proper decorum within a socially and economically determined social context, and also because it works as '*Energia* or *egon* . . . with a strong and vertuous operation' (*The Arte of English Poesie* (facsimile edition), 143). When Puttenham writes of similitude, he is thus not using the concept as the single, metaphysical goal of language in the form of a match between word and object, but rather as a performative means to a rhetorical end. 'Similitude' is but one figure among many: 'As well as to a good maker and Poet as to an excellent perswader in prose, the figure of *Similitude* is very necessary, by which we not only bewtifie our tale, but also very much inforce and enlarge it. I say inforce because no one thing more prevaileth with all the ordinary jugements than perswasion by *similitude*' (*The Arte of English Poesie* (facsimile edition), 240). Puttenham's account of similitude is pragmatic. He offers a descriptive elucidation of varieties of language in use, which does not overlook its embeddedness in social and material circumstances and relationships. Shakespeare does at times entertain an epistemological solution to the problems of social, erotic and epistemological difference, but such attempts are finally abandoned in favour of what we might call the poetics of performance and the performative. This leads to a conclusion that is the exact reverse of Fineman's. Whereas political and social difference precludes any kind of epistemological or representational solution to the gap between word and object, it is only through the performative in some of the sonnets to the dark woman that a solution – temporary, contingent, far from ideal, but none the worse for that – may be found.

In *How To Do Things With Words* John Austin breaks with the notion that propositions are the fundamental model of all language, claiming instead that there are other uses of language in which the correspondence of word to object plays no fundamental role. He calls these uses 'performatives'. A performative speech act transforms a situation, relationship or object in the world.[6] Provided that the convention exists and the circumstances are appropriate, the saying itself constitutes the action or performance. It acts upon the situation or object in question; it does not reflect or fail to reflect it. There is no gap between saying and circumstance, word and object. The performance may be rendered invalid by other factors

---

[6] J. L. Austin, *How To Do Things With Words* (Oxford and New York: Oxford University Press, 1975), 12.

in the situation, but they are a product of context and social agreement or disagreement. They are not metaphysically inscribed into language itself.

This Austinian notion of a performative as an illucutionary act differs from the performative effects of rhetoric, which are perlocutionary. By agreed and institutionalised convention, to perform an illocutionary act is at one and the same time to *do* something, to transform a situation in predetermined ways. To say 'I promise you I shall love you forever' does not describe anything in the world: *in* the saying it performs the act of promising and places the speaker under an ethical obligation. Perlocutionary acts, on the other hand, are rhetorical acts. There is no direct, conventional or internal, link between the speech act and its 'external' consequences. By performing the illocutionary act of promising I shall love you forever I may perform perlocutionary acts as divergent as winning your love in return, provoking your eternal scorn, or evoking undying admiration from an audience which reads my sonnets. I may equally be able to achieve any of these perlocutionary effects through a constative utterance such as 'My mistress' eyes are nothing like the sun'. Whereas there is no gap between saying and performance in the case of illocutionary acts, perlocutionary acts are mediated by every kind of contingent, material circumstance. Their effects may range from the intentional to the purely accidental. Such effects, however, are never enacted by convention *in* the making of the utterance. As Austin points out: 'Clearly *any*, or almost any, perlocutionary act is liable to be brought off, in sufficiently special circumstances, by the issuing, with or without calculation, of any utterance whatsoever, and in particular by a straightforward constative utterance (if there is such an animal)' (*How To Do Things With Words*, 110). A statement or description may have divergent perlocutionary effects (it may warn, surprise, alarm, seduce, shock and so on). The consequences of such an act are therefore contingent rather than conventional. Stanley Fish warns that if we ignore the distinction between the illocutionary and the perlocutionary in a general view of language-as-performance we extinguish the illuminating force of the philosophy of speech acts.[7] The technical term 'performative' applies to illocutionary acts, not to the rhetorical effect for perlocutionary force. This is true, but the power of Austin's distinctions also lies in their capacity to reveal not only the differences between constative, illocutionary and

---

[7] Stanley Fish, 'How To Do Things with Austin and Searle', in *Is There a Text in this Class* (Cambridge, MA, Harvard University Press, 1980), 197–245.

perlocutionary acts, but also the relationships among them. If Austin's notion of the illocutionary act shows us how 'saying makes things so' (*How To Do Things With Words*, 7), Shakespeare's plays and sonnets enable us to see the matrix of relations that both join and keep apart the complex, contextually bound, processes of representation, performance and performatives. The player-poet of the sonnets and plays seeks, through the institutionalised, conventional performative or quasi-performative, to create what he calls in sonnet 116 a 'marriage of true minds'. And as Engle argues so convincingly, the sonnets themselves reveal that such a marriage is part of the context-bound pragmatics of social existence and change (*Shakespearean Pragmatism*).

Many of Shakespeare's sonnets to the young man attempt to negotiate the unequal political and social relationship between player-poet and aristocratic patron via performative uses of language, by which the player-poet seeks less to persuade careless nobility through rhetoric than to bring about something *in* the saying of it. Negotiations between power and weakness, authority and subordination in the sonnets are bound up with illocutionary rather than constative uses of language, and such performatives are the means by which the player-poet negotiates a politics of self-authorization. Through their overt staging of the performative – their performance of the performative – *Antony and Cleopatra* and *As You Like It* render more explicit the nature of speech acts in the poems.

There is a memorable moment, in Act Five of *Antony and Cleopatra*, when both the historical Queen of Egypt and the boy actor representing her appear, impossibly, like a duck-rabbit figure glimpsed for a moment in *both* aspects simultaneously:

> CLEOPATRA Nay, 'tis most certain, Iras. Saucy lictors
> Will catch at us like strumpets, and scald rhymers
> Ballad us out o' tune. The quick comedians
> Extemporally will stage us, and present
> Our Alexandrian revels. Antony
> Shall be brought drunken forth, and I shall see
> Some squeaking Cleopatra boy my greatness
> I' th' posture of a whore.   (5.2.210–17)[8]

The 'impossible' perception of both aspects at the same time is, in contrast to two-dimensional figures such as the duck-rabbit drawing,

---

[8] All references to Shakespeare's plays are from *The Oxford Shakespeare*, ed. Stanley Wells and Gary Taylor (Oxford: Oxford University Press, 1987).

made possible by the bi-fold nature of theatrical performance, in which embodied action and spoken verse provide a double perspective by which 'Gorgon' and 'Mars' can be presented together. In a moment of self-reflexivity, a historical character represented on stage entertains the horrible thought of being audience to the unflattering representation of herself. Cleopatra's horror stems from the perceived inevitability of this event ('Nay, 'tis most certain'). It also reflects the powerlessness of the represented subject before the authority of representation and performance, embodied in the transformative shape of the player. The self-reflexivity that enables us to entertain at once the double aspect of Cleopatra as actor-boy and historical figure, as 'queen' *and* 'whore', is, nevertheless, also the re-mark of its own powerful effect. The capacity of representation to display its own limitations and precariousness by reflecting upon itself and the conditions of its own possibility is precisely the sign of its own massive authority. The scene calls attention to what Robert Weimann calls the 'bi-fold authority' of theatrical performance: the authority of the actor to represent, transform and limit the authority of a class who are also patrons and the pre-eminent audience of the theatre.[9]

Sonnet 23 also embodies the anxiety of representation through performance, but it expresses the other side of the 'bi-fold authority' embodied by the 'boyed' Cleopatra.

> As an vnperfect actor on the stage,
> Who with his feare is put besides his part,
> Or some fierce thing repleat with too much rage,
> Whose strengths abondance weakens his owne heart;
> So I for feare of trust, forget to say,
> The perfect ceremony of loues right,
> And in mine owne loues strength seeme to decay,
> Ore-charg'd with burthen of mine owne loues might:
> O let my books be then the eloquence,
> And domb presagers of my speaking brest,
> Who pleade for loue, and look for recompence,
> More then that tonge that more hath more exprest.
> >   O learne to read what silent loue hath writ,
> >   To heare wit eies belongs to loues fine wiht

Such anxiety stems from differences of situation and power that are encapsulated by the precarious social position of the player and his medium.

---

[9] Robert Weimann, 'Bi-fold Authority in Shakespeare's Theatre', *Shakespeare Quarterly*, 39.4 (Winter 1988), 401–17.

It is one of the key poems in the sub-sequence to the young man because it conveys like no other the vulnerable inarticulateness of the player-as-poet before the beloved in the public space of an aristocratic audience. It shows that the silence embodied by such an audience is a source of power rather than a sign of repression, and it asks that the reciprocity for which it pleads be allowed to be negotiated through silence: on the printed page rather than the resounding stage. The number of sonnets that continue to be informed by the player-poet's acute sense of his social inferiority and lack of authority shows that the retreat for which the sonnet asks is not granted. In many of these poems he seeks to resolve material differences of social rank in the competition for patronage by appealing to an epistemological argument based on truth and a denigration of the 'persuasive force' of 'ornament'. But his appeals to the 'poetics of a unified and unifying eye' (*Fineman, Shakespeare's Perjured Eye*, 15) are a cover for a much more forceful, performative, rhetoric. Such rhetoric does not seek an epistemological correspondence between sight, word and object but rather a series of pragmatically determined social and erotic consummations.

Sonnet 23's claim that it is the poet's silent appeal through the ear that can say 'more then that tonge that more hath more exprest' is probably an early reference to the rivalry with the unknown poet which is confronted explicitly in the sonnets following 76. It shows that abandoning the uncertain eloquence of the theatre for the unstaged, private muteness of the book (the consummation for which sonnet 23 pleads) does not avoid the 'bi-fold authority' of performance and representation. The performative power of verse may be imitated and even superseded, the private space that binds poet and reader invaded, by others more powerful, more favoured or more persuasive. It is the dynamic power of the rival poet's writing – 'the proud full saile of his great verse / Bound for the prize of (all to precious) you' (86) – that the player-poet fears. Such power is itself a form of the 'silent loue' that sonnet 23 offers, able not merely to reflect its addressee in its mirror of praise, but also to make its way into his heart.

The problem of representation and performance in *Antony and Cleopatra* arises from the difficulty of representing the historical (or mythical) beauty and allure of a figure who is marked beforehand by an irreducible difference from the actor-on-stage. Instead of being left out in silence, difference in the theatre is always on display, as it is in the situation from which sonnet 23 speaks. The *locus classicus* of such a representation is Enobarbus's enraptured and enrapturing account of Cleopatra's seduction of Antony on the river Cydnus where, significantly, Cleopatra is herself absent from the scene of representation. We should thus note the similarity between Enobarbus's account of Cleopatra, in which she is doubly absent, both as character on the stage and as an emblazoned object of praise, with sonnet 23, where the absence of material body and space is said to be the condition of successful epideixis. The absence of a boyed Cleopatra from the stage at this point is paralleled by her absence as female subject of poetic description. She is not described but rather conveyed via the traces of her invisible power ('a strange invisible perfume hits the sense' 2.2.219) that informs, moves or attracts everything around it. She is presented not as an emblazoned or scattered body, but as an ineffable potency which lies beyond the power and limits of representation: 'For her own person, / It beggar'd all description: she did lie / In her pavilion... / O'er-picturing that Venus where we see / The fancy outwork nature' (2.2.204–8). Which is to say that the only way in which she could be described is through tautology: 'she was only she'. Enobarbus's and the player-poet's encomia are thus as little descriptions as Antony's account of the Egyptian crocodile, a comic but telling instance of the essential surdity of the 'serpent of old Nile' (1.5.25): 'It is shap'd, sir, like itself, and it is as broad as it hath breadth: it is just as high as it is, and it moves with its own organs. It lives by that which nourisheth it, and the elements once out of it, it transmigrates' (2.7.41–4). 'Will this description satisfy him?' (2.7.43) Caesar asks mockingly and incredulously. But logically it is no different from the description 'you are only you' that the player-poet of the sonnets – he who 'purpose[s] not to sell' – peddles to the young man as the only truly 'rich praise' (sonnet 84) that he deserves and should expect. This is the kind of clear-sighted praise of which, presumably, only the player-poet's own 'silent loue' (sonnet 23) is capable.

Like Puttenham, Shakespeare deals with the problem of similitude in an unmetaphysical, flexibly strategic way, as different forms of social action impress themselves upon him. Take sonnet 21:

> so is it not with me as with that Muse,
> Stird by a painted beauty to his verse,
> Who heauen it selfe for ornament doth vse,
> And euery faire with his faire doth reherse,
> Making a coopelment of proud compare
> With Sunne and Moone,with earth and seas rich gems:
> With Aprills first borne flowers and all things rare,
> That heauens ayre in this huge rondure hems,

O let me true in loue but truly write,
And then beleeue me,my loue is as faire,
As any mothers childe,though not so bright
As those gould candells fixt in heauens ayer:
    Let them say more that like of heare-say well,
    I will not prayse that purpose not to sell.

Ostensibly an attack on mere 'ornament', the poem is in fact an excuse for a kind of inaction. Its persuasive force appears to arise from its conventional stance against 'painted beauty' (sonnet 21) and painted verse. Ostensibly a rejection of the 'coopelment of proud compare' that marks both conventional love and verse, it pushes its own rehearsal of such a comparison as far as it will go without actually becoming the thing it rejects. Furthermore, precisely its own 'coopelment of proud compare' between the lavishness of others and its own 'truth' is what carries its general denigration of similitude. This is not merely to stress that the poem indulges in the very ornament that it sets out denigrate, but also that such denigration is a deliberate action that attempts to affect the unequal power relations that subtend it. The plea in the third quatrain – 'O let me true in loue but truly write, / And then beleeue me, my loue is as faire, / As any mothers childe' – enjoins the young man to *allow* the player-poet to write in a particular style (of which its self-proclaimed lack of rhetoricity constitutes its most powerful rhetoric) as the condition of opening himself to be persuaded of the fairness of the poet's love and his own exemplary beauty. Moreover, it is more than simply an appeal to the addressee to be authorised to write without the ornament of similitude. It is a *quasi-performative*, by which the player-poet strives to create the conditions that will ensure belief. I call it a 'quasi-performative' because it rests on no clear-cut conventional form such as promising, warning, crowning or declaring war. Nevertheless it shrinks from abandoning the utterance to a merely rhetorical or perlocutionary force, since the effects of such force are notoriously unpredictable. The political request to be allowed to do something in the appeal, 'O let me true in loue but truly write', is overwritten by a conditional which seeks to make the uptake of belief its necessary (and not contingent) consequence. 'If true in love I could write truly' (i.e. without ornament), it says, 'then you would believe as a matter of necessity.'

Many of the sonnets to the young man attempt to negotiate the unequal political and social relationship between player-poet and well-born patron via such quasi-performatives. This may account for the sonnets that have often been taken to be unsatisfactory because the couplet runs counter to the first twelve lines, attenuating blame with acceptance or banishing suspicion with what appears to be groundless affirmation of the beloved's 'truth'. Such 'turns' may not be mirrors of the 'speaker's vain attempts to resolve the conflicts in his own mind' (Dubrow, *Captive Victors*, 222), but rather attempts, from a position of social and erotic vulnerability, to transform the relationship through the self-proclaiming power of the quasi-performative. This tactic is most successful, however, when the poet abandons the epistemological argument entirely, as he does in sonnet 138, and embraces the performative power of the lie – 'excellent falsehood!' (*Antony and Cleopatra*, 1.1.42) – to effect a mutual economy of accepted untruths.

When Astrophel cries out 'What may words say, or what may words not say, / Where truth itself must speak like flatterie?' (*Astrophil and Stella*, sonnet 35), he overlooks the power of words to transform, rather than merely to reflect, a situation. Better to have asked what words may *do*, for then he might have negotiated more successfully, as Shakespeare does, the dilemma between truth and flattery. We may see what words may do in a few key scenes of *Antony and Cleopatra* which bring out both the power of the self-authorising performative as a public act and its political vulnerability in an uncertain world. Take the declarative or performative authority which Antony and Cleopatra as joint rulers assume when they crown themselves, dividing the Eastern world between them and their children, and in the process legitimising the children themselves:

> CAESAR Contemning Rome, he has done all this and more
>   In Alexandria. Here's the manner of 't:
>   I' th' market place on a tribunal silvered,
>   Cleopatra and himself in chairs of gold
>   Were publicly enthroned. At the feet sat
>   Caesarion, whom they call my father's son,
>   And all the unlawful issue that their lust
>   Since then hath made between them. Unto her
>   He gave the stablishment of Egypt; made her
>   Of lower Syria, Cyprus, Lydia,
>   Absolute queen.
> MAECENAS   This in the public eye?
> CAESAR I' th' common showplace, where they exercise.
>   His sons he there proclaimed the kings of kings;
>   Great Media, Parthia, and Armenia
>   He gave to Alexander. To Ptolemy he assigned
>   Syria, Cilicia, and Phoenicia. She

In th' habiliments of the goddess Isis
That day appeared, and oft before gave audience,
As 'tis reported, so.
Maecenas Let Rome be thus informed.   (3.6.1–20)

The Romans who relate and listen to this report are affronted by the public, performative nature of these declaratives, which announce and display their own self-enacted authority in 'the public eye', 'the market place' and 'the common show-place'. Caesar's account not only picks out a plethora of illocutionary acts such as crowning, proclaiming, bestowing and dividing kingdoms; it also draws attention to the reflexive, and extremely vexing, self-constituting authority of such acts. Antony and Cleopatra constitute the very framework institutions of authority that give their performatives their power. Their self-authorising proclamations deny Roman authority and jurisdiction in ways that are very different from Antony's earlier dismissal. 'Contemning Rome', he now publicly enacts with his queen what was earlier little more than a gesture of personal impatience and insult: 'Let Rome in Tiber melt, and the wide arch / Of the rang'd empire fall' (1.1.35–6).

Maecenas, Agrippa and Caesar assume that such self-proclaimed authority may be undercut by appealing to the people of Rome to withdraw their authorisation of such behaviour. But the public space that such a display creates excludes or banishes the political authority of Roman citizenry itself, as Fish shows in a related analysis of *Coriolanus*:

What Coriolanus does opens the way for anyone who feels constrained by the bonds of a society to declare a society of his own, to nominate his own conventions, to stipulate his own obligations: suddenly there is the possibility of a succession of splinter coalitions, each inaugurated by the phrase Coriolanus hurls at those whom he has cast behind him: 'There is a world elsewhere.' (Fish, 'How to Do Things', 998)

In his description of the carefully staged series of Alexandrian declaratives, especially those that legitimise *family* relations, Caesar attempts to contradict that authority through a series of counter-declaratives. These seek to negate the legitimacy of the Egyptian display and distance Caesar himself from such contaminating action. If Caesarion becomes Julius Caesar's son through Antony and Cleopatra's legitimising display, then such a performative draws Octavius himself into the arena by relating him to Caesarion and Cleopatra. All this, powerfully symbolised by Cleopatra's self-authorising assumption of the role of the goddess Isis, means that the Alexandrian pageant does not merely say that 'there is a world elsewhere'. It constitutes such a world in its very pronouncements. Of course, as Coriolanus discovers, such a world is a fragile thing without the military power and the popular support to maintain it. *Antony and Cleopatra*'s apparent concern with transcendence in its last scenes, like the sonnets' similar preoccupations, should be seen in terms of the attempts by its defeated protagonists to maintain, and even extend, the show of self-proclaimed performative authority exemplified in the public coronation and division of empire.

We turn now to an exploration of the way in which the series of conceits upon the ornament of similitude in sonnet 21 is turned into the thought that the only true praise is to be found in tautology. This argument reveals a different, and extremely subtle, form of self-authorising performative by the player-poet. Obscuring the disingenuousness of the repeated claim that the poet has refrained from 'painting' his beloved and patron, since he has been the only one to see that he needed no such painting, these sonnets use the concept of 'true telling' as a tactic with which to dislodge rivals from the economy of patronage upon which the player-poet himself depends. The player-poet pretends to reveal the superficiality of the relationship of subservience and flattery that patronage involves as morally reprehensible, but he does not transcend that game. Rather, he tries to displace his eloquent rival from the beloved's favour. The argument is employed because it is thought to have a greater political and social force than that of the rival, not because its language is epistemologically 'more true'. And it proceeds as a series of actions involving exchange, spending, profit and loss.[10]

> WHO is it that sayes most,which can say more,
> Then this rich praise,that you alone,are you,
> In whose confine immured is the store,
> Which should example where your equall grew,
> Leane penurie within that Pen doth dwell,
> That to his subiect lends not some small glory,
> But he that writes of you,if he can tell,
> That you are you,so dignifies his story.
> Let him but coppy what in you is writ,
> Not making worse what nature made so cleere,
> And such a counter-part shall fame his wit,

---

[10] Thomas M. Greene, 'Pitiful Thrivers: Failed Husbandry in the Sonnets', in *Shakespeare and the Question of Theory*, ed. Patricia Parker and Geoffrey Hartman (London and New York: Methuen, 1986), 230–44.

> Making his stile admired euery where.
>   You to your beautious blessings adde a curse,
>   Being fond on praise,which makes your praises worse.
>
> (sonnet 84)

Performatively, the poem does not try to describe a unique object accurately. Rather it tries to find a speech act that will render a proper, i.e., appropriate, account of the *social* rather than the epistemological relationship between the praiser and the praised and simultaneously transform it in his favour. The quasi-performative noted in sonnet 21 is here presented generally in the third person, where its conditional logic is revealed more clearly: 'But he that writes of you, if he can tell / That you are you, so dignifies his story. / Let him but coppy what in you is writ, / . . . And such a counter-part shall fame his wit, / Making his stile admired euery where.' There is no description in the poem, save the tautology 'you are you' which, as I shall demonstrate shortly, is no description at all.

The sonnet argues against the notion that, since the patron may 'euer liue young' (sonnet 19) in the poet's 'gentle verse', the 'monument' (sonnet 81) that such poetry creates is worthy of the recompense that comes of patronage: that poetry indeed offers a 'world-without-end-bargain' (*Love's Labour's Lost*, 5.2.781). But if the player-poet's sonnets offer such a bargain, so can sonnets written by other poets. In contrast to claims made elsewhere that only through the power of his poetry will Time 'neuer cut from memory / My sweet loues beauty' (sonnet 63), this sonnet tries to *diminish* the 'store' contained within the poet's pen by suggesting that the exchange operates in the opposite direction. Such expense is in fact the patron's:

> Yet what of thee thy Poet doth inuent,
> He robs thee of,and payes it thee againe,
> He lends thee vertue,and he stole that word,
> From thy behauiour,beautie doth he giue
> And found it in thy cheeke: he can affoord
> No praise to thee,but what in thee doth liue.
>   Then thanke him not for that which he doth say,
>   Since what he owes thee,thou thy selfe doost pay,
>
> (sonnet 79)

The use of the third person and the past tense directs attention away from the present writing towards another text, already written, and so veils its own present theft. The mere 'copy' which sonnet 84 prescribes as the proper business of the poetry of praise, inverting the usual economy governing the relationship between poet and patron, finally serves to praise the poet himself. It is the patron who expends himself by glorifying the 'wit' and 'style' of the poet: here, crucially, the player-poet's poetic, social and sexual competitor. Within the context of such materially located rivalry, the sophistry of his argument should be apparent. It should warn us against taking at face value the player-poet's appeal to his own epistemological purity or rigour. His 'rich praise' (sonnet 84), both epideictically and logically empty, is no less an exercise of social force than the 'good words' that 'others write' (sonnet 85). Overwhelmed and fearful of the public space or world that imposes differences of rank, blood and social power, the player-poet hopes to persuade the young man to retreat to a private world in which promising faithfulness, declaring love and commanding trust will not be informed and distorted by the exigencies of such difference. The paradox that only in its perfect silence can the player-poet's breast speak truly is understandable given the uncertainties that accompany public declarations of love. As we have seen, however, the retreat from stage to page implored in sonnet 23 is not good enough, since even the page is invaded by the words of others competing for favour. The player-poet makes the painful, Derridean, discovery that language itself is always already marked by the material space and spacing of the stage, by the always-present possibility of intrusion and citation.[11] The tautology 'you are you' culminates a complex series of social actions which, despite being conceived in economic terms, in fact seek to obliterate freedom of exchange with the settled values of feudal relations. The tautology masquerades as the epitome of truthfulness. But it is in fact a double performative: it performs both a sophisticated form of definition and a remarkably audacious self-authorisation operating under the guise of humility. It marks a decisive move away from the epistemological argument that continues to inform his other sonnets.

When Shakespeare's player-poet claims that tautology is the highest form of praise, this is a performative utterance that does not describe the young man, but rather turns him into the paradigm from which beauty gets its name. As such a paradigm, the young man is beyond description. He is the standard from which words such as 'faire', 'kinde' and 'true' (sonnet 105) derive their meanings. It is logically and socially inappropriate to apply those concepts *to* him, since they are derived *from* him. We can see the logic of this argument more clearly by looking at

---

[11] This is in fact the philosophical lesson that Derrida draws in his encounter with so-called 'Speech Act Theory.' See Jacques Derrida, *Limited Inc*, ed. Gerald Graff (Evanston, IL: Northwestern University Press, 1988).

an example from Wittgenstein. The philosophical idea underlying such a conception is that words are given the meanings they have by virtue of selected paradigms in the world which then constitute the standard by which the concept is to be used. The standard metre in Paris is such a paradigm. To say that that piece of metal is a metre long is not to describe it, but rather to institute it as a rule for the concept 'one metre' within the practice of measuring length. If the standard metre is the length which settles just what a metre *is* then it is beyond truth or falsity. As the rule by which other lengths are to be judged it cannot itself be said to be one metre long, for what standard should we use to establish this? It is therefore in a logical sense beyond description except by a proposition that describes it as a paradigm. One can say that the standard metre is the measure by which we decide what a metre is, but one cannot say that it is one metre long.[12]

Shakespeare's argument about the young man in the sonnets implicitly invokes this logic. The tautology that 'you alone are you' is thus declaring: 'you are the standard by which we measure what beauty is, by which beauty gets its name'. The argument against the rival poet claims that if the young man is not an object that may be described (truly or falsely) as beautiful, but in fact the standard by which the concepts of fairness, truth and beauty are established, then it makes no sense to *describe* him as such. All one can do is proclaim him, over and over again, as the paradigmatic instance from which these concepts take their meaning: by which beauty gets its name! Although this view closes the gap between words and the world, it does not make the object the meaning of the word. Rather, it sees objects in the world as a manifold which, within the changing contexts of human practice, can be appropriated in different ways as rules for the use of words.[13] Shakespeare's argument shows that the 'ornamental' descriptions of other poets are not only logically vacuous or redundant, they also denigrate the paradigm as paradigm, reducing it from timeless rule to just another object among others. To praise the young man by a standard of beauty taken from some other paradigm or standard of reference empties the words of all meaning. It would be like judging that the standard metre is a metre long by using a tailor's tape measure. Or else it reduces his status as paradigm, it insults and degrades him, by subordinating him to a higher standard. The elevation of the young

---

[12] See Ludwig Wittgenstein, *Philosophical Investigations*, trans. G. E. M. Anscombe (Oxford: Blackwell, 1953), para. 50.
[13] For an extended account of this argument, see my *Literature and The Touch of the Real: Words in the World and Literary Theory* (Newark: University of Delaware Press, forthcoming).

man to the standard which gives beauty its name also accounts for why
the poems to him are so descriptively empty, why, as Thomas Greene
points out, 'the friend as an individual remains a "shadow", undescribed,
voiceless, hazy' ('Pitiful Thrivers', 235).

The argument is remarkable for its capacity to denigrate the
'ornament' of normal forms of praise on logical rather than rhetorical
grounds. Such forms of praise commit what Gilbert Ryle calls a category
mistake.[14] In the light of the category mistakes committed by rival poets it
now becomes clear why Shakespeare's verse should be 'so barren of new
pride / So far from variation or quicke change' (sonnet 76). It deals in definitions rather than descriptions, in the reiterated definition of concepts –
'faire, kinde, and true' – with reference to a paradigm case, which by
definition is 'still constant in a wondrous excellence' (sonnet 105), rather
than in the syntactical elaboration of mere description. Sonnet 79 exemplifies the logical economy by which the meanings of the words used in
descriptions of the young man are neither bestowed on him nor used in
propositions that could be true or false, but are rather derived from the
young man himself:

> Yet what of thee thy Poet doth inuent,
> He robs thee of, and payes it thee againe,
> He lends thee vertue, and he stole that word
> From thy behauiour,beautie doth he giue
> And found it in thy cheeke.

It is a philosophically subtle argument, and it would be hardly surprising if the young man himself failed to understand it. It renegotiates but
does not displace the complex imbrication of performative and material
power in the player-poet's situation. For the setting up and institutional-
isation of something as a universal paradigm is a social act. There has to
be general agreement to use a certain piece of metal as the standard rule
for what will count as a particular length. It has to be institutionalised
by a general agreement that then authorises the standard as such.

The young man's player-poet writes as if his beloved were intrinsically
constituted as such a paradigm by the authoring and authorising power
of nature (see sonnet 20). But of course it is his own human, rhetorical,
project to establish the young man as universal standard. Via the performative of determining the young man as the universal rule for the
concept of beauty and truth, the player-poet authorises the power of his
own verse over its subject. The logic of paradigmatic definition signalled

---

[14] Gilbert Ryle, 'Categories,' *Proceedings of the Aristotelian Society*, 38 (1937–8).

by tautology allows objects in the world to be appropriated in different ways as rules for the use of words. It closes the gap between words and the world and avoids Sidney's dilemma between flattery and truth in a situation in which words may say anything. But the appropriation of objects as paradigmatic instances is a performative speech act with far-reaching social implications, since it raises the question of authorisation: who has the right, or the power, to decide the standards by which words get their meanings? The player-poet engages in such appropriation first by elevating the beloved to the position of paradigm; then by proclaiming himself the only one who properly recognises that incomparable status. There is a sleight of hand here, since the self-authorising performative of the first move is performed under the guise of the humble descriptiveness of the second. It is the young man who must be persuaded that he is indeed the universal standard of beauty; once dazzled by his own status he will not notice that it is the actor-turned-poet's verse, not nature, that institutionalises him, retrospectively, as such: 'And him as for a map doth Nature store, / To show faulse Art what beauty was before' (sonnet 68). Replace 'Nature' with 'Shakespeare' and one has the properly secularised agent of such conceptual mapping.

Such agency has to be authorised in some communal way. How does the player-poet see his relationship to that empowering community? After witnessing the power of the self-authorising performative in the poems which deal with court rivalry, we therefore need to explore the player-poet's authoritative relationship to a broader community when the object of his affections is neither male nor fair, but female and black. If Shakespeare's player-poet can declare his independence of 'subbornd *Informers*' (sonnet 125) and 'frailer spies' (sonnet 121) by magisterially invoking the divine tautology 'I am that I am' in his own person (sonnet 121), the later sub-sequence shows a persona much less assured about the power of the performative to forge a 'world elsewhere'.

The opening poem of the sub-sequence, sonnet 127, begins with a confident elaboration of the argument sketched above regarding 'beauty's name' and its exemplification by some chosen standard. But the rest of the sequence almost immediately belies such confidence. The opening lines – 'In the ould age blacke was not counted fair, / Or if it weare it bore not beauties name' – are a variation on the theme that the meanings of words are open to change as and when new paradigms are authorised. This human appropriation and authorisation, which gives Shakespeare's argument its social and political dimension, sets my Wittgensteinian analysis apart from Platonic readings of this process. In days gone by, the poem suggests, even if beauty had included blackness, blackness would certainly not have counted as its paradigmatic instance. No one would have dreamed of teaching a novice Petrarchan poet the meaning of the word 'beauty' by pointing to a dark woman. But this has changed. Since 'each hand hath put on Natures power, / Fairing the foule with Art's faulse borrow'd face / *Sweet beauty hath no name*'. The concept of beauty has been emptied of content, since there are no longer indubitable paradigm cases by which to exemplify it and its relation to truth. Such apparent paradigms of fairness as there are are untrustworthy, for it is no longer possible to tell whether they have 'prophan'd' or not. To exemplify the concept of beauty via a woman who appears to be fair nowadays would be like trying to settle the length of a metre with a piece of elastic.

The crux of this poem's subtle argument lies in the logical operator 'therefore', which marks the transition from octave to sestet. For, taken as the reason why he has chosen a dark mistress, it confirms the player-poet's self-authorising power to revive the name of beauty by instituting a new paradigm, the now exemplary 'dark lady of the Sonnets'. In this subtly self-aggrandising poem, the poet no longer opposes an 'other world' of language users who persist in their own perverse usage, following their own paradigmatic samples. Instead (he implies), he effects a sea-change in the very concept of beauty through his choice of mistress: 'Yet so they mourne becoming of their woe, / That euery toung says beauty should looke so'. But such confidence does not last long. The agreement conveyed by 'every toung' is unusual in a sequence that finds itself not only at odds with the world at large but also with itself. Within a sonnet or two the poet acknowledges that his elevation of the mistress is hardly universal, nor is he willing to defend his authority in the matter: 'Yet in good faith some say that thee behold, / Thy face hath not the power to make loue grone; / To say they erre I dare not be so bold, / Although I sweare it to my selfe alone' (sonnet 131). His abject promise to declare her 'black' to be the ideal instance of beauty if only she would 'mourn for me' (sonnet 132) is hardly the gesture by which to declare a 'world elsewhere'. As the sub-sequence progresses, the poet internalises the difference between his unauthorised judgement of the mistress and a world that now stands 'hugely pollitick' (sonnet 124) against the madness of his private discourse, via the device, so extensively analysed by Fineman, of the contest between his heart and his eyes, indeed, all his senses, which now draw back in horrified disgust from a perversely persistent perversity: 'My thoughts and my discourse as mad mens are, / At random from the truthe, vainely exprest, / For I have sworne thee faire, and thought thee bright, / Who art as black as hell, as darke as night' (sonnet 147).

'At random from the truth, vainely exprest'. This is, of course, one aspect of 'lust in action' (sonnet 129). But it could also be applied to one of the most intriguing moments in *Antony and Cleopatra* when, in a surprising Petrarchan moment, the defeated Queen subjects Antony to a lover's extravagant blazon:

> CLEOPATRA His face was as the heav'ns, and therein stuck
> A sun and moon, which kept their course and lighted
> The little O o' th' earth.
> DOLABELLA   Most sovereign creature –
> CLEOPATRA His legs bestrid the ocean; his reared arm
> Crested the world. His voice was propertied
> As all the tunèd spheres, and that to friends;
> But when he meant to quail and shake the orb,
> He was as rattling thunder. For his bounty,
> There was no winter in 't; an autumn 'twas,
> That grew the more by reaping. His delights
> Were dolphin-like; they showed his back above
> The element they lived in. In his livery
> Walked crowns and crownets. Realms and islands were
> As plates dropped from his pocket.
> DOLABELLA   Cleopatra –   (5.2.78–91)

Dolabella cries out, surprised and horrified at what he perceives to be the madness, the eccentricity and excessiveness, of Cleopatra's 'thoughts and discourse'. As we saw above, the felicity of such discourse depends on the willingness of the audience to concur in both its truth and force. Dispassionately rejecting the falsity of Cleopatra's praise, but also horrified by its exorbitant power, Dolabella responds with a pitying but firm 'no' to her question: 'Think you there was, or might be such a man / As this I dreamt of?' (5.2.92). As many critics have pointed out, the question, with its subjunctive modification, is concerned as much with the powers of poetry as with the truth of history. It returns us to, or rather, anticipates, Cleopatra's concern later in the scene with the power of fiction to represent and transform her own historically specific figure into the stuff either of myth or political propaganda. Reading Cleopatra's praise of Antony in the way that the player-poet reads the 'full proud saile' (sonnet 86) of the rival poet's verse, Dolabella flatly denies the veracity of her dream. Being false to its object, a product of projection rather than truthful description, it is 'at random from the truthe', and because it is at random from the truth, it is 'vainely exprest'.

But as so often happens in this play, with its Chinese-box effects of audiences nested within wider audiences, we are free to answer Cleopatra's question differently, just as we were able, in the opening scene, to accept Philo's invitation to 'behold and see' by judging his judgement:

> Look where they come.
> Take but good note, and you shall see in him
> The triple pillar of the world transformed
> Into a strumpet's fool. Behold and see.
>
> (1.1.10–13)

What we, watching Philo and Demetrius watching Antony and Cleopatra, behold is a remarkable scene which gives full reign to the performative as a way of attempting to transform, successfully or not, a situation through the power of merely saying so. The scene is too long and complex to analyse in full here. We should merely note the way in which Antony institutes himself and Cleopatra as a paradigm of the 'nobleness of life' itself: 'the nobleness of life / Is to do thus: when such a mutual pair / And such a twain can do it, in which I bind, / On pain of punishment, the world to weet / We stand up peerless' (1.1.38–42). But it is one thing to make such a declaration in the private world of a lyric poem, as Donne, for example does, another to stage it publicly in one's capacity as the 'triple-pillar of the world'. Antony's theatrical declaration betrays precisely the difficulty of such self-fashioning and self-authorising public show: if Antony and Cleopatra can turn their sensuality into a paradigm of 'nobleness' only by binding 'the world' to acknowledge it on 'pain of punishment' then it fails as a performative. A performative is not empowered by the exercise of physical coercion, although it always exists within a material world.

I have argued elsewhere that if our own involvement in what we have communally instituted as the 'literary' stems at least in part from its capacity to show us the institution and relationships between the concepts of our language, it also opens the space for the constitution, however brief and unstable, of an imaginary consensus whereby paradigms may be shifted, concepts renegotiated. If it is Cleopatra rather than Philo who publicly refuses Antony's extravagant gesture, she does so in a powerfully ambiguous phrase: 'excellent falsehood!' This is to part-reject, part-deny, part-admire a claim that, if it is ostensibly 'at random from the truthe' and 'vainely exprest', may indeed, from the imaginary perspective of the theatre audience, fall beyond the limits of truth altogether. It is a critical commonplace that an ambivalence towards truth and lying, deceit and trust, marks Antony and Cleopatra's relationship throughout the play, and it is never fully settled one way or the other, just as it is never settled whether Antony is a 'strumpet's fool' or a Colossus whose 'legs bestrid the ocean'.

I am not saying that we are each left to decide for ourselves, for that would mean that we would finally settle on a truth, one way or another. Rather, I want to suggest that, just as performatives are logically independent of truth or falsity – of a correspondence with an entity that already exists in the world – but rather transform the world or bring about a situation merely in their saying, *Antony and Cleopatra* and the sonnets both represent and perform this transformative power of language in the imaginary space of theatrical and poetic production. If Cleopatra fears this process in her reflection upon what she will become at the hands of 'quick comedians' in Rome, she fully indulges in it in her 'dream' of Antony. The dream is not simply a fiction:

> But if there be, or ever were one such,
> It's past the size of dreaming. Nature wants stuff
> To vie strange forms with fancy; yet t' imagine
> An Antony were nature's piece 'gainst fancy,
> Condemning shadows quite. (5.2.95–99)

Such an Antony is not a product of fancy, since he is, like the young man of the sonnets, 'nature's piece 'gainst fancy'. On the other hand, he is not a mere empirical object of description. Rather, to '*imagine /* An Antony' is to see both how paltry mere fictions and how dull mere men are. Cleopatra speaks here of *an* Antony: not merely the man called Antony but the historical figure turned into generic type or paradigm. This is a philosophy of language and the imaginary that transcends classical oppositions between fact and fiction. Lying between truth and fancy, history and fiction – 'dolphin-like' as Antony's desires – such a figure is the object of a performative use of language that is neither true nor false, but rather enacts or brings into being the figure it speaks about. To read it as the object of a truth-claim is, like Dolabella, to miss its force entirely. But to see it for what it is, a different language game that could be said to constitute epideixis as such, is to find 'new heaven, new earth' (1.1.17), but without transcending the ones presently inhabited.

This is not a transcendentalising reading of either the sonnets or *Antony and Cleopatra*. Such a language game is still very much of this earth, even if it extends it beyond the limits dreamed of by positivist philosophy. We can see its mundane operation in one final moment of Act 5, when, re-enacting the self-authorising moment in the Alexandrian market place when she appeared 'in the habiliments of the goddess Isis' (3.6.17), Cleopatra proclaims herself, not 'whore' or 'mistress', but Antony's wife: 'Husband, I come' (5.2.282). We are reminded at once of Antony's earlier statement 'I am not married, Caesar' (2.2.129), poised ambivalently between being a mere description of an indubitable condition and a declaration of emotional, political and sexual independence.

The marriage ceremony is one of Austin's paradigm cases of the performative: a clear-cut case in which to say 'I do' and 'I declare you man and wife', by the appropriate people within a proper institution, is not to say of anything that it is true or false but to bring it into being, to make it so. More than any other play by Shakespeare, *As You Like It* explores the complexity of marriage as a self-initiating or self-authorising performative, especially with regard to the power of women not only to choose a mate, but to organise, through illocutionary acts both imaginary and non-imaginary, relationships within the society at large. Susanne Wofford's excellent essay on this issue argues that Rosalind represents the appropriation by marginalised 'others' – women as a sex and the theatre as an institution – of the power to transform social relationships through the performative.[15] The crux is Rosalind's self-authorised giving of herself to both father and husband, with the identically repeated 'To you I give myself, for I am yours' (5.4.114 and 115). To Wofford, Rosalind's first performative, by which she acknowledges herself as subject to her father, is in tension with the second, which harks back to an earlier, playful 'giving' of herself in the name of Ganymede.

As Wofford observes, the double theatricality of that giving calls into question Austin's apparent exclusion of speech acts 'said by an actor on a stage' as being '*in a peculiar way* hollow or void' (Austin, *How To Do Things With Words*, 22).[16] Celia's protest, 'I cannot say the words',

<hr />

[15] Susanne L. Wofford, ' "To You I Give Myself, For I Am Yours": Erotic Performance and Theatrical Performatives in *As You Like It*', in *Shakespeare Reread: The Texts in New Contexts*, ed. Russ McDonald (Ithaca, NJ: Cornell University Press, 1994), 147–69.

[16] I say 'apparent' because it is possible to read Austin's lectures as not excluding fiction from his account at all, but rather showing in the end that no such exclusion is possible. The exclusion on page 22 is thus provisional, a sleight of hand by which the philosopher covers his tracks. See my forthcoming *Literature and The Touch of the Real*.

when Rosalind and Orlando sweep her into their game by asking her to 'be the priest and marry us' (4.1.116–17), may stem from her fear of the magical power of the words as performatives rather than from ignorance or forgetfulness. The beneficial 'magic' that Rosalind claims to possess at the end of the play is no more than the magic of the performative – the transformative magic of words. Celia, knowing Rosalind's real sex and her love for Orlando, may suddenly find herself on the brink of confirming a headlong rush into real marriage in the guise of mere play. Mindful of the power of '[m]arriage *per verba de praesenti*', which, as the Arden editor reminds us, 'was still valid in the sixteenth century',[17] she may find that she cannot bring herself to use the transformative potency of 'words' that are, in effect, deeds.

F. Pollock and F. W. Maitland claim that '*sponsalia per verba de praesenti . . .* takes place if they declare that they take each other as husband and wife now, at this very moment'.[18] Agnes Latham observes that Rosalind is scrupulous about observing this grammatical requirement: she insists that Orlando replace the future tense, 'I will', for '*now*, as fast as she can marry us' (4.1.122–9; Latham, Introduction, 133). Rosalind's gift of herself to Orlando in Act 5 has already been preceded by their exchange in Act 4; it thus merely confirms 'I am yours', and, in effect, denies the proprietary claims of her father, which she has, however, just appeared to acknowledge. The two sentences, lexically and grammatically identical, thus constitute not only two different, but also two contradictory, speech acts. The identity of form hides the discrepancy of illocutionary force, as does the apparent constative 'for I am yours', which deliberately fails to draw attention to the different ways in which Rosalind might belong to, and might give herself to or withhold herself from, husband and father respectively. This is reminiscent of two other moments in which women are able to make use of the transitional point between father and husband to forge some kind of limited authority of their own: Desdemona in Act 1 Scene 2 of *Othello*, and Cordelia in the opening scene of *King Lear*, both of whom find space to oppose the wishes of their fathers by invoking a woman's duty to her husband. It is a much narrower space than that afforded to Rosalind-as-Ganymede, and it remains caught between the Scylla of the patriarch and the Charybdis of the spouse, but it does permit a degree of opposition and independence.

[17] Agnes Latham, Introduction, *As You Like It*, The Arden Shakespeare (London: Methuen, 1975), 133–4.
[18] F. Pollock and F. W. Maitland, *The History of English Law before the Time of Edward I* (1898), ii, 364ff., quoted by Latham, Introduction, 133–4.

In *As You Like It*, the move from constative to performative speech, culminating in the woman's appropriation of the right to 'go before the priest' by giving herself in marriage, is enacted by a shift from monological, Petrarchan doggerel issued by the male (in the form of Orlando's verse) to a gameful dialogue of illocutionary acts controlled by the female. Orlando's dreary poems, which do at least alert his beloved to his presence and devotion, are soon abandoned, not merely in the face of Jacques's and Touchstone's satirical criticism, but for the more engaging pastime of erotic dialogue so aptly characterised by Stephen Greenblatt.[19] When Rosalind sets the terms of the game, via the putative 'cure for love' supposedly practised earlier upon a love-sick youth, she gives an account of it in entirely performative terms:

He was to imagine me his love, his mistress; and I set him every day to woo me. At which time would I, being but a moonish youth, grieve, be effeminate, changeable, longing and liking, proud, fantastical, apish, shallow, inconstant, full of tears, full of smiles; for every passion something, and for no passion truly anything, as boys and women are for the most part cattle of this colour – would now like him, now loathe him; then entertain him, then forswear him; now weep for him, then spit at him, that I drave my suitor from his mad humour of love to a living humour of madness, which was to forswear the full stream of the world and to live in a nook merely monastic. And thus I cured him, and this way will I take upon me to wash your liver as clean as a sound sheep's heart, that there shall not be one spot of love in 't. (3.3.392–408)

The whole speech may be taken variously as an ironic threat, promise or prediction, seeking through quasi-fictitious performatives to demonstrate the ethical responsibilities as well as the light-hearted pleasures of love talk. If at the beginning of the scene we are reminded that the 'truest poetry is the most feigning' (3.3.16), then Rosalind demonstrates that even playful illocutionary acts carry the burden of transformative force. Among all the gameful speech acts of 'liking', 'loathing', 'forswearing', 'entertaining' and 'longing' in which Orlando and Ganymede/Rosalind indulge, promising carries a special, and entirely appropriate, weight. Twice Orlando's 'feigning' poetic expression of his love is called to account before a broken promise, and Rosalind's entire project of bringing together the 'country copulatives' (5.4.56) in an extravagantly self-authorised coup depends upon her prior exchange of solemn promises with each of the parties:

19 Stephen Greenblatt, 'Fiction and Friction', in *Shakespearean Negotiations* (Berkeley and Los Angeles: University of California Press, 1988), 66–93.

ROSALIND Patience once more, whiles our compact is urged.
   (*to the Duke*) You say if I bring in your Rosalind
   You will bestow her on Orlando here?
DUKE SENIOR That would I, had I kingdoms to give with her.
ROSALIND (*to Orlando*)
   And you say you will have her when I bring her?
ORLANDO That would I, were I of all kingdoms king.
ROSALIND (*to Phoebe*) You say you'll marry me if I be willing?
PHOEBE That will I, should I die the hour after.
ROSALIND But if you do refuse to marry me
   You'll give yourself to this most faithful shepherd?
PHOEBE So is the bargain.
ROSALIND (*to Silvius*) You say that you'll have Phoebe if she will?
SILVIUS Though to have her and death were both one thing.
ROSALIND I have promised to make all this matter even.
   Keep you your word, O Duke, to give your daughter.
   You yours, Orlando, to receive his daughter.
   Keep your word, Phoebe, that you'll marry me,
   Or else refusing me to wed this shepherd.
   Keep your word, Silvius, that you'll marry her
   If she refuse me; and from hence I go
   To make these doubts all even.   (5.4.5–25)

The 'boy' Rosalind 'can do all that he has promised' (5.4.1–2) only by extracting promises from all the other characters that she has skilfully insinuated as being commensurate with their desires. She knows that each of them will swear to act in ways that will to all appearances fulfil what they most deeply want. She can extract such promises for two reasons: she is uniquely in a position to know the whole gamut of related desires, and she is negotiating the compact in the third person rather than the first, as a 'boy' rather than a 'girl', possessed of a 'not damnable' (5.2.59) magic in which everyone desperately wants to believe. And she does have secure command of a certain kind of beneficial magic: the transformative magic of speech, in the form of the performative, which, in the tradition of all spelling, can make things so merely in the saying. This cannot be achieved on one's own, but requires 'interactive dialogue', arising out of a society bound together not only by commensurable goals and desires, but also by the fact that they take the illocutionary force of speech acts such as promising seriously. There is nothing to stop Rosalind's little cast from breaking their promises, and in a certain kind of society, such as that reflected in *Troilus and Cressida*, for example, that would indeed be the norm. We see the same ethical drive to take on the burden of speech as action at the end of *Love's Labour's Lost*, where promises are preludes to the possibility of erotic fulfilment. In a play concerned throughout with 'truth', Rosalind shows that such truth is less a matter of matching a word to an object (as Orlando, for example tries to do in his verse), than a mode of transforming human relationships through a certain kind of action, of which speech is an integral, but not a sole, part.

Returning now to Cleopatra's urgent vocative, 'Husband, I come' – which names Antony as he is called by Egypt (1.2.99) – we may ask if it is not a condensed form of the marriage ceremony: a unilateral declarative which transforms in the saying her relationship with Antony, and thereby effects our judgement of both of them. It is neither an 'excellent falsehood' nor a gesture of pure transcendence, but an acceptance that the title involves publicly accessible standards of behaviour, standards that are not self-authorised in a show of pride, such as is exemplified by Antony in 1.2., but are rather an independent measure of her condition: 'Now to that name my courage prove my title!' (5.2.283). Cleopatra's death is a kind of performative by which she lives up to that transforming 'title', and at the same time effects a transformation of its ideological values. If, through the performative power of her suicide, Cleopatra does not transcend the mundane world but rather subjects herself to its transformative institutions (of which the concepts 'husband' and 'wife' are an irreducible part) she nonetheless, by subjecting herself to such concepts, transforms the ideological thrust of the patriarchal institution in which they have their life. No theoretician of speech acts would accept Cleopatra's cry as an instance of the felicitous performance of the marriage ceremony. But the play invites us to do so: it asks us to accept the authority of a figure who is 'no more but e'en a woman, and commanded / By such poor passion as the maid that milks' (4.16.75–6), and in the absence of consenting husband or presiding clergyman, to claim for herself the right not only to choose but also to make her own husband.[20] Shakespeare's play thus effects the very opposite kind of transformation that Cleopatra so fears at the hands of comedians, imbuing her through its own transformative power with the ability and right to transform herself from whore to queen and self-fashioning and self-fashioned wife.

Let us return, finally, to the sonnets, especially 138: 'When my love sweares that she is made of truth, / I do beleeve her, though I know she

---

[20] See Mary Hamer, 'Cleopatra: Housewife', *Textual Practice*, 2.2 (September 1988), 159–79, who points out one of the cultural threats posed by Cleopatra insofar as she exemplifies the fact that Egyptian woman 'enjoyed one freedom that made them a scandal to the men of Rome: they were free to choose their own husbands' (163).

lyes', which enacts its own kind of transformative power. Edward Snow's reading of this sonnet both draws parallels with *Antony and Cleopatra* and also sees in it 'a moment of repose' and a 'subtle realignment of values'.[21] Against this view Nona Feinberg proposes a feminist argument that such repose is achieved through the silencing of the woman, so that in the end 'the sonnet celebrates the speaker's verbal power at the cost of the loss of the Dark Lady's voice'.[22] In chapter 2 I examine the silencing or scattering of the beloved through a discussion of what happens to the blazon when it is embodied in the theatre, especially when silence makes itself heard through the irreducible presence of the silenced body on the stage. It could be argued that the sonnet is the poetic form least able to accommodate another's voice in anything but the most cursory or indirect way. But this is to ignore a possibility that the theatre makes palpable, namely an original context of address and reception in which the response of the beloved, though not recorded in the poem itself, would not only have been possible, but likely. It is, we recall, precisely to avoid the unwelcome consequences and circumstances of such an address that the player-poet urges his patron audience to 'heare wit eies' (sonnet 23). The presence, and intrinsic power, of an audience to shape the poet's own voice and stance should not be overlooked in a discussion of whether sonnet 138 achieves a tone of repose, smugness or grim seriousness.

Few feminist critics who accept the general notion that Petrarchan sonnets in general necessarily exclude, silence or disembody the beloved as woman comment on the silence – almost always icily aloof, to be sure – of the young man in Shakespeare's sub-sequence. With this in mind it might be useful to compare sonnet 93 with the much more famous 138, since there are distinctive similarities of subject matter, even if they diverge in their final treatment of a common predicament.

> s o shall I liue,supposing thou art true,
> Like a deceiued husband,so loues face,
> May still seeme loue to me,though alter'd new:
> Thy lookes with me,thy heart in other place.
> For their can liue no hatred in thine eye,
> Therefore in that I cannot know thy change,
> In manies lookes,the falce hearts history

[21] Edward. A Snow, 'Loves of Comfort and Despair: A Reading of Shakespeare's Sonnet 138', *ELH*, 47 (1980), 462–38 (462 and 479).

[22] Nona Feinberg, 'Erasing the Dark Lady: Sonnet 138 in the Sequence', *Assays: Critical Approaches to Medieval and Renaissance Texts*, 4 (1987), 97–108 (108).

Is writ in moods and frounes and wrinckles strange.
But heauen in thy creation did decree,
That in thy face sweet loue should euer dwell,
What ere thy thoughts, or thy hearts workings be,
Thy lookes should nothing thence, but sweetnesse tell.
    How like *Eaues* apple doth thy beauty grow,
    If thy sweet vertue answere not thy show.

(sonnet 93)

While 138 is addressed to an audience apart from the player-poet and woman, so that not only her discourse but also the accommodation expressed by the poem are conveyed only indirectly, as a product of the poet-speaker's narrative point of view, this poem, at least implicitly, has the young man himself as its direct and primary audience. One would expect this to make it more intimate, achieving the 'mutuall render, onely me for thee' (sonnet 125) that sonnets 23 and 125 attempt to effect. But this is not so: sonnet 93 conveys as much alienation and uncertainty, distance and obeisance, as we find in the more overt poems of estrangement. The proximity of sonnet 93 to the much more well-known sonnet 94 prompts us to recognise, in the beloved whose face shows neither 'thy thoughts or thy hearts workings' in sonnet 93, the enigmatic and discomfiting 'Lords and owners of their faces' of sonnet 94. Furthermore, the silence of the beloved is here and in 94 – indeed, throughout the sub-sequence – a source of the young man's strength: the aloof, judgemental and mute power of the spectator.

It is across this distance, then, of both social power and inscrutable enigma, that the poet declares his decision to do what sonnet 138 announces in such a different mode: to 'liue, supposing though art true, / Like a deceiued husband'. This is no less than a paraphrase of the famous opening line of 138, and while the latter may lack the conventional flattery of lines like 'For their can liue no hatred in thine eye' and 'But heauen in thy creation did decree, / That in thy face sweet loue should euer dwell,' such flattery is in any case quickly and deftly undercut by the implication that this apparently gracious gift of nature may both be what puts 'faire truth vpon so foule a face' (sonnet 137) by hiding the 'falce hearts history' (sonnet 93) and the sign of promiscuity insofar as the beloved is unable or unwilling to 'frown' on anyone. That this inscrutably beautiful beloved is given no opportunity to speak, even indirectly, is a sign of an almost total asymmetry of power, but it acts in favour of the beloved rather than the poet, in the relationship. The decision by the poet to 'liue, supposing though art true, / Like a deceiued husband' is thus made entirely unilaterally, in an exasperated and fearful attempt to adapt to an intolerable situation in which all 'mutuall render' is excluded *a priori* both by the beloved's implacable silence and the double-edged argument that his heart may be in another place precisely because 'their can liue no hatred in [his] eye'. Directed as a monologue to the beloved, the poem engages less in description than in what I have called a quasi-performative: the attempt to effect or change a situation simply by saying so. There is no perlocutionary force in the argument, for what would it achieve? By the poem's own argument, to persuade the beloved to a change of heart would be pointless, for how would he know that such a change of heart had taken place? There is no way of knowing, since the beloved's heart is hidden by a face that exasperatingly does not 'alter when it alteration finds' (sonnet 116). So the poet simply has to console himself with the belief that the poem itself will bring into being the state of homo-geny for which it longs: it is an enactment of the adoption of a belief, a way of living. But such an enactment can be no more than a lonely tactic so long as the lie is lived and believed entirely unilaterally: 'so shall *I* liue, supposing thou art true'.

In contrast, as Snow argues, sonnet 138 in the very least reports, and perhaps also enacts, in a variety of nuanced ways which I need not re-hearse here, a kind of mutual rather than unilateral transformation of a relationship through the acceptance of a double kind of lying. And it is the pun on 'lie', in which consummating action obliterates differentiating similitude, that does the most work in this poem. The difference between 138 and 93 lies in the fact that in the latter the beloved shares (or is said to share) the decision to live in terms of a pair of fictions that finally constitute the relationship and its undoubted, if imperfect, consummations. In other words, the empowering Petrarchan distance, constituted in part by the absence of an answering voice, that marks not only sonnet 93 but the whole of the sub-sequence to the young man, is closed by the 'mutuall render' of the heterosexual couple's lying: to and with each other. To agree to engage in this relationship through the powers of the lie is neither to harp on 'what really is' nor to accept the shadows of mere fancy, but to bring forth a situation in the mode of what we may call an 'excellent falsehood'. It is in fact to abandon the idea of a 'simple truth' – one to which sonnet 93 still clings and from which it derives its pain – in favour of the shared power of the performative, by which 'saying makes things so'.

To say this is not to be complacent or smug about the sonnet or its poet. That the woman's voice is excluded or shaped by the poet is a truism.

This would formally be so even if she were to speak the entire poem in direct speech. Why sonnets in general do not resound with the voices of their addressees is the subject for another, perhaps Bakhtin-directed, study. Such silence is not always a sign of either disempowerment or even dismemberment, however. Plays such as *Antony and Cleopatra* and *As You Like It* display the exclusions, accommodations and enactments of the performative that may have marked the actual, historically embodied, situations of address, reception and response of the original performances of these now infuriatingly silent poems. I now turn to such embodied situations of address as they are examplified in *Love's Labour's Lost*, *Romeo and Juliet* and *Twelfth Night*.

CHAPTER 2

Embodiment: the sonnets, Love's Labour's Lost, Romeo and Juliet and Twelfth Night

It is one of the more telling ironies of literary history that a body of poems that proclaims its own capacity to rescue its addressees from the obscurity and ravages of time by immortalising them in the transcendental life of its own language should in fact have left their natures and identities a virtual blank. Despite attempts by literary biographers and historians to find out who the 'dark lady' and the 'fair friend' of Shakespeare's Sonnets were, the life that they lead – considered purely through the poems – is a linguistic or textual one. Whatever subjectivity or objectivity they enjoy appears at first sight to be merely grammatical, literally the outcome of the logical law that to speak about something entails nothing about its existence. To paraphrase Stephen Booth, the dark lady and the young man were almost certainly either actual historical people or fictions; the sonnets provide no explicit evidence on the matter.[1]

The recent trend, beginning with the New Criticism and culminating in recent poststructuralist theory, of rejecting biographical or dramatic accounts of the sonnets in favour of their textually self-reflexive and self-enclosed nature, may be attributed to a growing and increasingly self-conscious obsession with this truth. This critical tendency has emphasised not only the multiple and irreducible complexities and ambiguities of the language of the sonnets (Stephen Booth, Helen Vendler), it has also sacrificed their objects of address to the overriding idea that the poems are interesting above all for the way in which they constitute the subjectivity of their creator (Joel Fineman). Shakespeare's sonnets are taken to be less about the noble young man or the morally duplicitous dark lady of their address than about the grammatically necessary (rather than historically actual) poetic subject of their writing. This theoretical common ground underlies Heather Dubrow's suggestion that the sonnets do not enact a dramatic scenario but rather 'explore their

---

[1] *Shakespeare's Sonnets*, ed. Stephen Booth (New Haven, CT: Yale University Press, 1978), 545.

speaker's psyche',[2] Ann Ferry's claim that they for the first time establish an 'inward language' of 'the self',[3] Joel Fineman's argument that through his sonnets Shakespeare 'invented...an altogether novel but subsequently governing subjectivity in our literary history'[4] and Helen Vendler's exclusive interest in their representation of a 'solitary mind' at work,[5] despite otherwise prodigious differences among these critics. The historically situated embodiment of the sonnets within a nexus that included poet, addressee and audience, each embroiled in complex political, sexual and economic relations, has tended either to be reduced to the space of the psychological drama of the persona or suppressed in favour of a general poetic subjectivity that is in fact no less than the symptomatic expression of language in its march towards Lacan and Derrida.

This chapter interrogates the set of critical assumptions that dissolve the corporeality of the referent in a solution of textuality and subjectivity, by posing questions about the *embodiment* of addressee, the writer and the sonnet itself. I use *Love's Labour's Lost*, *Twelfth Night* and *Romeo and Juliet* to explore the sonnet form as it is literally incorporated into the material space of the theatre. In this space the corporeality of speaker and audience, or the real circumstances either of receipt or miscarriage, are difficult to ignore, and performative uses of language are set in fully developed contexts of interactive dialogue. The peculiarly theatrical mode of the sonnets and their self-conscious use of language as a form of social action demonstrate that however much the transcendence of the worldly conditions of distance and temporality are to be desired, such a removal from a material and social world is impossible. The poems rehearse again and again not the futility or emptiness of the ideal, but its incorrigible imbrication in the contingent, the real, the embodied. The ideal is always acknowledged as an inescapable desire; it is even presented as an inevitable condition of language itself.

The distinction between two different kinds of readings of the sonnets – between a contextualised and a decontextualised, or a textualised and

---

[2] Heather Dubrow, *Captive Victors: Shakespeare's Narrative Poems and Sonnets* (Ithaca, NY and London: Cornell University Press, 1987), 212.

[3] Ann Ferry, *The 'Inward' Language: Sonnets of Wyatt, Sidney, Shakespeare, and Donne* (Chicago: University of Chicago Press, 1983).

[4] Joel Fineman, 'Shakespeare's Ear', *Representations*, 28 (Fall 1989), 6. Fineman's argument is fully developed in *Shakespeare's Perjured Eye: The Invention of Poetic Subjectivity in the Sonnets* (Berkeley, Los Angeles and London: University of California Press, 1986).

[5] Helen Vendler, *The Art of Shakespeare's Sonnets* (Cambridge, MA: Harvard University Press, 1997).

embodied, treatment of address – is in fact represented as part of the action of *Love's Labour's Lost*. In Act 4 Scene 2, the sonnet addressed by Biron to Rosaline and sent via Costard is presented to Holofernes by Jaquenetta, who, thinking that it comes to her from Don Armado, asks the pedant to read it. After making characteristically inflated and pompous remarks about the Italian epigraph, Holofernes commands Nathaniel to read it aloud. This sonnet was subsequently published in *The Passionate Pilgrim* in 1599. In its theatrical context it expresses Biron's infatuation with Rosaline and his attempt to rationalise his broken promise to forswear the company of women. Nathaniel, the curate, never its intended recipient, thus disseminates Biron's sonnet to an audience even further removed from its original path of address. Moreover, if Holofernes is to be believed, Nathaniel's performance is aesthetically wanting: he 'find[s] not the apostrophas, and so miss[es] the accents' (4.2.119). Holofernes's subsequent 'supervision' of the 'canzonet' reveals that his own interest in the verses is that of a technical, self-inflating literary critic. The circumstances of address, although quite apparent from the letter and the sonnet itself, form no part of the pedant's aesthetic interest. These are considered to be a matter for the King and his court, and Jaquenetta and Costard are summarily dispatched to deliver Biron's missive to the 'royal hand' with the offhand remark that 'it may concern much' (4.2.140). Holofernes's own concerns are what we would now term formalist ones: he uses the 'accidental' appearance of the verses to show off his own supposed learning and wit by proclaiming the paucity of 'elegancy, facility, and golden cadence of poesy' (4.2.122) in the courtier's numbers. And yet, such a narrow, internal reading of Biron's sonnet extends beyond a purely formalist framework. Holofernes may not allow any specific biography of address to inform his reading of the poem (the fact that it comes from Biron, is addressed to Rosaline and is 'an action, something done for and to the beloved'[6]), but he does use its fortuitous appearance to confirm a sense of community which he delimits from that of the court. Biron's sonnet provides the cue for Holofernes's learned banquet, an occasion not only for 'prov[ing] those verses to be very unlearned, neither savouring of poetry, wit, nor invention' (4.2.156) to a circle of like-minded admirers, including a pupil and her father, but also for signalling the difference between the 'gentles' game' of love and his own pedantic 'recreation' of literary criticism (4.2.163).

---

[6] C. L. Barber, 'An Essay on the Sonnets', in *Elizabethan Poetry: Modern Essays in Criticism*, ed. Paul J. Alpers (New York: Oxford University Press, 1967), 299 – 320 (303).

Two issues present themselves. The first is the theoretical point that as an instance of social action a sonnet always finds itself within a particular circle of address. In this case it is addressed by the courtier Biron to the lady-in-waiting Rosaline, within a complex context in terms of which his vow of constant love is in the same breath the transgression of an earlier commitment to abstinence. The fact that the circle of original address can always be broken does not negate the significance of that origin. In enacting such a breaking of the circle, whether, as Holofernes remarks, 'accidentally, or by way of progression' (4.2.137–8), the scene under discussion in fact underlines the importance and significance of that original context. Holofernes correctly sees that the verses that have fallen into his hands 'may concern much' in social and political terms, which is why he dispatches Jacquenetta to the King with no further ado. The whole plot of the comedy turns upon this insight, which ostensibly has nothing to do with the aesthetic nature of the sonnet. At the same time, Holofernes's own use of the sonnet takes it out of that context and turns it into a 'literary' object: an aesthetic product which is treated in terms of its technical accomplishments, its display of wit or its lack of learning. Thus the distinction between formalist and social criticism is in fact made within the play itself.

Nor does the matter rest there. For we know that what was originally Biron's sonnet to Rosaline was further removed from the context of theatrical embodiment and address when it appeared in *The Passionate Pilgrim* as one of *Shakespeare's* 'Sugred sonnets' (Francis Meres, *Palladis Tamia*, quoted in *The Sonnets*, ed. Katherine Duncan-Jones, 1). I will come back to this later. For the moment I wish to underline the second point that seems to me to be made in this scene, namely, that even when the sonnet is disembodied, formalised, aestheticised by Holofernes, this move does not escape a further context of embodiment or circle of address. Holofernes as formalist literary critic uses the sonnet to cement a different kind of social relationship from that envisaged by its original author (Biron): Holofernes places himself at the centre of a learned circle of non or anti-courtiers who achieve their solidarity in part through the disparagement of the literary efforts of the court. Laughing at the 'gentles' game' proves to be the recreation of the learned middle classes, an enterprise which in fact encompasses the broader social relations that subtend the writing and performance of *Love's Labour's Lost* itself, especially in the class aspirations of its playwright. In its enactment of the movement of a sonnet beyond its original context of address, this scene distinguishes not merely between two kinds of literary reception and effect; it also shows that there is no purely formalist criticism, no simple interiority outside a context of address by which a sonnet may reflect either the psychological struggles of its author or constitute the moment-by-moment experiences of its reader.

In this brief scene we are thus made aware of three different levels on which a sonnet may be embedded in a context: the original context of address in which it is penned by Biron in order to express his love for and excuse his broken vow to Rosaline. This is followed by the formalist treatment of the sonnet as an example of inept technique and inadequate learning by an audience for whom it was not intended, but for whom it is nonetheless embedded as a form of class rather than sexual rivalry. Finally, the instance most removed from its 'origin' in the play, it is published beyond the contexts of social action represented and enacted on the stage, in an Elizabethan anthology as a representative of Shakespeare's verse. In the last, most removed context, the paradox invoked by the first line, 'If love make me forsworn, how shall I swear to love?', which arises directly from the plot of the play, would presumably have perplexed a contemporary reader.

As Arthur Marotti has noted, the formalist disembodiment of poetry from its context of original readers and social action, where it was a 'kind of social currency', and which we can now recognise in specific forms of literary criticism, was already occurring in contemporary dissemination of sonnets in printed anthologies: 'the texts in manuscript and printed miscellanies lost touch with their original contexts, as the very act of anthologizing dislodged poems from their place in a system of transactions within polite or educated circles and put them in the more fundamentally "literary" environment of the handwritten or typographical volume'. This process of recontextualisation, he adds, 'occurs in any formalist or ahistorical reading',[7] often with the result that 'the conventional literary language . . . used to express what were probably, in context, quite specific personal responses to social and political circumstances [comes] across to later readers as peculiarly contentless' (*John Donne*, 11). Most recent criticism of Shakespeare's sonnets does indeed treat them as if the last of these contexts, their literary recontextualisation, were in fact the norm: a disembodied appearance in print, leaving no or little trace of the original circumstances – social, political and erotic – which the play *Love's Labour's Lost* does indeed represent to its audience, at least in the case of Biron's sonnet. Taking our cue from the necessary embodiment,

---

7 Arthur F. Marotti, *John Donne: Coterie Poet* (Madison: University of Wisconsin Press, 1986), 12–3.

both physically and in terms of the represented situation of political and economic relations that is inescapable in the theatre, we can begin to understand the intervention of the sonnet as a form of social action in the place where it originally did its work. Its necessary embodiment in that context, constitutive of the address of one human body to another within the original circumstances of social action (even though they may seem to have dissolved in the textuality of the purely printed word) and rendered inescapable by the theatre, is precisely what is ignored in anti-biographical and anti-dramatic readings of printed sonnets. I now turn to the most well-known instance of the sonnet embodied on stage: the 'dialogue sonnet' in *Romeo and Juliet*.

Critics may differ in their views of the degree to which *Romeo and Juliet* is contained by or transcends the Petrarchan tradition, but they do not doubt that the popular tragedy bears the strong imprint of this essentially aristocratic poetic pastime. It is one thing to note the presence, whether as overriding motif or mere trace, of a different literary genre in a play. It is another to account for the mutual transformations that are wrought by their 'different greeting' (*Romeo and Juliet*, 1.5.89). For if the sonnet literary tradition to some degree set the terms of the play's language and story, as Jill Levenson argues,[8] the play itself ensures that the sonnet will never be the same again once it has passed through its essentially theatrical body.[9] The singularity of Shakespeare's sonnets is at least in part made possible by the transforming mode of the tragedy and its social world. Rosalie Colie notes the way in which literary devices are renewed in Shakespeare's plays through the capacity of the theatre to render literal or concrete things that are otherwise merely abstract or figurative.[10] By creating a social world in which family feuds are an integral part of the psychological and political dynamic, Shakespeare renders the received literary device of the Petrarchan oxymoron in the most palpable and

---

[8] Jill L. Levenson, 'The Definition of Love: Shakespeare's Phrasing in *Romeo and Juliet*', *Shakespeare Studies*, 15 (1982), 21–36 (22). See also '*Romeo and Juliet*: Tragical-Comical-Lyrical History', *Proceedings of the PMR Conference*, Augustinian Historical Institute, Villanova University, PA, 12.13 (1987–8), 31–46, and '*Romeo and Juliet* before Shakespeare', *Studies in Philology*, 81.3 (Summer 1984), 325–47.

[9] Gayle Whittier claims that 'in *Romeo and Juliet* the inherited Petrarchan word becomes English flesh by declining from lyric freedom to tragic fact through a transaction that sonnetizes the body, diminishes the body of the sonnet, and scatters the terms of the *blazon du corps*', 'The Sonnet's Body and the Body Sonnetized in *Romeo and Juliet*', *Shakespeare Quarterly*, 40 (1989), 27–41; reprinted in *Critical Essays on 'Romeo and Juliet'*, ed. Joseph A. Porter (New York: G.K. Hall, 1997), 82–96 (47). I shall argue that it is a mistake to deny such embodiment to the sonnet as such.

[10] Rosalie Colie, *Shakespeare's Living Art* (Princeton, NJ: Princeton University Press, 1974), 95.

material terms. This may seem close to Gayle Whittier's argument that in *Romeo and Juliet* the essentially disembodied, merely literary existence of the sonnet is fatally incorporated into the 'tragic fact' represented by the play. But her argument depends on an absolute generic difference between tragedy and lyric, 'fact' and 'freedom', the abstract and the material, so that their meeting on the stage inevitably results in the reduction, diminution or scattering of the lyric. By implication at least, Whittier regards the sonnet-as-lyric as essentially free of the constraints – material, political, psychological – that mark tragedy as drama and theatre. I shall argue that the opposite is in fact true. Far from being a realm of freedom, the Elizabethan sonnet, as a form of social action, was as constrained by social and political fact as theatrical forms of representation, as public and embodied a medium as any 'two-hours' traffic of [the] stage' (*Romeo and Juliet*, Prologue, 12). Rather than diminishing or scattering the body of the sonnet (and all it represents), *Romeo and Juliet* renders that body more concrete by restoring it to a social world from which history and criticism have extracted it.

From the early poems to the young man of rank, urging him to marry and have a son, through the idealising attempts to negate the space of social difference in the mutuality of 'private' love, to the bitter wit of the 'Will' poems to the dark woman, the player-poet seeks to reduce the gap between addresser and addressee that is the very condition of the Petrarchan mode. It has not escaped commentators or audiences that in *Romeo and Juliet* Shakespeare represents a moment of reciprocity via the archetype of incommensurability: a sonnet, uniquely shared by Romeo and Juliet in Act 1. Then there are the sonnets that introduce the first two acts of the play which, though not in dialogue, again speak with the shared voice of the theatre rather than the solitary voice of 'the mind in *solitary* speech' (Vendler, *The Art of Shakespeare's Sonnets*, 1–2). All of these sonnets are both caught in and made possible by a simultaneously constricting and sustaining web of social relations.

> Two households, both alike in dignity
> In fair Verona, where we lay our scene,
> From ancient grudge break to new mutiny,
> Where civil blood makes civil hands unclean.
> From forth the fatal loins of these two foes
> A pair of star-crossed lovers take their life,
> Whose misadventured piteous overthrows
> Doth with their death bury their parents' strife.
> The fearful passage of their death-marked love

And the continuance of their parents' rage –
Which but their children's end, naught could remove –
Is now the two-hours' traffic of our stage;
The which if you with patient ears attend,
What here shall miss, our toil shall strive to mend.

(*Romeo and Juliet*, Prologue, 1–14)

Is this a sonnet? It looks like one. It conforms to all the formal character-istics of what we now call a 'Shakespearean' sonnet. It has fourteen lines, it is in iambic pentameter, it observes the characteristic rhyme scheme and it has a structure that combines three quatrains and a couplet with the vestigial 'Petrarchan' division of octave and sestet. Shakespeare wrote it. Yet in certain respects it is utterly uncharacteristic. First, although only one person utters it, it speaks with the communal voice of a collective rather than the single voice of a lyrical subjectivity. Its primary mode is expostulatory or narrative rather than reflective. It is thoroughly public, openly addressing an audience of many rather than one. Vendler would not consider it a Shakespearean sonnet in the proper sense at all (*The Art of Shakespeare's Sonnets*, 5).

Levenson suggests that the prologue is a witty means by which a poetic convention can reduce a well-known story to its own, more confined dimensions: 'the cliché clichéd', as she aptly puts it ('The Definition of Love', 23). But perhaps the play serves to expand the sonnet: to display its social, embodied character. Like the 1609 Quarto, the opening sonnet is the product of a dramatist who turns his hand to sonnets rather than a sonneteer who dabbles in drama. In a play that is concerned with the difficulty of dividing private from public, these fourteen lines raise the question of the sonnet itself and the use to which it may be put as a form of social action. For they are not merely a declarative utterance, an exercise in simple narrative, or a self-conscious cliché. They speak on behalf of a joint-stock company in which the actor who utters them and the writer who wrote them are mutual members. Together they are in the business of negotiating a public relationship and pleading for the approval of a disparate audience. But the reciprocity of pleasure and financial reward that this sonnet pursues in its theatrical context is strikingly echoed in the many sonnets of 1609, which seek erotic consummation in similar terms, treating the private, inward, psychological concepts of personal devotion through the discourse of public transactions, political or economic. This sonnet as theatre strikingly reminds us of the role of its informing, public discourse in the transactions of the sonnet as lyric.

Coming between the two ostensibly declarative prologues, whose public show is carried on their faces, the lovers' sonnet is quieter, withdrawn from public appraisal and show. Masked from the public gaze, it seems, like its protagonists, a still point of personal contact. As such it appears to be totally different from the sonnets that precede and follow it, each of which is, in effect, a commentary on its genesis and predicament. The communal speech of those two sonnets is here remarkably split into a symbol of perfect reciprocity. The little room of the sonnet is, unusually, shared by two equal, interdependent, and – most important – embodied voices

> ROMEO (*to Juliet, touching her hand*)
>   If I profane with my unworthiest hand
>   This holy shrine, the gentler sin is this:
>   My lips, two blushing pilgrims, ready stand
>   To smooth that rough touch with a tender kiss.
> JULIET Good pilgrim, you do wrong your hand too much,
>   Which mannerly devotion shows in this.
>   For saints have hands that pilgrims' hands do touch,
>   And palm to palm is holy palmers' kiss.
> ROMEO Have not saints lips, and holy palmers, too?
> JULIET Ay, pilgrim, lips that they must use in prayer.
> ROMEO O then, dear saint, let lips do what hands do:
>   They pray; grant thou, lest faith turn to despair.
> JULIET Saints do not move, though grant for prayers' sake.
> ROMEO Then move not while my prayer's effect I take.
>   (*He kisses her*)
> ROMEO Thus from my lips, by thine my sin is purged.
> JULIET Then have my lips the sin that they have took.
> ROMEO Sin from my lips? O trespass sweetly urged!
>   Give me my sin again.
>   (*He kisses her*)
> JULIET   You kiss by th' book.
>   (*Romeo and Juliet*, 1.5.92–109)

The familiarity of this exchange-as-sonnet should not prevent us from acknowledging the uniqueness of its moment: in which the Petrarchan habit of speaking of one's beloved, or to one's beloved, or behind the back of one's beloved, is replaced by the reciprocity of speaking *with* one's beloved. This is, of course, obvious. But its very obviousness is liable to prevent us from remarking on the subtlety of that dialogue and its originality. Compare, for instance, this dialogue-sonnet to 128, which is similar in desire and image, but not in embodied reciprocity:

HOW oft when thou my musike musike playst,
Vpon that blessed wood whose motion sounds
With thy sweet fingers when thou gently swayst,
The wiry concord that mine eare confounds,
Do I enuie those Iackes that nimble leape,
To kisse the tender inward of thy hand,
Whilst my poore lips which should that haruest reape,
At the woods bouldnes by thee blushing stand.
To be so tikled they would change their state,
And situation with those dancing chips,
Ore whome their fingers walke with gentle gate,
Making dead wood more blest then liuing lips,
 Since sausie Iackes so happy are in this,
 Giue them their fingers,me thy lips to kisse.

Against the more distanced observation of the male persona in this sonnet, with its obviously unrequited yearning, and its proposed parcelling
out of favours, the sonnet-in-dialogue achieves the meeting of both fingers and 'liuing lips' as the consequence of its spontaneously mutual engagement. Everything that the Petrarchan tradition has yearned for over
thousands of years, *while making it a defining condition that it should not achieve
that desire within its own body or in its own time,* is achieved in the play's interaction: words, touch, kiss, given and taken, 'thou mine, I thine' (sonnet 108).
And it is achieved, not by destroying or negating the Petrarchan body,
but by inhabiting it afresh. The voice that Sidney banishes to the songs
of his sequence, Shakespeare the dramatist incorporates into the body
of the sonnet, giving it the power not merely to say 'yes', but to converse,
in interactive dialogue. The sonnet is thus constructed out of a series of
speech acts in which the conditional, the question, the response and the
plea are woven into a fabric of ever-closer, witty engagement.

In her commentary on this meeting, Whittier mixes acute perceptive-
ness with a dogged insistence on the essentially disembodied nature of the
sonnet as such. The 'encounter' sonnet marks a moment, she correctly
points out, in which 'voice and flesh reciprocate'. But such reciprocation
is hardly an example of 'the *sonnet's* corruption into the world of substance
and time' ('The Sonnet's Body', 53). I prefer to think of it as an extension
of the movement – tonally different, to be sure – towards carnality that
Mercutio represents: not a denial or contamination of the Petrarchan
impulse, but a sign of its actual engagement – in its Elizabethan forms
at any rate – in time and substance. The sonnet which Romeo and Juliet
jointly create calls for action, signalled by the stage directions introduced
variously by all editors since Pope, and unusually consummated by the

double kiss at the end. Whittier points out (and Shakespeare shows on other occasions) that the voice and the kiss appear to be incommensurable. One negates the other, as we see in Benedick's 'Peace, I will stop your mouth' (*Much Ado About Nothing*, 5.4.97) and Cressida's ambiguous invitation to be kissed when she asks to be silenced (*Troilus and Cressida*, 3.2.122). But such incommensurability is in fact only apparent or, at the very least, paradoxical: the kiss is not so much the negation of the voice as the culmination of its desiring power; the voice is the passage to the kiss. Benedick and Beatrice's kiss – the sign that Benedick is now a 'married man' – is in fact made possible by their 'own hands against [their] hearts' (5.4.91) in the form of mutually reciprocating sonnets. The theatre audience is made privy to at least one of those sonnets in truncated form in Beatrice's complex performative turn from 'maiden pride' to 'kindness':

> What fire is in mine ears? Can this be true?
>> Stand I condemned for pride and scorn so much?
> Contempt, farewell; and maiden pride, adieu.
>> No glory lives behind the back of such.
> And Benedick, love on. I will requite thee,
>> Taming my wild heart to thy loving hand.
> If thou dost love, my kindness shall incite thee
>> To bind our loves up in a holy band.
> For other say thou dost deserve, and I
> Believe it better than reportingly.
>> (*Much Ado About Nothing*, 3.2.106–16)

Beatrice and Benedick's mutual engagement in the world of the sonnet – despite their shared ironical stance towards Petrarch – is decisive in breaking their solitary poses. Their alignment of hands and hearts reminds us that the sonnet is a form of action, something produced through and by the body towards the union of both bodies and souls.

If Beatrice and Benedick require the publication of sonnets written separately to the beloved to attest to feelings that neither can finally deny, no prior sonnets are written or published by Romeo or Juliet. Romeo stumbles into a kind of Petrarchan mode in the garden in Act 2 Scene 1, but Juliet quickly cuts him short, confirming her love and eschewing vows as something that, since they always contain the possibility of falsehood, she would rather do without. The dialogue-sonnet in the previous scene and the overheard unburdening of Juliet's heart from the balcony short-circuits a whole world of conventional negotiations. The conventionality of such negotiations does not render them superficial or nugatory, however. On the contrary. If Juliet is pleased to be able to circumvent the necessary possibility of falsehood that lies in the vow as speech act, she is also disturbed by the suddenness with which conventional rites have been dispensed with:

> Fain would I dwell on form, fain, fain deny
> What I have spoke; but farewell, compliment.
> Dost thou love me? I know thou wilt say 'Ay',
> And I will take thy word. Yet if thou swear'st
> Thou mayst prove false. At lovers' perjuries,
> They say, Jove laughs. O gentle Romeo,
> If thou dost love, pronounce it faithfully;
> Or if thou think'st I am too quickly won,
> I'll frown, and be perverse, and say thee nay,
> So thou wilt woo; but else, not for the world.
>   . . .
> ROMEO Lady, by yonder blessèd moon I vow,
>   That tips with silver all these fruit-tree tops –
> JULIET O swear not by the moon, th' inconstant moon
>   That monthly changes in her circled orb,
>   Lest that thy love prove likewise variable.
> ROMEO What shall I swear by?
> JULIET   Do not swear at all,
>   Or if thou wilt, swear by thy gracious self,
>   Which is the god of my idolatry,
>   And I'll believe thee.
> ROMEO   If my heart's dear love –
> JULIET Well, do not swear. Although I joy in thee,
>   I have no joy of this contract tonight.
>   It is too rash, too unadvised, too sudden,
>   Too like the lightning which doth cease to be
>   Ere one can say it lightens.   (*Romeo and Juliet*, 2.1.130–62)

Coming so soon after their shared sonnet, this exchange conveys the alienation of the usual processes of erotic negotiation that is rehearsed so incessantly in the sonnets. Caught between a desire to dwell on the form that gives a public stability to such 'giddy' situations and the recognition that it is too late for such 'compliment', Juliet displays an unerring, if disconcerting for herself, understanding of the peculiar logic that underlies the performatives of love and the personal vulnerability which informs them. Juliet dares make Romeo's answer for him, in part to preclude the possibility of denial, but also to forestall the very possibility of falsehood that lies within every assent, ominously signalled by his unfortunate decision to swear by the moon. Even her suggestion that he should swear by himself, the subject of her new idolatry, is quickly brushed aside in the realisation that swearing under such circumstances is at best redundant, while at worst it opens up the possibility of 'infelicity'.

Whatever Romeo and Juliet have to say to each other as lovers in the balcony scene has already been said at the ball and has been signalled by the reciprocity of their kisses. Those kisses, which follow Juliet's demure invitation, act as the culminating moment of a sonnet that she co-creates almost without effort with her new lover. But that sonnet is unable completely to contain their sought-after reciprocity. Desire bursts forth again, not only in the subsequent encounter in the garden, but in the immediate passage of a new, but now interrupted, sonnet. The shared quatorzain in the earlier scene is thus followed immediately by the initiating quatrain of a new, dialogical sonnet. And in another constitutive paradox, the admired 'little room' of the sonnet is shown to be built upon a lack: its perfect structure of fourteen lines strives towards a fifteenth, in which the sonneteer may say, with Romeo: '*Thus* from my lips, by thine my sin is purged.' This quiddity of carnal union, denoted through a theatrical deixis that remains outside the sonnet's 'numbers' but which nevertheless informs them completely, is what both Juliet and Mercutio emphasise at other moments of the play. But such quiddity is hardly sufficient. Romeo's triumph is no more than the beginning of another sonnet, in which desire gathers itself up once again. The ancient conceit of the stolen kiss is, however, turned by Juliet into a reflection on the residual conventionality of Romeo's solicitation. Word and flesh come together in a different way in Juliet's charge that he kisses by the book. This is a reminder, perhaps, that there is no kiss but by the representations of the cultural. But it is also, in a movement of 'love's transgression' (1.1.182), the sign of her desire for a less bookish form of consummation. Both of these notions are encapsulated by the summons of the mother and the name of the father, which abruptly breaks off the second sonnet, just as it looks as if its terms are to be determined by Juliet, rather than Romeo:

> NURSE Madam, your mother craves a word with you.
> (*Juliet departs to her mother*)
> ROMEO What is her mother?
> NURSE   Marry, bachelor,
> Her mother is the lady of the house,
> And a good lady, and a wise and virtuous.

> I nursed her daughter that you talked withal.
> I tell you, he that can lay hold of her
> Shall have the chinks.
>
> ROMEO (*aside*)   Is she a Capulet?
>
> (1.5.110–16)

After the mutual intimacy of the sonnet Juliet is suddenly distanced by the third-person pronoun and the alienating proper name. The ties of the world have been kept at bay because both Romeo and Juliet are masked, and because neither of them knows the other's (divisive) proper name. They can forge the reciprocity represented by the sonnet only under the playful anonymity of the common name, through the fictional identities of 'pilgrim, saint, palmer', by which the networks of relationship that tie them to their families' names and distance them from those of others are suspended. The encounter exemplifies as theatre both Sidney's imploring desire for consummation with Stella as a *fictional* identity: 'I am not I, pitie the tale of me' (sonnet 45) and the desire in Shakespeare's 1609 Sonnets to loosen the ties of the proper name. I discuss the role of names in chapter 4. Such a loss of oneself in a fictional world is precisely what Juliet's 'pity' in the shared sonnet allows, although the moment of reciprocating identity loss that the lovers achieve is soon overwhelmed by a reality that has always been lurking on the outskirts of their private meeting. Tybalt has recognised Romeo even before he meets Juliet ('This, by his voice, should be a Montague' (1.5.53)), and his description of the internal conflict caused by the clash between his obedience to his uncle and his own 'wilful' anger ominously frames the 'different greeting' of Romeo Montague and Juliet Capulet:

> TYBALT Patience perforce with wilful choler meeting
> Makes my flesh tremble in their different greeting.
> I will withdraw, but this intrusion shall,
> Now seeming sweet, convert to bitt'rest gall.
>
> (1.5.88–91)

The encounter sonnet, created equally by Romeo and Juliet in a di-alogical[11] fusion of voices and desires, is framed by the two prologue sonnets whose communal voices act rather differently. By the beginning of Act 2, the voice of the company that speaks through the Prologue is merely implied rather than alluded to directly through the use of the

---

[11] It needs to be noted that 'dialogical' is not being used in its Bakhtinian sense here. Indeed, its sense is the very opposite of what Bakhtin meant by the word. No conflicted or competing social voices, no heteroglossia, are released in this sonnet. Its purpose is the very opposite: to fuse two voices into a single monological form.

first-person plural. Those fourteen lines thus appear to be no more than a convenient vehicle for the redundant summary of a narrative that would have been well known in any case. But, coming so soon after the unusual sonnet as vehicle of reciprocity in Act 1 Scene 5, its role is more complex:

> CHORUS Now old desire doth in his deathbed lie,
> And young affection gapes to be his heir.
> That fair for which love groaned for and would die,
> With tender Juliet matched, is now not fair.
> Now Romeo is beloved and loves again,
> Alike bewitchèd by the charm of looks;
> But to his foe supposed he must complain,
> And she steal love's sweet bait from fearful hooks.
> Being held a foe, he may not have access
> To breathe such vows as lovers use to swear,
> And she as much in love, her means much less
> To meet her new belovèd anywhere.
> But passion lends them power, time means, to meet,
> Temp'ring extremities with extreme sweet.

Cleverly representing the transformation of Romeo's desire in terms of the conflicts of the society at large, including its generational differences, this sonnet both explains the impossibility of conventional Petrarchan discourses in such a society and conveys in its structure the reciprocity achieved by Romeo and Juliet in the previous scene, even as it expresses the social barriers to such union. Romeo 'loves again', but this time he is also 'beloved'. And if he now has to 'complain' to his 'foe supposed', she in turn must 'steal love's sweet bait from fearful hooks'. Juliet's sexual desire and agency here inverts Petrarchan stereotypes of female silence and passivity.[12] Whereas the sonnet succinctly conveys the mutuality of the lovers' affection, it also recognises the unequal freedom that male and female lovers have to pursue their desires. The ideological forces that deny Romeo the conventional means to express his love trap the female – 'as much in love' – in a more concrete kind of domestic confinement: 'her means much less / To meet her new belovèd anywhere'. The Petrarchan

---

[12] Cf. John Donne's 'The Bait', and *Antony and Cleopatra*, 2.5.10–15:

> CLEOPATRA: Give me mine angle. We'll to th' river. There,
> My music playing far off, I will betray
> Tawny-finned fishes. My bended hook shall pierce
> Their slimy jaws, and as I draw them up
> I'll think them every one an Antony,
> And say 'Ah ha, you're caught!'

mode, of 'complaint' and 'vows', is thus represented as a real rather than a merely literary response to love, caught in the exigencies of a particular social and political context. As it happens, the mutuality of the lovers' now separated desire – represented, let us not forget, through a sonnet – renders that mode of preparatory negotiation unnecessary, as their reciprocating 'passion lends them power ... to meet'. Significant, too, is the sonnet's repeated use of the most common epithet for reciprocal, sensual love in the 1609 Sonnets – 'sweet' – especially in the union of the closing couplet rhyme: 'meet/sweet'. If the sonnet that acts as the Prologue to the play as a whole encapsulates the well-known narrative from which the drama is derived, this one both represents the reciprocity of the lovers and places Petrarchan discourse within an active, material and social context.

From the staged representation of active female desire and embodied reciprocity, I now turn to the ways in which the embodiment of the sonnet on stage may work against reciprocity, enacting the agency, even through silence, of the female 'no'.

Much recent feminist criticism of the Petrarchan sonnet tradition has remarked on the degree to which the addressee of the sonnet, despite her tradition idealisation – bordering at times on idolatry – is in fact reduced by the tradition to a silent, passive and, in the case of the blazon, dismembered, object. Nancy Vickers has persuasively argued that the Petrarchan reduces the beloved to silence and fragments her absent body in order to constitute the fullness of his own subjectivity. 'Silencing Diana is an emblematic gesture', Vickers argues,

> it suppresses a voice, and it casts generations of would-be Lauras in a role predicated upon the muteness of its player. A modern Actaeon affirming himself as poet cannot permit Ovid's angry goddess to speak her displeasure and deny his voice; his speech requires her silence. Similarly, he cannot allow her to dismember his body; instead he repeatedly, although reverently, scatters her throughout his scattered rhymes.[13]

Philip Sidney's *Astrophil and Stella* seems to confirm Vickers's argument insofar as the *sonnets* of the sequence do in fact assume Stella's silence as a condition for Astrophil's considerable volubility. Although many of the sonnets are addressed to Stella, and her physical presence is alluded to in some (the most well-known being number 47, 'Soft but here she

[13] Nancy Vickers, 'Diana Described: Scattered Woman and Scattered Rhymes', *Critical Inquiry*, 8 (1981–2), 265–79 (279).

comes' (line 12)), she is given a voice in none of them, despite the fact that the comments of Astrophel's courtly detractors appear quite frequently in both direct and indirect speech (sonnet 54).[14] On occasion Stella's remarks are alluded to as indirect discourse ('She in whose eyes *Love*, though unfelt, doth shine, / Sweet said that I true love in her should find' (sonnet 63, lines 3–4)), and in the famous 'grammar' sonnet (64) her double rejection 'No, no' is turned into a sophistical triumph by the convention 'That in one speech two Negatives affirm' (line 14).

Matters are different with the songs, however, where Stella is given, comparatively speaking at least, a quite considerable voice and presence. Although it represents Stella's direct speech, the Fourth Song does no more than re-enact the trap of sonnet 63. She says no more than 'No, no, no, no, my Deare, let be', nine times, the last of which is twisted, via a turn in the direction of Astrophil's argument, into an affirmation of love rather than its denial. The song is in fact no more than a more elaborately clever enactment of the process of silencing and manipulation to which Vickers draws our attention. As a reflection of her own autonomy Stella's participation serves her worse than silence would. The presence of her voice in the Eighth Song is, however, different. Not only does Stella speak with authority and some compassion in this song, but Sidney also embodies her response as the autonomous actions and speech of a fully human agent:

> There his hands in their speech, faine
> Would have made tongue's language plaine;
> But her hands his hands repelling,
> Gave repulse all grace excelling.
>
> Then she spake; her speech was such,
> As not eares but hart did touch:
> While such wise she love denied,
> As yet love she signified.
>
> '*Astrophil*' sayd she, 'my love
> Cease in these effects to prove:
> Now be still, yet still beleeve me,
> Thy grief more than death would grieve me.

And so she goes on, uninterrupted, for six more quatrains. Not only does this representation of Stella's response uncharacteristically embody

---

[14] I am ignoring the possibility that sonnet 83 is in fact spoken by Stella herself. For an intriguing essay on this possibility see Jonathan Crew, *Hidden Designs: The Critical Profession and Renaissance Literature* (New York and London: Methuen, 1986), 87ff.

her in a mode other than the pacifying and dismembering modes of epideixis – 'her hands his hands repelling' is hardly the stuff of conventional blazon – but her speech also silences both Astrophel and the poet. The song ends with the poet reflecting on both his and the hero's enforced muteness. This silencing is effected by the active intervention – the represented action – of the woman who intentionally absents herself and breaks both heart and verse 'with what she had done and spoken':

> Therewithall away she went,
> Leaving him so passion rent,
> With what she had done and spoken,
> That therewith my song is broken.

Stella speaks in one further song. In the Eleventh (and last) she is the initiator rather than the respondent in the exchange. As in the Eighth Song, the Eleventh represents her as a person trapped within a set of social and economic constraints rather than as the disembodied fragments of a poetic convention. Furthermore, her intervention brings the sequence to an end. The reiterated scattering which Vickers remarks as the condition of Petrarchism knows no end: it is endlessly and necessarily repeatable, as long as the addressee remains mute and as long as her *daunger* is limited to the cold heart ascribed to her by the poet and a simple reported 'no' of rejection. Petrarchism as a purely poetic convention knows no other narrative: it feeds on the necessity of an eternal 'no'. This monotony is one reason why Marotti can say that approached purely formalistically early modern sonnets appear to be peculiarly contentless. But by introducing an embodied response from the beloved, Sidney opens the whole cycle to what Bakhtin calls the 'event' of the utterance: a response that bears the traces of a complex set of social relationships and conflicts, rather than merely signalling the fragmentation of an epideictic object.[15] Stella is not merely allowed to 'speak her displeasure and deny his voice'. The fact of her response embroils both herself and the erotic relationship within a social context. Other, publicly pressing factors – the social pressures of 'tyrant Honour' or the family jealousies of 'lowts' with '*Argus* eyes' (Eleventh Song) – underlie her rejection, rather than the necessary because always-already written projection of feminine *daunger*.

The final act of *Love's Labour's Lost* embodies on stage the situation described in the songs of *Astrophil and Stella*, revealing that on the physical

---

[15] Mikhail Bakhtin, *Speech Genres and Other Late Essays*, trans. Vern W. McGee, ed. Caryl Emerson and Michael Holquist (Austin: University of Texas Press, 1986).

platform of the theatre the situation of address and reception of the sonnet is inescapable. No longer a fragmented and muted absence, the women are able not only to voice their displeasure but also to cause the disintegration of the sonnet itself. Their switching of masks and tokens shows how important it is for a declaration of Petrarchan love to find its proper mark: it is precisely by turning the anonymity, the blankness or facelessness that the convention imposes upon its addressee, against the lovers in a context of embodied action that the women are able to expose the hollowness of each courtier's claims to dote on a specific woman who, by definition, must surpass all others in beauty and desirability. The Princess and her women reveal and reject in their masking and swapping of favours precisely the paradoxically disembodying affects of the Petrarchan epideictic praise for 'a hand, a foot, a face, an eye, / A gait, a state, a brow, a breast, a waist, / A leg, a limb' (4.3.182–4). They confront such dismemberment with the active corporeality of their own bodies, which are able to trap the writers and reciters of sonnets into enacting what has always been the condition of their writing and their passion: as Biron puts it, 'we, / Following the signs, woo'd but the sign of she' (5.2.468–9). By forcing each of the lords to repeat the conventional declarations of love and praise that were expressed in their original sonnets directly to a completely different woman, the women themselves show the importance of the situation of address: their own assumed facelessness, in the form of their masks, emphasises both the signal significance, indeed the reality, of their faces and also exposes and negates their textual effacement by Petrarchan praise.

The most telling enactment of the power of the women literally to break the sonnet against their bodies rather than be incorporated into its dismembering textuality occurs when they refuse to allow Mote to set the terms of the courtiers' erotic address. In the actual encounter between body and text the women are able, simply by turning their backs on the men, to render literal, and thus nonsensical, the abstract hyperbole of the representative sonnet that Mote has conned:

> MOTE All hail, the richest beauties on the earth!
> BIRON (*aside*) Beauties no richer than rich taffeta.
> MOTE A holy parcel of the fairest dames –
>   (*The ladies turn their backs to him*)
>   That ever turned their – backs to mortal views.
> BIRON 'Their eyes', villain, 'their eyes'!
> MOTE That ever turned their eyes to mortal views.
>   Out . . .

BOYET True, out indeed!
MOTE Out of your favours, heavenly spirits, vouchsafe
        Not to behold –
BIRON 'Once to behold', rogue!
MOTE Once to behold with your sun-beamèd eyes –
        With your sun-beamèd eyes –
BOYET They will not answer to that epithet.
        You were best call it 'daughter-beamèd' eyes.
MOTE They do not mark me, and that brings me out.
BIRON Is this your perfectness? Be gone, you rogue!

                                        (5.2.157–73)

The actions of the women in this encounter are more dramatically telling than the consciously anti-Petrarchan stance of sonnet 130. In the sonnet the poet has to *tell* us that his 'Mistres when shee walkes treads on the ground'. The dramatist on the other hand can count on the actors' actual embodiment of such down-to-earth materiality to negate the power of the text to create and control the object and situation of its address.

Despite the sonnets' celebration of their own capacity, not simply to perpetuate the image of the beloved beyond the ravages of time, but also to constitute him or her through their creative force, this scene reminds us of the other side of that thought, evident in the anxiety of the sonnets to the young man of rank, that a sonnet needs to be 'marked' for it to be granted the power that it proclaims for itself. The women's negation of both the sonnet's descriptive and performative force by turning their backs on it thus enacts more economically than any other action in the play the suggestion that court poetry was primarily a form of social action, and that 'what distinguishes the individual from the type . . . arose from the situation, not the words'.[16] 'A jest's prosperity lies in the ear / Of him that hears it, never in the tongue / Of him that makes it' (5.2.848–50), Rosaline pointedly reminds Biron. She refers not only to the very different context of reception and address to which she asks him to commit himself by 'visit[ing] the speechless sick' (5.2.838), but also to the women's refusal to grant any prosperity to the King and his courtiers' wooing. This touches the broader relationship between dramatist/actor and theatre audience.

The power of the women to dictate the terms of address and reception is presented very strongly. The paradoxical rationalisation by which Biron seeks to pin the blame for his own and his companions' perjury on the women themselves ('Therefore, ladies, / Our love being yours, the

[16] John Stevens, *Music and Poetry in the Early Tudor Court* (London: Methuen, 1961), 208.

error that love makes / Is likewise yours' (5.2.763–5)) is given short shrift by a Princess who insists on the women's collective power to determine the terms of any 'world-without-end bargain':

> QUEEN We have received your letters full of love,
>   Your favours the ambassadors of love,
>   And in our maiden council rated them
>   At courtship, pleasant jest, and courtesy,
>   As bombast and as lining to the time.
>   But more devout than this in our respects
>   Have we not been, and therefore met your loves
>   In their own fashion, like a merriment.
>
> (5.2.70–77)

If one were to look at the sonnets penned by the courtiers outside the embodied context of such exchange and rebuttal (as one would, for example, if one encountered Biron's sonnet for the first time in *The Passionate Pilgrim*), one would hardly guess at the ways in which their performative and descriptive force is broken by the corporeal presence of the women – at the way in which their conventional blazon may be outfaced by the deliberate facelessness that the women assume towards it.

A similar process of outfacing the Petrarchan address is enacted in *Twelfth Night*, in the encounter between Viola as go-between and Olivia as unapproachable beloved. That scene, in which Olivia deliberately makes herself indistinguishable from her similarly veiled gentlewomen – an echo of the assumed anonymity of the women in Act 5 of *Love's Labour's Lost* – makes it clear that a sonnet has to find its proper address as a condition of both success and sense. This is borne out by the abrupt stay in Viola's recitation after only one line, as it dawns on her that the sentiments, though hackneyed, are not merely conventional or textual. To have any sense they need to be addressed to the person for whom they were written. A substitute, as Olivia pretends to be, will not do:

VIOLA The honourable lady of the house, which is she?
OLIVIA Speak to me, I shall answer for her. Your will.
VIOLA Most radiant, exquisite, and unmatchable beauty. – I pray you, tell me if this be the lady of the house, for I never saw her. I would be loath to cast away my speech, for besides that it is excellently well penned, I have taken great pains to con it. Good beauties, let me sustain no scorn; I am very 'countable, even to the least sinister usage. (*Twelfth Night*, 1.5.161–9)

What is at stake here is the very concept of love itself. For the asymmetrical nature of the possibility of substitution indicates that we are mid-way between a purely impersonal negotiation and the full-blooded ideal of romantic and companionate union. It is perfectly in order for Cesario to articulate Orsino's desires, but a similar understudy cannot replace the beloved at whom such desires are directed. To address the petition to a substitute, the substitute her/himself suggests, would be to 'cast away' the 'speech', to waste both labour and spirit. Viola manoeuvres Olivia into revealing her face to create the very condition of possibility of her 'penned' and 'conned' speech.

The situation embodies an aporia that, as Fineman has demonstrated and Elizabethan poets constantly reflect, marks the limits of epideixis: 'What may words say, or what may words not say / Where truth it selfe must speak like flatterie?' (Sidney, *Astrophil and Stella*, sonnet 35). In the abstract context of print the inadequacy of words to their object is entirely grammatical. We cannot tell whether the signifieds generated by the poem are or are not adequate to their referent. At most we may be persuaded, as Finemen argues of the 'dark lady' sonnets, of the postmodern axiom that words and images are *essentially* incompatible, that any eye is doomed to be 'perjured', and that the very speaking of language attests to an essential inadequation between signifier and referent. The referent simply disappears in this apparatus or, as Stephen Booth has put it in a different, though related, theoretical context, 'the grammatical dominates; after all, what a reader beholds is not the speaker of the poem but the poem itself'.[17]

But what happens when the grammatical is brought into contact with the referential, in the form of both speaker and addressee, as happens in the theatre? Or else, if we follow the injunctions of critics who wish to keep alive the thought of historical and physical contexts of address and reception, in the reading of sonnets to an audience which includes the beloved?[18] In such a context the double reference of words such as 'love' – both as the feeling expressed by the poet and as the beloved to whom the poem is addressed – would be palpable, embodied before our eyes. The supposed inadequacy of the conceptual to the referential could not simply be settled in advance. Two issues are at stake here: not simply

---

[17] Stephen Booth, *An Essay on Shakespeare's Sonnets* (New Haven, CT and London: Yale University Press, 1969), 121.

[18] For a discussion of this possibility in relation to *Astrophil and Stella*, see Clark Hulse, 'Stella's Wit: Penelope Rich as Reader of Sidney's Sonnets', in *Rewriting the Renaissance: The Discourse of Sexual Difference in Early Modern Europe*, ed. Margaret W. Ferguson *et al.* (Chicago and London: University of Chicago Press, 1986), 272–86.

the philosophical problem at the heart of all epideixis, namely, the now well-known problem of difference between that which is spoken and that which is spoken about, but a further difference, analysed frequently by Robert Weimann, between the positions of power and authority that mark the person representing and the figure represented.[19] In *Love's Labour's Lost* the asymmetry of power relations is embodied in the unequal relationship that exists between player and audience. Both the masque of Russians performed by the King of Navarre and his courtiers and the sorry pageant of the Nine Worthies offered by the learned bourgeoisie are dashed 'like a Christmas comedy' (5.2.462) because of the social power that lies in such spectators to denigrate the performative illusion and the human dignity of the 'comedian'. Sonnet 54 of Spenser's *Amoretti* expresses the vulnerability of the Petrarchan lover precisely in terms of such differences of power, by which the 'ydle spectator' indifferently abuses her capacity to destroy performance and performer alike:

> Of this worlds Theatre in which we stay,
> My loue lyke the Spectator ydly sits
> beholding me that all the pageants play,
> disguysing diuersly my troubled wits.
> Sometimes I ioy when glad occasion fits,
> and mask in myrth lyke to a Comedy:
> soon after when my ioy to sorrow flits,
> I waile and make my woes a Tragedy.
> Yet she beholding me with constant eye,
> delights not in my merth nor rues my smart:
> but when I laugh she mocks, and when I cry
> she laughes, and hardens euermore her hart.
> What then can moue her? if nor merth nor mone,
> she is no woman, but a sencelesse stone.[20]

But the invocation of the stage here is purely conventional: it does little more than extend Petrarchan commonplaces in stock theatrical terms. It is the work of a poet who merely finds a theatrical metaphor useful. Shakespeare's treatment of the immense power of the spectator and converse vulnerability of the player in his sonnets combines an acute social consciousness with lived theatrical concreteness. Here is sonnet 23:

[19] See Robert Weimann, 'Shakespeare (De)Canonized: Conflicting Uses of "Authority" and "Representation"', *New Literary History*, 20.1 (Autumn 1988), 65–81 'Representation and Performance: Authority in Shakespeare's Theater', *PMLA*, 107.3 (May 1992), 497–510; 'Bi-fold Authority in Shakespeare's Theater', *Shakespeare Quarterly*, 39.4 (Winter 1988), 401–17.

[20] *The Poetical Works of Spenser*, ed. J. C. Smith and E. de Selincourt (London: Oxford University Press, 1929). I owe the suggestion to look at this sonnet to Michael Spiller.

> AS an vnperfect actor on the stage,
> Who with his feare is put besides his part,
> Or some fierce thing repleat with too much rage,
> Whose strengths abondance weakens his owne heart;
> So I for feare of trust,forget to say,
> The perfect ceremony of loues right,
> And in mine owne loues strength seeme to decay,
> Ore-charg'd with burthen of mine owne loues might:
> O let my books be then the eloquence,
> And domb presagers of my speaking brest,
> Who pleade for loue,and look for recompence,
> More then that tonge that more hath more exprest.
>   O learne to read what silent loue hath writ,
>   To heare wit eies belongs to loues fine wiht

The negotiation of the unequal power relations that Shakespeare invokes by referring to himself as an 'vnperfect actor on the stage' is more telling than the static asymmetry of action and response to which Spenser refers. Far from being a merely literary conceit, the unequal relationship of spectator and actor, Petrarchan suitor and beloved, includes almost insurmountable class and economic differences. Such differences inform at least a fifth of the poems addressed to the man of rank by the poet and player. The player-poet's lowly social position is more than once conveyed in terms of his vassalage and the disgrace that his mere presence or name may bring upon his beloved patron. Unlike Spenser's poem, Shakespeare's displays not merely the fear or mockery that puts the disregarded actor beside his part, but also the *grotesque* nature of his own feelings, which are felt to transgress both propriety and expression: 'some fierce thing repleat with too much rage'. In this state of impotent power, of eloquent silence, negotiation with and to the beloved's face would prove too much; it would be inadequate and impossible.

If both the silence of the spectator and his own dumb-struck stage-fright are marks of his exposure and vulnerability it might seem paradoxical that the player-poet seeks to resolve such material inequality through another kind of silence: the silence of the written word. The political and cultural inequality of the relationship between addresser and addressee is reflected in the asymmetrical ways in which silence and speech are distributed across player and audience. The stage-fright paradoxically expressed in the opening line arises from the player-poet's acute sense of vulnerability and inadequacy, both as 'vnperfect actor' and on account of the socially inappropriate strength of his passion for the silent, distant patron. Whereas the silence of stage-fright is a sign of the player-poet's social inadequacy, the absence of the patron's voice from the poem is a mute expression of the latter's overwhelming authority. The sonnet owes its existence to that fact that, as a poet, the player, however 'vnperfect', is able to make that silence speak: through the mute eloquence of the written word. By urging the patron to withdraw to the more private space of the page, and also by enacting such a withdrawal through the poem itself, the player-poet hopes to be able create a mutual space in which the 'injurious distance' (sonnet 44), imposed by his inappropriate theatricality and his place in the theatre as social institution, may be diminished.[21] Eloquence is, unusually, here the source of impotence rather than a sign of accomplishment, and the poem itself is a paradoxically eloquent plea to be allowed to 'leaue out difference' (sonnet 105) by moving into a private sphere with the beloved as poet rather than as tongue-tied player. Only via the eloquent silence of writing, which matches the powerfully significant silence of the patron, will player-poet be able to take up a less abject and exposed position. It is in order to achieve this consummation that the speaker (who in the world of the poem does not (yet) abandon the exposed role of player) resorts rather desperately to a series of performatives: 'O let my books. . . . O learne to read'. Through these illocutionary acts the beloved is urged to negate the differences in rank and love – differences historically exemplified by the public distance of stage and spectator – in the supposedly undifferentiated exchange of written texts.

The whole poem is built on a series of paradoxes which suggest that the 'perfect ceremony of loues right' lies in the willingness of the beholder to 'heare wit [with] eyes' rather than in any formal features of any particular address or behaviour. This is a telling inversion of Shakespeare's habitual invocation to his early audiences, in plays as diverse as *A Midsummer Night's Dream* and *Henry V*, to see with their ears. The poetic move attempts to transcend the corporeality of the body, negating the emotional and political reality of the situation of address. In the deft definition of 'loues fine wiht [wit]' in the final line it also constitutes a lesson by the poet to the beloved on the art of reading. The final couplet thus presumes to instruct the beloved on how to attend to the letter's expressive silence rather than the social situatedness of the 'speaking brest' which, for social and political reasons. the sonnets remind us, may by its very presence 'prophane' the young man's 'sweet beloued name' (sonnet 89). The move from spoken address to written word, therefore,

---

[21] I explore the relationship between privacy and theatricality in the sonnets in the next chapter.

is an attempt to transcend the socially marked differences of voices and bodies in a material encounter (to 'leaue out difference'), and it is the daring of this sonnet to suggest that love consists in the 'wit' that 'read[s] what silent loue hath writ' and so 'heare[s] wit [with] eyes'.

Returning now to the encounter between Olivia and Viola, we can begin to understand something of the renegotiation of power relations that this scene represents. Viola's fearlessness, despite her claim that she is 'very countable', in her allotted role breaks through the veil, literal and metaphorical, that Olivia erects between herself and Viola/Cesario's erotic overtures. The first obstacle is based on blood and class. This is evident in the reference to her 'sauciness' (1.5.189) and lack of 'courtesy' (1.5.199) and the deliberately slighting question 'Are you a comedian?' (1.5.175). Viola's response is deftly ambiguous, deflecting the insulting allusion to the lowly profession of the player, while in the same breath alluding to the mystery of the double theatrical role that she plays as Orsino's understudy and as the boy Cesario: 'No, by my profound heart: and yet, by the very fangs of malice, I swear, I am not that I play' (1.5.176–7). Viola thus embodies the tension that is evident in sonnet 23 between the cultural and erotic vulnerability of sonneteer as petitioner/player, and the power of the petition itself over the beloved. The power of the latter is compounded in this instance by the petitioner her/himself taking on some of the aloof mystery of the Petrarchan beloved. Furthermore, unlike the situations in *Love's Labour's Lost*, the position of player, protagonist of feigning, is an enabling rather than constraining one: 'What I am, and what I would, are as secret as maidenhead: to your ears, divinity; to any other's, profanation' (1.5.206–8).[22]

As in the earlier comedy, however, the staging of the encounter between praiser and praised allows the beloved to deflate commonplace Petrarchisms by parodically insisting upon their literal sense. Instead of 'remaining the described and inscribed, passively subject to an entire process through which [her] identit[y] [is] re-written',[23] Olivia achieves, through the knowing 'inventory' of her own beauty, a deft and witty depreciation both of the argument of the first seventeen sonnets and of the more general Petrarchan scattering discussed above:

[22] See Susanne Wofford, ' "To You I Give Myself, For I Am Yours": Erotic Performance and Theatrical Performatives in *As You Like It*', in *Shakespeare Reread: The Texts in New Contexts*, ed. Russ McDonald (Ithaca, NY: Cornell University Press, 1994), 147–69, for an excellent account of the way in which the use of performative language in the theatre may be seen to lay a claim for the authority of theatrical performance itself.

[23] R. L. Kesler, 'The Idealization of Women: Morphology and Change in Three Renaissance Texts', *Mosaic*, 23. 2 (Spring 1990), 107–25 (112).

VIOLA 'Tis beauty truly blent, whose red and white
    Nature's own sweet and cunning hand laid on.
    Lady, you are the cruell'st she alive
    If you will lead these graces to the grave
    And leave the world no copy.
OLIVIA O sir, I will not be so hard-hearted. I will give out divers schedules of
    my beauty. It shall be inventoried and every particle and utensil labelled
    to my will, as, item, two lips, indifferent red; item, two grey eyes, with lids
    to them; item, one neck, one chin, and so forth. Were you sent hither to
    praise me? (*Twelfth Night*, 1.5.228–38)

The affinity with sonnet 130 is clear enough. The difference between
the two contexts, however, lies in the fact that on the stage the parody
is not merely a corrective redescription by a man of his 'mistress' in the
face of a poetic convention. It is embodied by a woman whose ironical
mimicry of the language of sonnets allows her to play words off against
the visible integrity of her face before a theatre audience and refuse the
Petrarchan disembodiment and dismemberment of the beloved in its
scattered rhymes. R. L. Kesler suggests that sonnets depend upon the
necessary absence of ideal feminine perfection, for which they act as
substitutes:

The perfection of woman as an ideal in the sonnet is also part of its ruse, not
only in the sense that it is co-opted by its fragmentation and re-assembly at the
hands of the male, but also in that it is only pointed to by these descriptions and
never itself presented. Like the 'represented world' itself, it lies always beyond
the sonnet, inaccessible to direct perception. ('The Idealization of Women', 115)

But such emphasis on the signifier to the exclusion of the referent is
possible only in print. The embodiment that characterises both the stage
and an actual context of direct address renders Kesler's argument less
compelling. Clearly, what is at stake in the exchange between Olivia
and Cesario is not 'truth' or a 'represented world' but rather kinds of
social action: having dismissed Orsino's 'feigned' text as 'heresy', Olivia
is nonetheless moved by what Cesario might *do*:

        OLIVIA Why, what would you?
        VIOLA Make me a willow cabin at your gate
           And call upon my soul within the house,
           Write loyal cantons of contemnèd love,
           And sing them loud even in the dead of night;
           Halloo your name to the reverberate hills,
           And make the babbling gossip of the air
           Cry out 'Olivia!' O, you should not rest

> Between the elements of air and earth
> But you should pity me.
> OLIVIA You might do much.   (2.1.256–66)

Nowhere could the affinity of language and action be clearer: making a willow cabin at Olivia's gate is not different in kind from ceaselessly re-echoing her name – 'spending again what is already spent' (sonnet 76) – and, as it turns out, this very speech is action enough to move Olivia's heart, informed as it is by Viola *as woman's* sudden opportunity to express her suppressed feelings for Orsino.

The scene ends with the invocation of the very economy upon which the sonnets dwell so insistently. The money that Olivia offers to Cesario in recompense for 'her pains' is not a straightforward cancellation of debt but rather its displacement: it is offered to be spent *for herself*, an exemplary case of 'increasing store with loss, and loss with store' ('I thank you for your pains. Spend this for me') (2.1.273). By refusing the symbolical obligations that such spending would incur, Cesario holds herself aloof from the system of erotic and economic exchange, but without recognising that her self-proclaimed blazon of parentage and disguise in fact traps her within it: 'I am no fee'd post, lady. Keep your purse. / My master, not myself, lacks recompense' (lines 274–5). The scene ends with a curious reinscription of Petrarchism as Olivia, having originally outfaced its power through her parodic self-blazoning, herself falls prey to it:

> OLIVIA 'What is your parentage?'
> 'Above my fortunes, yet my state is well.
> I am a gentleman.' I'll be sworn thou art.
> Thy tongue, thy face, thy limbs, actions, and spirit
> Do give thee five-fold blazon.   (lines 279–83)

The staged scene thus makes clear to what degree the blazon of 'perfection' is conditional upon that of blood: it is presumably only the condition of Cesario's blood and birth that allows Olivia to 'reason thus with reason fetter' and give her love 'unsought' (3.1.153–4).

In an earlier part of this chapter I suggested that the necessary embodiment of addresser and addressee in the theatre forestalls both the dismemberment and the silencing of the addressee. I have looked at two scenes from *Love's Labour's Lost* and *Twelfth Night* in which women in the position of addressee literally outface the scattering and silencing blazon. As we move more deeply into the latter play, however, such embodiment is complicated in ways that begin to approximate the fraught triangular relationship between Shakespeare, the young man and the dark mistress. Despite Fineman's claim of a 'lusty misogyny' (*Shakespeare's Perjured Eye*, 17) in the sonnets that is said to be 'recognizably Shakespearian', it is significant that in the comedies it is universally women who find themselves wronged, 'tongue-tied' and rendered vulnerable by the arrogance and duplicity of men. If *Love's Labour's Lost* shows us anything, it is that the women who mock when the men laugh, laugh when they cry and generally harden their hearts to the suitor's advances are anything but hard-hearted or senseless.

The affinity between Helen in *All's Well That Ends Well* and the poet of the sonnets has often been noted, and is the subject of analysis in chapter 5, below. Fewer commentators have seen the similarities between the player-poet and Viola. Her disguise as a man evokes an androgyny that is constantly in play in the sonnets. She also combines the paradoxical power and vulnerability of the player-poet in the sonnets. Unlike the self-composed aristocratic women of *Love's Labour's Lost*, or even Olivia in *Twelfth Night*, Viola occupies a liminal position, both socially and erotically, which is not at all unlike that of the man, newly divorced from home and family, who attempts to negotiate a political and sexual path between a beautiful young patron and the supposedly duplicitous 'dark woman'. I say 'supposedly' here, because it strikes me as odd that critics have almost universally taken Shakespeare at his word on this point. Why do we invoke the moral weight of the word 'whore' (duplicitous in its own way) to the dark woman, but fail to use anything like that language of the young man of rank or the player-poet himself? Is it possibly, as Nona Feinberg has suggested, that, unlike Sidney, Shakespeare in his sonnets does not simply disallow the woman's speech: he silences the silences themselves, obscuring the violence and significance of the repression? It is a process of silencing, moreover, that persists to the present day, not only in criticism, but in the fabric of our social life. That is why we should perhaps interrogate the dogmatic refusal, now ingrained in all criticism and scholarship that wishes to avoid universal professional derision, to address the biographical problem of the identity of the dark woman. Is such reticence merely an objectively scientific desire to venture no further than the empirical evidence allows? Or does the aversion to biography of so much contemporary criticism obscure a revulsion, signalled by sonnet 129 amongst others, at the embodiment of this woman specifically and woman in general? For to confine the 'dark lady' to the limits of Shakespeare's text is to refuse to hear her voice, to neglect to imbue her with a humanity that would belie her status as a mere sign of 'otherness' or symbol of duplicity. Samuel Schoenbaum, for example, argues that ' "the opposition between Fair Youth and Dark Lady" needs no reference to a particular woman to explicate it . . . for it is "perfectly comprehensible in terms of moral and poetic symbolism" ' .[24] He thus dismisses A. L. Rowse's questionable claim that the 'dark lady' is Emilia Lanyer with the comment that there were in any case plenty of other promiscuous women in Elizabethan London. I have no quarrel with Schoenbaum's deflation of Rowse's historical claims. But should we not weigh up the ideological implications of a commitment to a 'system of moral and poetic symbolism' in which one of the elements can simply be reduced to a whore (one amongst many) against Rowse's attempts to restore a historical embodiment and humanity to a woman who would otherwise be a mere cipher? As Lorna Hutson reminds us, 'a "moral and poetic symbolism" that is "perfectly comprehensible" is one which is still *working*, still creating an evaluative language in which to articulate experience and authorize desire' ('Why the Lady's Eyes', 155).

It is significant that in his early account of 'who the dark lady was', Rowse projects upon her all the qualities that we find in sonnets 126–54, thereby simply endorsing the moral and poetic symbolism that he finds in Shakespeare's verse as a whole:

We soon learn that the Dark Lady is a very equivocal lady; she is, in fact, a bad lot, as Shakespeare knows very well . . . We are told that besides being false in tongue, she is proud and wilful, tyrannising over both Shakespeare and the younger man . . . she is a calculating woman – Shakespeare refers to her as 'cunning'. . . He had found no constancy or trust in her, but duplicity and breach of faith; she was temperamental and spoilt . . . All in all, with his characteristic candour and openness, he has told us everything about the Dark Lady, except her name.[25]

But has Shakespeare told us 'everything' about her? This is an example of the excesses to which biographical criticism can lead, in the form of a *petitio principi* by which an assumption about Shakespeare's character predetermines the assumed truth and completeness of his texts. Let us look at another crossed lover telling us 'everything' about his 'dark lady':

---

[24] Samuel Schoenbaum, 'Shakespeare, Dr Forman and Dr Rowse', in *Shakespeare and Others* (London: Scholar Press, 1985), 76, quoted in Lorna Hutson, 'Why the Lady's Eyes are Nothing Like the Sun', in *New Feminist Discourses: Critical Essays on Theories and Texts*, ed. Isobel Armstrong (London and New York: Routledge, 1992), 154–75 (155). See also, Samuel Schoenbaum, *Shakespeare's Lives*, new edition (Oxford: Clarendon Press, 1991), 328–30, 493–8, and 550–9.

[25] A. L. Rowse, *Shakespeare's Sonnets: The Problems Solved* (London: Macmillan, 1973), xxx–xxxiii.

What? I love, I sue, I seek a wife? –
A woman, that is like a German clock,
Still a-repairing, ever out of frame,
And never going aright, being a watch,
But being watched that it may still go right.
Nay, to be perjured, which is worst of all,
And among three to love the worst of all –
A whitely wanton with a velvet brow,
With two pitch-balls stuck in her face for eyes –
Ay, and, by heaven, one that will do the deed
Though Argus were her eunuch and her guard.
And I to sigh for her, to watch for her,
To pray for her – go to, it is a plague
That Cupid will impose for my neglect
Of his almighty dreadful little might.
Well, I will love, write, sigh, pray, sue, groan:
Some men must love my lady, and some Joan.
(*Love's Labour's Lost*, 3.1.184–200)

Setting aside the difference in tone between Biron's meditation here and the sonnets about Will's dark-eyed beloved, we can recognize similar obsessions: with the perversity of desiring the 'worst' of women, but also with the assumed sexual voracity of all women, here, as in the sonnets and in plays such as *Othello* and *Antony and Cleopatra*, conceived as being both attractive and repulsively fearsome. Most important, however, is the fact that the dramatic context makes it clear that these are no more than wild obsessions. They are projections for which there is not merely no evidence, but which the play itself reveals as a feature of the men rather the women. If there are any 'German clocks . . . ever out of frame' they are the King and his courtiers rather than Rosaline and her companions.

I have no intention of whitewashing Shakespeare's dark woman. I wish rather to make a theoretical request that we allow the embodied context and action of the theatre to flesh out the obfuscations and imposed silences that a certain reading of the sonnets encourages. When Rowse encounters the voice of the 'dark lady' he has purportedly discovered – in the poems of Emilia Lanyer – he quickly abandons the 'facts' provided by Shakespeare's 'characteristic candour and openness'. He sees instead a woman who, though no more chaste or faithful than the figure in the sonnets, is now sympathetically embodied in struggles and forms of social action which are not limited to 'doing the deed' with poor Will and everybody else. From being one more 'whore' among many, she becomes 'an exceptional, dominating personality'. She is the next best 'woman poet of the age, second to Mary, Countess of Pembroke', who shows 'a natural aptitude for pentameter and rhyme ... highly educated, well read in the Bible and those classics to the fore in the Renaissance'.[26] Her struggle to improve her status through her intellectual superiority differs little from Shakespeare's own efforts, and Rowse extols her feminism as a product of women's general oppression at the time: 'Her status was beneath what she considered her due; it was maddening to be so much more intelligent and to have got nowhere with it. But this was the lot of women, dependent on men for their status. This made her a feminist unexampled in that age ... she stands up squarely for her sex' (*Discovering Shakespeare*, 48–51). In addition to making her poetry available, Rowse allows her to express her own personal and ideological condemnation of the cruelty and duplicity of men:

'Women deserve not to be blamed', they should not condemn each other, but leave that to 'evil-disposed men who – forgetting they were born of women, nourished of women, and that if it were not by the means of women they would be quite extinguished out of the world and a final end to them all – do like Vipers deface the wombs wherein they were bred'. (*Discovering Shakespeare*, 53–4)

'We know now', Rowse concludes, glancing at what he had previously supposed Shakespeare had told us of her, 'what a very remarkable woman she was, a powerful personality. No doubt, when young and beautiful, musical, with a foreign flavour about her, and with that background, distinguished if equivocal, with her pride and spirit, she must have been ravishing, if not always ravishable' (*Discovering Shakespeare*, 54). I quote extensively from Rowse not because I endorse his specific claims about the biographical identity of the 'dark lady', but to reveal how humanly and ideologically confined and confining the criticism is that refuses to interrogate or move beyond what is conceived as the internal 'moral and poetic symbolism' of the texts conceived in a disembodied way. With his discovery of Emilia Lanyer's poetry – with the discovery of her voice and her life – Rowse turns the duplicitous whore of Shakespeare's sonnets into a 'very remarkable woman', and he does so without revising his sense of her moral or sexual behaviour.

It should be clear that when I question the recent revulsion from biography I am not proposing a return to the Romantic tendency to regard the text as little more than a window on to the unique consciousness

---

[26] A. L. Rowse, *Discovering Shakespeare* (London: Weidenfeld and Nicholson, 1989), 47–9.

behind it.[27] On the contrary, I wish to question the mere displacement of such concerns, which may be seen in the move from a unique personal consciousness to the structural interiority offered by recent concerns with 'poetic subjectivity'. In proposing that we move from textuality to embodiment I am attempting to reincorporate the sonnets within a set of social practices in which silence is, as feminism and gay studies have shown us, a palpable indicator of the power relations that subtend the writing and dissemination of poetry. In its concern with the possibilities of human practice my argument is in keeping with the logical truth to which I allude in the opening paragraph of this chapter. Even if the dark woman and the young man were fictions, my concern with embodiment, demonstrated by an appeal to the fictions of Shakespeare's dramatic characters, would still hold.[28] In other words, I am suggesting that biographical criticism is a matter of *grammar* (in the Wittgensteinian sense) rather than fact, a mode of reading and writing rather than a Romantic search for personal detail. By 'grammar', Wittgenstein means the sum of the language games, their rules and the forms of life from which they spring in which a concept or a related group of concepts have their use.[29] I am arguing that the Wittgensteinian 'grammar' of the concept of a persona or character necessitates the kind of embodiment that Rowse engages in his later exploration of the sonnets' mistress *as* Emilia Lanyer, even if she was not *actually* Emilia Lanyer. Asked what the history of the 'dark lady' is in conventional accounts of the sonnets which pay no heed to this biographical grammar, we would have to reply in the words of Viola/Cesario: 'A blank . . . she never told her love' (2.4.110). It is either ignored completely, or she has it told for her.

I have argued that the necessary embodiment of address and reception on the stage precludes the silencing and scattering of the woman

---

[27] See Margareta de Grazia, *Shakespeare Verbatim: The Reproduction of Authenticity and the 1790 Apparatus* (Oxford: Clarendon Press, 1991), for an account of the shift towards seeing the plays and poems as an expression of Shakespeare's unique and authentic consciousness.

[28] Michael Spiller, in *The Development of the Sonnet: An Introduction* (London: Routledge, 1992) is as much against the 'biographical' view as anybody: 'If there is a critical bias [in his book], it is against the view of the sonnet as a piece of lyrical autobiography – if that view needs opposing' (x). He argues very deftly and convincingly, however, that 'the situation and feeling presented in the sonnets come from Shakespeare's own life' (153), by adducing internal evidence from the modes of representation in the sonnets themselves. His argument rests on the fact that they offer very little of the circumstantial information that would have been known only to an actual, specific addressee, and which fictional mimesis necessarily fills in for an audience. The mode of this argument about the importance of the circumstances of discursive practices is close to my own.

[29] See Hans-Johann Glock, *A Wittgenstein Dictionary* (Oxford: Blackwell, 1996), 150–4.

that we may find in Petrarchan verse. We have seen occasions in both *Love's Labour's Lost* and *Twelfth Night* on which the embodied speech of women – their ability to contrast the force of address self-reflexively with the presence of their own bodies – literally outfaces the Petrarchan address. More important, perhaps, muteness on stage speaks itself as such: it reveals itself as silence, showing also the exercise of power that has enforced it. If the present voices of women on stage outface the speech of men, we are *faced* by the enforced silence of someone such as Helen, Viola or Catherine in the final act of *Henry V*.[30]

I now trace some of the complex patterns of silence and address that mark the triangular relationships among Orsino, Olivia and Viola/Cesario, marking the ways in which they reflect on a similarly fraught triangular relationship among Shakespeare, the young man and the dark woman of the sonnets. There can be no straightforward correlation between any of these figures: both gender and the direction of desire are complexly different. Thus if the male, middle-class player-poet feels himself marginalised by the social superiority of the beautiful aristocratic male and the moral duplicity of a woman whose unconventional beauty did not preclude her from engaging in a rival sexual relationship with the well-born youth, it is in fact Cesario/Viola who suffers that splitting and marginalisation. She is the hopeless and silent suitor to Orsino, 'pricked out' by her enforced disguise for Olivia's pleasure, while mutely pledging a love that she can reveal only by betraying herself.

The dramatic situation in which Viola/Cesario is caught thus reproduces some of the precariousness of Shakespeare's own position. She doubles the difference suffered by Helen in *All's Well*, for she adds to it the peculiar 'defeat' worked by doting nature and lamented in sonnet 20. The performing practices of the Elizabethan stage furthermore allow the androgynous beauty of sonnet 20 to be embodied in the doubly cross-dressed figure of a boy actor playing Viola playing the boy Cesario.[31] Compare the sonnet with a selection of Orsino's remarks, both on the nature of women's beauty in general and the attractiveness of Cesario in particular:

---

[30] See David Schalkwyk, 'Shakespeare's Talking Bodies', *Textus: English Studies in Italy*, 13 (2000), 269–94.

[31] For a discussion of cross-dressing, see Jean E. Howard, 'Cross-Dressing, the Theatre, and Gender Struggle in Early Modern England', *Shakespeare Quarterly*, 39.4 (1988), 418–40 and Stephen Orgel, *Impersonations: The Performance of Gender in Shakespeare's England* (Cambridge: Cambridge University Press, 1996).

A womans face with natures owne hand painted,
Haste thou the Master Mistris of my passion,
A womans gentle hart but not acquainted
With shifting change as is false womens fashion,
An eye more bright then theirs,lesse false in rowling:
Gilding the obiect where-vpon it gazeth,
A man in hew all *Hews* in his controwling,
Which steales mens eyes and womens soules amaseth.
And for a woman wert thou first created,
Till nature as she wrought thee fell a dotinge,
And by addition me of thee defeated,
By adding one thing to my purpose nothing.
    But since she prickt thee out for womens pleasure,
    Mine be thy loue and thy loues vse their treasure.

For they shall yet belie thy happy years,
That say thou art a man. Diana's lip
Is not more smooth and rubious; thy small pipe
Is as the maiden's organ, shrill and sound,
And all is semblative a woman's part.

(Twelfth Night, 1.4.30–4)

ORSINO There is no woman's sides
    Can bide the beating of so strong a passion
    As love doth give my heart; no woman's heart
    So big, to hold so much. They lack retention.
    Alas, their love may be called appetite,
    No motion of the liver, but the palate,
    That suffer surfeit, cloyment, and revolt.
    But mine is all as hungry as the sea,
    And can digest as much. Make no compare
    Between that love a woman can bear me
    And that I owe Olivia.

(Twelfth Night, 2.4.92–102)

Like most critics, Fineman takes Shakespeare's account of the dark lady's essential duplicity at face value. Indeed, his thesis depends upon the momentous historical necessity of woman as overriding figure or trope of difference and duplicity: 'With her "insufficiency" and with her "unkindness" the lady introduces a fundamental heterogeneity into the tradition of homogeneity . . . in sexual terms, the lady stands for an alienating heterosexuality that, in the context of the poet's relation to the young man, intrudes upon and interrupts the poet's homosexual ideal' (*Shakespeare's Perjured Eye*, 21). This crucial heterogeneity is marked not only by the 'nothing' that distinguishes her from those who, like Shakespeare and the young man, have the 'one thing' that pricks them out for 'womens pleasure', it is also apparent in an essential duplicity that is expressed in her conduct and written all over her face: in the 'fairness' that is at the same time 'the badge of Hell' (*Love's Labour's Lost*, 4.3.250). Fineman argues that the essential duplicity or paradox that the dark lady expresses in the sonnets gives rise to what he calls a 'Shakespearian' (but also a Lacanian) desire: 'Desire no longer originates in a source outside the self... the poet's desire is now determined as an effect occasioned by the language that *he* speaks' (*Shakespeare's Perjured Eye*, 24). The combination of moral duplicity and sexual difference ('Thy blacke is fairest in my judgements place' (sonnet 131)) in the desired woman (all desired women?) is in fact no more than the figure of a particular species of desire discovered by Shakespeare, one which is predicated upon the essential return of loss: 'Such desire has the power to generate its own desire, for lust is always lusting after the love that lust has lost, in accord with a structure of continuous erotic nostalgia whose yearning is continually refeeding itself *because* "consum'd with that which it was nourish'd by"' (*Shakespeare's Perjured Eye*, 24).

Such desire is represented in *Twelfth Night* as being particularly Orsinian, not universal. Fineman's analysis rejuvenates the tired critical cliché that Orsino is in love with love, by showing how such a desire feeds upon a projected difference between men and women, which the embodied events of the play in fact contradict. The desire which claims to be 'all as hungry as the sea, / And can digest as much' (2.4.100–1), is by definition both insatiable and self-sustaining, and does indeed, as Fineman argues and sonnet 20 proclaims, discover itself through the disparagement of the duplicitous other, the fair foul, of woman. But the embodiment of Viola as boy on stage contradicts the logic of Orsino's desire. It reveals that women are not necessarily duplicitous and shifting, and so denies this vital, projected difference upon which both Orsino and Fineman insist. It also shows, like sonnet 20, that difference and identity are not monolithic categories. Both sonnet 20 and Viola-in-disguise suggest that sexual difference need not block the fulfilment of desire. It may be an enabling condition:

> And for a woman wert thou first created,
> Till nature as she wrought thee fell a dotinge,
> And by addition me of thee defeated,
> By adding one thing to my purpose nothing.

In the light of Orsino's – and the player-poet's – disparagement of the 'shifting change [which] is false women's fashion' as the condition of a male desire 'as hungry as the sea', we should ask why the comedies give the lie to this dogma of the constancy of male desire. They systematically show, as Orsino puts it elsewhere, how 'Nought enters there, / Of what validity and pitch soe'er, / But falls into abatement and low price / Even in a minute' (1.1.11–14). Why do only women display the constancy that the sonnets proclaim as the essence of masculine love? If the difference that the sonnets require in order to establish 'the subjectivity effect required by a postidealist literariness' (Fineman, *Shakespeare's Perjured Eye*, 25) can be contradicted on the stage, how seriously can we take claims about the historical and philosophical inescapability of such difference?

No easy answer presents itself to these questions. The embodied representation of social relations on stage, however, precludes the transcendence of the political – of 'policy' and 'accident' – that the player-poet attempts to achieve in the sonnets. The 'difference' that the player-poet claims to leave out of his 'hugely pollitick' (sonnet 124) verse – 'to constancie confin'd' (sonnet 105) – refers to his rhetorical and erotic integrity. But it also encompasses inequalities of social class and rank. In the theatre such difference cannot be discursively 'left out' in the name of an idealised love that will admit no impediment to the marriage of true minds. As Leonard Tennenhouse points out: 'On stage ... [as in real life] the dress of various candidates ... would have indicated all the distinctions of rank and the matching and mismatching partners in a visually political game.'[32] We have already seen how in the first encounter between Cesario and Olivia the sameness of blood and class is the condition of possibility of any relationship whatsoever: Olivia's desire for Cesario is wholly consequent upon her reading correctly the submerged blazon of 'noble blood' in Cesario's carriage and bearing. The ease with which Sebastian takes Cesario's place confirms the overriding significance of the difference (and sameness) signalled by parentage.

Within such a context there is little ideological space for a man totally beyond the pale of blood to approach the already unattainable aristocratic woman or man. The only character in Shakespeare's plays who manages to achieve that is Bottom – in a dream, as the unknowing instrument in the battle of the sexes between the king and queen of the fairies. Malvolio flaunts such a fantasy, but he suffers ridicule, gross indignity

[32] Leonard Tennenhouse, *Power on Display: The Politics of Shakespeare's Genres* (London: Methuen, 1986), 62.

and mental torture as a result. There is no absolute gap between the imaginings of Malvolio and the projected illusions considered in sonnet 114 ('Or whether doth my minde being crown'd with you / Drinke vp the monarks plague this flattery?'). Nor should we accept the repeated proclamation in the sonnets that the player-poet's love transcends all worldly concerns any more readily than Olivia accepts Orsino's similar protestations:

> Once more, Cesario,
> Get thee to yon same sovereign cruelty.
> Tell her my love, more noble than the world,
> Prizes not quantity of dirty lands.
> The parts that fortune hath bestowed upon her
> Tell her I hold as giddily as fortune;
> But 'tis that miracle and queen of gems
> That nature pranks her in attracts my soul.
>
> (2.4.78–85)

When Shakespeare wishes to convey 'how hard true sorrow hits' (sonnet 120) in love women are almost always the victims, trapped in the web of social and erotic differences that the sonnets would like to, but finally cannot, leave out. Viola's vulnerability in her crossed love for Orsino differs from the player-poet's for the young man because the latter can speak his love, whereas Viola is committed to remaining silent about hers. But her embodiment in the theatre makes that silence speak.

> ORSINO ... Make no compare
> Between that love a woman can bear me
> And that I owe Olivia.
> VIOLA Ay, but I know –
> ORSINO What dost thou know?
> VIOLA Too well what love women to men may owe.
> In faith, they are as true of heart as we.
> My father had a daughter loved a man
> As it might be, perhaps, were I a woman
> I should your lordship.
> ORSINO   And what's her history?
> VIOLA A blank, my lord. She never told her love,
> But let concealment, like a worm i' th' bud,
> Feed on her damask cheek. She pined in thought,
> And with a green and yellow melancholy
> She sat like patience on a monument,
> Smiling at grief. Was not this love indeed?
> We men may say more, swear more, but indeed

Our shows are more than will; for still we prove
Much in our vows, but little in our love.
ORSINO But died thy sister of her love, my boy?
VIOLA I am all the daughters of my father's house,
And all the brothers too; and yet I know not.

(2.5.100–21)

Forced not only to suggest her own love through the indirection of a
'sister' who is in fact herself as persona, but also to defend all of her
sex against Orsino's misogynist slander, Viola-as-Cesario can speak only
from a position of alienation: as an other both masked and revealed by
the truth/falsity of herself-as-man. We see a classic double bind here. As
boy, Cesario can know nothing of the truth of women's, love; as woman,
Viola could only lie about it. And the truth of Viola's 'sister's' love can
speak only through her death. This tale is recounted in *Love's Labour's
Lost*, when the story of Katherine's sister's death through love provides
a telling prelude to the collective decision by the women to expose the
men's 'shows' for being 'more than will'. But it is especially effective
here. For Viola's embodiment of her enforced silence exposes the trap
that otherwise would remain concealed and thus all too effective.

The player-poet declares: 'WHEN my loue sweares that she is made of
truth, / I do beleeue her though I know she lyes.' Does he have a choice?
Is this paradox not a self-inflicted condition of the dogma which holds
that, as Hutson has so tellingly put it, no woman's eyes can ever be like
the sun if to be like the sun is to have the political and metaphysical
power to 'Flatter the mountaine tops with soueraigne eie... Guilding
pale streams with heauenly alcumy' (sonnet 33)? Or that the story of
woman is 'still all one, euer the same' (sonnet 76), namely, 'Fairing the
foule with Arts faulse borrow'd face' and 'Slandring Creation with a false
esteeme' (sonnet 127)? Of course, the difference between the 'flattering'
and 'guilding' of the 'soueraigne eie' and 'heauenly alcumy' and the
'slandring' of 'Creation' with 'Arts faulse borrow'd face' is tenuous. The
gap between them as male and female principles, hardly capable of being sustained across the sequence as a whole, is severely questioned on
the comic stage. This interrogation is effected precisely by the embodied
androgyny of the comic heroine, forced through political and sexual vulnerability to adopt the mask of a young man. In *Twelfth Night*, specifically,
Viola/Cesario seems to rearticulate subject positions and relationships
that are so complexly negotiated in the sonnets between the young man,
the dark woman and the poet himself. For, combining the political vulnerability and the erotic abjectness of the desiring subject in the sonnets,

s/he nonetheless embodies as actor/character the androgynous object of desire of sonnet 20. The split subject that critics have noticed in the poet of the sonnets is thus combined in the theatrically embodied figure of Viola/Cesario.

At the end of the exchange between Cesario/Viola and Orsino, the former tellingly leaves the question about her 'sister's' (and thus her own) death open. This hiatus is almost filled in the final act, when it appears for a moment that Orsino will kill Cesario, both to punish him for his erotic rivalry and to spite the woman who, in pursuing the 'boy' servant, has insultingly rejected him. This is a moment of crucial transference, as in the process of threatening to kill Olivia if he cannot have her, Orsino discovers that her understudy and his supposed rival is in fact the 'thing he loves':

> ORSINO Why should I not, had I the heart to do it,
>   Like to th' Egyptian thief, at point of death
>   Kill what I love – a savage jealousy
>   That sometime savours nobly. But hear me this:
>   Since you to non-regardance cast my faith,
>   And that I partly know the instrument
>   That screws me from my true place in your favour,
>   Live you the marble-breasted tyrant still.
>   But this your minion, whom I know you love,
>   And whom, by heaven I swear, I tender dearly,
>   Him will I tear out of that cruel eye
>   Where he sits crownèd in his master's spite.
>   (*To Viola*)
>   Come, boy, with me. My thoughts are ripe in mischief.
>   I'll sacrifice the lamb that I do love
>   To spite a raven's heart within a dove.
> VIOLA And I most jocund, apt, and willingly
>   To do you rest a thousand deaths would die
>
>   (5.1.115–31)

The conviction of woman as 'cruel' (5.1.108), 'perverse' and 'uncivil' (5.1.110) tyrant is abandoned 'even in a minute' (1.1.14) for the male rival in love, in a gesture that combines violence with lust. Do we not recognise this reiteration of the dance of difference and sameness, of self and other, in all those half-bitter, half-abject sonnets that proclaim both their attraction-in-disillusionment and their readiness to 'make [his] loue' so 'engrafted' to the 'store' (sonnet 37) of the beloved that the poet is happy to be obliterated, engulfed or even killed by it, 'consum'd with that which it was nourish'd by' (sonnet 73)? There are many sonnets in this vein. Sonnet 37, the double pair of sonnets, 57 and 58, and 71 and 72, and the sequence 87 to 92, spring to mind. They express the attitude of Viola to her 'master's' 'cruel love', 'happy to have thy love, happy to die!' (sonnet 92). But above all, the scene resonates to the paradoxical thought in sonnet 147, that 'desire is death'.

Petrarchan roles are at once displaced as, for a moment, the direction of desire from abject male to cruel female switches through a relay of homosocial rivalry, which is revealed to be the real circuit of erotic desire, between Orsino and the 'master('s) mistress', Cesario/Viola (sonnet 20 and 5.1.384). Particularly apparent on stage is the sustained sexual ambivalence of the Cesario/Viola figure who, despite being transferred from the blocked homosexual relationship with Olivia to the allowed heterosexual one with Orsino, remains embodied in all senses as the 'Master Mistris' of sonnet 20:

> Cesario, come –
> For so you shall be while you are a man;
> But when in other habits you are seen,
> Orsino's mistress and his fancy's queen.
> (5.1.381–4)

The theatre is able to enact, in ways that are impossible in the poems, the material splitting of confused identity (the master mistress of passion) into two discrete figures which, no matter how alike, are able to transform differences into sameness: in the form of a pair of relationships that are matched in terms of blood and sex. This is why Fineman contrasts the movement of 'presentation' or recovery of loss in the comedies with the continual re-enactment, as the very condition of representation and desire, of the loss of the self in the sonnets:

the principal figures of Shakespearean comedy tend rather regularly, and not only in the festive comedies, to find whatever they may have lost in the course of their misadventures . . . it is reasonable to characterize Shakespearean comedy as a drama of presentation, a drama in which, as a corresponding consequence, characters arrive at a kind of personal and interpersonal 'oneness'. (*Shakespeare's Perjured Eye*, 301)

My own discussion of the embodiment of the situation of Petrarchan reception and address in *Love's Labour's Lost* and *Twelfth Night* has interrogated both the tendency to posit a monolithic and all-encompassing closure in the comedies and the emphasis upon 'principal' characters. For, as I have shown, the material embodiment of a character on the stage not only makes a response necessarily possible, it also forces us to read or hear silences as such and enquire about the conditions of their enforcement, rather than pass over them in silence. In one sense, neither the dark woman nor the beautiful young man are 'principal characters' in the sonnets: they are too silent, even if they are immensely powerful.

At the end of *Twelfth Night* there is a technical problem which is almost bound to go unnoticed at the level of the signifier or signified, but which has to be addressed by actor and director at the level of the embodied referent. I usually bring this problem to the attention of my students by asking them to describe in precise detail how they would get everybody off the stage for Feste's final song if they were to direct the play. They then become aware of a silent, unnoticed, but physically present figure who has to be made to disappear, but whose disappearance is all the more noticeable because he is marginal and mute and cannot, without strain, be swept off in a mêlée of like-minded characters. I am of course referring to the character that Leslie Fiedler drew to our attention in *The Stranger in Shakespeare*: Antonio, whose combination of selfless devotion and bitterness at his social and sexual alienation and rejection are echoed time and time again by the player-poet of the sonnets:

> His life I gave him, and did thereto add
> My love without retention or restraint,
> All his in dedication. For his sake
> Did I expose myself, pure for his love,
> Into the danger of this adverse town,
> Drew to defend him when he was beset,
> Where being apprehended, his false cunning –
> Not meaning to partake with me in danger –
> Taught him to face me out of his acquaintance,
> And grew a twenty years' removèd thing
> While one would wink, denied me mine own purse,
> Which I had recommended to his use
> Not half an hour before.   (*Twelfth Night*, 5.1.76–88)

'His life I gave him' – this may be said of Shakespeare's relationship to the young man who now lives only through the 'blacke lines' (sonnet 63) of the sonnets. Of course, Antonio is mistaken in the particular substance of his accusation, but in general terms his account is true enough. Upon being seduced into Olivia's arms and bed, Sebastian does indeed '[grow] a twenty year... / While one would wink', echoing Orsino's earlier reflections on the capacity of love to consume and negate everything (1.1.11–14). Furthermore, the effortless substitution by which Cesario can be exchanged for Sebastian is for both sexual and social

reasons not available to Antonio. After the bitterness of betrayal, all that
is left Antonio is to wonder and be silent, the joy of discovery and reunion
turning into the bewilderment of loss and uncertainty 'even in a minute':

> ANTONIO Sebastian are you?
> SEBASTIAN Fear'st thou that, Antonio?
> ANTONIO How have you made a division of yourself?
> An apple, cleft in two, is not more twin
> Than these two creatures. Which is Sebastian?
>
> (5.1.218–22)

These are the last words that Antonio speaks. They remind us of sonnet
144: 'Two loues I haue of comfort and dispaire / Which like two spirits
do sugiest me still.' We may well ask 'Which is Antonio?' considering the
investment that he has made in a love suddenly multiplied and alienated
through 'use'. And does he really not know 'Which is Sebastian?' after
having spoken to him? Or has Sebastian become the signifier of a love
confined to silence, rather than an object of loss? Whatever the case,
he is mute from now on to the play's supposedly festive closure. It is a
muteness which, because he is a body and not a word, the theatre forces
to speak its own silence as the printed page does not.

There are two things that one might say in conclusion. The first, which
emphasises the affinity between Antonio and the poet of the sonnets, is
that the sonnets are themselves, perhaps, a display of muteness, an attempt to express, as the paradoxes of sonnet 23 ('As an vnperfect actor
on the stage') do so well, that 'whereof one cannot speak'.[33] The second
point, which takes up the fraught, unspeakable situation of social and
personal powerlessness in a situation of overwhelmingly powerful passion, is that, if Antonio is the real stranger in *Twelfth Night,* the stranger
in the sonnets is the player-poet himself, whoever that self might signify.

---

[33] Ludwig Wittgenstein, *Tractatus Logico-Philosophicus,* trans. C. K. Ogden (London: Routledge and
Kegan Paul, 1922), section 7.

CHAPTER 3

Interiority: the sonnets, Hamlet and King Lear

The last chapter closed by raising two issues: 'that whereof one cannot speak' and the question of the 'self' in the sonnets. Both have tended to be discussed in contexts that are very different from – indeed often in opposition to – the conditions of embodiment upon which I have been focusing. Commentators have often conceived of that which must be passed over in silence as the product or possession of an 'inner' being, itself regarded as the real or authentic 'self' in contradistinction to whatever 'actions that a man might play' (*Hamlet*, 1.2.84). This contrast between 'privacy' and 'theatricality' has been central to critical discussion of Renaissance literature for some time. In conjunction with a cognate pair, the interior and the public selves, they have formed the crux of an intense debate. Margareta de Grazia noted over a decade ago that *Hamlet* and Shakespeare's sonnets have occupied a central place in the critical movement towards discovering a properly conceived 'interior' self.[1] Almost ten years before that, Anne Ferry saw in *Hamlet* and the sonnets the culmination of a sense of an 'inner life' or 'real self'[2] that is only half-wrought in the poetry of Wyatt and Sidney. Ferry's argument was countered by materialist critics such as Francis Barker, Catherine Belsey and de Grazia herself, who insisted that such construction of 'subjectivity as the (imaginary) property of inner selfhood' is an anachronistic projection of a later, properly bourgeois and thoroughly ideological, sensibility.[3] More recently, Katherine Eisaman Maus has struck back. In *Inwardness and the Theatre of the English Renaissance* she adduces historical evidence to the effect that the distinction between the outer and the inner selves was

[1] Margareta de Grazia, 'The Motive for Interiority: Shakespeare's *Sonnets* and *Hamlet*', *Style*, 23.3 (Fall 1989), 430–44.

[2] These phrases are emphasised in the title of Ann Ferry's Introduction: 'The *inner life*, the *real self*, and Hamlet', in *The 'Inward' Language: Sonnets of Wyatt, Sidney, Shakespeare, and Donne* (Chicago: University of Chicago Press, 1983).

[3] Francis Barker, *The Tremulous Private Body: Essays on Subjection* (London and New York: Methuen, 1984), 31.

not only available in the early modern period, but was also a pervasive and vexed issue in the culture, especially in its religious politics.[4] More recently still, Ramie Targoff has argued that 'non-conformist opponents of the theatre and the highly conformist ecclesiastics of the English church' shared a 'profound conviction in the transformative power of public performance'.[5] That is to say, both groups believed not so much in the separation of an unknowable inner from a public outer self, as Maus argues, as in the efficacy of public performance to shape the inner self in its own image. The English church defended public prayer and the non-conformists attacked the theatre on the same grounds: out of a shared belief that performance inevitably *becomes* the man or woman.

The issue of inwardness and performance, or privacy and theatricality, is the subject of two kinds of critical conflict, then. On the one hand, there is a debate, even within materialist and historicist criticism, about the historical status of the concepts.[6] The question is whether the early modern period had access to a theory of subjectivity based on an interior self, or whether this is merely an anachronistic projection of later criticism. Early materialist critics had a considerable ideological investment in the argument against interiority. It enabled them to posit a decisive historical break between the early modern period and the era of bourgeois subjectivity proper, and at the same time to offer their own readings of the period based on the theoretical centrality of public life. On the other hand, many feminist critics invested heavily in the existence of a properly female interiority that could be said to have been invented by women writers, both as a bulwark against a hegemonically patriarchal public world and as a means of authentic female expression with which contemporary readers could identify. Both forms of criticism claim to be historical, but each sees evidence that serves its present needs. This is in itself no great crime. But it leaves the claim to be doing historical criticism in a peculiar position. What is the search for evidence for or against theories of inwardness or interiority in the period meant to achieve? What relationship exists between the ecclesiastical notion of the transformative performance of prayer or the theatre, for example, and the meaning of

[4] Katherine Eisaman Maus, *Inwardness and the Theatre of the English Renaissance* (Chicago and London: University of Chicago Press, 1995).

[5] Ramie Targoff, 'The Performance of Prayer: Sincerity and Theatricality in Early Modern England,' *Representations*, 60 (Fall 1997), 49–69 (50).

[6] An earlier essay in which Maus outlines her argument (against Belsey and Barker) that the distinction between private and public selves was prevalent in the early modern period is, for example, included in a recent collection representative of materialist readings of Shakespeare: *Materialist Shakespeare*, ed. Ivo Kamps (London and New York: Verso, 1995), 157–80.

Hamlet? And how do theories of the public and the private impact upon the workings of Shakespeare's sonnets?

All the participants in the debate acknowledge evidence contrary to their own positions, but they differ in the weight they accord it. So, Barker does not deny that Hamlet claims to have 'that within which passeth show' (*Hamlet*, 1.2.85). He downplays it as a merely prototypical anticipation of a later philosophical and ideological moment. What Ferry and Maus regard as a signal historical moment Barker dismisses as an aberration. Maus sees the distinction between the inward and the performative self maintained by persecuted and disempowered groups as a sign of the currency of the private in the early modern period. Targoff interprets the same evidence as an exception that proves the contrary rule 'that the mainstream English population increasingly clung to the reliability of visible appearances' ('The Performance of Prayer', 59). This is in itself a curious claim. But it is also difficult to see how it is supposed to sway our view of complex symbolic artefacts such as *Hamlet* or the sonnets. Assuming for the moment that the 'mainstream English population' (whatever that might be) were anxiously steadfast in this belief, does that mean that Shakespeare's play automatically reflects this orthodoxy? I suspect that whatever reasons the orthodox clergy had for endorsing the performative aspects of prayer, like anyone else their belief in the reliability of outward appearances in everyday life was not held as a dogma, but varied pragmatically from occasion to occasion. Sometimes one trusted what one saw, at other times one did not. And one adjusted one's behaviour accordingly. There is and was nothing metaphysical about this. This is not to say that people did not have metaphysical theories. The issue is to accord them their proper place both within the daily lives of people living in complex relations with one another and the world, and in what used to be called the 'literary system'.

Maus has observed that the debate is confused by a tendency to conflate two quite different things: a philosophical argument, derived from a distinctly modern and postmodern body of writing, which regards the self as an essentially social product, and a historical argument that denies early modern inwardness in order to avoid anachronism. The latter does not follow from the former. It is a fundamental mistake to believe that the philosophical dependence of the concept of inwardness upon social or public forms of life and expression means that 'inwardness simply vaporizes, like the Wicked Witch of the West under Dorothy's bucket of water' (*Inwardness*, 28). The task is to see how the concept of inwardness is used in the period, what work it does and how precisely it is articulated with complementary, public concepts. Maus chooses to examine the concept as it is employed in forensic and religious discourses: as one pole of the distinction between the knowable, but superficial and deceptive, 'outer' person and the unknowable, but deeply true, 'inner' being. She makes a convincing case for the wide-ranging deployment of this distinction for historically specific political, religious and legal ends, especially in cases where the pressures of interrogation and persecution rendered the difference between what the heart feels and the tongue speaks useful, if not indispensable. The problem of inwardness in the period is thus in her view the problem of 'other minds', but not in the radically sceptical form in which the very existence of other minds is put in doubt. Rather, it is what happens *in* those minds, what they contain, that is forever secret, essentially unknowable (*Inwardness*, 7).

In a more recent, less theoretically vexed, essay called 'The Silent Speech of Shakespeare's Sonnets', George T. Wright pursues the question of 'inwardness' in relation not to the forensic problem of discovering the inner self, but to the development of the resources of 'inner speech' in Shakespeare's sonnets and plays.[7] Taking a line that is very different from my own emphasis on the embodiment of the sonnet's voice via the plays, Wright sees in the sonnets an essentially (or perhaps only predominantly) silent voice: one disembodied, spoken in and speaking about absence, without sound, above all, unperformed. It is 'speech without speech' or, perhaps more accurately, speech inside speech. The differences upon which Wright dwells in his attempts to distinguish the two different kinds of speech are absence and disembodiment. The unsounded speech of the sonnets is solitary, rehearsed only 'as if' the writer were present to the addressee. Because unsounded, it is 'not really a voice; it does not speak, it makes no sound, it does not share with actual voices (or even whispers) the physical characteristics of pitch, volume, timbre, and accent; it is unheard' ('Silent Speech', 142).

Wright's essay is most suggestive when he claims a deep, internal connection between the silent speech of the sonnets and the 'inward' speech of such figures in Shakespeare's plays in whom we recognise an (often troubled, sometimes evil) interiority: Hamlet, Richard III, Prince Hal, Henry IV, Cassius, Brutus. Exploring a not entirely untravelled critical path that takes us through the sonnets to the plays, Wright suggests that Shakespeare fashions from the poems' command of silent, internal

---

[7] George T. Wright, 'The Silent Speech of Shakespeare's Sonnets', in *Shakespeare's Sonnets: Critical Essays*, ed. James Schiffer (New York: Garland, 1999), 136–58.

speech the sense of deep inwardness that characterises his dramatic characters: 'an authentic inner voice becomes available after 1593 or so to many of Shakespeare's characters, who speak this private or intimate language from the stage as no one had ever done before' ('Silent Speech', 147). If the inner speech of the sonnets is, in Wright's felicitous phrase, a 'play without a play', then the added context of the play itself may indeed change certain material aspects – sound, accent, pitch, volume, as Wright points out – but it cannot change it as language, as speech. In other words, Wright's historicist argument that the sonnets are the workshop for the fashioning of an 'inner speech' that renders stage characters more 'authentic' – certainly more capable of representing states of mind, feelings and a continuous internal form of consciousness – means that 'inner speech' cannot be a radically different language from sounded, public or theatrical speech. If the historical connection between them is to be sustained, then the silent language of interiority in the sonnets cannot differ *as language* from the sounded discourse of intimate inwardness on the stage. In this respect, Saussure is right: the perception of language as such is independent of its material aspects. Furthermore, for the silent speech of the sonnets to carry the weight of language as speech act – and not merely to hover as empty, ghostly forms – the 'inner ear' must be able to 'hear' tone, volume, timbre, pitch, even accent. These do not have to be sounded to register: they are the traces of exteriority that are borne in the very silent listening of the deepest inwardness. Most important, the conventional force of the performative, derived from the world of public discourse, should in principle be alive in all inner speech. Unsounded or not, the performatives of promising, threatening, imploring, declaring and so on must be capable of being reproduced when I speak to myself, or when I imagine myself speaking to an absent person, or when I rehearse an absent person's imagined speech to someone far away.[8]

It should be clear that the 'inwardness' that Wright wishes to trace through the 'silent speech' of the sonnets, and the forensic 'interiority' that Maus correctly emphasises in her historicist study, are different, though perhaps related, concepts. The former is not – or only tangentially – concerned with what is hidden, secret or unknowable. On the contrary, Wright's double emphasis on the passage of such speech into

---

[8] For a classic statement of this argument, see V. N. Voloshinov, *Marxism and the Philosophy of Language*, trans. Ladislaw Matejka and I. R. Titunik (Cambridge, MA: Harvard University Press, 1986). But see also Jacques Derrida, *Speech and Phenomena* (Evanston, IL: Northwestern University Press, 1973) for a different form of the argument.

the plays, and his emphasis on its recognisable nature, even in its most intensely 'private' moments, suggests that while we are indeed dealing with a realm that is distinct from what is 'outside', it is hardly unknowable or even an index of the unknowable. In other words, Wright suggests that the private and the public are distinct concepts, but they are not separated by radically different languages. The same language inhabits both. This means that, while Maus is right in insisting that early modern inwardness cannot be dissolved in a solution of postmodern philosophy and historicism, her own forays into the radical unknowability of the interior self cast little light on the language of inwardness attributed to the sonnets and plays such as *Hamlet*.

I am arguing that there is something misleading about a historicism that seeks to determine the meanings of literary texts on the basis of theories that may or may not have been held by the 'mainstream population' of the time. The scholarship offered by the monographs and essays that I have cited so far undeniably contributes to the history of ideas. But as a series of moves in determining what plays and sonnets can or cannot mean it is hardly decisive. Participants in the debate conflate the history of subjectivity with the history of its representation. They assume that if something is not represented in the literature of the period then it simply did not exist: literature is taken to be symptomatic of human life in general, indeed, completely mimetic of it (despite the current revulsion from mimesis). If we take subjectivity as, not something 'within' which 'passeth show', but a manifold of speech acts or language games that a particular culture needs to conduct the complex procedures and interactions of its social life, it becomes more questionable to attribute this to ourselves or the 'modern' period but to deny it of others on supposedly historical grounds. Human subjectivity does not belong to any one culture or period; it does not arise at any discernible historical moment; it is born with language itself. We should not be misled by the undeniable historical case that techniques for the representation of such speech acts do develop historically, but it is a mistake to believe that this represents the development of human subjectivity itself. To do so is to attribute a considerably reduced intellectual, emotional and spiritual life to anybody beyond the narrow confines of the European Enlightenment and its postmodern manifestations.

I am talking here about what Wittgenstein calls the 'forms of life' that inform the language games available to a group or a culture in their daily practices, not any theory that they might hold about the subjectivity that their linguistic practices make available to them. Such theories do change, develop, regress, but they are in a strict sense beside the point regarding the availability of human subjectivity as such. I want to suggest, therefore (before I go on to discuss Shakespeare's *Hamlet* and his sonnets), that whatever *theories* the English population – of whatever stream or tributary – held, are irrelevant. Here is Wittgenstein on the best way of illustrating the meaning of a particular speech: 'The contexts of a sentence are best portrayed in a play. Therefore the best example for a sentence with a particular meaning is a quotation in a play. And whoever asks a person in a play what he's experiencing when he's speaking?'[9] When the philosopher tries to demonstrate the nonsensical nature of a widespread and apparently philosophically rigorous and commonsensical belief that the meaning of a word is the thing for which it stands, he includes within his demonstration concepts that pertain to inwardness or interiority. The theory to which he is opposed holds that just as the word 'table' stands for (and therefore derives its meaning from) the object in the world to which it corresponds, so the word 'pain' means what it does through its correspondence with an inner state or feeling. Indeed, the correspondence theory soon collapses the relations between words and material objects into an 'interior' relationship established through an inner process called 'meaning' or 'intention'. The word is connected to the thing via my 'meaning' it in a particular way. In terms of this picture I am most secure when I mean by a word an inner state that only I can know. Wittgenstein argues that this is a fundamentally mistaken notion of how language works.

If what I shall call 'concepts of inwardness' get their meaning from whatever interior state a person happens to be experiencing, Wittgenstein argues, this would be like someone who has a box which, s/he claims, contains a beetle which only s/he can see.[10] The moment anyone else tries to inspect this beetle the box shuts quickly and firmly. In such circumstances the beetle would in fact be redundant. It would not matter one way or the other whether there was or was not a beetle in the box. All we have to work with is the box itself, with or without its beetle. This is not to deny that there is a beetle in the box: we do not know, and it does not matter. By analogy we have only the words in public circulation to work with. Any interior 'beetle' that is supposed to give them life or meaning, but which is hidden from the view of all but a single person, is redundant. Words work without interior states to back them up. And to bring this

---

9   Ludwig Wittgenstein, *Last Writings*, vol. 1, ed. G. H. von Wright and Heikki Nyman, trans. C. G. Luckhardt and Maximilian A. E. Aue (Chicago: University of Chicago Press, 1990), 38.
10 Ludwig Wittgenstein, *Philosophical Investigations*, trans. G. E. M. Anscombe (Oxford: Blackwell, 1953), 293.

out, Wittgenstein suggests that the paradigm case for explanation of a meaning of a word is its use in a sentence in a *play*. Because of the distance between actor and character, no appeal to 'inward states' in the speaker (actor) can be invoked to account for the meaning of the word or sentence. Whatever interior state the actor is experiencing is irrelevant to what s/he is saying: 'whoever asks a person in a play what he's experiencing when he's speaking?' And we understand utterances in plays perfectly well, even those that express or speak of 'interior states' that the actor is palpably not experiencing. This argument underscores the claim made above, namely, that 'inner' and 'outer' speech, whatever their material differences, are not different languages. There is therefore a passage from one to the other, exemplified historically in a variety of Shakespeare's texts, so that it makes perfect sense to say that the language of inwardness is constituted by public life. The meanings of the words used of inward states are not those states themselves, but rather publicly derived rules and uses. That does not, however, mean that inwardness disappears: the distinction between the interior and the exterior has a *use* in the language, however much of a social product language may be.[11] Consequently, it is invalid to collapse inwardness into outwardness, the private into the public, on the grounds that language is social. In short, we should take care not to deny the conceptual distinction between these different concepts.

In the light of this argument, the systematic choice of a play, *Hamlet*, as either the epitome or, at the very least, the anticipatory instance, of modern interiority should strike us as being especially interesting. For whatever interiority the play carries is purely conceptual. That is to say, we cannot attribute such interiority to anything hidden within the actor speaking, as Hamlet himself appears to do when he claims to have 'that within which passeth show'. Whatever Hamlet 'has within', in this metaphysical sense of being hidden, is like the beetle in the box: irrelevant, redundant. Interiority is a function of linguistic use in publicly accessible contexts, as our understanding of the play itself demonstrates. But that is not to say that interiority as a concept 'vaporises'.[12] Ferry claims that in *Hamlet* and his sonnets Shakespeare learned, via Sidney, to posit an interior that was not simply obscured by 'outward show'. She

---

[11] Maus's work is useful in demonstrating that such a use is not confined to a post-Enlightenment age, but is alive in the general discourses of the early modern period.

[12] See also Lynne Magnusson, *Shakespeare and Social Discourse: Dramatic Language and Elizabethan Letters* (Cambridge: Cambridge University Press, 1999), 'To emphasize the outward determination or the social orientation of utterances need not be to deny them any relation to inward states or individual psychology' (55).

claims that Shakespeare asserts a radical difference by which the heart is 'unknowable, inexpressible, and that therefore it may defy judgement' (*The 'Inward' Language*, 205). This inner, hidden self, which in effect cannot be 'unpacked' because it is beyond language and judgement, is the invention of what, in the modern world proper, Ferry claims, came to be regarded as the 'real' self. I am claiming, on the contrary, that *Hamlet qua* play demonstrates that interiority is a matter of the meaning (the public use) of concepts. Whatever Elizabethans, jointly or severally, may or may not have believed about the inner and the outer man is, strictly speaking, irrelevant to the play of concepts in the drama.

Following Wittgenstein's suggestion, we can see that theatricality may, in fact, best enable us to see the proper place and operations of interiority. I want to take this suggestion further by claiming that the same is true of the lyric. The lyric may appear to be different from the theatre. There, surely, the beetle is undeniable; the lyric is the pure expression of inwardness, the vehicle whereby one 'unpacks' one's heart. But as far as the meanings of words are concerned, Hamlet on the stage and Shakespeare writing sonnets are in exactly the same position: the paradigm case, even for as intimate a thing as the heart, is the theatre. This claim requires further elaboration and careful qualification, for it is clear that the lyric and the theatre are not the same things. For the moment I wish merely to register the Wittgensteinian point that the theatre is the *model* case for investigating concepts of interiority, for in it we are less likely to look for the meanings of words (even ones pertaining to interiority) in the emotional states of the speakers. This argument contradicts Ferry and Maus, who hold that the 'inwardness *topos*' prevalent in the early modern period affirms a radical interiority which 'escapes theatrical representation' (Maus, *Inwardness*, 15). It is, however, consistent with Wright's suggestion that the plays and sonnets share a common language of 'inner speech', and even with his claim that Shakespeare's mastery of the representation of interiority is the product of a particular historical moment.

To invent a poetic subjectivity is not the same thing as inventing human subjectivity. Shakespeare is remarkable for showing us, both theatrically and poetically, the rich drama of both public and private life as it is enacted and embodied in the language games and speech acts that constitute language in its relation to lived experience. In a special sense, then, interiority is not opposed to theatricality: it is inextricably imbricated in it. The 'interiority' ascribed to Hamlet and the speaker(s) of the sonnets should not be sought in any supposedly new theory about the difference between an inner and an outer self. It resides in the way in which the play and the poems represent or enact a complex play of speech acts, public or private: in the linguistic representation of 'thought', conveyed in a series of related and conflicting judgements, propositions, questions, estimations, expressions of feeling, exclamations and so on. Shakespeare's mastery of the representation of the manifold of speech acts and their relationships that make up human discourse and thought makes certain of his speakers appear to convey what we now like to think of as a properly interior self: what Ferry misleadingly calls a 'real self'. It is entirely plausible that people removed from us historically should not have had this or that theory, or even that they should have had different concepts. But that is not to say that they were incapable of forming judgements, making promises, engaging in intellectual exploration, expressing feelings, and performing a myriad of speech acts which make up the texture of language in use.

There is no moment in the Shakespearean canon in which the relationship between words and the heart is more consequential than in the opening scene of *King Lear*. Lear's unwavering confidence in the absolute power of his public performatives to command and remake the world – as he demands demonstrations of love, divides and alienates his kingdom with a series of sweeping gestures, warns, chastises and, finally, disinherits and banishes – is matched by his uncomplicated belief that love may be expressed and weighed in the arena of public contest. Everyone knows that whereas Goneril and Regan are prepared to indulge in the King's charade, Cordelia feels that the expression of filial love requires a different language game, another kind of speech act. Just what that language game is, is not made clear in this scene (though it is in the course of the play). This uncertainty leads to the understandable conclusion that love is essentially inexpressible, irreducibly private, certainly beyond mere words. But instead of standing in opposition to the speech act by which love is ostensibly expressed, the belief in the fundamental inadequacy of language is most powerfully present in the very rhetoric by which (false) love strains to make itself heard. Here is Goneril:

> Sir, I do love you more than words can wield the matter;
> Dearer than eyesight, space, or liberty;
> Beyond what can be valued, rich or rare;
> No less than life; with grace, health, beauty, honour;
> As much as child e'er loved, or father, friend;

> A love that makes breath poor and speech unable.
> Beyond all manner of so much I love you.
>
> (*King Lear* (1608 Quarto), 1. 1.50–6)

'A love that makes breath poor and speech unable' is precisely the state that informs the expressive muteness of sonnet 23, where the player-poet, like Lear's daughter, is exposed to the agonistic display of a public arena. In the face of her sister's precedent and her father's demand, Cordelia feels that she can say nothing (though she can *do* much, merely by remaining silent – see the discussion in the previous chapter). The difference between speech and action is brought out by a telling equivocation between the Quarto and the Folio texts: 'What shall Cordelia do?' (1.1.57) she asks in the former; 'What shall Cordelia speak?' (1.1.62) in the latter. If Cordelia quite literally speaks 'nothing', her silence is itself a form of action, a performative that rejects the language game that the King insists on playing as inappropriate. Cordelia consequently resolves to *say* nothing, but also to carry on *doing* what she has always done: to 'love and be silent' (1.1.62).

Cordelia may seem to represent a paradigm case of unknowable or unspeakable inwardness. This appears to be signalled by her aside, 'I am sure my love's / More ponderous [richer – Quarto] than my tongue' (1.1.77–8) and by the more open declaration to her father and the assembled court: 'I cannot heave / My heart into my mouth' (1.1.89–90). But she is not entirely true to her word. She responds, not with complete silence, but in the language game of public, social obligation – a language game that is appropriate to the context:

> I love your majesty
> According to my bond, nor more nor less.
>
> (1.1.92–3)

If a larger audience than merely her father has read in this meticulous statement a certain aloofness, even a calculated hard-heartedness, it is because they miss the way in which it exposes the inappropriateness to the occasion of the kind of speech act that the King demands, and in which her sisters are all too willing to indulge. Deprived from the beginning of even the rhetoric whereby words may be declared inadequate to love (since that rhetoric is already part of her sisters' declarations), but unable to remain completely silent, Cordelia speaks publicly of love in public terms: of duty, bonds and obligations. Does this mean that there is another kind of love, a deeper, more intimate and private kind, which is, if not unknowable, then certainly beyond language? No. It merely means that within a context of public competition no language game is available or appropriate in which to speak of such love. Kent does not doubt Cordelia's love. Nor do we. Nor, indeed, do we doubt Kent's own (different) love for Lear. Within this context, to refuse to speak is itself a declaration of love, although that in itself is not sufficient. Through the combination of subsequent speech and action the play subsequently confirms our initial impressions of their respective loves, and Lear himself comes to recognise their love in different, more intimate contexts of speech and action. One of the things that Lear learns when his speech acts no longer have the power to transform the world into his own image of it, are the language games and their surroundings that make speaking of love and appreciating it possible. Despite appearances, then, Cordelia's inability to 'heave her heart into her mouth' does not signal her possession of a deep inwardness impervious to language or show. It demonstrates her sensitivity to the surroundings that make or mar love talk. That sensitivity confirms my argument that whereas the public and the private are distinct concepts, they are distinguished by differences in language games (which include behaviour and context) rather than the incompatibilities of speech and silence, outwardness and inwardness.

The pressures of Cordelia's situation are instantly recognisable in the like struggles of the player-poet to negotiate the often-incompatible demands of love and duty in a similarly competitive, public show. Take sonnet 85, from the 'rival poet' sequence:

> MY toung-tide Muse in manners holds her still,
> While comments of your praise richly compil'd,
> Reserue their Character with goulden quill,
> And precious phrase by all the Muses fil'd.
> I thinke good thoughts,whilst others write good wordes,
> And like vnlettered clarke still crie Amen,
> To euery Himne that able spirit affords,
> In polisht forme of well refined pen.
> Hearing you praisd,I say 'tis so, 'tis true,
> And to the most of praise adde some-thing more,
> But that is in my thought,whose loue to you
> (Though words come hind-most) holds his ranke before,
>   Then others,for the breath of words respect,
>   Me for my dombe thoughts, speaking in effect.

The paradox of the player-poet as an 'vnlettered clarke' repeats itself more generally throughout the poem, which is written precisely to declare: 'I thinke good thoughts, whilst others write good wordes'. The sonnet offers a glimpse of the public nature of the compliment against which it subtly aligns its own more inward appreciation. Even if the 'richly compil'd' and 'precious phrase' of the rival poetry is conceived as being written, it extends beyond the intimate space between addresser and addressee. It circulates more widely, either on the page or, as the sonnet itself suggests, it is read out aloud in a company of which the player-poet is a member. He is expected at the very least to add his own voice to the sentiments expressed: 'Hearing you praisd, I say 'tis so, 'tis true.' With this self-quotation, like the 'Amen' earlier, offered as direct speech, the sonnet draws an implied distinction between the enforced, voiced speech of the public occasion and the silent thoughts of a more personal devotion. Rather than being entirely internal and unvoiced, however, such love occupies a paradoxical, liminal relationship between 'dombe thoughts' and the 'breath of words' – in the form of the more intimate, less public kind of writing exemplified by the poem itself. The reticent strains of his public voice, sounded as a mere endorsement of the praise of others, are contrasted with the elaborate logic of the sonnet itself, which announces itself as a private document: the 'speaking in effect' of the player-poet's 'dombe thoughts' in their written form. The poem thus presents a perfectly cogent distinction between the public and the private. But despite the language of silent interiority, its very performance repudiates the idea that the private is something fundamentally inexpressible or unknowable. The poem seeks precisely to make 'dombe thoughts' speak 'in effect', but without negotiating the debilitating world of public self-display. Like sonnet 23, it shows that words may be saved from mere breathiness in the properly private (but not unknowable) language of writing. And like that sonnet it is a lesson, an attempt to teach the young man of rank how to accommodate himself to such a language.

Hamlet is hardly recognised as a play in which sonnets figure promi-nently. It does, however, contain a prominent sonneteer. Like Benedick before him, Hamlet tries his hand at rhyme to express his admiration and desire for the 'most beautified Ophelia' (2.2.110), admitting openly, if ambiguously, that he is 'ill at these numbers' (2.2.120). Ophelia speaks of Hamlet's many 'tenders of affection' (1.4.100), underscored by 'all the vows of heaven' (1.4.114), and in their painful encounter in 3.1, she expresses her (enforced) desire to return his 'remembrances' (3.1.95) orig-inally accompanied by 'words of so sweet breath composed / As made the things more rich' (3.1.100–1). If Hamlet is indeed, as she puts it, the 'glass of fashion and the soul of form' (3.1.156), displaying, amongst other things, the 'courtier's ... tongue' (3.1.154), then it is probably safe to assume that 'the music of his honey vows', which she admits to have 'sucked' (3.1.159), would have arrived in the shape of a sonnet or, indeed, a number of sonnets.

Like the sonnets in *Love's Labour's Lost*, Hamlet's verse does not remain within the private space between himself and his beloved. It is monitored by her father, alienated and redistributed to the King and Queen, where it is read out in the public space of the court, subjected to Polonius's 'literary' criticism, turned into the object of forensic enquiry and, pre-sumably, finally returned to him by Ophelia at her father's behest. It is in the public domain. Yet it is also indubitably private, its privacy as violated as Ophelia must feel hers to be when Hamlet, uninvited, en-ters her closet in his own silently eloquent dumb-show, his 'doublet all unbraced / ... his stockings fouled, / Ungartered, and down-gyved to his ankle' (2.1.79–81). Hamlet as sonneteer is thus as embroiled as any sonneteer in the problem of what words may say in a society not merely given over to flattery and lies, but in which the general encroachment of the public upon the private world renders the latter extremely precarious.

Such encroachment is material. It is the product of a particular social world, not the result of any metaphysical or philosophical truth. Any number of confusions, not least the theoretical reduction of the private to the public, are liable to arise from a failure to observe the distinction between what I shall call metaphysical and material anti-theatricality. For clarification, let us turn to the *locus classicus* of early modern 'interiority', Hamlet's response to his mother's injunction to abandon his mourning disposition:

> QUEEN GERTRUDE Good Hamlet, cast thy nightly colour off,
> And let thine eye look like a friend on Denmark.
> Do not for ever with thy vailèd lids
> Seek for thy noble father in the dust.
> Thou know'st 'tis common – all that lives must die,
> Passing through nature to eternity.
> HAMLET Ay, madam, it is common.
> QUEEN GERTRUDE   If it be,
> Why seems it so particular with thee?
> HAMLET Seems, madam? Nay, it *is*. I know not 'seems'.
> 'Tis not alone my inky cloak, good-mother,
> Nor customary suits of solemn black,
> Nor windy suspiration of forced breath,
> No, nor the fruitful river in the eye,

> Nor the dejected haviour of the visage,
> Together with all forms, moods, shows of grief
> That can denote me truly. These indeed 'seem',
> For they are actions that a man might play;
> But I have that within which passeth show –
> These but the trappings and the suits of woe.
>
> (1.2.68–86)

Cited most frequently as a signal historical moment in the assertion of a hidden interiority beyond theatrical representation, Hamlet's response is hardly simple. What ontological reality does he affirm in the curt 'Seems, madam? Nay, it *is*'? Let me suggest that it is not primarily an ineffable inwardness, but rather his *singularity*. If losing fathers is common, then Hamlet asserts the uncommonness of his persistent grief in contrast to those around him that have been happy to turn from death to life, from 'funeral baked meats' to 'marriage tables' (1.2.79–80). He thus reiterates, in words this time, what all 'outward show' – his clothing, demeanour, actions – proclaims from the moment he enters: his difference from the society around him.

Having done that, Hamlet does indeed wish to signal a further difference: a grief, an inwardness, that lies beyond what Derrida has called 'iterability', or representation itself.[13] He can do this only through words, and such words, paradoxically, can be no more than gestures. It is as if he feels that any action that can be repeated by someone else (including himself) is too gross, or too promiscuous, to 'denote [him] truly' (*Hamlet*, 1.2.83). Glimpsing this metaphysical 'revulsion from representation',[14] Ferry and Maus in different ways attribute a notion of something within that – whatever such a thing is – is by definition inexpressible. As such, it lies beyond anything that can bear meaning. It may, in this sense then, be meaningless: a beetle in a box. Of course, such a thing does not lie within the player that plays Hamlet. But let us entertain the idea that it lies within the character Hamlet. It is something towards which the character can only gesture, momentarily, mutely. The player, in turn, represents that attempt at representation, in a gesture of a gesture: lying beyond imitation it is no more than a glimmer, an anti-concept. But it also singles Hamlet out, signalling more than anything his difference from the world of Denmark. As such it paradoxically signifies its other

---

[13] Jacques Derrida, *Limited Inc*, ed. Gerald Graff (Evanston, IL: Northwestern University Press, 1988).

[14] Robert Weimann, 'Shakespeare (De)Canonized: Conflicting Uses of "Authority" and "Representation"', *New Literary History*, 20. 1 (Autumn 1988), 64.

side: not an inwardness that is metaphysically unknowable, but one that, like Cordelia's love for her father and the player-poet's devotion to his friend, cannot be expressed because no context is appropriate for its expression. Such inwardness is an effect, not of 'considering too curiously' (*Hamlet*, 5.1.201) (that is to say, metaphysically), but of feeling oneself at odds in and with one's society.

In short, Hamlet thinks that his inability to express his innermost feelings signals the metaphysical ineffability of such a state, but we can see that it is a product of his material circumstances. He is caught in a society that has robbed the language games that make the expression of inwardness possible, of their efficacy. Both senses of an inexpressible inwardness trade on a kind of anti-theatricality, but we should be careful to keep them apart. Metaphysical anti-theatricality recoils from signification itself: from whatever is capable of being duplicated, rehearsed, repeated. It clings to the notion of 'presence' which Derrida deconstructs. It thinks it lives in the 'private language' that Wittgenstein shows to be logically impossible (*Philosophical Investigations*, 243ff.). Material anti-theatricality is very different. Its target is not representation *as such*, but rather the possible effects of theatricality as a mode of behaviour in a particular situation. In a context in which people are systematically and dishonestly ostentatious about feelings that they do not have, or about roles they do not deserve, such an anti-theatrical position prefers to keep its own counsel, to downplay the 'actions that a man might play' and refuse to be 'played on' as a pipe (*Hamlet*, 3.2.352). In its quest for personal integrity it refuses to 'heave its heart into its mouth'. Its silence is performative, not empty.

If language games signify properly only in the surroundings that make them possible, then in the absence of such surroundings the words and gestures by which they are usually played will be empty, as sounding brass. In a society in which every gesture is potentially hollow the modes of personal integrity will be silence rather than speech, substance rather than form, plainness rather than ornament. But such choices are made in the ordinary world: they are themselves 'actions', 'forms' or 'moods', and are thus not predicated upon an essentially unknowable and inexpressible 'inside'. There may come a time when the society is so corrupt that one is at a loss to say or do anything, since its politics or morality has degenerated to the point where the face of integrity is indistinguishable from every other. But to have to make one's way in such a society (as Hamlet, Cordelia, and the player-poet of the sonnets, in their different ways, do) is not to be confronted by the 'problem of other minds', as Maus puts it (*Inwardness*, 7). In such a situation one is not faced with the philosophical problem of whether anything exists outside one's own mind, or whether there is an interior 'something' that is literally unrepresentable because it is metaphysically not amenable to re-presentation. It is the problem of finding adequate ways of living among people who are not so much intrinsically unknowable (merely by virtue of being *other* minds), but are rather all too transparently shallow and duplicitous. Hamlet and the player-poet of the sonnets might seem to entertain metaphysical forms of anti-theatricality from time to time. They are, however, attempting to negotiate what I have called the *material* problem of inwardness, even if they sometimes misrecognise it as a metaphysical one.

Jonas Barish reminds us that the concept of theatricality carries pejorative overtones even today, and they are almost invariably contrasted with those of interiority.[15] To be theatrical is to banish privacy – the inner, the personal, the protected, the secret, the deep, the intimate, the certain – in favour of 'show' – the outer, the public, the vulnerable, the exposed, the superficial, the common and the duplicitous. Between these two sites language itself is in an anomalous position. Preserver of the private, it is also the medium of the theatrical. In the most anti-theatrical moments silence must be declared the only true sign of truth. The paradox that such a declaration entails is obvious. *Hamlet* the play speaks in every way against the philosophical anti-theatricality that in the view of some critics its protagonist expresses.[16] The tragedy as a whole demonstrates the irreducibility of all the concepts that I have aligned above with theatricality to that which 'passeth show'. Or rather, the play demonstrates that privacy is inextricably imbricated in the forms, moods and shows of public life, but also (and this is important) that it is not reducible, as a concept, to the public. Critics who regard Hamlet's disavowal of that 'which passeth show' as the sign of a momentous affirmation of unknowable inwardness seldom consider his intimate relationship to representation, show, theatre and theatricality in the rest of the play. They seldom ask whether the theory of inwardness that they find in his early speech is in fact sustained by the play as a whole.

There are at least four major moments in which the issue of theatricality and its discontents is revisited in detail: the arrival of the players in

---

[15] Jonas Barish, *The Anti-Theatrical Prejudice* (Berkeley and Los Angeles: University of California Press, 1991), 1.

[16] See Barker, *The Tremulous Private Body*. Jeffrey Masten discusses this issue, drawing a somewhat different conclusion from my own, in 'Circulation, Gender, and Subjectivity in Wroth's Sonnets', in *Reading Mary Wroth: Representing Alternatives in Early Modern England*, ed. Naomi J. Miller and Gary Waller (Knoxville: University of Tennessee Press, 1991), 76.

Act 2 Scene 2; Hamlet's encounter with Ophelia in the following scene; Claudius's prayer scene in Act 3 Scene 3; and Hamlet's excoriation of his mother a scene later. None of these scenes offers a homogenous *theory* of inwardness and theatricality, although each explores their conceptual relationships and differences.

In Act 2 Scene 2, theatricality is not merely a metaphor or vehicle for the distinction between outwardness and inwardness; furthermore, inwardness itself is considerably less inscrutable than Hamlet's opening lines might suggest. If Hamlet's early opposition to 'actions that a man might play' stems from what I have called a 'metaphysical' aversion to performance (and this is not settled), he is by no means dismissive of the men who play such actions. In fact, he greets their arrival with considerable enthusiasm, he displays an intimate knowledge of the politics and sociology of the theatre and treats the players themselves with an easy familiarity combined with singular respect. Theatricality is presented not as a philosophical idea but as a set of material social conditions, actions and techniques. Hamlet is more concerned with the politics of the theatre wars, the pressures of audience expectations and the practical problems of a boy player's voice breaking too soon than with the problems of scepticism that arise from 'considering too closely' the discrepancies between the 'exterior' and the 'inward man' (2.2.6). Later, before the performance, he is certainly concerned with theatrical practice – with the appropriate use of gesture and word to convey a realistic sense of human behaviour and passion – but this is a matter of technique. It carries no intrinsic sense of the inscrutability of 'that within which passeth show'. If anything, Hamlet assumes that one *can* convey passion adequately, provided one adjusts and controls one's body properly: 'suit[ing] the action to the word, the word to the action' and 'o'erstep[ping] not the modesty of nature' (3.2.17–19).

Especially striking are Hamlet's thorough knowledge of and interest in the theatre, the easygoing warmth of his relationship with the common players and the respect with which he treats them and commands others to treat them. The royal endorsement of the players both as men and as the 'abstracts and the brief chronicles of the time' (2.2.527–8) differs markedly from the supercilious contempt that the aristocrats in the court of Theseus display towards the players in *A Midsummer Night's Dream*, when they use the performance as a vehicle for their own superiority and wit. Both Hamlet and Theseus insist that, as a nobleman, treating lesser people with respect enhances 'your own honour and dignity' (*Hamlet*, 2.2.534). Only Hamlet suits the action to the word. But

Hamlet does more than honour the players with his grace: upon their arrival he relaxes for the first time, pursuing matters of what we might call 'ordinary life' in which he has a rich, detailed interest. For the first time Denmark seems more than a prison. His discourse with his supposed friends, Rosencrantz and Guildenstern, changes, upon the arrival of the players, from guarded accusation and enigmatic aphorism to unselfconscious enquiry and genuinely warm banter. It is clear that the players *do* delight him; everything he does and says in their company speaks of a different man, one who suddenly no longer 'seem[s] most alone in greatest company'.[17] One suspects that Hamlet is able to relax among the players precisely because they are *not* 'politicians': they are honest men trying their best to sustain a difficult and thankless trade in the face of the vicissitudes of politics and fashion.

If this seems like special pleading on the part of Shakespeare the player-dramatist, it should also be considered special pleading by Will, the player-poet of the sonnets. The relationship between the persona of the sonnets and the protagonist of the tragedy lies less in the mutual expression of an inexpressible inwardness than in the inescapability of a certain kind of theatricality in each text. At one level, the player-poet of the sonnets is pleading to be 'used' after a properly noble sense of 'honour and dignity'. The 'oblacion, poore but free' (sonnet 125) that he offers to the young man is the honest gift of a man who is like the players in *Hamlet*. They are at once contrasted to 'pittiful thrivors' (sonnet 125) such as Rosencrantz and Guildenstern or Polonius. Both Hamlet's consciously friendly respect for the players and his unusual ease in their company bespeaks Shakespeare as player-poet's desire to promote his own company as morally and personally superior to 'others who', in the poet's absence, are 'all too neere' (sonnet 61) his own dark lord. Act 2 Scene 2 presents Hamlet as a double figure: an ideal model for the young nobleman of the sonnets and as an expression of the player-poet's own struggle with the problem of theatricality in 'these last so bad' days (sonnet 67).

This conflation of the noble prince and common player should come as no surprise, considering the sonnets' tension between a 'mutuall render' (sonnet 125) which 'leaues out difference' (sonnet 105) and their acute and painful acknowledgement of the social distance between lover and beloved. In this respect, Hamlet's wish to hear a play – 'never acted, or, if

---

[17] Philip Sidney, *Astrophil and Stella*, in *The Poems of Sir Philip Sidney*, ed. William A. Ringler Jr. (Oxford: Clarendon, 1962), sonnet 27.

it was, not above once . . . caviar to the general' and which 'pleased not the million' because of its quality ('an excellent play' (2.2.437–43)) – aligns him more with the creators of such material than with a courtier, such as Polonius, who is 'for a jig or a tale of bawdry, or he sleeps' (2.2.503–4). The inclusion of Polonius among those who would not appreciate a play 'very much more handsome than fine' (448–9) complicates what appear at first to be Hamlet's scornful reflections on class. Despite his pretensions to literary taste, Polonius and doubtless many others of his class are included among the 'million' whose taste for 'sallets' and ostentatious display would confine a play such as Hamlet describes to a single performance. So too, perhaps, is the young man of the sonnets, whose love for 'affectation' renders him blind to the 'honesty' that his player-poet claims for his own work.

There are both metaphysical and material senses to theatricality in this scene. Hamlet's interaction with the players invites us to contrast their basic honesty with the social duplicity of the members of the court that surround him. But at the same time, the player's passion in his delivery of the Hecuba speech does raise the issue of the relationship or discrepancy among passion, action and word that is encapsulated by considering performance in metaphysical terms. Hamlet is amazed by neither the player's duplicity nor his inscrutability, but rather by his uncanny ability to move himself and others in the absence of any immediate, personal cause: 'What's Hecuba to him, or he to Hecuba / That he should weep for her?' (2.2.561–2). This is the *energeia* of which the anti-theatricalists were so suspicious, but of which both Puttenham and Sidney write with undisguised approval.[18] Hamlet's reflection on the marvel of the player's capacity to make 'his whole function [suit] / With forms to his conceit' (2.2.558–9) offers a contrary perspective on his earlier insistence on the emptiness of 'outward forms' and their incapacity to express the 'something' in the heart. As both Wittgenstein and Hamlet, in their different ways, remind us, the *player* has 'nothing' in the heart (2.2.571); or, to put it more accurately, the player need feel no inward passion whatsoever for his or her words to be imbued with the most powerful force and meaning.

We should not underestimate how 'monstrous' (2.2.553) this insight seems to those who are committed to the opposing metaphysics, by which words are essentially inner things. Hamlet's own language begins to break down when he thinks too nicely on this 'monstrosity'. It seems to him

---

[18] Note Sidney's comment on the lack of *energeia* in contemporary poets. Does he mean that they lack real passions, or that their language does not move the reader?

that if the player had the 'motive and the cue for passion' that he has, the player would

> drown the stage with tears,
> And cleave the general ear with horrid speech,
> Make mad the guilty and appal the free,
> Confound the ignorant, and amaze indeed
> The very faculty of eyes and ears.   (2.2.562–6)

But this is merely an instance of the over-acting that he himself prohibits before the performance. If the player could be so moved and so moving without any personal or interior stake in the event, then a properly interior passion should surely intensify the force of the speech. But Hamlet himself knows that this is false reasoning. The player is so moving because he justly captures the force of human passion by suiting action to word – nothing else. Whatever passion he himself experiences is irrelevant to the force and meaning of what he is saying. He may feel nothing, yet still render the speech with the most powerful passion and persuasion. When the Prince considers his own inadequacy it is perceived in terms of his incapacity for speech rather than action:

> Yet I,
> A dull and muddy-mettled rascal, peak
> Like John-a-dreams, unpregnant of my cause,
> And can *say* nothing –
> (2.2.564–671; emphasis added)

Strange. When Hamlet does manage in due course to work himself into a vituperative rage he soon realises both its futility and emptiness:

> Bloody, bawdy villain!
> Remorseless, treacherous, lecherous, kindless villain!
> O, vengeance! –
> Why, what an ass am I? Ay, sure, this is most brave,
> That I
>
>   . . .
>
> Must, like a whore, unpack my heart with words
> And fall a-cursing like a very drab,
> A scullion!   (2.2.583–90)

This is Hamlet finally 'unpack[ing] [his] heart' under the pressure of a properly inward passion. But his words ring as emptily as any ham actor's. The interiority claimed earlier is here shown to be as vacant as the monstrous fiction or 'nothing' of the player who performs the Hecuba speech. Once he recovers himself, Hamlet turns once again to the theatre as the ideal vehicle for his purposes, but not before he has branded the unpacking of the heart as a peculiarly (and contemptibly) female preoccupation.

There is little in Act 2 Scene 2, then, to endorse the claim to unrepresentable interiority that Hamlet makes in Act 1 Scene 2. If anything, the encounter with the players and reflections on performance undercut it considerably, showing that unpacking the heart produces 'nothing': hollow words. Hamlet's words, the emptiness of which he himself acknowledges, but which are supposed to arise from the fullness of an inward passion, are in fact less forceful than the 'monstrous' fictionality of the player who has *nothing* within that passes show. Nor does the rest of the scene contradict this fact. Claudius sends for Rosencrantz and Guildenstern because he believes that they might discover what is wrong with Hamlet. But he does not talk of a hidden interiority that fails to match a manifest exterior. He is confident on the basis of what he can see that 'not th' exterior nor the inward man / Resembles that it was' (2.2.6–7). Furthermore, Hamlet's sorry pair of friends are very bad at concealing their real purpose. He sees through them immediately: 'You were sent for, and there is a kind of confession in your looks which your modesties have not craft enough to colour. I know the good King and Queen have sent for you' (2.2.281–3). Wittgenstein cautions against the sceptical disposition, which wants to generalise the fact that we find some people inscrutable into a universal, metaphysical condition, by reminding us of the difference between individual cases: 'We also say of some people that they are transparent to us. It is, however, important as regards this observation that one human being can be a complete enigma to another' (*Philosophical Investigations*, 223). That is to say, the fact that some people find it easy to 'smile and murder while [they] smile' (*3 Henry VI*, 3.2.182) cannot be extrapolated across all cases into a general sceptical principle. For Hamlet, the idea is unusual enough to warrant immediate recording in his 'tables': 'My tables, / My tables – meet it is I set it down / That one may smile and smile and be a villain' (1.5.107–9). Wittgenstein argues that whether or not we find people enigmatic will be connected with degrees not only of personal but also cultural and social familiarity. This is not, he says, 'because of not knowing what they are saying to themselves' but because 'we cannot find our feet with them' (*Philosophical Investigations*, 223). Hamlet's oft-remarked ability to see through others (Targoff, 'The Performance of Prayer', 64) is not merely a product of character but of social situation; just as, I shall argue shortly, the player-poet of the sonnets encounters his dark lord as an enigma through the inequalities of power that mark their relationship. That Hamlet fails in his reading of Claudius at prayer does, perhaps as Targoff suggests, 'reflect negatively upon the transformative force of both theatrical and devotional practice' (63). But whatever theory it may or may not endorse, it reflects the differences between the language games in which concepts of interiority get their meanings. Such differences tend to be overlooked in the search for whatever general theory prevails in a specific play, author or the culture as a whole. It is the product of a language game, Wittgenstein argues, that one can hear God speaking only to oneself and not to others. In other words, God's speech is a concept different from yet related to human speech. When Hamlet, seeing Claudius at prayer, assumes (mistakenly) that he is in a state of true devotion, he reveals a difference between language games or concepts; he does not endorse any theory about the essential inscrutability of human interiority.

Recent criticism has sought to render interiority both more material and materialist by translating psychic into material space: in the form of the semiotic significance and day-to-day roles of the closet as the most private and 'inward' of rooms in the aristocratic house in the early modern period.[19] Is it significant that a play supposedly so concerned with its protagonist's interiority should never withdraw him into this most private of spaces, even for his most intimate speeches, but rather represent him as the violator of others' closets, those of his mother and his lover, Ophelia? In this play it is women who are precluded from retiring into what *The English Secretorie* calls 'a room proper and peculier onely to our selves'.[20] Privacy is a space systematically denied them. This is apparent in the systematic control that Ophelia's brother and father exercise over her affections. They render her relationship with the Prince in brutally public terms. Even in death, Ophelia is subjected to graveyard gossip, religious controversy and the indignity of Laertes's and Hamlet's histrionics within her very grave.

Like Cordelia in the opening scene of *King Lear*, Ophelia is forced to enact her most intimate feelings in the public eye, in terms of language games that are either completely inappropriate or surrounded

---

[19] See Alan Stewart, 'The Early Modern Closet Discovered', *Representations*, 50 (Spring 1995), 76–99; Patricia Fumerton, *Cultural Aesthetics: Renaissance Literature and the Practice of Social Ornament* (Chicago: University of Chicago Press, 1991); and Robert Girouard, *Life in the English Country House: A Social and Architectural History* (New Haven, CT: Yale University Press, 1978).

[20] Angel Day, *The English Secretorie* (London: 1592), 109; quoted in Stewart, 'The Early Modern Closet Discovered', 83.

by contexts that render them meaningless. She, too, finally resorts to relatively impersonal and public discourses – the modes of performance, song and folklore – to 'unpack her heart'. In its enigmatic distraction, Ophelia's discourse, though considered 'nothing', is taken seriously for the first time. It becomes the object of intense interpretive effort and anxiety:

> Her speech is nothing,
> Yet the unshapèd use of it doth move
> The hearers to collection. They aim at it,
> And botch the words up fit to their own thoughts,
> Which, as her winks and nods and gestures yield them,
> Indeed would make one think there might be thought,
> Though nothing sure, yet much unhappily.
> QUEEN GERTRUDE 'Twere good she were spoken with, for she
> may strew
> Dangerous conjectures in ill-breeding minds.
> Let her come in. (4.5.7–16)

Like Hamlet's similarly carnivalesque use of aphorism and popular saw, Ophelia for once renders herself incapable of being 'spoken to', even by royal command. Popular songs and ballads allow her a discursive space free of her usual gendered constraints within the family and the court. It is as if Cordelia were to occupy the place of Lear's Fool. Unlike Hamlet, Claudius or even Gertrude,[21] Ophelia is allowed no language for an interior self that is not at the same time wholly public and thus amenable to having the 'heart of [its] mystery' 'plucked out' (3.2.353). If she is herself unable to speak except in the most indirect ways about this condition, it is brutally and painfully anatomised by a female sonneteer writing some two decades after *Hamlet* was first performed:

> If ever love had force in humaine brest?
> If ever he could move in pensive hart
> Or if that hee such powre could but impart
> To breed those flames whose heat brings joys unrest.
> Then looke on me; that ame to thes adrest,
> I, ame the soule that feeles the greatest smart;
> I, am that hartles trunk of harts depart

---

[21] See, for example, in this very scene:

> QUEEN GERTRUDE To my sick soul, as sin's true nature is,
> Each toy seems prologue to some great amiss.
> So full of artless jealousy is guilt,
> It spills itself in fearing to be spilt. (4.5.17–20)

> And I, that one, by love, and grief oprest;
> None ever felt the truth of loves great miss
>   Of eyes, till I deprived was of bliss;
>   For had he seene, hee must have pitty show'd;
> I should nott have bin made this stage of woe
>   Where sad disasters have theyre open showe
>   O noe, more pitty hee had surely beestow'd.[22]

Ophelia lacks Pamphilia's lacerated self-awareness of the impossibility of privacy in her social and erotic world, but we can see in her public display a similarly tortured condition which draws attention to its deep privations through a peculiar kind of histrionics. Such histrionics manages to speak dumbly, if shockingly, through gesture and song:

> (*Sings*) By Gis, and by Saint Charity,
> Alack, and fie for shame!
> Young men will do 't if they come to 't,
> By Cock, they are to blame.
> Quoth she 'Before you tumbled me,
> You promised me to wed.'
> So would I 'a' done, by yonder sun,
> An thou hadst not come to my bed.
>   (*Hamlet*, 4.5.58–65)

The issue is not simply that the private is subsumed by the public, or that the private offers a deep, inexpressible sense of self beyond the social, but rather that a society in which the private is always invaded by the public is pathological – as Hamlet puts it – 'rotten'. Mary Wroth staging herself as the exemplum of abuse, Ophelia showing that her 'nothing's more than matter' through the display of her abuse (4.5.174), Hamlet thinking that the 'play's the thing' in which he'll 'catch the conscience of the king'(2.2.606–7) and the player-poet of the sonnets struggling to forge the intimate space of writing through the public discourses of his poems, are all struggling in different but related ways against that pathology.

Only in a public life in which behaviour and values run so violently athwart his own can the Prince of Denmark feel so intensely the impossibility of all expression, the corrupt vacuity of all show. This sense extends to his own capacity for representation, which he feels to be attenuated, if not diminished entirely. It also blocks his capacity to allow Ophelia the very humanity that is systematically denied him on his return from Wittenberg. This accords with the position of the player-poet

---

[22] Sonnet 42, in *The Poems of Lady Mary Wroth*, ed. Josephine A. Roberts (Baton Rouge and London: Louisiana State University Press, 1983).

in Shakespeare's sonnets, whose anti-theatricality is close to Hamlet's, and whose stance towards women is similarly problematic.[23]

One of the chief counter-discourses of Petrarchism involves the violent disavowal of theatricality, but it is simultaneously intrinsic to the discourse. Petrarchan poets are caught in the trap of having to disavow, through the necessarily public, theatrical 'show' of their verse, the superficiality of mere display. Such dislike of histrionic ostentation paradoxically marks Hamlet's own peculiar histrionics over Ophelia's grave. His exorbitant parody of Laertes's Petrarch-like display is at the same time a desperate effort to display what he has been forced to suppress:

> HAMLET Why, I will fight with him upon this theme
> Until my eyelids will no longer wag.
> QUEEN GERTRUDE O my son, what theme?
> HAMLET I loved Ophelia. Forty thousand brothers
> Could not, with all their quantity of love,
> Make up my sum. – What wilt thou do for her?
> KING CLAUDIUS O, he is mad, Laertes.
> QUEEN GERTRUDE (*to Laertes*) For love of God, forbear him.
> HAMLET (*to Laertes*) 'Swounds, show me what thou'lt do.
> Woot weep, woot fight, woot fast, woot tear thyself,
> Woot drink up eisel, eat a crocodile?
> I'll do 't. Dost thou come here to whine,
> To outface me with leaping in her grave?
> Be buried quick with her, and so will I.
> And if thou prate of mountains, let them throw
> Millions of acres on us, till our ground,
> Singeing his pate against the burning zone,
> Make Ossa like a wart. Nay, an thou'lt mouth,
> I'll rant as well as thou.
> KING CLAUDIUS (*to Laertes*)　　　This is mere madness.
>
> (5.1.263–81)

If Ophelia can give expression to her position only 'by indirection', Hamlet addresses Laertes directly, but the effect of his address is anything but direct. Ostensibly a parody of Laertes's overblown rhetoric, Hamlet's intervention is the action of one who can no longer contain that which 'passeth show'. Declaration of love or parody of such declaration? His utterances and actions perform both at the same time, just as

[23] The psychoanalytical studies which attribute the 'problem' in the play to Hamlet's incapacity to cope with his mother's sexuality (and by extension that of all women, including Ophelia) should be well known. See, among others, Jacqueline Rose, '*Hamlet* – the *Mona Lisa* of Literature', *Critical Quarterly*, 28 (1986), 35–49 and Janet Adelman, *Suffocating Mothers: Fantasies of Maternal Origin in Shakespeare's Plays* (London and New York: Routledge, 1992).

Shakespeare's supposedly anti-Petrarchan sonnets remain twinned with the very conventions that they parody. It is precisely the conventionality of Laertes's expression of grief that frees Hamlet to engage in what is essentially a dialogical appropriation of that expression, through which he can declare, in a parodic third voice, an aspect of himself repressed by his overwhelmingly public existence at Elsinore. Of course, we are left free to judge the adequacy of Hamlet's performative. His 'love' for Ophelia is not something that lies *within* Hamlet; it is something made evident or obscured by his behaviour at other moments in the play. Perhaps the best conclusion – one which I shall pursue in the discussion to follow of the sonnets – is that 'love', at least in one of its aspects, is rendered impossible by the material dissolution of the private by the public.

Sonnet 23 ('As an vnperfect player on the stage') might be regarded as one of the central texts in the sub-sequence to the young man of rank. Its anti-theatricality differs from Hamlet's insofar as it speaks from the position of a common player who finds himself exposed and vulnerable, indeed overwhelmed, by the occasion of having to speak before an audience whose taciturn gaze reduces him to silence. That this tongue-tied player has 'that within that passeth show' is at most submerged in the sonnet. The player-poet's problem is not an essentially inexpressible inwardness, but rather the unbearable social pressure of the occasion which makes him forget his lines, reducing him, as player, to nothing. Like Hamlet's anti-theatrical histrionics, the anti-theatrical stance entertained by the player-poet stems from his position within a particular society: as a man of the theatre. His entertained antipathy to the theatre paradoxically takes the theatrical form of forging a space in which he can act the part of a poet.[24] The renunciation of the theatrical in sonnet 23 is thus material, not metaphysical, even though we discover that the player is pleading to be allowed to replace speech and gesture with written verse as the 'domb presagers of [his] speaking breast'. The player's lowly social status combines with the exposed publicity of his place on the stage to make any 'mutuall render' between himself and the gazing man of rank impossible. Acutely aware of more assured rivals who are much more at home than he on the different, aristocratic stage of courtly compliment,

---

[24] For an account of the social struggles of the professional poet, especially one from the theatre, who attempts to break into the amateur world of courtly patronage, see Alvin Kernan, *The Playwright as Magician: Shakespeare's Image of the Poet in the English Public Theatre* (New Haven, CT and London: Yale University Press, 1979).

he thus asks to be allowed to play a different role, that of the less exposed, less public, poet, whose silent words may, in the more intimate, private space of *reading*, speak more eloquently: 'O learne to read what silent loue hath writ; / To heare wit eies belongs to loues fine wiht.' The 'difference' which this sonnet wishes to 'leaue out' is thus not the difference between feeling and language, the inner and the outer, but the material difference of rank that is proclaimed all-too-clearly by his position in the public theatre and in the stagey space of English Petrarchism.

That space should remind us of the complexities of audience. Aside from Francis Meres's intriguing comment about Shakespeare's 'sugar'd sonnets' among his 'private friends', and Marotti's speculations about manuscript circulation (which is maddeningly silent about Shakespeare),[25] we do not know the conditions under which Shakespeare's sonnets circulated. Were they passed on only to close friends (the coterie) in manuscript? Were they presented directly to the young man? Or were at least some of them also read or recited aloud, in company, perhaps in the presence of the beloved, in a theatrical enactment of the conditions of address described in sonnet 23? And what does a coterie audience entail? It is often assumed to have been a group of friends essentially sympathetic to the poet. But might such a group not be more fractured, less harmonious, or discrepant, as is suggested in some of Sidney and Wyatt's sonnets? Or were the poems variously circulated under different conditions of audience and address? In each case the presence of others (as auditors) would make a difference to the force of the sonnet: retroactively, upon the speaker who might feel uncomfortably vulnerable in the public glare of the address ('As an vnperfect actor on the stage' (sonnet 23)); tangentially, upon an audience of co-auditors who may in fact be the chief targets of a poem ostensibly directed at someone else ('Hence, thou subbornd*Informer*!' (sonnet 125)); or directly, at an addressee signalled out rhetorically by the poem itself ('Why didst thou promise such a beautious day?' (sonnet 34)). The sonnet might work tangentially in different directions, complicating an apparently direct or simple address by the mere fact that others are privy to it. *Hamlet*, again, provides a useful instance of such layered audience effects: in both Claudius's and Hamlet's awareness, throughout the play, but especially in Act 1 Scene 2, of being the object of others' gazes, and in the multiple scenes of staged overhearing, spying, rivalry and scrutiny involving

[25] Arthur F. Marotti, *Manuscript, Print, and the English Renaissance Lyric* (Ithaca, NY: Cornell University Press, 1995).

Ophelia, Polonius, Hamlet, Gertrude, Horatio, the players and Laertes. Though apparently trivial and tangential, Polonius's pretensions to literary criticism, combining both paternal and aesthetic disapproval in the case of Hamlet's own 'sonnet' to Ophelia and the players' performance, and Hamlet's counter-criticism, should not be overlooked. Poetry and theatre are not merely pleasant adjuncts to this world of erotic and political machination, but parts of it.

The oppressive, intrigue-ridden court of Denmark, which seems so like a prison to Hamlet but not to his school friends, is not unlike the world of the sonnets. These poems present not merely lyrical personae, but a social world glimpsed both in peripheral and focused vision. I have already explored ways in which one may glean both the sonnet's power and weakness as a form of social action via plays in which sonneteering is an integral part of the action, such as *Love's Labour's Lost* and *Twelfth Night*. The sonnets' relation to *Hamlet* opens our eyes to the dark world in which they are so self-consciously situated and to the equally dark lord that inhabits it so luminously, 'like a iewell (hunge in gastly night)' (sonnet 27). The sonnets' relationship to *Hamlet* does not reside in their shared invention of an essentially private modern interiority, or even in their undoubted demonstrations that such inwardness has an inextricable stake in the public world. It lies rather in their representations of the debilitating effects of a world in which the personal or the private can find no space for itself within the public or social world. This relationship allows us to review both formalist ideas of the lyric as an essentially private rehearsal of '*solitary* speech', which 'deliberately strips away most social specifications',[26] and the historicist conviction that the private simply *is* the social. What Vendler regards as the essence of the lyric in general is in fact merely a strategy that the poems entertain but ultimately cannot sustain. Far from endorsing the opposing, materialist position, however, that failure demonstrates the debilitating consequences of the reduction of the personal to the social.

I have suggested that sonnet 23 seeks to remove itself from the public gaze by moving away from the theatrical space of open address: away, precisely, from a public world. It seeks to persuade the beloved to retreat to the safer, more secluded world of writing where, it is hoped, a relationship might be established that is untrammelled by social distance or vulnerable display. The poems that follow sonnet 23 both seek to establish this removed but shared space where a 'mutuall render, onely me

[26] Helen Vendler, *The Art of Shakespeare's Sonnets* (Cambridge, MA: Harvard University Press, 1997), 2.

for thee' can be achieved, and also to register the impossibility of such a shrinking of distance between player-poet and aristocratic beloved. Sonnet 25 is an example of the former. It affirms the desirability of a total withdrawal from a world in which people who boast of 'public honours and proud titles' risk at the same time an equally 'publike' fall, painfully vulnerable to the 'frowne' through which 'they in their glory die':

> LEt those who are in fauor with their stars,
> Of publike honour and proud titles bost,
> Whilst I whome fortune of such tryumph bars
> Vnlookt for ioy in that I honour most;
> Great Princes fauorites their faire leaues spread,
> But as the Marygold at the suns eye,
> And in them-selues their pride lies buried,
> For at a frowne they in their glory die.
> The painefull warrier famosed for worth,
> After a thousand victories once foild,
> Is from the booke of honour rased quite,
> And all the rest forgot for which he toild:
>> Then happy I that loue and am beloued
>> Where I may not remoue,nor be remoued.

In an effort to escape the vulnerability of such a public life – in which the 'The painefull warrier famosed for worth' can in an instant be 'from the booke of honour rased quite' – the couplet proclaims the player-poet's own static transcendence of such political vicissitudes: 'Then happy I that loue and am beloued / Where I may not remoue, nor be remoued.' But the poem nowhere shows how such an intimate and mutual still point might be achieved. In opposition to the world of action evoked in the body of the poem, the passive voice of the couplet unconvincingly removes the poet (and, by implication, the beloved) from the realms of human volition and agency. The agency that the player-poet attributes to himself ('happy I that loue' and 'Where I may not remove') is empty since in political terms it is powerless. The poem does not show how the capricious 'stars' of the first line or the more earthly purveyors of the 'frownes' in line 8 are to be avoided. The beloved is present only as the frame of the poem – its 'absent cause' as it were. And yet he is also at the centre of the shifting power play of aristocratic life that the poem wishes to avoid.

In the face of the uncertain effects of political agency, sonnet 25 elides both the poet and the beloved's agency in its affirmation of a passive mutuality. In other poems, less concerned to withdraw from the theatre of political service and ambition, the lover's despair at the malign influence of his stars and the pain of the beloved's frowns is all too evident. Coming so soon after 23, 25 is a paradoxically eloquent address to the audience of the earlier poem which now affirms his withdrawal into the privacy for which the earlier poem does no more than wish. But such public eloquence defeats the purpose of the withdrawal: it acknowledges the persistent pressure of a world that the poem proclaims to be well lost, and which it continues to inhabit and fear. Sonnets 25 and 23 thus share a double audience: the rivals who enjoy a greater political status than the player-poet, but who also suffer the potential of still greater disappointment, and to whom 25 is directed as a childish boast, and the beloved to whom the poem is obliquely addressed as the quasi-performative of a wished-for state, rather than (as it appears grammatically to be), a description of an achieved one.

Sonnet 26, 'the first epistolary sonnet' as Vendler puts it (*The Art of Shakespeare's Sonnets*, 148), self-consciously uses its epistolary form, not to endorse the anti-theatrical, intimate privacy sought at the end of sonnet 23, but to acknowledge and affirm precisely the pressures of the public world that the previous sonnet seeks to disclaim:

> Lord of my loue,to whome in vassalage
> Thy merrit hath my dutie strongly knit;
> To thee I send this written ambassage
> To witnesse duty, not to shew my wit.
> Duty so great,which wit so poore as mine
> May make seeme bare,in wanting words to shew it;
> But that I hope some good conceipt of thine
> In thy soules thought (all naked) will bestow it:
> Til whatsoeuer star that guides my mouing,
> Points on me gratiously with faire aspect,
> And puts apparrell on my tottered louing,
> To show me worthy of their sweet respect,
>> Then may I dare to boast how I doe loue thee,
>> Til then, not show my head where thou maist proue me

The address, 'Lord of my loue', is self-consciously formal and deferential. It confirms the social 'vassalage' imposed upon the lowly addresser by the social 'merrit' of the nobleman, and expresses the player-poet's open acknowledgement of the obligation to 'witnesse duty' to such rank. The anadiplosis in the repetition of 'duty' across quatrains 1 and 2 stresses the inescapability of public, courtly values here, in contrast to both sonnet 23 and sonnet 25. The poem is addressed as much to an audience that is 'in fauor with their stars' as to the potent 'Lord'. Vendler remarks quite rightly that sonnet 26 is an extended apology. But what is it apologising for? If we take the poem's proximity to 25 as significant, rather than arbitrary, then it may be seen as an appropriately apologetic response to noble displeasure at the hubris of 25. Having been chastised for his earlier presumption, the player-poet now shows that he can be as eloquently servile as the worst, and affirms his proper place in the public order of things. The 'stars' that are dismissed in the opening gesture of sonnet 25 are here embraced, indeed they are implored to 'point on me gratiously with faire aspect', so that he may dare to display himself and his love for the well-born beloved in public: 'then may I dare to boast how I doe loue thee, / Til then, not show my head where thou maist proue me'. This sonnet – a speech act of extended, public apology – retracts the claims of happy mutuality and reckless transcendence made in the couplet of the previous poem. To love in this political world is to be *allowed* to love. The pressures of 'duty' and 'merrit' must be acknowledged, but not without a proper show of civic decorum. Such decorum may itself demand the muting of public display, especially considering the addresser's acute sense of the imbrication of dress and address: of the disgraceful display of his own 'tottered louing' or 'bare' duty, inadequately clothed.

The extensive commentary by New Historicist and materialist critics on the social and political significance of clothing, and the relationship between theatrical display of costume and the semiotics of apparel underlying the Sumptuary Laws, should draw our attention to the way in which sonnet 26 rehearses, if unwillingly, the essentially theatrical display of public love, proclaiming through its concern with the semiotics of dress its addressee's own disgraceful social origins and profession. And yet, paradoxically, in the very imagery (which is in this poem more concrete and material than mere imagery) of dress and undress, a wistful desire for transcendence remains. Why, in a poem so aware of the public significance of full costuming, should the young aristocrat's 'soules thought' be 'all naked': 'In thy soules thought (all naked) will bestow it'? The parentheses emphasise the 'bareness' of this aspect of an otherwise properly attired nobleman. Katherine Duncan-Jones suggests that this is a 'paradoxical suggestion that what is *naked* in the friend – his most intimate and unvarnished impulse and thought – has the capacity to clothe,

enrich and adorn his friend's unvarnished *duty*'.[27] Yes. But the paradox
has a chiefly ideological significance: it asks the young man (once again)
to disregard and abandon the sumptuary semiotics that marks him as
the unattainable man of rank beside the player-poet's 'tattered' lowliness.
Such 'nakedness', like the intimate space of writing at the end of sonnet 23, suggests the possibility of a relationship untrammelled by public
conditions and signs, in which 'merrit' may be more than mere high
rank and 'duty' disrobed to reveal unadorned love. In the very acknowledgement of the necessity of sumptuary hierarchy, the player-poet wishes
to create a space for 'nakedness', in which the differences between his
'tattered' loving and the young man's sumptuous friendship may be set
aside.

There is thus what Vendler usefully calls a 'shadow' poem at work
in sonnet 26, which considerably complicates the sonnet's ostensible
attitude to public display. On the one hand, it entertains the hope of
a 'consummation devoutly to be wished' (*Hamlet*, 3.1.65–6) by hinting
(via the nobleman's 'all-naked' thought) at a Hamlet-like dissatisfaction
with sumptuary exhibition in favour of 'that within, which passeth show'.
On the other, it openly confirms that it is impossible to escape the system
of social hierarchy in which clothing is a central symbol. It is not sufficient
for the poet to feel that his love comes from the 'heart', as an interior
'truth'. Such 'love' (or is it 'duty'?) has to take its place, or be repudiated,
in a world of public values, 'in eies of men' (sonnet 16). If it is mere
'duty' then it has a necessarily public shape; if it is something more
than that then the necessary publicity of its address always threatens
it since it is in every way transgressive. The nakedness to which the
poem appeals may appear to be a repudiation of the theatrical tenor
of public life. However, the paradox that Duncan-Jones points out re-
affirms the need for the tattered ('tottered') player-poet to be 'apparelled',
especially since it evokes the common practice of aristocrats to hand
their second-hand clothing down to the players. The graciousness of the
young man equips the petitioner to play the role of lover, but despite the
player-poet's best efforts, that role continues to be conceived in theatrical
terms.

Vendler claims that the invocation of slavery and vassalage in sonnets
such as 26, 57 and 58 is an indulgent and exaggerated metaphor: 'his
appropriation of the term *slave* leads us less to pity him than to resist

[27] Katherine Duncan-Jones (ed.), *The Sonnets*, The New Arden Shakespeare (London and New York: Routledge, 1997), 162.

his equation between real slavery and his own infatuation' (*The Art of Shakespeare's Sonnets*, 174). It is certainly exaggerated. But Shakespeare's self-consciously inferior position enables him to literalise the conventional Petrarchan image of 'slavery' as erotic infatuation. The sonnets explore, in ways that Sidney's do not because of their differences in both class and audience, the complex entanglements of 'love' *and* 'duty'. To see the imbrication of these two concepts, rather than their separation, as we now tend to do, is to see that being both in love and in duty is not an *interior* state but a liminal social condition. It is an amalgam of the public and the private that has to negotiate a fresh passage across a linguistic terrain of publicly settled historical meanings. Shakespeare's sonnets are striking precisely for their pioneering charting of this territory.

When sonnet 58 declares bitterly, 'That God forbid, that made me first your slaue, / I should in thought controule your times of pleasure', 'God' is not merely Cupid.[28] The poem's resentment, conveyed more forcefully if we read these lines as an oath, arises from the player-poet's frustrated sense of helplessness at his inferior social status, ironically invoked as part of a social reality ordained by God. The double possibility of reading 'God' as *both* the Judeo-Christian Almighty and the Greco-Roman erotic deity exemplifies the sonnet's wracked tension between 'love' and 'duty'. How does one combine the feudal sense of 'love' or 'duty' which pervades this poem, as it does so many others, with a friendship (erotic or otherwise) in which power is not the absolute prerogative of only one person? How does one assert a moral *right* to consideration and respect, and to express one's displeasure at the behaviour of the beloved, when the political inscriptions of love make such behaviour scandalous? How does one reconcile two competing concepts of love in the same ideological world and persuade one's more powerful beloved to accept that reconciliation?

Viewed more broadly, this dilemma is a feature of the historical tension between competing conceptions of marital relationships. We can glimpse its complications by imagining the working out of the merely suggested relationship between Beatrice and Don Pedro in *Much Ado About Nothing*. Would Beatrice be able to retain the sharp-witted independence that she shows towards Benedick, or would her 'shrewdness' be transformed into

---

[28] Vendler follows most editors in reducing the upper case 'God' of the Quarto to lower case, although there are no compelling reasons to do so. This is not a major crux, although it is an interpretative one, and the tradition merely confirms the tendency to ignore the full social and political dimensions of these poems. See Vendler's commentary on sonnet 58, *The Art of Shakespeare's Sonnets*, 277–9.

Kate's 'shrewishness' in *The Taming of the Shrew*? Whatever the outcome, I am suggesting that Beatrice would have to be represented as negotiating something like the passage between love and duty that the player-poet forges in the sonnets. She would be as constrained as the player-poet in what she could say and how she could say it. That is perhaps why the dramatist, in a metaphor apposite to the present discussion, makes her demurral invoke sartorial inappropriateness:

No, my lord, unless I might have another for working days. Your grace is too costly to wear every day. But I beseech your grace, pardon me. I was born to speak all mirth and no matter. (*Much Ado About Nothing*, 2.1.306–9)

Beatrice's proclivity for speaking 'all mirth and no matter' would be available to the player-poet of the sonnets only if the relationship involved a lover who exercised no political power over him. The sonnets of *Much Ado* are the undeniable public signs of an already agreed commitment – 'A miracle! Here's our own hands against our hearts' (5.4.91–2) – but they are not the means by which love is forged. That is the work of theatre.[29]

Sonnet 58 manages the remarkable feat of simultaneously offering an apology and levelling an accusation. It is an outburst of anger and frustration that tries to excuse its excess as it grows more excessive. The poem rewrites sonnet 26 and repudiates 25, in a painful, *Hamlet*-like re-hearsal of the impotence of speech acts when they are deprived of the proper contexts of social authority that give them their force. Its most painful moment comes in the Job-like 'Oh let me suffer / . . . Without accusing you of injury'. The pain comes not so much from the suffering itself as from the perceived obligation to suffer in silence. Its force lies in its paradoxically helpless *occupatio*. Pleading to be allowed (or to be given the strength) to bear its burden without complaint, like so many of the poems to the dark young man of rank it develops an exquisite poetics of blame. The private haven of 'silent loue' projected in sonnet 23, and the withdrawn patience proclaimed in the couplet of sonnet 26, now constitute an unbearable constraint. What conceptual resources are available to someone who has publicly acknowledged the 'principle of absolute feudal sovereignty' (Vendler, *The Art of Shakespeare's Sonnets*, 278) in a relationship from which he at least expects both the mutuality of recip-rocated love and the *moral* right to circumscribe the beloved's 'liberty'?

---

[29] See Jean Howard, 'Renaissance Antitheatricality and the Politics of Gender and Rank in *Much Ado About Nothing*', in *Shakespeare Reproduced*, ed. Jean Howard and Marion F. O'Connor (New York: Routledge, 1987), 163–87.

The erotic and the political are again fused: the sexual liberty that the young lord assumes is derived from a political freedom denied his petit-bourgeois lover in an order supposedly ordained by God. If there is a shadow poem within sonnet 58, it interrogates the bi-fold concept of love-as-duty. Given your absolute power, both political and erotic, given the fact that you have removed yourself completely from the ambit of my blame, it asks, can we call this love?

The third quatrain, in which the young lord's free reign is granted, reinforces the poem's bifocal exploration of love:

> Be where you list, your charter is so strong,
> That you your selfe may priuiledge your time
> To what you will, to you it doth belong,
> Your selfe to pardon of self-doing crime.

On the one hand, the strength of his political 'charter' endows him with the privilege of doing as he likes and grants him the sole prerogative of blame and forgiveness for his own behaviour. In the strictest sense, the bestowing performative of 'Be where you list' is hollow, since the poem is itself acutely aware of the speaker's lack of authority to grant such a privilege. Unusually, this is a descriptive masquerading as a performative. In other poems, the right to accuse is attributed to others, more nearly the young man's equals, who perceive through his deeds that he 'doest common grow' (sonnet 69). This move allows the lowly player-poet at least indirectly to 'accuse' the young man of 'injury', but it remains within a sphere of public, political discourse and privilege. In its other sense, the 'priuiledge' that the quatrain attributes to the young man is more limited, more intimate. He is not granted unlimited power to do as he pleases and then to pardon his own wrongdoing. Rather, the claims and rights that stem from duty and those that arise out of love should be differentiated. The young man's social position gives him the right to do as he wishes *vis-à-vis* his friend, but to claim that right, including the privilege of being above criticism and blame, is to offer a travesty of love. The poet is therefore to 'wait' in two different senses: in the sense of a servant attending upon a lord, and in the sense of a friend hopeful of a response which acknowledges the moral, and not merely the feudal, qualities of the right to love and be loved. The poem suggests that these two senses are, strictly speaking, incommensurable, just as in sonnet 23 public speaking seems to be incompatible with the proper expression of love. But, like Pamphilia, it can find no way out of 'love's' labyrinth.

The tension between metaphysical and material privacy is negotiated in the early sonnets on absence, where the desire to fuse lover and beloved in an essentially untheatrical space is constantly undercut by the necessity of social and physical distance. Sonnet 24, for example, attempts to conceptualise the untheatrical 'nakedness' invoked in sonnet 25 by using a traditional conceit of two lovers looking at their reflections in the other's eyes. The poem appears to contract the physical distance felt so acutely in sonnet 26 to the tiniest gap, while simultaneously expressing a spontaneous mutuality. But as it tries to exemplify such community, it abruptly comes up short against the social distance and difference of the young man. Such difference is exemplified by the sun's asymmetrical affinity with the dark lord of the poet's dreams, which, paradoxically, makes him opaque:

> Now see what good-turnes eyes for eies haue done,
> Mine eyes haue drawne thy shape, and thine for me
> Are windowes to my brest, where-through the Sun
> Delights to peepe, to gaze therein on thee . . .

The perfect mutuality of eyes mirroring their shared reflections is abruptly unsettled by the very image in which the poet seeks to bask. The sun, peeping through the eyes to gaze upon the young man lodged within the poet's breast, reminds the poet that no sun shines on his own image lodged within the dark lord's breast. Or at least, he has no access to such an image:

> Yet eyes this cunning want to grace their art
> They draw but what they see, know not the hart.

The dark lord's opacity is unlike Hamlet's inscrutable interiority insofar as the player-poet is perfectly able to show his own inwardness, in the form of the brightly illuminated image of the young man within his own breast. The 'cunning' that eyes 'want' remains metaphysical, though, insofar as the last line reasserts the traditional hiddenness of the interior – the 'hart' – of the other.

The companion poem to this sonnet, 46, seeks to solve the problem simply by sharing out the 'spoils' of the young man's sight in terms of the traditionally metaphysical separation of inner and outer, as the domains of heart and eye, respectively:

> As thus, mine eyes due is thy outward part,
> And my hearts right, their inward loue of heart.

But this is mere fantasy. Vendler notes that the consummation that the player-poet seeks is in fact the 'image' of the young man. One way of regaining the mutuality sought in sonnet 24 – to recapture the young man as a *presence* – is to reduce the young man phenomenologically: to his image, either as he appears to the dreaming poet, or as the picture lodged in his heart and projected through his wakeful eyes: 'So either by thy picture or my loue, / Thy selfe away, are present still with me' (sonnet 47). This move has two consequences, however. By a process of metaphorical contamination, the fair friend is transformed into a dark lord: one whose proper element is 'darknes' (sonnet 27) and 'gastly night' (sonnet 27). He is 'darkely bright...bright in darke directed' (sonnet 43), a 'shadow' (sonnet 37), a 'faire imperfect shade' (sonnet 43) who can 'euery shadow lend' (sonnet 53), and around whose strange 'substance' 'millions of strange shadowes...tend' (sonnet 53); he is also a 'graue' (sonnet 31), the receptacle of 'precious friends hid in deaths dateles night' (sonnet 30). As imagined presence, then, the young man is transformed into a creature whose darkest interiority is not hidden from sight, but revealed as darkness itself. What is more, as every phenomenologist knows, the reduction of the object to a merely internal image, necessitated by the desire for its pure presence in consciousness, brackets out the physical and the material.[30] Their physical presence, however, is the real object of desire in these sonnets. The only place where the player-poet can possess the beloved is in the recollection of the dream or the projection of imagination: in 'thought'. But 'thought', which promises to deliver the poet from the condition of absence, in due course 'brings in his revenges' (*Twelfth Night*, 5.1.373).

Sonnet 44, for example, opens with a yearning desire to transform flesh into thought in order to overcome the absenting effects distance and space: 'If the dull substance of my flesh were thought, / Iniurious distance should not stop my way.' But the player-poet is soon brought up by the realisation that the presence promised by reduction of space and time to 'thought' is no more than a 'shadow', which renders the spatial condition of absence and the heavy weight of time even less bearable:

> But ah, *thought kills me that I am not thought*
> To leape large lengths of miles when thou art gone,
> But that so much of earth and water wrought,

---

[30] See Edmund Husserl, *Ideas: An Introduction to Pure Phenomenology*, trans. W. R. Boyce Gibson (London: George Allen and Unwin, 1931).

I must attend,times leisure with my mone,
Receiuing naughts by elements so sloe
But heauie tears,badges of eithers woe.

(Emphasis added)

The alternative strategy available to the player-poet lies in the conventional thought that lover and beloved are in fact one. This thought is variously entertained in the conceit that the poet, in praising the young man, is actually praising himself, or in the strained idea that the triangular distance between poet, dark lord and dark woman is somehow reduced by their communal promiscuity: 'But here's the ioy, my friend and I are one / Sweete flattery, then she loues but me alone' (sonnet 42). Such strained conceits arise from a craving for mutuality that finds the spacing of theatricality impossible to endure. A love-object who contains 'all' within him or herself is an object of desire (or 'will') that shrinks the distance between lover and beloved, interior and exterior, known and unknowable, to 'nothing'. But the double meanings of words such as 'all', 'will' and 'nothing' point to separation rather than union, making the distinction between 'loue' and 'loues use' especially problematic. The poems that entertain the possibility that dark lord and poet are 'one' – if only because the lord somehow encompasses *all* the world – repeat, in a different key, the sonnets that urge the dark woman to accommodate the poet's 'will' in her own 'spacious will', on the grounds that his 'one' can be accounted 'nothing'. I discuss the latter more fully in chapter 4 below. The later poems provide an excuse for the display of wit through writing, but the same subject in the earlier poems threatens writing altogether with another kind of 'nothing': silence. Sonnet 44 attempts to reduce the distance between lover and beloved through 'thought', but sonnet 39 shows why this is both metaphysically and materially undesirable: why there is a necessary separation between (writing) desire and (written) object in both a philosophical and a social sense:

OH how thy worth with manners may I singe,
When thou art all the better part of me?
What can mine owne praise to mine owne selfe bring;
And what is't but mine owne when I praise thee,
Euen for this,let vs deuided liue,
And our deare loue loose name of single one,
That by this seperation I may giue:
That due to thee which thou deseru'st alone:
Oh absence what a torment wouldst thou proue,
Were it not thy soure leisure gaue sweet leaue,

> To entertaine the time with thoughts of loue,
> VVhich time and thoughts so sweetly dost deceiue.
> And that thou teachest how to make one twaine,
> By praising him here who doth hence remaine.

We have come full circle from sonnet 23. There the distance constituted by theatricality overwhelms the player striving to declare love through the concept of public duty. He tries to overcome that distance in the private space of poetry. But such writing threatens to produce mere narcissism, producing more than an epideictic moment which, as Fineman claims, merely reflects the writer back to himself. In order to maintain the ideal of mutual affection and the 'oblacion, poore but free' (sonnet 125) of socially ordered duty he is therefore forced to reinstitute the original 'iniurious distance'. It is now precisely 'this seperation' that allows the poet to 'giue:/ That due to thee which thou deseru'st alone'.

In the sonnets that deal directly with the rival poet, the bourgeois player in his new role as quasi-courtly poet soon discovers that there is a theatrical condition to writing that incessantly interposes itself between desire and consummation. Defending himself against the 'iniurious distance' that, as Derrida reminds us, informs writing itself, he turns to perhaps the most intensely metaphysical anti-theatricality of all: the Platonic notion of the intrinsic goodness of stasis, the evil of change.[31] Under this regime constancy in love is considered to be incompatible with the kind of poetic practice that indulges in 'variation or quick change' (sonnet 76) and ostensive show:

> MY loue is strengthned though more weake in see-ming
> I loue not lesse,thogh lesse the show appeare,
> That loue is marchandiz'd,whose ritch esteeming,
> The owners tongue doth publish euery where.
>
> (sonnet 102)

The player-turned-poet deprecates theatricality as much in terms of class ('marchandiz'd') as in the claim that his own verse is 'to constancie confin'd' (sonnet 105). Such constancy is displayed through the proclaimed stasis of the verse itself, which, 'still all one, euer the same' (sonnet 76), 'one thing expressing', is said to 'leaue out difference' (sonnet 105). This is a variation on an earlier theme, by which the uncertain attempts to drive a wedge between 'love' (which is constant) and 'style' (which changes) ('Theirs for their stile ile read, his for his loue' (sonnet 32)) assert

---

[31] See Karl Popper, *The Open Society and its Enemies, Volume I, The Spell of Plato* (Princeton, NJ: Princeton University Press, 1971), 37: 'In brief, Plato teaches *that change is evil, and that rest is divine.*'

a devotion somehow independent of its means of expression. Difference proves to be doggedly persistent, however. If the theatre is the exemplary medium of the kind of distance and difference imposed by mimesis between truth and appearance, poetry does not transcend that representational gap: it is embroiled in an irreducible theatricality of its own. Furthermore, the very argument that the beloved is the exemplum of unchanging beauty, which the poet merely copies, brings its own Platonic sting. This is apparent in sonnets 92–4, where constancy brings with it a further debilitating, and thoroughly theatrical, 'iniurious distance':

> In manies lookes,the falce hearts history
> Is writ in moods and frounes and wrinckles strange.
> But heauen in thy creation did decree,
> That in thy face sweet loue should euer dwell,
> What ere thy thoughts, or thy hearts workings be,
> Thy lookes should nothing thence, but sweetnesse tell.
>   How like Eaues apple doth thy beauty grow,
>   If thy sweet vertue answere not thy show.
>
>   (sonnet 93)

In this consideration of the 'truth' of those that are the 'Lords and owners of their faces' (sonnet 94), the anti-theatrical metaphysics of Plato and the discourses of Petrarchan deigesis reach their limit, in questions that are social and political rather than metaphysical. Here the direction of the gaze in sonnet 23 is switched. In sonnets 93 and 94 the inscrutable aristocrat, rather than the player-poet, is the object of the gaze. But that does not mean that relations of power have changed. His own anti-theatrical argument, which posits an essential gap between appearance and reality, renders the gazer powerless before the stony-faced object of his affection.

Sonnet 125 – usually considered to be the last but one addressed to the young friend – offers a final, complex negotiation of the intricacies of the public and the private, rendered all the more inscrutable by the poem's uncertainties of address:

> VVER't ought to me I bore the canopy,
> With my extern the outward honoring,
> Or layd great bases for eternity,
> Which proues more short then wast or ruining?
> Haue I not seene dwellers on forme and fauor
> Lose all,and more by paying too much rent
> For compound sweet;Forgoing simple sauor,

Pittifull thriuors in their gazing spent.
Noe,let me be obsequious in thy heart,
And take thou my oblacion,poore but free,
Which is not mixt with seconds,knows no art,
But mutuall render onely me for thee.
　　Hence,thou subbornd*Informer*, a trew soule
　　When most impeacht,stands least in thy controule.

To whom is the poem addressed? To what charge does it respond? Under what circumstances was it composed and/or delivered? There are at least two different addressees. On the one hand there is the young man to whom the two rhetorical questions in the first eight lines are addressed, and who is subsequently offered the plain exchange of simple reciprocity: 'mutuall render onely me for thee'. On the other is the 'subbornd *Informer*' whose suddenly noticed presence shatters the quiet request for mutuality. They are unlikely to be the same figure. To whom would the informer present his intelligence if not to the young man from whom reciprocity is sought? Such an intelligencer is presumably feared and hated because his information threatens the relationship that the poem itself tries to forge.

I have been arguing that the sonnets aim to establish a space for that relationship out of the glare of the public eye. Such a space is imagined as a withdrawal from stage to page, where to 'heare wit [with] eies belongs to loues fine wiht [wit] (sonnet 23)'. I have also argued that that goal is systematically thwarted by the intractable nature of the public life in which the relationship and the sonnets exist. This penultimate sonnet in the young-man sequence registers one last-ditch, vain attempt to achieve a personal reciprocity that has proved impossible through the gestures and actions of public life, such as the ostentatious bearing of the 'canopy' with which the poem opens. Such a 'canopy' includes, among other things, the sonnets themselves. They are public documents ('my extern') through which the player-poet has 'honoured' the 'outward', and through which, if some of those poems are to be believed, he has 'layd great bases for eternity'.

Is the player-poet responding to an (implicit or otherwise) accusation by the beloved that whatever he has done to honour him has in fact been informed all along by self-interest? Or is he responding to a request to be more ostentatious in his 'honouring' by contemptuously rejecting the supposed rewards that are promised for such behaviour, citing his familiarity with the 'actions that a man might play' within a world in which personal devotion is rendered impossible by the expectation of 'forme and fauor'? Given the ambiguity of the question, it is difficult to tell. The sonnet is, however, clear in its general rejection of public or external fraud in favour of simple, personal reciprocity. It rejects the pitiful economy of inevitable bankruptcy with poised contempt, but that poise is unbalanced by the fact that it is not sufficient merely to offer the gift of private 'obsequiousness' or 'oblacion': the player-poet has to implore the young man to accept such a gift: '*let me be* obsequious in thy heart, / And *take thou* my oblacion, poore but free'. In the felt need to beg the young man to accept his gifts of devotion and submissiveness, the poet hardly leaves behind the public world of hierarchy and rank that constitutes the 'pitiful thriving' from which he wishes to escape. Furthermore, although it might seem as if he is also forgoing the economy of profitless loss that marks those who 'lose all, and more by paying too much rent' and the 'waste and ruining' of his own forms of 'honouring', the request in the third quatrain is not merely an abject plea to be *allowed* to be devoted and servile. It asks (following the language game of sonnet 126) for some form of 'profit', certainly for an equal exchange: 'mutuall render, onely me for thee'. And at the still point of simple reciprocity, from which the economy of the public world is ostensibly excluded, the pressure of that world continues to make itself felt in the shadowy form of the 'subbornd*Informer*'.

Who is this informer? From whence does he come? If we imagine the sonnet as a miniature play-script, then he makes his entrance between the final quatrain and the couplet, interrupting a private dialogue between the player-poet and young man, and forcing the player-poet to declare openly and publicly his freedom from both moral taint and the public world. The very aim of the poem, to forge a private, personal space of 'mutuall render', would then be negated by the intrusion of a figure that embodies the impossibility of privacy. The sonnet seems to suggest that that figure is conjured into existence – brought to mind – by something that is said in the poem: perhaps the claim, contradicted by the 'forme and fauor' of the sonnet itself, that the offered 'oblacion' is 'free', pure, and 'knows no art'. But then who is the audience of this little scenario? It cannot be the primary addressee, the young man, for he is merely a character, together with the player-poet and the informer, in the scene. The audience is thus different from either of the addressees: it is a third, anonymous, entity that can take in and weigh up not only the argument but also the switches of address. It is the kind of audience that might watch a play. To read the poem from the position of such an audience would be like watching Hamlet or Cordelia acting within their respective worlds.

If, however, we imagine trying to read it as if we were the young man to whom the poem has been sent – the one to whom the plea for private mutuality is addressed – then the sudden intrusion of the informer causes considerable difficulty. The poem does not say: 'Call off this wretched informer of yours.' It addresses the informer *directly*. Is it possible that the sonnet is meant to be read out aloud, to an assembled company including the characters both alluded to and addressed directly in the sonnet: the 'pitiful gazers', with the young man of rank at the centre, the spy perhaps being one of the assembled group? If so, we have a scene charged with performative force. First, drawing attention to himself as a figure of public attention, the speaker contemptuously dismisses the social economy of self-serving subservience that constitutes the very occasion of address. He then pleads, in a direct address to the nobleman, for a private space in which duty may be pledged and love shared without compromise. But then, in an abrupt turn, he picks out one of the company, denounces him as a spy and publicly declares his own freedom and integrity.

Unlikely and melodramatic as it may seem, one can imagine such a scenario from the stuff of the poem. It makes sense, certainly more sense than the scenario in which the young man is the solitary addressee of both utterances. Like all the other scenarios I have sketched, it displays a desire for a private space of pure reciprocity. But it enacts, in the twofold direction of address that constitutes the very structure of the poem, the impossibility not only of separating the personal from the public, but also of preventing the debilitating encroachment of the one upon the other – a trespass figured acutely in the person of the spy. Like Hamlet's histrionic disavowal of histrionics, which is blind to his own refusal or incapacity to save Ophelia from the corrosive effects of Denmark as prison, the sonnet's public declaration of independence undermines its own force. It fails to create a private or personal space; rather, in the strained publicity of its declaration it merely acknowledges the intrusion and predominance of the very domain that it seeks to escape.

Shakespeare's anti-theatrical tactics in the sonnets, with their complex interweaving of social and metaphysical concerns, demonstrate that the 'iniurious distance' that theatricality in all its forms always imposes can never be reduced to a space in which 'dull substance' (sonnet 44) is dissolved into thought. Both writing and thought, which are supposed to effect the reduction, bear constant witness to the very opposite truth: 'But ah, thought kills me that I am not thought' (sonnet 44). In place of the anti-theatrical desire for an intimate, private space in which difference and distance are abolished, Shakespeare's sonnets attest not only to the public, and essentially theatrical, character of verse, but also register an acceptance of the player-poet's proper situation in 'the wide worlds common place' (sonnet 137). At first 'shamed by that which [he] bring[s] forth' (sonnet 72), he appears in the end to accept not only that he is indelibly marked, if not exactly 'subdu'd', like the 'Dyers hand' 'to what [he] workes in' (sonnet 111). His acceptance of the 'publick meanes which publick manners breeds' (sonnet 111) is finally an acknowledgement of the impossibility of any reduction of the theatrical to the pure spacelessness of interiority.[32]

But to note the systematic failure of both the metaphysical and material attempts in the sonnets to forge a private space free from the pressures of public life is neither to reduce the private to the public, nor to hanker after an ideal personal existence untainted by the social. If human existence is at every level informed by the social – as indeed it is – that does not mean that privacy or interiority does not exist, or that these concepts are mere epiphenomena of the social. Both the sonnets and *Hamlet* demonstrate the debilitating effects upon their members of societies that do not allow them the space for what we might call a personal or private life. If we feel in the closing couplet of sonnet 125 the player-poet's signal failure to achieve reciprocity throughout the sequence as a whole, then we need to return to *King Lear* to see how such personal reciprocity may be preserved even in the face of the most brutal public pressures.[33]

In Act 5, Lear and Cordelia are captured by Edmund. Cordelia, feeling that she could endure the tyranny of her sisters, but distraught at what this might mean for her father, suggests that they confront them at once. He demurs, suggesting a withdrawal to prison, which he imagines as a sanctuary from the world:

> CORDELIA (*to Lear*) We are not the first
> Who with best meaning have incurred the worst.
> For thee, oppressèd King, I am cast down,
> Myself could else outfrown false fortune's frown.
> Shall we not see these daughters and these sisters?
> LEAR No, no, no, no. Come, let's away to prison.
> We two alone will sing like birds i' th' cage.

---

[32] This of course leaves open the question of the misogynist sonnets to the dark woman, where the Platonic divide between what the eye sees and what the heart feels or the tongue pronounces, returns with a vengeance. Alvin Kernan, in *The Playwright as Magician*, suggests that the move from the young man to the dark woman represents the acceptance of the theatrical. This would, however, need to be explored in terms of gender politics rather than mere metaphor.

[33] Thanks to Jacques Berthoud for drawing this passage to my attention in the context of my argument.

When thou dost ask me blessing, I'll kneel down
And ask of thee forgiveness; so we'll live,
And pray, and sing, and tell old tales, and laugh
At gilded butterflies, and hear poor rogues
Talk of court news, and we'll talk with them too –
Who loses and who wins, who's in, who's out,
And take upon 's the mystery of things
As if we were God's spies; and we'll wear out
In a walled prison packs and sects of great ones
That ebb and flow by th' moon.
(*King Lear* (Folio text) 5.3.3–19)

In Lear's fantasy of a life removed from the pressures of the political world we can recognise striking elements of the player-poet's similar desires for withdrawal with the object of his love: in the portrait of perfect reciprocity ('When thou dost ask me blessing, I'll kneel down / And ask of thee forgiveness; so we'll live'), in the sardonic distance from the ins and outs of court intrigue, in the culminating idea that the constancy of achieved reciprocity will 'wear out / . . . packs and sects of great ones / That ebb and flow by th' moon', and in the fantasy that, rather than being the objects of spies and informers, they will, as 'God's spies', take upon themselves the 'mystery of things'. Lear transforms the thought of the prison, entertained by Hamlet as the epitome of the destruction of the personal by a rotten public life, into the very space in which the personal may be preserved from public intrusion.

Even without the tragic knowledge of the play's close, it is clear that such a fantasy is unsustainable, as unsustainable as the player-poet's dream of a role untouched by 'publick manners'. And yet, despite its acknowledgement of the impossibility of severing the personal from the social, this moment in *King Lear* enacts, through its interactive dialogue, the fragile but inestimable value of the personal. Believing at the beginning of the play that there is nothing outside the public discourse of political power, Lear then dreams that there may be a private realm – exemplified by the hermetic space of the prison – that can escape that discourse. He is wrong on both counts. But between the two he learns how to take upon himself the language games of personal relations. In contrast to the early language game of public avowal, by which he had attempted to force a declaration of personal love from his daughter, he now imagines and – more importantly – embodies, an intimate discourse of reciprocal love and forgiveness. As in all the humane moments in this play, the smallest gestures count: the repeated use of the first-person pronoun in its most common, non-royal, sense, and the simple pleasures of shared human intercourse: of praying, laughing, singing, telling old tales. The painful vulnerability of such things should not make us value them less, nor should it lead us to conclude that the personal or the private is obliterated by the public. We see them, enacted and embodied, before our eyes, in this very exchange: not merely talked about, but incarnate, performed through interactive dialogue.

Of all Shakespeare's plays, *King Lear* embodies most acutely the complex sense for which I have argued throughout this chapter, that while the private or personal is informed by the social, it cannot be reduced to or dissolved into it. *Hamlet* and Shakespeare's sonnets offer a related, but not identical, perspective on this relationship. Neither of them appears to be able to take upon themselves, to inhabit, the language games of personal relations that we see, momentarily, in Lear's interaction with his daughter, and Edgar's with his father. Hamlet and the player-poet are both finally reduced to monological histrionics. Hamlet rants his love over the body of a woman for whom they are too late and not enough. The player-poet tries in vain to keep the prying public at bay through the empty performative that concludes his penultimate sonnet to the young nobleman, or through the reduction of his mistress's person to the 'wide worlds common place'. If any sort of reciprocity is indeed achieved in the 1609 sonnets, then it lies, not in any withdrawal into a space untouched by the public, or in the ideal matching of word and object, but in the moments, like the ones in *King Lear*, in which failure is recognised and the personal embodied in the acceptance and understanding of mutual fault and forgiveness:

> THat you were once vnkind be-friends mee now,
> And for that sorrow,which I then didde feele,
> Needes must I vnder my transgression bow,
> Vnlesse my Nerues were brasse or hammered steele.
> For if you were by my vnkindnesse shaken
> As I by yours, y'haue past a hell of Time,
> And I a tyrant haue no leasure taken
> To waigh how once I suffered in your crime.
> O that our night of wo might haue remembred
> My deepest sence,how hard true sorrow hits,
> And soone to you,as you to me then tendred
> The humble salue,which wounded bosomes fits!
>   But that your trespasse now becomes a fee,
>   Mine ransoms yours,and yours must ransome mee.

(sonnet 120)

In the previous chapters I explored the performative dynamics, evident in this sonnet, through which words may achieve reciprocity through their power not merely to describe, but to transform human relationships and the world from which they take their life. In the next I look at the performative power of the names and naming events to fix the concept of the self explored above in given networks of personal and social relations.

CHAPTER 4

Names: the sonnets, Romeo and Juliet, Troilus and Cressida and Othello

I have argued that the concept of the performative, of what words may do rather than merely say, transforms the notion of 'truth' in Shakespeare's sonnets and plays in decisive ways. The power of language not to reflect but to transform the world through forms of social action unites the sonnets and plays such as *Antony and Cleopatra* or *As You Like It*, where conditions of sufficient social or personal cohesion enable the performative to do its proper work. Such work depends upon particular kinds of imagined or real social worlds, worlds in which the requisite speech acts and language games are sustained by what Lars Engle has called the 'thick deeps' of contingent rather than transcendental certainty.[1] We can respond to Cleopatra's transformations of herself and her lover, or the player-poet's elevation of the young man into the paradigm instance of 'truth', or the accommodations of mutual falsehood in the dark-woman poems, because the texts themselves work within vital frameworks of consensual linguistic practice. These constitute the performative power of their speech acts, even when such acts empower certain kinds of withdrawal or escape from a wider social or political realm. Many acts of this kind are self-authorising. They do not merely conform to the settled conventions and sanctioned capacities that are constitutive of the performative as it appears in Austin's and Searle's more conservative moments of analysis. They forge their own authority at the very moment of linguistic action, renegotiating in discursive ways conditions of social or personal disempowerment. The impotency that is the abiding condition of the sonnets to the young man of rank may to some degree be transcended through the mobilisation of empowering speech acts under the guise of other, less presumptuous forms of discourse.

[1] Lars Engle, *Shakespearean Pragmatism: Market of His Time* (Chicago and London: University of Chicago Press, 1993).

Chapter 3 above shows that is not sufficient for speech acts to conform to particular linguistic forms. To take effect they need contexts that, as Wittgenstein puts it, give them their life. Plays such as *Hamlet* and *King Lear* demonstrate that a particular kind of society, marked by certain kinds of political power or social pressure, may render certain language games nugatory. The very possibility of a 'private' life may be excluded by a relentlessly public environment that is inimical to the conditions that allow its members the linguistic and emotional space to forge relationships and identities protected from public scrutiny and interference. This is not to say that the 'private' is a mere epiphenomenon of the 'public', or that there is metaphysically speaking no such realm or concept as the private. Rather, a certain kind of public realm – exemplified by the worlds of the two great tragedies, and also reflected in the sonnets – may empty the discourses or language games of private life of meaning. In the following pages I bring the arguments developed earlier together under the rubric of names, both 'proper' and 'common'. I show first, in a reading of *Romeo and Juliet*, how proper names tie private lives to public existence: to inescapable networks of social relations. I then discuss the ways in which imagined worlds may offer alternative significations to fixed names in *Troilus and Cressida*. Finally, I discuss the ways in which naming events themselves act as performatives, fixing or transforming identities and relationships in the context of *Othello*.

When Juliet, reflecting on the name of the rose and the name of her love, engages in what Jacques Derrida rightly calls 'the most implacable analysis of the name',[2] she is faced with the fact that the names of roses and the names of men work in disparate ways. The names of men (and also women) attest to a web of irreducible social relations:

> Romeo, Romeo, wherefore art thou Romeo?
> Deny thy father and refuse thy name
>
>   ...
>
> 'Tis but thy name that is my enemy:
> Thou art thyself, though not a Montague.
> What's a Montague? It is nor hand nor foot
> Nor arm nor face nor any other part
> Belonging to a man. O be some other name.
> What's in a name? That which we call a rose
> By any other word would smell as sweet;
> So Romeo would were he not Romeo call'd,

---

[2] Jacques Derrida, *Acts of Literature*, ed. Derek Attridge (London: Routledge, 1992), 427.

> Retain that dear perfection which he owes
> Without that title. Romeo, doff thy name,
> And for thy name, which is no part of thee,
> Take all myself.   (*Romeo and Juliet*, 2.1.75–91)

In a strangely inverted blazon of her love, Juliet wishes to reduce the distance represented by Romeo's name to the presence of immediate deixis by which, as in Shakepeare's sonnets, one can dispense with proper names. Being neither 'hand nor foot / Nor arm nor face nor any other part / Belonging to a man', Romeo's name is, as Derrida puts it, 'inhuman' (*Acts of Literature*, 427); 'no part of him,' he should be able to put it aside, substituting for it precisely that which his name resists, Juliet herself.

This desire to strip the object of denomination is related to the frequently reiterated (and conventional) thought in the sonnets that language corrupts nature: 'I never saw that you did painting need, / And therefore to your faire no painting set' (sonnet 83). But I have argued that part of the unconventionality of Shakespeare's sonnets lies in their clear, self-conscious recognition of the performative, rhetorical nature of this claim. Names *do* count in the sonnet sequence as inexorably as they do in *Romeo and Juliet*, even though their pragmatic context is now hidden from us, and in spite of their player-poet's attempts to evade their ideological weight. What matters in the sonnets, as in the play, is the *use* of the respective names: as markers of social difference, matrices of ideological meaning, networks of social relations. The player-poet desires as much as Juliet that the beloved should 'doff his name' and 'for his name' 'take all myself'. The young man's soul, 'all naked', would then be free of the social, political burden of the player's name. It would transcend the painful 'blots' and 'guilt' that 'remaine' (sonnet 36) with the player-poet, at least in part because of his own name. For that name is linked to the sonnets, both by the generic title – 'SHAKE-SPEARES SONNETS' – that contains it, and by 'that which [he] bring[s] forth' (sonnet 72) through his 'publick meanes which publick manners breeds' (sonnet 111).

The absence of proper names in the sonnets has both a logical and an ideological import. Logically, it suggests – even if it does not prove – their autobiographical nature. Ideologically, it intimates the desire of the player-poet to substitute the burdensome name of the beloved with 'all' of himself. That 'all' must, however, be suitably cleansed of his own, improper name, which, according to a certain perspective, is no part of a man. But against the wish to reduce the social significance of the proper name, both the sonnets and *Romeo and Juliet* enact the inexorable rigidity of the proper name.[3] Logically, Juliet's invocation of her love in his absence, even if it is to urge him to abandon his name, demonstrates that she has to do so in his name: 'Romeo'. This speaks of both an essential separability and inseparability of bearer and name. One can call (to) Romeo (or anyone else) in his absence only because the name is not part of him. On the other hand, that one can call to him is an indication of the inseparability of his name from himself – not as hand or foot or face, but as a social creature. This 'inhumanity' of the name paradoxically constitutes Romeo's very humanity, for it is what ties him to a particular family and social world:

This analysis is implacable for it announces or denounces the inhumanity or ahumanity of the name. A proper name does not name anything which is human, which belongs to the human body, a human spirit, an essence of man. And yet this relation to the inhuman only befalls man, for him, to him, in the name of man. He alone gives himself this inhuman name. *And Romeo would not be what he is, a stranger to his name, without his name.* Juliet, then, pursues her analysis: the names of things do not belong to the things any more than the names of men belong to men, and yet they are quite differently separable. (Derrida, *Acts of Literature*, 427; emphasis added)

To adopt Saul Kripke's way of speaking,[4] Romeo is Romeo in *all* possible worlds, even in a world in which he has denied or renounced his name. The name of the rose is different from the name of Romeo, for 'Romeo' ties its bearer to a set of obligations, relations and values in a way that the word 'rose' does not tie the flower. Romeo may try to set himself apart from those ties, even if the logic of the proper name means that it will dog him forever, like his shadow. Romeo is thus, paradoxically, Shakespeare's character who *renounces* his name: 'Romeo would not be what he is, a stranger to his name, without his name.'

In contrast to Kripke, who claims that a proper name has a referent but no sense (or, to use different terms, a denotation but no connotation, a referent but no signified), both the tragedy and the sonnets assert the inescapable ideological significance, sense or connotation of the name at the same time as they affirm Kripke's conception of the proper name as a 'rigid designator'. Recall that Kripke argues against the traditional view that a proper name is an abbreviation of a set of descriptions that are true

[3] For a fuller discussion of this in the context of current philosophical debates, see my '"What's in a name?": Derrida, Apartheid, and the Name of the Rose', *Language Sciences*, 22.2 (April 2000), 167–92.
[4] Saul Kripke, *Naming and Necessity* (Cambridge, MA: Harvard University Press, 1980).

of someone in favour of a concept of rigid designation independently of any descriptive properties in order to allow for the possibility that such descriptions may turn out to be false. The name has to be able to pick out precisely the person of whom the set of descriptions does turn out to be false. It does so, in Kripke's view, not through any meaning that it may have (and which might match its bearer through the latter's contingent properties), but through an original act of baptism and a series of reference-preserving, causal links in the subsequent use of the name.

As Shakespeare represents the proper name, there is no consolation for Juliet in the apparent truth that changing the name of the rose will not affect the properties of the flower. For while this is also true of Romeo emblazoned as a collection of body parts, it is not true of him as member of a human community, as someone she may or may not love. The play shows that Romeo would not be able to escape the fate of his name by exchanging his 'proper' name for the 'common' name of Juliet's 'love' ('be but sworn my love'): 'She knows it: detachable and dissociable, aphoristic though it may be, his name is his essence. Inseparable from his being' (Derrida, *Acts of Literature*, 426). This is why Romeo cannot 'tear the word' (2.1.99): because *he* has not written it, because his name has been written before him, is essentially other to him, is inexorably social.[5] Romeo's sudden vision of his name as the perpetrator of violence against both his beloved and his enemy thus conveys the play's insight into the social and ideological web in which he, Juliet, indeed, every member of the society, is caught:

> As if that name,
> Shot from the deadly level of a gun,
> Did murder her; as that that name's cursed hand
> Murdered her kinsman.
>
> (*Romeo and Juliet*, 3.3.101–4)

Romeo's name, understood both as the carrier of social identity and as the marker of rigid designation, ties him inexorably to the tragic events of the play. It makes it impossible for him and Juliet to escape the web of social determination into a private world of love, just as the player-poet of the sonnets consistently fails to transcend the public world by reducing the distance of the stage to the mutuality of the page.

---

[5] Romeo's predicament (which is equally Juliet's) is summed up by Louis Althusser when he claims of a child that from the moment of conception 'it is certain in advance that it will bear its Father's Name ... Before its birth the child is always-already ... appointed as a subject in and by the specific familial ideological configuration in which it is "expected" once it has been conceived' (*Lenin and Philosophy and Other Essays*, trans. D. Brewster (London: New Left Books, 1997)), 176.

Notwithstanding its autobiographical capacity to do without proper names, 'SHAKE-SPEARES SONNETS' expresses a desire, like Juliet's, to obliterate the differences that proper names represent. I have discussed the player-poet's wish to close the distance imposed by the ideological signification of the socially marked names of the actor and the aristocrat. Compare Viola's Petrarchan moment in *Twelfth Night*, when she moves Olivia by entertaining the ceaseless invocation of her name. To Olivia's question, 'What would you do?' Viola replies:

> Make me a willow cabin at your gate
> And call upon my soul within the house,
> Write loyal cantons of contemnèd love,
> And sing them loud even in the dead of night;
> Halloo your name to the reverberate hills,
> And make the babbling gossip of the air
> Cry out 'Olivia!' O, you should not rest
> Between the elements of air and earth
> But you should pity me.
>
> (*Twelfth Night*, 1.5.257–65)

Here the repetition of the proper name is fundamental to the rhetoric of erotic persuasion. It is a climactic consummation of the preparatory 'loyal cantons of contemnèd love' that are taken up and echoed by the elements themselves via the unselfconscious self-confidence of the speaker. But Viola's social status and gender are temporarily masked by her assumed name, Cesario. Taken in by the latter, but uncertain whether the former might provide a barrier to an erotic relationship, Olivia's very first thought is of the 'parentage' of her suppliant:

> OLIVIA You might do much.
>   What is your parentage?
> VIOLA Above my fortunes, yet my state is well.
>   I am a gentleman.   (1.5.266–9)

When the player-poet of the sonnets asks, rhetorically, 'What's in the braine that Inck may character / Which hath not figur'd to thee my true spirit?' (sonnet 108), 'parentage' may well come to mind. For it is one of the urgent fantasies of the sonnets that differences of class may be sublimated by considerations of the agelessness of love, assumed to transcend 'outward forme' (sonnet 108):

> What's new to speake, what now to register,
> That may expresse my loue,or thy deare merit ?
> Nothing sweet boy,but yet like prayers diuine,

> I must each day say ore the very same,
> Counting no old thing old,thou mine,I thine,
> Euen as when first I hallowed thy faire name.
> So that eternall loue in loues fresh case,
> Waighes not the dust and iniury of age,
> Nor giues to necessary wrinckles place,
> But makes antiquitie for aye his page,
>   Finding the first conceit of loue there bred,
>   Where time and outward forme would shew it dead,
>   (sonnet 108)

Although the player-poet looks back at a time when, in a punning echo of Viola's projected devotion, 'first I hallowed thy faire name', his sonnet does not, despite its concern with devout repetition, invoke that 'faire name' even once. 'Hallow' and 'halloo' are close enough to suggest that at least one of the things that the player-poet might be expected to 'say ore the very same' as part of a litany of repeated devotion is the beloved's proper name. But it is absent from a cycle that pointedly celebrates its own constant repetitiveness; it is absent even from this sonnet, which tantalisingly refers back to the initial moment in which the lover 'hallo(w)oed' the beloved's name through Viola-like iteration.

Notwithstanding my argument that the autobiographical mode of the sonnets renders proper names pragmatically redundant, the complete absence of the 'hallowed name' of the beloved remains remarkable. The perfect reciprocity sought and claimed through the pronouns, perfectly balanced and paired, in 'thou mine, I thine' cannot, it seems, be achieved through the pairing of proper names. It is as if the singularity of the beloved needs to be stripped of the very qualities that dog Romeo. He needs to be reduced to the common name 'love' or the simple, pristine adjectives, 'faire, kinde, and true' (sonnet 105). These alone can bear the constant iteration that 'leaues out difference' in sonnet 105. Sonnet 111 makes it clear that in ideological terms the player-poet's own proper name is incompatible with that of his beloved. Caught in a network of social relations, of which Shakespeare's involvement in the profession of the common player is presumably paramount, his name not only 'receives a brand' – his very 'nature is subdu'd / To what it workes in, like the Dyers hand':

> o FOR my sake doe you wish [with] fortune chide,
> The guiltie goddesse of my harmfull deeds,
> That did not better for my life prouide,

Then publick meanes which publick manners breeds.
Thence comes it that my name receiues a brand,
And almost thence my nature is subdu'd
To what it workes in,like the Dyers hand,
Pitty me then,and wish I were renu'de,
Whilst like a willing pacient I will drinke,
Potions of Eysell gainst my strong infection,
No bitternesse that I will bitter thinke,
Nor double pennance to correct correction.
 Pittie me then deare friend,and I assure yee,
 Euen that your pittie is enough to cure mee.

In its quiet desperation the poem struggles to find the resolution of his apparently incorrigible condition. At first the beloved is asked, as in sonnet 29, merely to align himself with the player-poet, so that the latter will not have to 'beweepe' his 'out-cast state' 'all alone'. The mere thought of the beloved is held to be sufficient to transcend the vicissitudes of fortune in the early sonnet, but it is excluded here. Far from being a force above the player-poet's condition that can magically transform it, the beloved is drawn into this poem, first as a someone who can 'chide with fortune' and then, more conventionally, as a Petrarchan beloved from whom a transforming compassion may be sought. But it is unclear how such pity should wipe out stains that are essentially *social* in nature – tied to the player-poet's 'name', and exemplified by the difference between his 'branded' name and the 'honour' that belongs to the beloved's name.[6]

This abiding social difference is rehearsed in other sonnets. It is encountered in sonnet 36, where the player-poet acknowledges the 'shame' that his own name represents, in public, to the beloved: 'I may not euer-more acknowledge thee, / Least my bewailed guilt should do thee shame, / Nor thou with publike kindnesse honour me, / Vnless thou take that honour from thy name.' It is also present in sonnets 71 and 72. In these poems, the abject player-poet seeks to renounce his name through the fantasy of his own death and urges the beloved to avoid the infection of his contaminated and contaminating name: 'Do not so much as my poore name reherse / But let your loue euen with my life decay. / Least the wise world should looke into your mone /And mock you with me

---

[6] Cf. sonnet 36:

  I may not euer-more acknowledge thee,
  Least my bewailed guilt should do thee shame,
  Nor thou with publike kindnesse honour me,
  Vnlesse thou take that honour from thy name.

after I am gone', and 'My name be buried where my body is, /And liue no more to shame nor me, nor you'. Sonnet 89, too, acknowledges the disgrace that stems from the player-poet's use of the beloved's name: 'in my tongue, / Thy sweet beloued name no more shall dwell, / Least I (too much prophane) should do it wronge: /And haplie of our old acquaintance tell'.

Each of these poems is a plea for the rehabilitation of the offending name through some action on the part of the beloved. The mere thought of the young man is no longer sufficient. If sonnets 105 and 108 represent the timeless repetition of the beloved's name and qualities as a form of appropriate worship, in which no 'disgrace' or 'state' can be too bad for him to 'hallow' the name of the addressee, the other poems are informed by a much more secular grasp of social contamination that breaks with the spiritual, religious strain of Petrarchan devotion. The 'disease' of which sonnet 111 complains is thus not the Petrarchan condition of unrequited or irrational love, but the 'base infection' of an inferior social class and unacceptably public occupation: 'I am shamed by that which I bring forth' (sonnet 72). Sonnet 111 represents the limits of spiritual sublimation. Its conventional plea for compassion from the beloved is contradicted by its own firm sense of the incorrigibility of its infection. Being part of a general social condition decreed by 'guiltie...fortune' (sonnet 111), it is not only impervious to the most bitter medicines or forms of correction, it is dangerously infectious to the very person who is supposed to be the agent of its eradication. Any 'honour' done to the name of the player-poet necessarily subtracts from the 'honour' of the beloved's own name. The poignancy of this poem lies in its incapacity to focus on the agent of either disgrace or release, despite its shifting attempts to find traditionally idealist, Petrarchan solutions to a problem that is essentially material and social. Far from being the medium of release, as he is conceived to be in sonnet 29, the aristocratic beloved is an essential part of the problem, as much victim of 'fortune' as an agent of erotic and social alienation.

Like Romeo, then, 'Will' is trapped by a proper name that marks his place within a set of social relations over which he has only limited control. The 'pittie' for which Sonnet 111 pleads is much more complex than mere personal love or liking: it involves the creation of reciprocity through the repudiation of the social considerations that produce public conditions of hierarchy, difference and separation. Given that Romeo cannot repudiate the network of social, familial and conflictual relations that constitute his name, this test of personally given reciprocity – of compassion or 'pity' – is faced and passed by Juliet. Caught for a moment in the conflicting oxymorons produced by her own loyalty to her family (and its name) and her love for her enemy, Juliet's 'pity' obliterates the differences represented by her lover's name:

> Beautiful tyrant, fiend angelical!
> Dove-feathered raven, wolvish-ravening lamb!
> Despisèd substance of divinest show!
>
> (*Romeo and Juliet*, 3.2.75–7)

This parody of Petrarchan oxymoron represents Juliet's struggle to come to terms with the disjunction of the names 'Romeo' and 'Tybalt' and what they represent over and above her personal desires. The scene shows her bearing the consequences of her reciprocating 'pity', which, far from forging a private world in which names have been forgotten, has brought new, and deeply contradictory, public affiliations distributed in conflicting ways across the names 'Romeo', 'Tybalt', 'husband' and 'cousin':

> NURSE Will you speak well of him that killed your cousin?
> JULIET Shall I speak ill of him that is my husband?
>   Ah, poor my lord, what tongue shall smooth thy name
>   When I, thy three-hours wife, have mangled it?
>   But wherefore, villain, didst thou kill my cousin?
>   That villain cousin would have killed my husband.
>   Back, foolish tears, back to your native spring!
>   Your tributary drops belong to woe,
>   Which you, mistaking, offer up to joy.
>   My husband lives, that Tybalt would have slain;
>   And Tybalt's dead, that would have slain my husband.
>
> (3.2.96–106)

Wracked by these unfamiliar, contradictory affiliations and filiations, however, Juliet soon finds in the thought of Romeo's banishment the death of all the world, the obliteration of everything that has tied her to her family. The 'death' of Romeo's name through banishment negates all else:

> 'Tybalt is dead, and Romeo banishèd.'
> That 'banishèd', that one word 'banishèd'
> Hath slain ten thousand Tybalts. Tybalt's death
> Was woe enough, if it had ended there;
> Or, if sour woe delights in fellowship

And needly will be ranked with other griefs,
Why followed not, when she said 'Tybalt's dead',
'Thy father', or 'thy mother', nay, or both,
Which modern lamentation might have moved?
But with a rearward following Tybalt's death,
'Romeo is banishèd' – to speak that word
Is father, mother, Tybalt, Romeo, Juliet,
All slain, all dead. 'Romeo is banishèd' –
There is no end, no limit, measure, bound,
In that word's death.   (3.2.112–26)

Insofar as Juliet's new affiliation with Romeo has replaced every other filiation, the final line of sonnet 111 is perfectly correct. Nothing more is required than the beloved's 'pity', for such 'pity' would necessarily involve, as Juliet's does, the suspension of the social network and the differences held by the proper name by a renewed embracing of the name through total reciprocity, through the negation of the world that Donne imagines and celebrates so powerfully in his poetry. *Romeo and Juliet* is unique among Shakespeare's plays in its representation of such reciprocity, even if its brief living moment is confirmed more ominously in the embrace of mutual death. The romantic comedies and late romances represent the passage to such reciprocity – its promise and in some cases, its consequences – without actually representing it on stage. But in the only other tragedy which celebrates a marriage, *Othello*, untrammelled reciprocity of every kind is notoriously postponed forever. I shall discuss *Othello* and the imbrications of names and marriage in due course.

The proper name as a mark caught in a supra-individual (and some would say inhumane) network of social relationships underlies the tragedy of *Romeo and Juliet*. It embodies the web of the social, the public and the political that entwines, from the beginning, Romeo and Juliet's apparent flight into the private world of erotic reciprocity. The sonnets less explicitly, but no less cogently, explore the desire to escape, or at least reduce, social ties and differences through the exigencies of the proper name, although the very different worlds of the poems to the man of rank and the common woman mean that the proper name is employed in different ways. The fact that it is impossible for both Romeo and Will to 'tear the word' of their names does not mean that some degree of suspension of the public or social world is neither desirable nor possible. And the capacity of *Romeo and Juliet* as theatre to create a world in which both Petrarchan and counter-Petrarchan discourses are living modes of social intercourse, rather than merely literary devices, offers a perspective on the imbrication of the public and private, the political and the erotic, in the form of the name.

Like *Romeo and Juliet* and the sonnets, *Troilus and Cressida* explores the burden of the proper name, but it does so in a different mode. The story is woven around names that bring with them centuries of accumulated (and sometimes contradictory) ideological signification. But its primary pair of lovers also illustrates the process by which certain human figures may become the paradigmatic or defining instances of the conceptual or ideal. 'Troilus', 'Cressida', 'Pandarus' are not merely 'rigid designators' of historical figures; they point to the ideological process whereby these names have come to epitomise the concepts of 'fidelity', 'faithlessness' and 'pimp'. The performative quality of this process is underlined and ironised by the dramatist's decision to make the characters themselves agents of their future idealisation and de-idealisation. Ironically unaware of the generic self-reflexivity of the moment, Troilus, Cressida and Pandarus turn themselves, through the performative action of the jussive, into the historical paradigms that precede Shakespeare's play in the signification of their respective names:

> TROILUS But alas,
> I am as true as truth's simplicity,
> And simpler than the infancy of truth.
> CRESSIDA In that I'll war with you.
> TROILUS O virtuous fight,
> When right with right wars who shall be most right.
> True swains in love shall in the world to come
> Approve their truth by Troilus. When their rhymes,
> Full of protest, of oath and big compare,
> Wants similes, truth tired with iteration –
> 'As true as steel, as plantage to the moon,
> As sun to day, as turtle to her mate,
> As iron to adamant, as earth to th' centre' –
> Yet, after all comparisons of truth,
> As truth's authentic author to be cited,
> 'As true as Troilus' shall crown up the verse
> And sanctify the numbers.
> CRESSIDA Prophet may you be!
> If I be false, or swerve a hair from truth,
> When time is old and hath forgot itself,
> When water drops have worn the stones of Troy
> And blind oblivion swallowed cities up,
> And mighty states characterless are grated

> To dusty nothing, yet let memory
> From false to false among false maids in love
> Upbraid my falsehood. When they've said, 'as false
> As air, as water, wind or sandy earth,
> As fox to lamb, or wolf to heifer's calf,
> Pard to the hind, or stepdame to her son',
> Yea, let them say, to stick the heart of falsehood,
> 'As false as Cressid'.

PANDARUS Go to, a bargain made. Seal it, seal it. I'll be the witness. Here I hold your hand; here, my cousin's. If ever you prove false one to another, since I have taken such pain to bring you together, let all pitiful goers-between be called to the world's end after my name: call them all panders. Let all constant men be Troiluses, all false women Cressids, and all brokers-between panders. Say 'Amen'.

TROILUS Amen.

CRESSIDA Amen.

PANDARUS Amen.   (*Troilus and Cressida*, 3.2.164–203)

This scene is remarkable for its rehearsal of the speech acts of a certain kind of Petrarchan verse, and also for the way in which, by self-consciously exposing peculiarly Shakespearean variations on that theme, it reveals some of the building-blocks of the Shakespearean sonnet. It is itself built out of two sonnets, or a sonnet followed by a near-sonnet. As such it ironically echoes, in serial form, the dialogue sonnet that marks Romeo and Juliet's first encounter. Cressida's speech is a complete fourteen lines; Troilus's a more ominous thirteen. Unlike their counterparts in the earlier tragedy, these 'sonnets' are not shared in a moment of mutual dialogue.[7] On the contrary, the general Petrarchan perspective of love as war is given a fresh twist in the rivalry for truth between the lovers themselves. The beloved takes the place of the competing lover, in a 'virtuous fight, / When right with right wars who shall be most right'. Against the monological nature of the sonnet when it is confined to the page, the woman now rivals the male poet's claim of 'truth' in a sonnet of her own. Such exposure has its disadvantages, as we shall see. For the moment it is enough merely to note the public, confident nature of Cressida's stance. She steps into the role of Petrarchan poet, spurring Troilus on from a hapless and merely conventional declaration of his own 'truth', to a reflection on the ways in which such conventions are established and transformed.

---

[7] Thanks to Lars Engle for drawing this to my attention. I discuss the 'palmer's kiss' sonnet from *Romeo and Juliet* in chapter 2, above.

Troilus's claim to renew in his own name the tired inventory of Petrarchan comparison reflects on the reinvention of poetic language through the invocation of a particular name as a conceptual paradigm, and the historical, iterative process by which such freshness is in turn worn away into cliché. Mercutio notes such erosion when he invokes the paradigm of beauty central to the story of Troy to ridicule Romeo's Petrarchan infatuation:

Now is he for the numbers that Petrarch flowed in. Laura to his lady was a kitchen wench – marry, she had a better love to berhyme her – Dido a dowdy, Cleopatra a gypsy, Helen and Hero hildings and harlots, Thisbe a grey eye or so, but not to the purpose. Signor Romeo, bonjour. There's a French salutation to your French slop. You gave us the counterfeit fairly last night. (*Romeo and Juliet*, 2.3.36–44)

'Counterfeit' works across both speech acts here, infecting the 'numbers' imputed to Romeo, and thereby the very process by which 'true swains in love ... Full of protest, of oath and big compare' use similes derived from historical paradigms such as Helen. Fashioning himself as just such a paradigm of truth, Troilus is looking forward to being drawn into the inventory of fresh 'invention' (sonnet 105) rather than abandoned as an instance of 'truth tired with iteration' (*Troilus and Cressida* 3.2.172). But looking backward from a historical perspective by which the name 'Troilus' has itself become 'tired with iteration', Shakespeare's play can reflect on the peculiarity of a convention by which truth is defined diachronically, by invention, rather than through the constancy of unchanging repetition. This double perspective is, as Engle has shown, one of the major preoccupations of the sonnets' concern with value (*Shakespearean Pragmatism*). 'What's aught' as Troilus asks elsewhere, 'but as 'tis valued?' (2.2.51).

But constancy – unvaried repetition – works against invention, as the Shakespeare of the sonnets knows well enough. To 'confine' oneself (and one's verse) to 'constancie' (sonnet 105) is not merely to write 'all still one, ever the same' (sonnet 76), but to risk running against the grain of truth in a world transformed everywhere by alteration. Nowhere is this expressed more clearly than in sonnet 115, which offers a powerful counter-argument to the more famous sonnet that immediately follows it and a counter-perspective on the abrasive process of time in sonnets which precede it:

> THOSE lines that I before haue writ doe lie,
> Euen those that said I could not loue you deerer,
> Yet then my iudgement knew no reason why,
> My most full flame should afterwards burne cleerer.

But reckening time,whose milliond accidents
Creepe in twixt vowes,and change decrees of Kings,
Tan sacred beautie,blunt the sharp'st intents,
Diuert strong mindes to th'course of altring things:
Alas why fearing of times tiranie,
Might I not then say now I loue you best,
When I was certaine ore in-certainty,
Crowning the present,doubting of the rest:
　Loue is a Babe, then might I not say so
　To giue full growth to that which still doth grow.

The sonnet opens with an unorthodox admission, not that love grows with time (Donne says that),[8] but that his earlier claims of perfect love have now been shown to be untrue. A first reading would see the opening lines as a general admission of the untruthfulness of Petrarchan claims, but the whole quatrain unfolds the suggestion that the earlier claims have been rendered invalid by the growth rather than the falling off or prevarication of love. Truth is subject to the process of time and change, constituted by time's 'milliond accidents', rather than transcending them. To be true, or to produce truth that will last, is to withhold claims that might in due course be rendered invalid by an inevitable and inescapable process of accident. Whereas the other sonnets concerned with time are generally involved in the processes of decay, wearing away and loss, this poem is concerned with the way in which time inhabits human judgement and action. Time will always 'tan sacred beauty', as it does in the other sonnets. But the second quatrain focuses chiefly on the way in which it interposes between human intention and fulfilment, vow and performance, decree and enactment. That is to say, the sonnet is interested in the way in which time seeps into all human endeavour, not merely destroying it, but living in and through it. Such endeavour may therefore either wax or wane with time; love may be destroyed or it may grow, even though we tend to see only its destruction. Its insight into the inhabiting work of time produces a crisis regarding any statement or vow that might be rendered false by what is yet to come, rather than what has already happened. Such a crisis arises from being 'certaine ore in-certainty' based on present experience or judgement, since the mere fact of time must render all things uncertain. One may be wrong about the perfection of one's love at any given moment, not only because one may fall out of love, but because one may fall ever more deeply in love.

---

[8] See, for example, 'Love's Growth'.

The process of time sketched by the sonnet thus works in two directions: time consolidates as much as it destroys, rendering any certainty which 'crowns the present' radically problematic. This robs the player-poet of the one source of consolation to which he could turn in the other sonnets on time: the certainty that his love will live on in his verse, since he is now precluded even from making any absolute claims about that love. It is as much a lie to 'giue full growth to that which still doth grow' as it is to vow 'new hate after new loue bearing' (sonnet 152).

In the vows of the protagonists in *Troilus and Cressida* we can see the ways in which various degrees of blindness to the analysis of time presented in sonnet 115 cloud their attempts to 'crown the present' by turning their names into, respectively, paradigms of timeless devotion and infidelity. Precisely by offering his name up for the fresh invention – the 'quicke change', 'new found methods' and 'compounds strange' (sonnet 76) – that is the business of the Petrarchan poet, Troilus undermines his self-appointed status as the paradigmatic, transhistorical instance of truth. In general terms, we can see that the long historical tradition of the Petrarchan sonnet as it is received in England is precisely what generates its most productive paradox. The sheer historical weight of its conventionality demands both fidelity and renewal: 'all in war with Time for loue of you, /As he takes from you, I ingraft you new' (sonnet 15). The hubris that infects Troilus in his claim to be the true representative of true simplicity in love touches the speaker of the sonnets too. The latter's defiance of time in sonnet 123, for instance – 'No! Time, thou shalt not boast that I doe change!' – is every bit as bombastic as Troilus's utterance. The vow with which this sonnet concludes – 'Thy registers and thee I both defie, /.... / This I doe vow, and this shall euer be, / I will be true dispight thy scyeth and thee' – its hollowness in direct proportion to its rhetorical effort, stands in defective contrast to Juliet's quick suspicion of lovers' promises and Cressida's similar reticence.

Cressida's own part in the chorus of speech acts is less conventional because she appropriates a gendered speech position that belongs, traditionally, to the male. But she also understands, as Troilus does not, both the obliterating and constitutive effects of time. In this respect she 'wars' with her lover in more than merely personal terms. And in Shakespeare's own concession to the demands of poetic variation in the two speeches, her invocation of her own name as the paradigm marker of sexual betrayal recalls both the sonnets' 'war with time' (sonnet 15) and their apparent gendering of falsehood in the form of the 'woman collour'd il' (sonnet 144):

> When time is old and hath forgot itself,
> When water drops have worn the stones of Troy
> And blind oblivion swallowed cities up,
> And mighty states characterless are grated
> To dusty nothing, yet let memory
> From false to false among false maids in love
> Upbraid my falsehood.
>
> (*Troilus and Cressida*, 3.2.181–7)

Cressida's use of her conditional sets her apart from her lover. Troilus calls upon his name as 'truth's authentic author' of its own accord, as it were, in an exorbitant act of self-authorisation. He does not begin to entertain the possibility of change posited as an inevitable consequence of either 'wastfull time' (sonnet 15) or the more insidious 'million'd accidents' of sonnet 115. This very claim to truthfulness imputes a deleterious forgetting, a conspicuous lack of truth, in his own view of himself. Cressida, on the other hand, is fully conscious of the necessity of change over time. She is as aware as the player-poet of the inescapable wearing away of the stones of Troy – the immemorial erosion of 'mighty states' – and the equally inevitable falsehood of 'false maids in love'. 'If I be false' – here Cressida entertains the thought of herself as an actor in a different possible world, a world which, of course, readers and audience 'remember' (in the future) as the 'true' world of 'false Cressid'. Just as the young man's beauty is supposed to live on in the lines of the sonnets, so Cressida's treachery, entertained here merely as a possibility, will live on – and in fact has already lived on – in her name. The play can thus embody a process that the sonnets, caught in speculative speech acts that are as yet tied to the moment of their production, can only promise. But, of course, the very 'iteration' by which the sonnets establish their 'truth' guarantees change, if only through the wearing away of invention into cliché.

I have argued that sonnet 138 represents a much more satisfactory accommodation to a mutuality of 'falsehood' than the vulnerable idealism which seeks 'truth' in the inscrutable constancy of power. I have also questioned the way in which the 'faire, kinde, and true' of the dark lord of the sonnets is assumed as a given. In other words, I have suggested that the player-poet has not, *pace* Rowse, 'with his characteristic candour and openness... told us everything about the Dark Lady, except her name'.[9] We have tied together the disparate performatives and descriptions that make up 'SHAKE-SPEARES SONNETS' by substituting our own names for those maddening absences: the 'poet', the 'fair

---

9 A. L. Rowse, *Shakespeare's Sonnets: The Problems Solved* (London: Macmillan, 1973), xxxiii.

friend', the 'dark lady'. These are not proper names, however. They are epithets, abbreviated descriptions that we have pressed into service as proper names. They act ideologically, attributing value as much as they maintain constancy of reference. They condense the semantic total of a certain selection of speech acts into a designating phrase that is only apparently rigid, or rather, that has the empty rigidity of a tautology. By picking out only certain descriptions and holding them together under a title that is itself a shorthand description, such designating epithets run foul of Kripke's most important insight about proper names as rigid designators: that they allow for alternative descriptions, other possible worlds, different ideological significations for their referents. Could the 'fair friend' be a 'dark lord'; the 'dark lady' a 'sweet love', or the 'poet' a series of shifting speech-act positions shared among the three of them, the latter suggested especially by the rich undecidability of the name 'Will'? We need to subject the critical habits which project these epithets upon already determined 'characters' in the sonnets to critical scrutiny.[10]

As Juliet analyses it in her famous speech in Act Two of *Romeo and Juliet*, 'Romeo' is a true proper name: a rigid designator that can neither be 'torn' nor abandoned, for it designates Romeo in all possible worlds. 'Troilus' and 'Cressida' on the other hand, as the characters themselves invoke their names in the scene under discussion, are turned into epithets: carriers of a particularly ideological, semantic weight: the (intrinsically) 'true' knight, the (inevitably) 'false' woman. But they also, necessarily, act in the play as rigid designators. As such they allow the dramatist to explore modalities different from those entertained by Troilus and Cressida themselves or carried within folk memory. They allow for an alternative exploration of the very thing that, in Cressida's utterance, her name will keep alive 'out to the ending doome' (sonnet 55). Unlike the 'dark lady' and the 'fair friend' of the sonnets, whose respective 'fairness' and 'darkness' are merely bundles of circularly derived propositions collected under ideological signs, the 'truth' that Troilus appropriates to himself and the 'falsehood' that Cressida entertains of herself may be

---

[10] See Heather Dubrow, '"Incertainties now crown themselves assur'd": The Politics of Plotting Shakespeare's Sonnets', *Shakespeare Quarterly*, 47 (1996), 291–305; reprinted in *Shakespeare's Sonnets: Critical Essays*, ed. James Schiffer (New York: Garland, 1999); 113–34. In this essay Dubrow subjects the critical and ideological assumptions underlying the reading of the sonnets which regards them as a narrative of mutual homosocial or homosexual love destroyed by the dark duplicity of woman to devastating criticism. I am deeply indebted to her argument that there is no evidence for the traditional ascription of addressees to the poems, although the logical terms in which I analyse the issue here are very different from hers.

qualified by different modalities embodied by the *play* that bears their names. All the characters in this play, from the point of view of an attending audience, are therefore the products of a certain kind of 'madness of discourse', an instability in the 'rule of unity itself' (5.2.144–5).

Does Cressida bear the burden of this falsehood as inexorably as Romeo bears his name or the dark lady has traditionally borne hers? Not necessarily. Seen in the light of the meditation in sonnet 115 on the constitutive necessity of time, Cressida's fantasy is much closer to reality than Troilus's self-absorbed affirmation of himself as the incarnation of absolute truth. Furthermore, the rigid designation of the proper name allows that name to be used in a different possible world: a world in which Cressida does not bear the *ideological* weight of her name. It is possible to write a play in which the names 'Troilus' and 'Cressida' appear as rigid designators of Homer's characters, but in which they do not act as the defining instances of (male) truth and (female) infidelity. The theory of rigid designation explains how we can entertain the possibility that Troilus was not faithful, Cressida not faithless; or, for that matter, that Homer was not a single poet but an oral collective, or that Shakespeare did not write 'Shake-speare's' plays.[11] The question that names in *Troilus and Cressida* raise is not whether Cressida is false or not, but whether her name is inevitably the epitome of falsehood, its paradigm case or essence. The theatricality of *Troilus and Cressida* can achieve what the sonnets considered as mere text on a page cannot: in 'the two-hour traffic of our stage' the players' medium can combine the embodiment of character with the phenomenological fusion of change through time and space, in order to present figures whose historical paths may be charted differently. As Robert Weimann has argued, the theatre itself possesses a 'bi-fold authority' by which a character, especially a historically received one, both 'is and is not' him or herself. This doubleness constitutes in part the de-idealisation that theatre as an embodied art entails.

I have emphasised the idea that the sonnets present us with a world every bit as particular as those of the plays. Human action and belief can be understood and appraised only within the context of a specific, human world. Since that world is not fully recoverable from the poems, I have brought them into relation with the fuller universes of Shakespeare's

---

[11] For a classic account of the 'descriptive' theory of names, see John R. Searle, *Speech Acts: An Essay in the Philosophy of Language* (Cambridge: Cambridge University Press, 1969), 157–75. For the counter-theory of 'causal reference', see Saul Kripke, *Naming and Necessity*.

dramatic works in order to offer contexts in terms of which we might make greater sense of their intensely wrought but incomplete fragments. Plays such as *Troilus and Cressida* share the sonnets' concern with the problem of the ideal, not as something Platonic that transcends time and practice, but rather as a necessary condition of language and thought that is appropriated again and again *from* the world to stand as a governing paradigm, a rule for the mobilisation of concepts. In *Troilus and Cressida* and to a different degree in *Othello*, Shakespeare inverts the process of idealisation that I have traced in the sonnets that elevate the young man to a linguistic rule of beauty. The theatrical embodiment upon which I have built much of the argument of earlier chapters here serves to de-idealise, turning rule back into sample, reducing paradigm to mere 'instance'. Helen as embodied woman, materially present on stage, cannot sustain the timeless role of her name as the governing idea of beauty. This grand disillusionment is re-enacted more locally in the figure of Cressida, in whom we witness both painful idealisation and de-idealisation. The inversion of the process of idealisation in *Troilus and Cressida* is achieved in particularly theatrical ways. 'Helen' as received idea is no more than a proper name: a thin mark around which a series of reported events conglomerate. We know her, notoriously, as the 'face that launched a thousand ships' (or, in Troilus's commercialising paraphrase, as the 'pearl / Whose price hath launched a thousand ships' (2.2.81–2)). The play offers no description of that face: like the young man and the 'serpent of old Nile', she is who she is. She is the standard by which other women are judged. But, as an embodied figure on the stage – her 'greatness' 'boyed' by a 'squeaking' youth – she is also a highly contested standard: her value is the function of a certain masculine wilfulness, her beauty 'painted' by the blood of brawling warriors. In a play in which status is the product of performative discourses as much as actual performance, we are from the beginning acutely aware of the questioning irony of Troilus's observation of her lack of intrinsic merit, of the fact of her elevation through certain kinds of action: 'Helen must need be fair / When with your blood you daily paint her thus' (1.1.90–1). In the context of Helen as transhistorical ideal, her embodiment on stage is a let-down, a counter-ideal that speaks against a whole tradition of paradigmatic elevation through the mere quiddity of incarnation. The stage exemplifies her 'monstrosity', engendered, like the 'monster in love', by the gap between 'infinite will' and 'confined execution' (3.2.78–9). That Shakespeare's play deliberately presents her as idle, vacant and indulgent merely adds to a process that begins with the very materiality of the player's body.

Such de-idealising of the paradigm is as much a product of embodiment, of the theatre as such, as the staging of women's silence discussed in chapter 2. Even the epic figures of Hector, Ulysses, Agamemnon, Achilles and Priam, which have historically encapsulated the heroic ideals of a classical golden age, no longer comply in their embodied forms with the matchless names of history. As commentators have repeatedly noted, the heroes who come down the long path from Homer carry their celebrated names as mere ciphers of qualities that are equalled in neither their behaviour nor speech.[12] Even in the most intimate circles, character and reputation are not inscribed on the face; ideal and essence fail to shine through either word or deed. In this world, as in the later, fallen Petrarchan realms of praise and compliment, worth means being 'dress[ed] ... up in voices' (1.3.375). 'Truth tired with iteration' shares its depletion with the similarly exhausted, reiterative modes of Petrarchism. The embodiment of Helen on stage necessarily turns ideal into instance, concept into flesh. If a paradigm such as 'Helen of Troy' is a historical sample necessarily withdrawn from its circulation in ordinary propositional discourse, so that it can become the measure by which such language games are played, then a play such as *Troilus and Cressida* recirculates it within such discourse, reducing its status as ideal paradigm to local instance.[13]

If something may be elevated to ideal status – such as the young man as the defining rule for 'beauty' – it may also be de-idealised, reduced from its governing or defining status to one more 'instance' or object among many. Whereas *Antony and Cleopatra* reveals the elevation of instance to paradigm, it is now generally held that *Troilus and Cressida* traces the opposite movement by registering a deep sense of disillusionment or de-idealisation. Such a de-idealising movement is clear enough in the trajectory of desire and rejection in Troilus's view of Cressida. This trajectory, which unfolds over time on the stage, is compressed into moments of simultaneous desire and revulsion in the sonnets. The process of idealisation and disillusionment constitutes the conceptual framework of the play itself, which, in its belated literary moment, enacts again and

---

[12] This is not to ignore the fact that for many Elizabethans, the ancient Greeks represented a distinctly unheroic society. See T. J. B. Spencer, '"Greeks" and "Merrygreeks": A Background to *Timon of Athens* and *Troilus and Cressida*', in *Essays on Shakespeare and Elizabethan Drama in Honor of Hardin Craig*, ed. Richard Hosley (Columbia: University of Missouri Press, 1962), 223–33.

[13] See Ludwig Wittgenstein, *On Certainty*, ed. G. E. M. Anscombe and G. H. Von Wright, trans. Denis Paul and G. E. M. Anscombe (Cambridge: Blackwell, 1979), 81–8.

again a corrosive de-idealisation of all its supposedly heroic characters, further wearing away a 'truth tired with iteration' through its own reiterative movement of theatrical time. At the same time, if that 'wearing away' of the ideal has become a commonplace of criticism of the play, I want to argue that the play and the sonnets demonstrate the dogged persistence of the idealising or generalising impulse as a condition of language itself. The corrosive disillusionment of these two works is conditional upon their contrary modes of idealisation, upon which they not only trade, but which they also perpetuate.

In the theatre the body cannot be totally transformed into script or text: an excessive remainder escapes such textualising, providing a space for different ways of seeing the body as a material 'instance' rather than as a wholly conceptualised ideal. The theatre neither confirms nor escapes essence; it shows the mode by which 'instances' shuttle between being distilled as 'essence' and then de-essentialised as multifarious 'instance' once again. The 'monstrosity' of love, of which Cressida reminds Troilus, lies in its entrapment between ideal and instance or, as Troilus puts it: 'this is the monstrosity of love, lady, that the desire is boundless and the act a slave to limit' (3.2.75–7). Taken back to its Latin roots, the monstrous is the instance, the example, that which can be pointed at or shown. Its abnormality as monster arises from its oscillating in a liminal position between the absolute and the empirical, the ideal and the instance, the desire and the act. Such monstrous liminality is apparent in Troilus's fervent expectation of the erotic delights to come, of the incarnation of the ideal:

> I am giddy. Expectation whirls me round.
> Th'imaginary relish is so sweet
> That it enchants my sense. What will it be,
> When that the wat'ry palates taste indeed
> Love's thrice-reputed nectar?   (3.2.16–20)

The giddiness that Troilus experiences here could be said to be the precursor – the other side of the coin – of the ailment that pervades sonnet 129 and sonnet 147 alike:

> MY loue is as a feauer longing still,
> For that which longer nurseth the disease,
> Feeding on that which doth preserue the ill,
> Th'vncertaine sicklie appetite to please:
> My reason the Phisition to my loue,
> Angry that his prescriptions are not kept

> Hath left me,and I desperate now approoue,
> Desire is death,which Phisick did except.
> Past cure I am,now Reason is past care,
> And frantick madde with euer-more vnrest,
> My thoughts and my discourse as mad mens are,
> At randon from the truth vainely exprest.
>   For I haue sworne thee faire,and thought thee bright,
>   Who art as black as hell,as darke as night.
>
> (sonnet 147)

In the most obvious way, the self-recriminating disillusionment, ex-pressed in the closing couplet of this sonnet as a kind of 'madness of dis-course', is matched by Troilus's discovery of Cressida's unfaithfulness. But such an infected madness afflicts Troilus from the very beginning, when, even before disillusionment exposes her darkness, swearing Cressida fair and thinking her bright itself constitutes the most brutal of tortures. The simplest statement of the beloved's fairness – speaking 'no more than truth', as Pandarus puts it (1.1.64) – has painful perlocutionary effects. The standard Petrarchan idea that the unrequited lover is tormented or diseased by his mistress's lack of pity is pushed to grotesque limits, not unsurprising in a play which imbricates love at every point with war and sickness. The lover's heart, alternatively wounded by the beloved's cruelty or ruptured by the lover's own disease, is a festering sore, into which the emblazoned parts of the beloved are poured, as into a sewer. Every reiteration of the blazon of fairness constitutes further laceration:

> I tell thee I am mad
> In Cressid's love; thou answer'st 'She is fair',
> Pourest in the open ulcer of my heart
> Her eyes, her hair, her cheek, her gait, her voice;
> Handlest in thy discourse, O, that her hand,
> In whose comparison all whites are ink
> Writing their own reproach, to whose soft seizure
> The cygnet's down is harsh, and spirit of sense
> Hard as the palm of ploughman. This thou tell'st me –
> As true thou tell'st me – when I say I love her.
> But saying thus, instead of oil and balm
> Thou lay'st in every gash that love hath given me
> The knife that made it.
> PANDARUS I speak no more than truth.
> TROILUS Thou dost not speak so much.   (1.1.51–65)

Troilus's contorted syntax is symptomatic of the madness he decries. It releases from Panadarus's simple comment, 'she is fair', a torrent of anguished hyperbole that transfers the subjective agency of praise to the world itself through a series of surprising associations: we pass from Cressida's hand, to ink, to 'all whites', which 'write their own reproach' through their now comparatively inky darkness. Far from being an example of truth's simplicity, Troilus's extravagant conceit mystifies the process by which the sought-after ideal is established. Thwarted desire, unable to accept the limits of truth ('Thou dost not speak so much'), projects into the very substance of the world its own hyperbolic operations, but not before reminding us, through the associations of 'hand', 'ink' and 'writing', of Cressida's own fateful agency. By the end of the scene, when he is able more soberly to entertain the likelihood of achieving his prize, Troilus returns to the more settled, though nonetheless unsettling, language of commerce, trade and colonial plunder:

> Her bed is India; there she lies, a pearl.
> Between our Ilium and where she resides
> Let it be called the wild and wand'ring flood,
> Ourself the merchant, and this sailing Pandar
> Our doubtful hope, our convoy, and our barque.
>
> (1.1.100–4)

The eager, hyperbolic anticipation of Troilus's earlier speech remains, but he now presents a different world, of practical action and adventurous merchandising.

In his anticipatory giddiness, Troilus conceives Cressida as being no less than the thrice-distilled drink of the gods. Tasting her will supposedly confer immortality on a palate that is mortal not only in its 'mouth-watering' appetite, but also in its lack of substance, in the 'wateriness' by which everything it ingests 'falls into abatement and low price / Even in a minute' (*Twelfth Night*, 1.1.13–14), like the 'vncertaine sicklie appetite' in sonnet 147.[14] How different is Troilus's fear of 'death', of 'losing distinction in [his] joys' (*Troilus and Cressida*, 3.2.20–5), from Juliet's fearless summoning of 'loving, black-browed night', so that Romeo might

---

[14] Most editors gloss 'watr'y palates' as '(mouth)-watering', but the literal sense may be that the palate is indeed *watery*, like the 'spirit of love' that, as Orsino imagines it,

> Receiveth as the sea, naught enters there,
> Of what validity and pitch so e'er,
> But falls into abatement and low price
> Even in a minute! So full of shapes is fancy
> That it alone is high fantastical.
>
> (*Twelfth Night*, 1.1.11–15)

shine luminously upon her 'like fresh snow upon a raven's back' (*Romeo and Juliet*, 1.1.65). Whether the difference between Troilus's and Juliet's anticipatory celebrations of carnal pleasure are necessarily gendered remains to be seen. Both the sonnet and the play struggle to locate the place of the madness that they enact: does it lie in the object of desire, thought fair, but actually 'black'? Does it lie in the perverse nature of (male?) sexual desire, which relentlessly pursues a life-threatening poison, 'like rats that raven down their proper bane' (*Measure for Measure*, 1.2.121), thereby proving 'desire is death'? Or will it instead fling itself back in revulsion from the 'hell' that it had earlier sought as 'heaven'? Or does it lie in discourse itself, in the sinuously deceptive coils of syntax and disseminating scattering of semantics which render the 'rule of unity itself' a mere fiction? We might, for the moment, suggest an answer of sorts to Troilus's nervously self-centred question – 'what will it be?' (*Troilus and Cressida*, 3.2.18) – by turning to sonnet 129:

> TH'expence of Spirit in a waste of shame
> Is lust in action,and till action,lust
> Is periurd,murdrous,blouddy full of blame,
> Sauage,extreame,rude,cruell,not to trust,
> Inioyd no sooner but dispised straight,
> Past reason hunted, and no sooner had
> Past reason hated as a swollowed bayt,
> On purpose layd to make the taker mad.
> Made In pursut and in possession so,
> Had,hauing,and in quest,to haue extreame,
> A blisse in proofe and proud and very wo,
> Before a ioy proposd behind a dreame,
> > All this the world well knowes yet none knowes well,
> > To shun the heauen that leads men to this hell.

Vendler has taught us to see this sonnet not merely as a disgusted outburst against lust, but as a complex recreation of two distinct, lived moments, both of which are represented by Troilus in the less compressed dimensions of drama: the forward-looking moment of eager, idealising anticipation, subsequently 'corrected' by the retrospective, disillusioned movement of experience (Vendler, *The Art of Shakespeare's Sonnets*, 553). In *Troilus and Cressida* this disillusioning moment is already apparent on the very morning after Troilus has tasted the 'thrice-reputed nectar' when, in contrast to the aubade in *Romeo and Juliet*, he is not only all too willing to leave Cressida's bed, but happy to collude in her uncle's greasy comments. Later, Troilus's desperate attempt to hold an idealised Cressida together in one breath with the woman he sees before him with Diomedes could be said to rehearse the 'bi-fold authority' of this sonnet:

> Within my soul there doth conduce a fight
> Of this strange nature, that a thing inseparate
> Divides more wider than the sky and earth,
> And yet the spacious breadth of this division
> Admits no orifex for a point as subtle
> As Ariachne's broken woof to enter.
>
> (*Troilus and Cressida*, 5.2.150–5)

Both this passage and the sonnet struggle to make sense of a 'thing inseparate' that 'divides more wider than the sky and earth'; both see this division in the 'rule of unity itself' as a kind of madness that infects reason; and both attribute this madness to the dark plague of sexuality. But the most remarkable thing about sonnet 129 is its preoccupation with language. It is packed, cluttered with words, an effect achieved not only by its repetitive chiasmi, but by the lines which forgo the usual, semantically thin words that forge syntax for catalogues of heaped adjectives. The poem does not present merely a subjective emotion, obsession or drive but the effort of language to possess the world. That is why it has seemed to many to be a 'definition' poem. And so it is. But it is an extremely complex definition. Or rather, it enacts the complexity of definition itself: the movement by which flesh is made word. The poem is a performance of the very thing of which it speaks: the way in which 'all labour / Mars what it does; yea, very force entangles / Itself with strength' (*Antony and Cleopatra*, 4.15.47–9). It traces the movement that can be predicated of the whole of *Troilus and Cressida* itself, the movement by which the ideal is de-idealised and re-idealised. This movement is essentially linguistic. It is impossible outside discourse, and the excessive 'wordiness' of the sonnet expresses exactly this necessity. It is also why the phenomenon of which the poem deals is not beastly but irreducibly human, 'entangled' not only in the 'strength' of 'will', but in the web of meaning, value and truth that living within language and society necessitates.[15] If it enacts

---

[15] Compare the Duke's moralising attempts to reduce the sexuality from which Pompey lives to the 'beastly' in *Measure for Measure*:

> DUKE ... 'From their abominable and beastly touches
> I drink, I eat, array myself, and live.'
> Canst thou believe thy living is a life,
> So stinkingly depending? Go mend, go mend.

the process by which an ideal may be reduced to an instance of enraged disillusionment, it does not rest there.

Whatever the sonnet has to say about the nature of lust, its pursuit of the workings of language is unflinching. As the poem expands from the narrow scope of what appears to be personal experience (but is never stated as such) to encompass what 'the *world* well knowes', the semantic force of the line as it moves from 'heauen' to 'hell' undergoes a complementary reduction. It changes from the idealising and idealised abstraction of the love object as 'heauen' to the material 'instance' of 'hell' as the female genitalia. This movement might seem anti-Petrarchan, a complete abasement of that whole discourse of idealisation. But sonnet 129 carries within it the opposite, Petrarchan movement towards the idealising of 'hell' as 'heauen', in a ceaseless oscillation. The poem is strikingly 'bi-fold' insofar as it does not simply move from ideal to defect, from 'spirit' to 'waste', from 'heauen' to 'hell'. By underlining the continuous movement from 'heaven' to 'hell', the couplet insists on an equally unstoppable motion in the opposite direction, by which 'hell' is elevated and pursued as 'heauen' once more. Even as it decries the contaminating urgency of lust, the sonnet thus recognises the idealising force that informs such carnal pursuit.

The modal positions that Troilus and Cressida respectively occupy in Act 3 Scene 2 appear to correspond to those traditionally assumed to be inscribed in the sonnets: the presumed fidelity of the 'man right fair' seems to match the 'truth' of Troilus, while the promiscuity of the 'woman colloured il' (sonnet 144) is assumed to correspond to Cressida's faithlessness. At the time of their invocations of their names Cressida is not yet unfaithful. Yet such a possibility is entertained exclusively for her, not her lover. The subject positions that can be adopted by men and women, through the modalities of different speech acts, are clearly related to the struggle in the sonnets with the possibility of falsehood in the 'fair friend', the certainty of falsehood in the 'dark woman' and the ambivalent self-recrimination of the poet who is shaped by both modes. The *copulatio*

> POMPEY Indeed it does stink in some sort, sir. But yet, sir,
> I would prove –
> DUKE Nay, if the devil have given thee proofs for sin,
> Thou wilt prove his. – Take him to prison, officer.
> Correction and instruction must both work
> Ere this rude beast will profit.
> *(Measure for Measure, 3.2.292–301)*

Pompey is denied the opportunity to put his proof. Given the chance, I suspect, he would prove, like sonnet 129 and *pace* the Duke/Friar, the *humanity* of such 'touches'.

by which Cressida projects her anticipated falsehood posits a world in which women are always already untrustworthy: 'yet let memory / From false to false among false maids in love / Upbraid my falsehood'. Cressida is herself aware of the ways in which women are always already trapped in an inescapable cycle of falsity – of necessarily being what they are not – through the expectation that they are expected to mask their erotic desires.

This awareness is expressed in a particularly clear-sighted way in the form of a sonnet with which Cressida brings Act 1 Scene 3 to a close. Like sonnet 126, it is in rhyming couplets:

> Words, vows, gifts, tears, and love's full sacrifice
> He offers in another's enterprise;
> But more in Troilus thousandfold I see
> Than in the glass of Pandar's praise may be.
> Yet hold I off. Women are angels, wooing;
> Things won are done. Joy's soul lies in the doing.
> That she beloved knows naught that knows not this:
> Men price the thing ungained more than it is.
> That she was never yet that ever knew
> Love got so sweet as when desire did sue.
> Therefore this maxim out of love I teach:
> Achievement is command; ungained, beseech.
> Then though my heart's contents firm love doth bear,
> Nothing of that shall from mine eyes appear.
> (*Troilus and Cressida*, 1.3.278–91)

This passage is not merely a conglomeration of fourteen lines. It has the structure that we have come to expect from the 1609 Quarto of sonnets: three logically distinct quatrains, followed by a concluding couplet that succinctly conveys Cressida's double course of action and position. Unusually, it presents the female, Petrarchan beloved speaking directly to an audience that excludes her lover, in a confession of why she is adopting the female Petrarchan role of withholding her favours – as if Rosaline (in *Romeo and Juliet*), or the dark mistress or Stella were suddenly to bare their hearts. The message is striking not so much for what it tells us about Cressida's heart or character, but for its revelation of the role of the Petrarchan mistress: a fantasy figure constructed out of the generic necessity of endlessly deferred desire. By self-consciously drawing attention to her required role as a 'false maid in love', Cressida unfolds the iron but unspoken law of the Petrarchan mode: once the beloved is won, the Petrarchan mode is done. Cressida is therefore already marked, before she gives up her name as the epitome of falsehood, by an *imposed* falsehood, which she carries by virtue of being both a sexual and a social, female, being:

> ULYSSES   Fie, fie upon her!
>   There's language in her eye, her cheek, her lip;
>   Nay, her foot speaks. Her wanton spirits look out
>   At every joint and motive of her body.
>   O these encounterers so glib of tongue,
>   That give accosting welcome ere it comes,
>   And wide unclasp the tables of their thoughts
>   To every ticklish reader, set them down
>   For sluttish spoils of opportunity
>   And daughters of the game.   (4.6.55–64)

Unburdened by Romeo's reticence, which refrains from assuming to know what the female body speaks, or to whom that speech is addressed ('I am too bold. 'Tis not to me she speaks' (*Romeo and Juliet*, 2.1.56)), Ulysses articulates an attitude by which the non-idealized body has always already been turned into the very idea of disillusionment. Such violent inscription recalls the 'fair paper', the 'most goodly book, / Made', in Othello's anguished phrase, 'to write "whore" upon' (*Othello*, 4.2.173–4).

When Othello justifies his marriage to Desdemona before the Signory of Venice by reporting her response to the 'story of [his] life':

>   My story being done,
>   She gave me for my pains a world of kisses [sighs – Q].
>   . . .
>   She thanked me,
>   And bade me, if I had a friend that loved her,
>   I should but teach him how to tell my story,
>   And that would woo her   (*Othello*, 1.3.157–165)

it fulfils a fantasy expressed by Astrophil:

>   Then thinke, my deare, that you in me do reed
>   Of Lover's ruin some sad Tragedie:
>   I am not I: pitie the tale of me.
>   (*Astrophil and Stella*, sonnet 45)

It is Othello's *tale* that moves Desdemona. She would fall in love with a substitute were he to tell it. How do such narratives and their relation to 'character' and 'identity' bear upon the roles of names in *Othello*?

The play's names have long been a topic of discussion. Scholars have sought the philological origins of Desdemona and Othello in Greek and Italian.[16] It has been argued that Iago and even Rodrigo suggest a web of historical and ideological connections to the arch-enemy, Spain, via their references to Santiago Matamoros, the 'Moorslayer', and El Cid Campeador, Don Rodrigo Diaz, the liberator of Spain from Moorish rule, respectively.[17] I shall ask, however, how such references relate to the *use* of names in the play through the multiple 'naming events' by which bodies are inscribed with the indelible character of imposed names.[18] From the question of the proper name as rigid designator I move to the more unstable relationships among proper names, common names and epithets, and their shifting use by people other than the bearer of the name. Such uses are performative. They inform and are informed by the relations of power and vulnerability, and they seek to consolidate, transform or negate those relationships through the actions of naming and renaming.

The two avenues along which the names in *Othello* have tradition-ally been explored show two things about the proper name that are, if not contradictory, then certainly in tension. Attempts to discover the meaning of a name such as Desdemona in Greek (either 'ill-starred' or 'God-fearing' (Kahane, 'Desdemona')) follow a Cratylitic desire to make the name match its bearer. Despite our recent attachment to the idea of the arbitrariness of signs, we derive a special satisfaction from the matching of name and the fate or nature of a character in a literary text. Such correspondence attests to the aesthetic design of the author. The name designates an individual in a literary text and, through its meaning, anticipates the plot in which that individual is involved. The meaning of a name may also convey dramatic irony. The character is usually unaware of the significance of her name – the fact that her des-tiny is inscribed, from the beginning, in the hidden (to her) meaning of

---

[16] Henry and Renée Kahane, 'Desdemona: A Star-Crossed Name', *Names*, 35.1–2 (1987), 232–5; F. N. Lees, 'Othello's Name', *Notes and Queries*, 8 (1961), 139–41; T. Sipahigli, 'Othello's Name. Once Again', *Notes and Queries*, 18 (1971), 147–8; Robert F. Fleissner, 'The Moor's Nomencla-ture', *Notes and Queries*, 25 (1978), 143; Samuel L. Macey, 'The Naming of the Protagonist in Shakespeare's *Othello*', *Notes and Queries*, 25 (1978), 143–5.

[17] Barbara Everett, 'Spanish Othello: The Making of Shakespeare's Moor', *Shakespeare Survey*, 35 (1982), 101–12; John Rea, 'Iago', *Names*, 34 (1986), 97–8; and Eric Griffin, 'Un-sainting James: Or, *Othello* and the "Spanish Spirits" of Shakespeare's Globe', *Representations*, 62 (Spring 1998), 58–99.

[18] The analysis that follows is deeply indebted to Carrol Clarkson's superb account of names in Dickens in 'Naming and Personal Identity in the Novels of Charles Dickens: A Philosophical Approach', unpublished DPhil thesis, University of York, England (November 1998). See also, Carrol Clarkson, 'Dickens and the *Cratylus*', *British Journal of Aesthetics*, 30.1 (January 1999), 53–61.

her name. Desdemona does not know that her name signifies her fate, that she is 'ill-starred' in name. Cressida, on the other hand, challenges her fate in her name, thereby calling it into being. We should thus distinguish between 'external' and 'internal' perspectives on a character's name. In the first, the match between character and name is controlled or decided from outside the world of the play. In the 'internal' view, characters in the fictional world see, change or impose particular significance in a proper name through their use of it (Clarkson, *Naming and Personal Identity*). The significance or meaning of a name may thus be invoked or changed *within* the fictional world to inscribe a particular meaning upon a character. *Troilus and Cressida* offers one view of such inscription, whereby a designator, such as 'Cressida' or 'Pandarus', takes on common signification: 'unfaithful woman' or 'whore', 'go-between' or 'pimp'. The inexorable move towards tragedy in *Othello* is marked by a continuous inscription of characters through events of un-naming and re-naming through which the proper name is turned into or replaced by a common name or epithet. The displacement of names is thus not the least of the multiple substitutions so frequently noted in *Othello*.[19]

If the philological interest in characters' names emphasises the meaning of a proper name, the genealogical assimilation of 'Iago' to 'Santiago Matamoros', for example, attests to ways in which even a proper name without any connotation may call up a network of social and historical relations. Apart from any meaning that it may or may not have, as the designator of a specific referent the proper name is the locus of affiliations and filiations that entangle that individual, partly but crucially constituting her identity. Romeo cannot 'tear his name' precisely because he is powerless as an individual to rip the web of social relations and their demands that it entails. The claim that Iago is derived from Santiago Matamoros calls attention to his affiliation with the historically hated Spaniard. And Shakespeare's invention of the name 'Othello' (supposedly by adding to the first syllable of 'Oth-oman' the Italianate '-ello') suggests the conscious and paradoxical or ironical affiliation of the man to the Turks he is employed to fight. Such an affiliation is enacted in the tragic ending, when Othello the Moor executes just such 'a malignant and a turbaned Turk' (5.2.362) by killing himself.

The tension between the two views of the proper name – the one seeking like Cratylus an identification of name as signifier and its designated

---

[19] For an account of displacements that does not focus on names, see Michael Neill, 'Changing Places in *Othello*', *Shakespeare Survey*, 37 (1984), 115–31.

object, so that the name becomes a description or definition of the object; the other emphasising not the meaning of the name but its role as a place-holder in a network of relations – appears in the double designation or designation-description: 'Othello, the Moor'. The proper name, 'Othello' – Shakespeare's addition to the more descriptive designation, 'the Moor', in Cinthio's *Hecatomithi* – introduces a tension between name as designation and name as meaning. But the descriptive designator 'Moor' is rendered unstable through interactive dialogue and its repeated naming events. The play's play with names renders undecidable the significance of this term and complicates its function as a proper name.[20] Nor is such play merely formal: it involves the use of names in relations of power and struggle. Interactive dialogue allows characters to be abused – *un*-named – through the performative act of re-naming. Clarkson describes this process especially succinctly:

> To call someone by name is to place that person in linguistic relation to oneself. To abuse that person's name; wilfully to misuse it; to refuse to use it at all – these are all actions within a naming event which radically redefine the terms of the relations between namer and named. One's proper name thus has a negative potential in that it can become a vulnerable linguistic site of personal abuse and exploitation. But then this is only so ... *because* one of a name's many uses is to constitute a sense of self. (*Naming and Personal identity*, 88)

Othello presents a manifold of such abusive naming events. The play's much noted representations of racism turn either on specific characters' refusal to use Othello's proper (in all senses of the word) name, or their substitution of the proper name with a common name or an epithet that is then used as a proper name: 'thick-lips' (1.1.66), 'black ram' (1.1.88), 'Barbary horse' (1.1.13–14). Each of these uses contaminates the designator 'Othello' by displacing it with a descriptive phrase that is mobilised as a supposedly proper name. Othello is renamed, dislocated from his sense of himself, by the new name's mobilisation of meanings and associations which stem from its place in an ideologically loaded discourse. In the specific events of its interactive discourse, however, the play also repeatedly represents non-racist naming events through which Othello's Moorish affiliations are endorsed or elevated, by calling him 'noble Moor' (2.3.130; 3.4.26; 4.1.266), 'warlike Moor' (2.1.28) or 'valiant Moor' (1.3.47). This

---

[20] For a fine historical account of the complexity and polysemy of the term 'Moor', see Michael Neill, ' "Mulattos", "Blacks", and "Indian Moors": *Othello* and Early Modern Constructions of Human Difference', *Shakespeare Quarterly*, 49.4 (Winter 1998), 361–74.

means that when characters refer to Othello only as 'the Moor', the affiliations or associations of the name cannot be reduced, as often happens in criticism, willy-nilly to its role in a putative system of racist discourse. The inflection of this name is a product of the interaction of individual use and discursive system: one's name, as Clarkson reminds us, has a potential that may be mobilised either negatively or positively. When Emilia refuses to refer to Desdemona's husband as 'Othello' after the murder, pointedly referring to him simply as 'the Moor' ('The Moor has killed my mistress', 5.2.174), she is invoking affiliations that (ironically) align her with her husband. For Othello himself at the end of the play, the appellation 'Moor' produces a dislocation of self that he subsequently enacts through his split suicide:

> Set you down this,
> And say besides that in Aleppo once,
> Where a malignant and a turbaned Turk
> Beat a Venetian and traduced the state,
> I took by th' throat the circumcisèd dog
> And smote him thus.
> (*He stabs himself*)   (5.2.360–5)

Like the tales that win Desdemona's pity, Othello's havering uncertainly between the perfect tense of a historical event and the performative present through which it is actually enacted instantiates Astrophil's curious disavowal, 'I am not I'. And it does so at the very moment in which Othello invites us to 'pity the tale of me'. The self can be split between two instances of the first-person pronoun because it can be divided between two names, 'Venetian' and 'Turk', each bearing a mutually exclusive web of affiliations and values. Our pity is elicited precisely because we recognise the incorrigibility with which Othello is moved towards that dissociation of selfhood ('I am not I') through the competing pressures of different naming events. That Othello comes to see himself as being split between these networks is in part at least due to the ways in which he has been progressively un-named and re-named in the specific kinds of narrative in which Iago embroils both his name and Desdemona's. Such narratives work not merely descriptively but performatively, bringing things about in the saying or naming, but they work only by masking their performative force behind the appearance of description. Iago turns Othello from the 'noble Moor' to the 'turbaned Turk'. But such a splitting of self across two names is not merely debilitating. The notion of himself as 'Venetian' is precisely what *allows* Othello the agency to take the 'circumcisèd dog' 'by th' throat', and to reclaim his affinity with Desdemona through a dying kiss, however discomfited we may feel about the ways in which such actions resonate ideologically.

Othello thus contains two different modes of the proper name. The one, in Clarkson's felicitous expression, is revealed in the fact that while names may be arbitrary with regard to their referents, they are not arbitrary with regard to other names (*Naming and Personal Identity*, 129). The other is revealed in the ease with which someone's proper name may be abused by turning it into or displacing it with a common name, the connotation or meaning of which marks or stigmatises its bearer. I have focused so far on the abuses of Othello's name, which transform him into someone other than he is. What about Desdemona? The extensive critical focus on Othello as protagonist in earlier criticism and as racial Other in more recent commentary has tended to shift Desdemona to the periphery. If Othello suffers conflicting inscriptions of affiliation through the abuse of his name, Desdemona bears the brunt of the process by which a person may be stigmatised and transformed by the substitution of her proper name by a common name: indeed, by the most common of names, 'whore'. And she suffers this at the hands of Othello himself. Before I embark on the analysis of this process, in which the question 'Am I that name?' will be paramount, I turn briefly to the sonnets for an extended exemplification of the play between proper and common names in a pair of poems that move between the pursuit of sexual favour and indulgence in jealous condemnation.

In the poems to the dark woman the player-poet seeks reciprocity, not by idealising or 'hallowing' the name of the mistress, but by the witty, irreverent reduction of his own proper name to the commonest of names. If Sidney's 'Astrophel' proclaims the highly abstracted and elevated nature of the protagonist as the lover of a star, Shakespeare's 'Will' is not merely a more mundane proper name, its punning relation to a variety of common nouns allows its properness to be elided in the particular and single-minded quest for erotic union. Sonnets 135 and 136 are further exercises in the obliteration of the proper name that I have traced in the sonnets to the young man of rank and *Othello*, but to a very different effect and within a dissimilar social world. Insofar as they are rhetorical responses to a woman who refuses the poet's solicitations they may be regarded as Petrarchan.

WHO euer hath her wish,thou hast thy *Will*,
And *Will* too boote,and *Will* in ouer-plus,
More then enough am I that vexe thee still,
To thy sweete will making addition thus.
Wilt thou whose will is large and spatious,
Not once vouchsafe to hide my will in thine,
Shall will in others seeme right gracious,
And in my will no faire acceptance shine:
The sea all water,yet receiues raine still,
And in aboundance addeth to his store,
So thou beeing rich in *Will* adde to thy *Will*,
One will of mine to make thy large *Will* more.
   Let no vnkinde,no faire beseechers kill,
   Thinke all but one,and me in that one *Will*.

                   (Sonnet 135)

IF thy soule check thee that I come so neere,
Sweare to thy blind soule that I was thy *Will*,
And will thy soule knowes is admitted there,
Thus farre for loue, my loue-sute sweet fullfill.
Will, will fulfill the treasure of thy loue,
I fill it full with wils,and my will one,
In things of great receit with ease we prooue.
Among a number one is reckon'd none.
Then in the number let me passe vntold,
Though in thy stores account I one must be,
For nothing hold me,so it please thee hold,
That nothing me,a some-thing sweet to thee.
   Make but my name thy loue,and loue that still,
   And then thou louest me for my name is *Will*.

                  (sonnet 136)

If we accept G. Blakemore Evans's argument that the italics of the Quarto are authorial, then the difference between 'Will' and 'will' in these lines raises the question of the proper name in a different key.[21] Though the punning resonance in the capitalised word to the 'six senses of will' that have been distinguished in these poems should not be ignored,[22] attention to the multivalence of the pun should not blind us to the specific use of the proper name in this context. For the manic repetition of the proper name in the first two lines of sonnet 135 divides and redistributes

---

[21] G. Blakemore Evans (ed.), *The Sonnets* (Cambridge: Cambridge University Press, 1996), 275ff.

[22] *Ibid.*, 253. The six senses, as Evans catalogues them, are: '(a) wish, desire, choice, intent (in both noun and associated verb forms), wilfulness . . . (b) carnal desire, lust . . . (c) shall (expressing definite intention) . . . (d) penis . . . (e) vagina . . . (f) the Christian name Will[iam] (i.e. William Shakespeare and probably at least one other)'.

the excess, which appears at first to be wholly the attribute of the woman, on to the man (or men) who plague(s) her. (The sonnet may refer to three Wills: player-poet, young friend and the woman's husband.) The 'Wills' that 'vexe' her without let ('still'), and among whom the poet regards himself as 'more then enough', are unbearably excessive ('in ouer-plus'). The poem's continuous sliding of proper into common and common into proper names effects precisely what is structurally impossible in *Romeo and Juliet* but constantly attempted in *Othello* – the displacement of the proper name as rigid designator by the common name as a locus of meaning. The dogged persistence of proper names in *Romeo and Juliet* conditions the heightened celebration of sexuality as both a moral and a tragic quality. The erasure of the distinction marked by the proper name in sonnets 135 and 136 destroys everything that *Romeo and Juliet* simultaneously celebrates and laments: the individuality of its protagonists and their entrapment in a network of social relations. It dissolves the distinguishing mark of subjectivity (which is also the defining condition of love) into the semantic and moral morass of farce, by which, in a joky tautology, 'all' – proper name, desire, future, intention, male and female sexual organs – may be 'reckon'd none' (or 'nothing') (sonnet 136).[23]

In tone and feeling, sonnet 135 could not be further from Juliet or Othello's tragic relation to names. For it dissolves, through the reduction of the singular 'Will' to the common 'will', the very distinction that Juliet upholds in committing herself to the difference between 'Romeo' and 'Paris'. Othello is brought to believe that this distinction is destroyed by his wife's supposed accommodation to Cassio's 'will'. Like other young women who wilfully refuse the wills of their fathers by insisting on the singularity of their choice (preferring 'Lysander' above 'Demetrius', for example), Juliet exercises a will which is not totally different from the seldom noticed erotic resistance of her dark sister in the sonnets. In their keenness to emphasise the promiscuity of the latter, commentators tend to overlook the fact that sonnets 127–52 remain deeply Petrarchan insofar as they systematically try to overcome a resisting object of desire. Will's woman is both wholly promiscuous and maddeningly chaste: she is 'tyrannous' and 'cruel' (sonnet 131), but also the 'wide world's common

---

[23] But see Capulet's invitation to Paris to come to the ball so that he may

> . . . hear all, all see,
> And like her most whose merit most shall be,
> Which on more view of many, mine, being one,
> May stand in number, though in reck'ning none.
>
> (1.2.28–31)

place' (sonnet 137). The poems thus appear to be written out of a deep sense of frustration at being rejected by a woman whose aloofness is hardly conventional. Like all Petrarchan mistresses, the dark woman of the sonnets keeps saying 'No', but only to the player-poet himself (or so he says).

Shakespeare's modes of persuasion differ from traditional Petrarchan rhetoric insofar as, unconventionally, the object of desire is perhaps just choosy. The main persuasive device of sonnets 135 and 136 thus negates the logical basis for such discrimination. It extends Theseus's argument that, since there is no difference between Lysander and Demetrius, Hermia might as well take the latter, or the Nurse's suggestion that Paris is an unexceptional substitute for Romeo. Its carnivalesque wit and playfulness run contrary to a system that makes class, blood and female chastity the determining factors in the choice of sexual partners. Indeed, this pair of sonnets is carnivalesque in the now well-known Bakhtinian sense of the term. Their reduction of the social distinctions signified by the proper name to the undiscriminating openness of what Bakhtin calls the 'grotesque body' represents at least an imaginative form of release from the social hierarchy and constraint that is central to both Petrarchan and the patriarchal modes of dealing in and with women.[24] In *Romeo and Juliet* this carnivalesque impulse is represented by Mercutio, who reduces Petrarchan idealism to the mundane materiality of the body porous to the world – 'an open-arse, and . . . popp'rin' pear' (2.1.38).

Sonnet 135 slides from proper name to common name, so that the singularity of the person(s) designated by the name Will, being 'reckon'd none', is obliterated in an undifferentiating sea of sexual desire and the nameless copulation of generic organs – of 'wills'. Following this logic of the negation of 'one', one more penis should make no difference. The woman is asked to allow the name of the penis to count for nothing: to dissolve the differentiating particularity of the proper name, 'Will', into the most common name, 'will'. This request is, of course, a plea for reciprocity, and it bears a perverse relation to the similar pleas to the young man of rank to disregard the differences inscribed in the player-poet's proper name. But it belongs to a different world: one in which there appear to be no differences of rank and blood, certainly none that offer any felt obstacles to the relationship. All such inequalities are merely inconsistencies of 'will', and the linguistic carnival of the poem

---

[24] Mikhail Bakhtin, *Rabelais and his World*, trans. Helene Iswolksy (Bloomington: Indiana University Press, 1984).

seeks to elide even those differences. The proliferation of senses in the excessive punning of the sonnets, as always, results in the obliteration of distinctions, so that by the end of the poem a whole erotic world is contracted into the meeting of 'wills'.

It could be argued that the sonnet's obliteration of the proper name in the undifferentiated *mélange* of common organs represents the ultimate retreat into the private: into an impossible world in which the social disappears altogether. Sonnet 136, however, reverses the argument of 135 by reaffirming the singularity of the proper name as rigid designator, and reasserting a traditional desire for a more limited reciprocity, by which the poet seeks, not the indiscriminate sexual union of sonnet 135, but a relationship in which both constancy and the singularity of his necessarily social identity are reasserted: 'Make but my name thy loue, and loue that still, / And then thou louest me for my name is *Will.*' Having rehearsed the negation of his singularity via the early modern conceit that 'one' is not a number, the poet now enjoins the woman not to forget his name, to love him *for* his name, to count his singular desire. The sonnet thus re-affirms Will as a proper name, to which the woman is enjoined to commit herself ('love that *still*'), although the name has by now wittily accumulated associations that the woman has been shown to love well enough. 'Will', as the proper name that both distinguishes the player-poet from his rivals and marks his rejection by the woman, has by the end of these twenty-eight lines become a paradigm instance of their shared sexual desire and its instruments of consummation. It is supposed to command unstinting commitment from the woman precisely because of her promiscuous desires. But by reaffirming it as his own, the player-poet circumvents the plethora of 'wills' (or 'Wills') that compete for her 'will', urging her instead to fix solely upon him through the proper designation of his name.

Far from being trivial exercises in obscenity or misogyny, sonnets 135 and 136 thus reveal, through their playful manipulation of proper and common name, a logical basis for the distinction between love and lust, tragedy and farce. The excess that these two sonnets perform is not the sexual voraciousness of 'dark' female desire. It is the wilful, male impulse to obliterate all distinctions in the headlong pursuit of sexual gratification. Such a pursuit is recognised (and not only in sonnet 129) as 'had, hauing, and in quest to haue, extreame', and it is attached, here at least, to the proper name of the male. At the same time, read against the aristocratically patriarchal conceits of sonnets 1–17, with their emphasis on self-directed conservation of the male line – in which women are the 'maiden gardens yet vnset' or 'vn-eard wombs' ready for the 'tillage' of the young man's 'husbandry' – these two sonnets are a liberating affront to particular, patriarchal expectations of female chastity and obedience. Such expectations are flouted by Juliet in her heterodox commitment to the bearer of the proper name Romeo to the exclusion of all other males. No such accommodation is available in the world of *Othello*, however. In that play male anxiety about female sexuality refuses the self-deprecatory play with the properness of its own name. Instead it inscribes the female designator with its own projected meaning, writing 'whore' where 'Desdemona' once stood.

In one of the most unbearable scenes of Othello, we watch Desdemona struggling with her inability to speak her name. It is, of course, *not* her name; it is the black name for which her whiteness – this 'fair paper' (4.2.73) as her husband puts it – appears always already to have been prepared. The idea of woman as fair paper or book evokes at once the inscriptions of the sonnet tradition as whole, in which woman is generally written as fairness, and Shakespeare's sonnets in particular, in which she is sealed as darkness. But reading *Othello* and Shakespeare's sonnets together allows us to see the peculiar arbitrariness of that dark inscription, an arbitrariness made horribly clear in Othello's renaming the alabaster Desdemona 'whore'.

I have remarked on the readiness with which most readers take the player-poet at his word regarding the duplicity and faithlessness of the woman of the sonnets. She is assumed in biographical accounts to be one of the countless prostitutes of London. Or else formalist critics take whatever the sonnets tell us about her as the sum total of her properties, since to ask whether she is really as faithless as the player-poet claims would be as egregious an error as to indulge in speculation about Lady Macbeth's children. The formal approach fixes her as whore. The biographical approach at least allows for a re-evaluation of her qualities. By giving her a local habitation and a name, however historically questionable, in the shape of Emelia Lanyer, A. L. Rowse is at least forced to reconsider the assumption that Shakespeare has 'told us everything about her'. The proper name, Emilia Lanyer, designating a person active within a complex set of social relationships, refuses the reductive ideological and moral flattening of the inscribed common name, 'whore'. *Othello* records the flattening and denigration of such renaming, in which the connotation-free designation of the proper name, with its manifold ties to a wide variety of human and social characteristics and forms of agency, is replaced by the overwhelming simplicity of a common meaning that is alien to the person renamed in such a way. Such substitution reduces a plural sense of personal identity to a mark that is literally unbearable and unspeakable by the subject herself.

Desdemona's bewildered response to the repeated naming events by which her husband calls her 'whore' (4.2.89) and 'strumpet' (4.2.84) with the question, 'Am I that name?' (4.2.121), testifies to the powerful degree to which identity is constituted through the proper name (or its displacement by a common noun) in mouths other than that of the bearer of the name. The question, 'Am I that name?', thus reveals a close relationship between 'I am' as an existential and a nominal proposition. Both *Othello* and the sonnets invoke the existential propositions, in either their tautological or contradictory forms, in order to distance the speaker from nominal ties. Iago's 'I am not what I am' (1.1.65) is thus closely related to the player-poet's inverted decree, 'I am that I am' (sonnet 121), insofar as their shared refusal to close the proposition 'I am' with a proper name renounces the social bonds that are usually tied to the proper name. When Desdemona thus asks, 'Am I that name?', she is not merely asking about a label but trying to plumb the depths of herself. Iago's cruelty is more intense for being so casual: 'What name, fair lady?' he asks (4.2.122), underlining the starkness of the disparity between his appellation ('fair lady') and the one he invites her to utter ('whore'). But she cannot utter it. She can do no more than allude to it as a doubly removed object of indirect speech: 'Such as she said my lord did say I was' (4.2.123). Why can Desdemona not bring herself to say the name, if all she would be doing is reporting Othello's speech? Because she senses, in the depths of her soul, that to say the name would be to declare it as her own. Having had her proper name displaced by Othello's insistent, performative re-naming events – see his insistent repetition of the words 'strumpet' and 'whore' against her in 4.2 – she fears that she has no control over the performative outcome of her own utterance of the word. She feels that if she says it out loud she would not merely be reporting what someone else has said – merely mentioning the word, as John Searle would say[25] – but rather declaring it her name: calling out her own, proper name.

Lisa Jardine claims that the fact that Emilia overhears Othello's slander transforms its nature completely. An accusation that moved from

---

[25] For a discussion of the difference between 'use' and 'mention' pertinent to literary studies, see the polemic between Jacques Derrida and John R. Searle collected in Derrida's *Limited Inc*, ed. Gerald Graff (Evanston, IL: Northwestern University Press, 1988).

the private to the public sphere without being gainsaid in public, she suggests, was taken to transform the subject into a whore:

> Othello's doubt is ended, and with it his jealousy, when a case of defamation is perpetrated against Desdemona, and the case is not answered – 'She turn'd to folly, and she was a whore' (v.ii.133). From that point on he acts with complete certainty of her guilt . . . [D]oubt has given way to certainty . . . for Othello, the certainty that entitles the cuckolded husband to seek retribution upon his wife, hinges on that substantial defamation, perpetrated by Othello himself – who 'being a very suspicious man, hath some tyme audiently caulde . . . [his wife] "hore"'.[26]

Anticipating Jardine's argument that the uses of language may change or gain performative dimensions through the introduction of a public context, Madeleine Doran has argued from the historical perspective of Roman law that a man's 'good name' might be lost through an essentially public form of *infamia* or infamy.[27] Crucial to Doran's and Jardine's accounts is the fact that *mala infama* contaminates the name as the locus of personal identity, and that it does so independently of fact. It is not a description that may match or not match its object, but rather an event that transforms the name-bearing object through the imposition of another name. Doran writes that counter-performatives existed in public discourse that could remove *infamia* through forms of *restitutio*, but she adds that it was unclear whether they did in fact have complete power of restoration:

> A man's good name . . . can be taken away as surely by rumour of guilt as by such openly recognized guilt as might lead to an indictment in court; and . . . restoration of it, though possible legally, is difficult, and may in fact be impossible, since the opinion of a man held by the community is not controllable by law . . . the idea that a man's good name is proper to him by virtue of his being a man, not merely an adjunct given him by society, has the consequence . . . that to lose his name is to lose himself. (Doran, 'Good Name in *Othello*', 198)

Desdemona appears to feel the change from a private to a public context intensely. Emilia is unperturbed about using the name in public when Iago unsuccessfully tries to trap Desdemona into doing so, but she is equally aware of the public weight of such a charge: 'He called her whore. A beggar in his drink / Could not have laid such terms upon his

---

26 Lisa Jardine, ' "Why should he call her whore?"': Defamation and Desdemona's Case', in *Addressing Frank Kermode: Essays in Criticism and Interpretation*, ed. Margaret Tudeau Clayton and Martin Warner (London: Macmillan, 1991), 124–53 (144).

27 Madeleine Doran, 'Good Name in *Othello*', *Studies in English Literature 1500–1900*, 7 (1967), 195–217.

callet' (4.2.125–6). The intensely public nature of Desdemona's situation, together with her extreme vulnerability, informs her fear that she would transform herself into the name by uttering it. Her insecure reticence thus stems from her incapacity to place herself at the subjective centre of certain kinds of speech act. In a wonderfully intelligent paper Kenneth Gross claims that 'the characters always hear each other's words as if they were alien, uninterpretable rumours. The game not only makes the questions unanswerable and the words ambiguous, but leaves the words in a deep sense unutterable, unperformable.'[28] To this one wants to say yes and no. Certain words (or rather speech acts) are certainly unutterable or unperformable by someone like Desdemona. Once the private space between herself and her husband has been reduced to nothing by slander, she no longer has access to any public space through which she may perform crucial speech acts: through which she might speak, as Bourdieu puts it, 'not only to be understood but also to be believed, obeyed, respected, distinguished'.[29] Slander is not, as Gross claims, a 'limiting-case of language' ('Slander and Skepticism', Gross, 830); it is its very possibility.[30] And Desdemona can 'find no terms in which to condemn Othello's accusations' (Gross, 'Slander and Skepticism', 838), less through her personal weakness or inadequacy than because, isolated on the military outpost of Cyprus, she is robbed of the conditions that would give such speech acts life. In saying this I am reiterating the argument in chapter 3 above that in certain kinds of society private language games are rendered impossible. In the relatively familiar public world of the Signory Desdemona finds no difficulty in justifying herself and deflecting the imposition of certain kinds of discourse upon her, but she cannot do so on Cyprus.[31]

It is a mistake to speak generally about conditions of discourse in *Othello*, as if all words bend to the same necessity. In the marginal world of the threatened island, Othello's capacity to make certain utterances 'perform' is infinitely greater than that of his wife, even if it is in certain respects dwarfed by Iago's exceptional facility in making words transform

---

[28] Kenneth Gross, 'Slander and Skepticism in *Othello*', *ELH*, 56.4 (Winter 1989), 819–52.
[29] Pierre Bourdieu, 'The Economics of Linguistic Exchanges', *Social Science Information*, 16 (1977), 645–68 (648).
[30] For an extended argument to this effect, see Jacques Derrida, *Limited Inc*.
[31] Lynne Magnusson, 'Language and Symbolic Capital in *Othello*', *Shakespeare Survey*, 50 (1997), 91–9: 'Desdemona does not enter the play as the stereotypical silent and modest woman, but rather as an aristocratic speaker whose discourse is full of the assurance and self-confidence of her class habitus' (94). I am arguing that her capacity for speech in the sense that Bourdieu means it is severely curtailed by the change in public and private space on Cyprus.

situations. In an essay that proceeds from a different theoretical base, but is nonetheless very close to my own project, Lynne Magnusson argues that it is the social site from which speech acts are produced, not the 'essential nature' ('Language and Symbolic Capital', 93) of a character, that determines the possibility of their production and reception. We are liable to overlook the shifting use of words as various speech acts are mobilised through action if we insist too much on what language as a whole does in the play or on the instrinsic nature of signs conceived as things separate from use.

R. W. Zandevoort systematically perpetuates this error by speaking of signs, first, as if they were fixed, coded entities, and then claiming that when they are used to a variety of purposes the sign 'effectively contradict[s] itself', and is consequently 'subversive of the conventions which give codes their meanings'.[32] Signs cannot contradict themselves; only signs put to use in particular speech acts can do so. Nor is Iago's project the 'systematic...attack upon the possibility of signification at large' (Zandevoort, 'Putting Out the Light', 116). If anything, Iago demonstrates the enormous power and effectiveness of signification as a performative act. Such power belongs to actor and ruler alike. To Zandevoort's claim that Iago 'insinuates himself as an infinitely mutable sign whose want of fixed referent calls into question the authority of all other signs' (114) we should respond that it is unclear how a person, or even a character, could be a sign without a fixed referent. What Zandevoort is trying to say, I think, through the mists of Saussurean semiotics, is that Iago, like the Vice of old and the early modern player who succeeded the morality actor, is not tied existentially to the effects and consequences of the speech acts he adopts and discards. Iago can speak of the crucial centrality of one's 'good name' in one context and its insignificance in another because he is not invested in social discourse in the way that Cassio, Desdemona or Othello are. Such detachedness gives him an insuperable advantage against characters who understandably assume that he invests his language games with a normal sense of social identity and moral responsibility. It is his lack of an invested relation to human language – characteristic of the histrionic irresponsibility of old Vice – that makes him so deeply inhuman, so deeply *other* as a character. That is why it is silly to talk of Othello's 'enormous naiveté' (Zandevoort, 'Putting Out the Light', 112), or his 'idiot metaphysics' (Gross, 'Slander

---

[32] R. W. Zandevoort, 'Putting Out the Light: Semantic Indeterminacy and the Deconstitution of Self in *Othello*', *English Studies*, 75 (1994), 110–22 (116).

and Skepticism', 827), or Desdemona's weakness or complicity in the face of such inhumanity.[33]

Iago is a fantasy image of the player-poet of the sonnets, who is himself too invested in the discourses of social inferiority to be able to play fast and loose with them. Iago is the figure – a careless play of performatives – that the player-poet would like to be. If Iago is invested in any social feeling, then it is the envy and resentment at the ways of the world betrayed by the player-poet: at his inferior social position, his inability or unwillingness to play the game whereby

> Many a duteous and knee-crooking knave
> That, doting on his own obsequious bondage,
> Wears out his time much like his master's ass
> For naught but provender, and when he's old, cashiered.
> Whip me such honest knaves. Others there are
> Who, trimmed in forms and visages of duty,
> Keep yet their hearts attending on themselves,
> And, throwing but shows of service on their lords,
> Do well thrive by 'em, and when they have lined their coats,
> Do themselves homage.   (*Othello*, 1.1.45–54)

It would be a mistake to identify either of these positions of service too exactly with the player-poet. What we can recognise, however, is the reach and sharpness of this analysis and diagnosis in those sonnets in which the player-poet either bemoans his fate or looks on with contemptuous detachment at such 'dwellers on forme and fauor' who 'lose all, and more by paying too much rent' (sonnet 125). Othello, one could say, loses all, and more. Iago's resentment and analysis of his inferior social position, signalled in his contempt for Cassio as courtier, his deep understanding of both the centrality and arbitrariness of 'good name' and 'reputation' and his sexual resentment signal a structural affinity with the player-poet of the sonnets. In Iago's unfathomable misogyny, too, there is more than an echo of the disgusted resentment that is projected upon the mistress of the sonnets. Furthermore, Iago's displacement of Desdemona in a quasi-erotic attachment to Othello, signalled especially in the terrible parody of the marriage ceremony at the end

---

[33] Stanley Cavell warns us against this mistake: 'I . . . ask that we not, conventionally but insufferably, assume that we know more about this woman [Desdemona] than this man [Othello] knows her – making Othello some kind of exotic, gorgeous, superstitious lunkhead', *The Claim of Reason: Wittgenstein, Skepticism, Morality, and Tragedy* (Oxford: Oxford University Press, 1982), 488. See Carol Thomas Neely, 'Women and Men in *Othello*', *Shakespeare Studies*, 10 (1978), 133–58, for a discussion of critical responses to Desdemona.

of Act 3, underlines the play's affinity with the dark love triangle in the sonnets:[34]

> ([*Othello*] *kneels*)
>   Now, by yon marble heaven,
>   In the due reverence of a sacred vow
>   I here engage my words.
> IAGO   Do not rise yet.
>   (*Iago kneels*)
>   Witness you ever-burning lights above,
>   You elements that clip us round about,
>   Witness that here Iago doth give up
>   The execution of his wit, hands, heart
>   To wronged Othello's service. Let him command,
>   And to obey shall be in me remorse,
>   What bloody business ever.
>   (*They rise*)
> OTHELLO   I greet thy love,
>   Not with vain thanks, but with acceptance bounteous,
>   And will upon the instant put thee to 't.
>   Within these three days let me hear thee say
>   That Cassio's not alive.
> IAGO   My friend is dead.
>   'Tis done at your request; but let her live.
> OTHELLO Damn her, lewd minx! O, damn her, damn her!
>   Come, go with me apart. I will withdraw
>   To furnish me with some swift means of death
>   For the fair devil. Now art thou my lieutenant.
> IAGO I am your own for ever.
>   (*Exeunt*)   (3.3.463–82)

This catalogue of hellish performatives – oaths, declarations of loyalty and love, constancy and service – offers a distorting glass that reflects the complex forms of rivalry, jealousy, misogynistic rage, and powerful homosocial and/or homosexual fantasies of the marriage of love and duty in Shakespeare's sonnets. If there is a single sonnet that suggests *Othello* more than any other, it is the poem in which triangular desire plays itself out in a remarkably similar scene of devilish temptation and doubt:

> TWO loues I haue of comfort and dispaire,
> Which like two spirits do sugiest me still,
> The better angell is a man right faire:

---

34 See, for example, Robert Matz, 'Slander, Renaissance Discourses of Sodomy, and *Othello*', *ELH*, 66 (1999), 261–76.

The worser spirit a woman collour'd il.
To win me soone to hell my femall euill,
Tempteth my better angel from my sight,
And would corrupt my saint to be a diuel:
Wooing his purity with her fowle pride.
And whether that my angel be turn'd finde,
Suspect I may,yet not directly tell,
But being both from me both to each friend,
I gesse one angel in an others hel.
   Yet this shal I nere know but liue in doubt,
   Till my bad angel fire my good one out.

(sonnet 144)

This poem recalls (or anticipates) the triangular relationship of Iago, Desdemona and Othello, but it inverts those relations. It reminds us, as Stanley Cavell has remarked, of the 'demon' and 'hell' that lurk in the last two names. The play provides a double perspective in which the woman is now 'comfort', now 'dispaire'; now the 'better angell', now the 'worser spirit'. In this reading a subjectivity such as Othello occupies the position of the player-poet, caught between two loves that are both incarnations of doubt. Of course, the positions do not match exactly. Othello is not trapped by the uncertainty of whether Desdemona is betraying him with Iago, although he does think that she is doing so with Cassio. We may, however, see in the sonnet the pathology of projection and rivalry that mark Othello's relationship with his ancient and his wife. And the play's perspectives may in turn alert us to the pathology of the poems themselves. Othello's collapse into groundless but uncontrollable rage and disgust at the dark uncontrollability of female sexuality allows us to entertain the thought that sonnet 144 – indeed, all the poems in which the mistress's supposedly profligate sexuality are excoriated – records, not the certainty of betrayal, but the lacerations of doubt and projection whereby the female beloved is turned into a 'worser spirit' or the 'wide worlds common place' (sonnet 137), while the male remains the 'better angell' to be rescued from her fiendish consumption. The 'marriage' between Iago and Othello in the passage above, signalled by Iago's resounding performative, 'I am your own for ever' (3.3.482), and occasioned by Othello's final resolution to eradicate the 'fair devil' (3.3.814), provides a terrifying parody of the implicit desire in the sonnets for 'mutuall render', uncontaminated by social difference or the rivalry of female sexuality.

The player-poet of the sonnets sees ugliness and darkness but is bewildered by his attraction to it; Othello, on the other hand, sees beauty and fairness but is bewildered by the fact that it may in fact be ugly and dark. But the reiterated pathology of the sonnets comes to an end in the play because Othello believes that killing the thing he loves (see *Twelfth Night*, 5.1.117) will forge a path out of the madness that is lived in the darkness of the sonnets for the woman: of loving what you hate, of being attracted to what is essentially ugly. This is the 'cause' with which Othello reassures his soul: to allow Desdemona to live would mean to perpetuate the living hell in which the player-poet resides, trapped by his disease into 'feeding on that which doth preserve the ill' (sonnet 147). Othello, feeling himself progressively bewitched by 'balmy breath, that dost almost persuade / Justice to break her sword' (5.2.16–7), entranced by 'the whiter skin of hers than snow, / And smooth as monumental alabaster' (5.2.4–5), encapsulates the dilemma of sonnet 148:

> O ME ! what eyes hath loue put in my head,
> Which haue no correspondence with true sight,
> Or if they haue,where is my iudgment fled,
> That censures falsely what they see aright ?
> If that be faire whereon my false eyes dote,
> What meanes the world to say it is not so ?
> If it be not,then loue doth well denote,
> Loues eye is not so true as all mens:no,
> How can it? O how can loues eye be true,
> That is so vext with watching and with teares?
> No maruaile then though I mistake my view,
> The sunne it selfe sees not,till heauen cleeres.
> O cunning loue,with teares thou keepst me blinde,
> Least eyes well seeing thy foule faults should finde.

Despite the lingering kisses through which Othello postpones the murder, he ultimately refuses to live the dilemma that is ceaselessly reiterated in the sonnets. Better to 'kill thee / And love thee after' (5.2.18).

'How can loues eye be true?' sonnet 148 asks. Cavell reminds us that, in the moments before he kills her, Othello turns Desdemona to stone (*The Claim of Reason*, 489). If the player-poet comes close to turning his dark lord to stone, or finding him, ultimately, 'as stone' (sonnet 94), he marks his difference from the 'loues eye' that plagues Othello by refusing to transform his mistress in this way. Such holding back is one of the most remarkable things about Shakespeare's sonnets. It enables the poet to delineate the troubling relationship of 'loues eye' to the idea or the ideal in ways that do not merely settle on either simple disillusionment or idealisation.[35] The transformations traced in this chapter through the performative power of names and naming events have tended to work against the interests and desires of individuals. I now turn to ways in which individual subjects, especially women, may use the agency of performative action to transform themselves from a mere name to the thing itself in *All's Well that Ends Well.*

[35] See Cavell's claim that *Othello* 'is a play . . . in which not a marriage but the idea of marriage, or let us say an imagination of marriage, is worked out' (*The Claim of Reason*, 486).

CHAPTER 5

Transformations: the sonnets and All's Well that Ends Well

In the previous chapter I traced the ways in which a name may act as more than a mere designator in the worlds of Shakespeare's plays and sonnets. From its action as a focal point of ineradicable social relations and ties in *Romeo and Juliet* and the sonnets, through its idealising and de-idealising use in *Troilus and Cressida* and the dark-woman poems, to its transformative power in the naming and re-naming events of *Othello*, I have argued that the proper name may be as much part of the performative dimensions of language use as more syntactically elaborate utterances. In this chapter I pursue the question of names as one thread within the broader text of *All's Well that Ends Well* and its much noted relationship to Shakespeare's sonnets. Helen's predicament represents the limits of what names can do. Being merely 'the name and not the thing' (*All's Well*, 5.3.310), she has to seek performative modes of action beyond language that can transform her from 'name' to 'thing'. The framing analysis for the role of names in *All's Well* includes an extended re-examination of the much noted affinities between the play and the sonnets, the politics of gender and class in the play and the poems, and the subject positions and embodied situations of address of the sonnets that are represented within in the play.

All's Well that Ends Well has long been recognised as a play intimately connected with the felt experience of slighted love under the pressures of class inequality in the sonnets. G. Wilson Knight claims that it 'recalls the Sonnets more nearly than any other play'.[1] More recently, Susan Snyder notes that the reworking of the original story from Boccaccio signals

---

[1] E. M. W Tilyard, *Shakespeare's Problem Plays* (Harmondsworth: Peregrine, 1951), 106; G. Wilson Knight, *The Sovereign Flower: Shakespeare as the Poet of Royalism* (London: Methuen, 1958), 157–8; Muriel Bradbrook, 'Virtue is the True Nobility: A Study of the Structure of *All's Well that Ends Well*', *Review of English Studies*, 26 (1950), 289–301 (301); Roger Warren, 'Why Does It End Well?: Helen, Bertram, and the Sonnets', *Shakespeare Survey*, 22 (Spring 1969), 79–92.

the common origin of both the sonnets and the play in 'Shakespeare's own experience',[2] and Richard Wheeler argues that, while '*All's Well* imposes a rigorous, compensatory, even vindictive dramatic structure upon a love that in the Sonnets repeatedly betrays the dedicated idealization Shakespeare brings to it', Helen's love for Bertram nonetheless also extends into the play 'the eloquent adoration that Shakespeare lavishes on the young friend'.[3]

Whatever one may think about such links it is clear that *All's Well* and the poems induce a similar, paradoxical sense of admiration and enigma, engagement and discomfort. *All's Well that Ends Well* opens up a world that is glimpsed intermittently in the dispersed shards of the sonnets. It represents an intense and exorbitant erotic desire rendered almost impossible by the extent of its social ambition. It also offers as the unworthy object of that desire a spoilt, self-absorbed young aristocrat who flees heterosexual union in marriage on the one hand, while seeking a brief, lust-driven seduction on the other. What the sonnets are forced to suggest by rhetorical indirection, because of the way in which their protagonist is caught within each moment and situation of address, the play can display with greater freedom and detachment. Shakespeare's player-poet has to create the conditions for his acceptance as a member of the society of supplicants, even before any particular request has been made or wish granted. By displacing the uncertainty of response, which is generically and contextually central to the writing of a sonnet as a means of real social action, on to a theatrical space in which the represented audience can be taken for granted rather than encountered as a force to be deflected, moulded or appropriated, Shakespeare finds a degree of freedom that eludes him as a sonneteer. When Susan Snyder claims that in its relation to the sonnets *All's Well that Ends Well* is 'one giant act of displacement' ('The King's Not Here', 31), she is perhaps thinking of precisely the freedom of the dramatist to create a world in which personal preoccupations or predicaments may be 'worked through' in ways not available to the sonneteer. The socially engaged poet lacks the power to control the contexts of his reception, or to represent more detached forms of judgement on those contexts in the shape of characters from which he can distance himself.

---

[2] Susan Snyder, 'The King's Not Here: Displacement and Deferral in *All's Well that Ends Well*', *Shakespeare Quarterly*, 42.1 (Spring 1992), 20–32 (30).

[3] Richard P. Wheeler, *Shakespeare's Development and the Problem Comedies: Turn and Counter-Turn* (Berkeley, Los Angeles and London: University of California Press, 1981), 60.

The connections between *All's Well that Ends Well* and Shakespeare's sonnets are worth pursuing for their illumination of the complexities of the comedy as much as the vexed issues of sexuality, identity and performative interaction in the poems. But they should not be pursued by equating any role in the sonnets with any single character in the play. The notion of multiple 'subject positions' offers a more useful tool for exploring the ways in which the interactive world of the play is informed by the shadow world of the sonnets. Bertram, variously charged in the course of the play for his youthful failings – 'proud, scornful boy' (2.3.152), 'rash and unbridled boy' (3.2.28) and 'foolish idle boy' (4.3.220) – is clearly a severely disillusioned rewriting of the 'sweet' and 'lovely boy' (sonnets 108 and 126) of the sonnets. And Helen embodies the self-effacing longing for a love object placed beyond reach by socially inscribed hierarchies expressed by the player-poet of the sonnets. And yet the parallels do not work consistently. The unspeakable sexual desire branded as 'ambitious' that we recognise in Helen is differently gendered in the sonnets. Furthermore, the player-poet shares Bertram's darker attitude towards female sexuality. To see Helen as the embodiment of Shakespeare's unspeakable desire for his 'friend' is to eroticise that 'friendship' and to further complicate the gendering of the player-poet's desire. This complication hardly exists in the play. Helen's love is frankly erotic. Her dotage on Bertram displays an urgent physicality that is certainly present in the sonnets, but there it is split between the player-poet and his distinctly unchaste female object of desire. It is difficult to equate the poems to the dark mistress with any woman in *All's Well that Ends Well*, unless we recognise in Bertram's slander of Diana the persistent attitude of the lover to his mistress, perhaps to all women, in the sonnets. In some respects the player-poet of Shakespeare's sonnets resembles Bertram as much as he does Helen. And then there is Paroles. Paroles is frequently dismissed for being the 'villain' of the play, derided by external critic and internal aristocrat alike for his wordiness, his cowardice and, above all, the temerity with which he assumes the ambitious roles of gentleman and friend to Bertram. But he bears a more than passing resemblance to our player-poet. He is a sonneteer and Bertram's rival in love, and his habit of making himself 'a motley to the view' through his upstart profession of words, fictions and 'borrowed flaunts' (*The Winter's Tale*, 4.4.23) brings public disgrace to his aristocratic companion.

If the subject positions represented and explored in the sonnets may be distributed across different forms of interaction and relationship in *All's Well that Ends Well*, the First Folio itself represents character and role in relational and provisional, rather than monolithic and permanent ways. *All's Well that Ends Well* in particular works against the 'transcendent unity' ascribed by modern modes of thought 'to the notion of individual, isolated character' (Cloud, '"The very names of Persons"', 93). This has been obscured by the editorial practice of reducing the multiplicity of speech tags in the Folio to a single, arbitrarily chosen, 'proper' name or epithet. Writing of editorially imposed lists of dramatis-personae (coupled to arbitrary, conservative descriptions), Random Cloud states:

> These lists imply that characters are solid entities,
> The Countess
> that pre-exist their functions in the play, rather than illusions
> now *mother* now *Old Countess* now *Lady* . . .
> built up out of the simultudinous dynamic of *all* the ingredients of
> dramatic art, of which character is only a part.[4]

'Now *mother* now *Old Countess* now *Lady*' aptly describes the sense of 'character' to be gleaned from Shakespeare's sonnets: now *counsellor*, now *lover*, now *player*, now *friend*, now *aristocrat*, now *lecher*, now *beauty*, now *whore*, now *mother*.[5] If we wish to explore these contrasting and overlapping aspects of 'character', developed differentially through interaction, we need to distribute them across the roles or subject positions of *All's Well that Ends Well*.

My argument in the Introduction above that the absence of proper names from the sonnets is a logical pointer to the autobiographical nature of the 1609 sonnets does not depend upon any unitary conception of character or experience. Nor is it vitiated by Random Cloud's indication of the changing, relational nature of the name tags in *All's Well that Ends Well*. My view of the autobiographical mode of the sonnets is compatible with the notion that the presentation of self and its relation to others is liable to vary through that very interaction. Montaigne's sense of the dispersal of self through different moments and perspectives is underscored by the sonnets' enactment of a similar disjunction:

---

[4] Random Cloud, ' "The very names of Persons": Editing and the Invention of Dramatic Character', in *Staging the Renaissance: Reinterpretations of Elizabethan and Jacobean Drama*, ed. David Scott Kastan and Peter Stallybrass (London and New York: Routledge, 1991), 88–96 (91). Cf. Susan Snyder, 'Naming Names in *All's Well that Ends Well*', *Shakespeare Quarterly*, 42.3 (Fall 1992), 265–79. Snyder's argument that readers would be better able to sustain imaginatively a unified conception of the main characters if 'character names of minimum importance are not featured in the text' (279) is made on behalf of the very tradition that Random Cloud attacks.

[5] See Naomi Miller, 'Playing "the mother's part": Shakespeare's Sonnets and Early Modern Codes of Maternity', in *Shakespeare's Sonnets: Critical Essays*, ed. James Schiffer (New York: Garland, 1999), 347–68.

Even sound authors are wrong in stubbornly trying to weave us into one invariable and solid fabric . . . Anyone who turns his prime attention on to himself will hardly ever find himself in the same state twice. I give my face this face or that, depending upon which side I lay it down on. I speak about myself in diverse ways: that is because I look at myself in diverse ways. Every sort of contradiction can be found in me, depending upon some twist or attribute: timid, insolent; chaste, lecherous; talkative, taciturn; tough, sickly; clever, dull; brooding, affable; lying, truthful; learned, ignorant; generous, miserly and then prodigal – I can see something of all that in myself, depending on how I gyrate; and anyone who studies himself attentively finds in himself and in his very judgement this whirring about and this discordancy. There is nothing I can say about myself as a whole simply and completely, without intermingling and admixture.[6]

There are two sonnets in the body of *All's Well that Ends Well*. Strangely, they have been passed over by all of the critics who have explored the parallels between the play and Shakespeare's sonnets in thematic and psychological terms. The first is hardly a 'good' sonnet, considered in 'literary' terms. Compared even to the poorest of the 1609 Quarto, it plods. Yet it comes out of a remarkable situation of address:

> I am Saint Jaques' pilgrim, thither gone.
> Ambitious love hath so in me offended
> That barefoot plod I the cold ground upon
> With sainted vow my faults to have amended.
> Write, write, that from the bloody course of war
> My dearest master, your dear son, may hie.
> Bless him at home in peace, whilst I from far
> His name with zealous fervour sanctify.
> His taken labours bid him me forgive;
> I, his despiteful Juno, sent him forth
> From courtly friends, with camping foes to live,
> Where death and danger dogs the heels of worth.
> He is too good and fair for death and me;
> Whom I myself embrace to set him free.

(3.4.4–17)

It is an epistolary sonnet, addressed to the Countess by Helen. Her steward reads it out publicly, before the other members of the court. Unusually, it is a sonnet addressed by a woman to another woman, read aloud by a man. It concerns unrequited love. But its circuit excludes the object of desire in a direct appeal to the mother-in-law. It is therefore a public declaration, not only of female desire, but also of such desire

---

[6] Michel Montaigne, *The Essays of Michel de Montaigne*, trans. and ed. M. A. Screech (Harmondsworth: Penguin, 1991), ii.1, 'On the inconsistency of our actions', 373–7.

rejected and transformed. It recalls, glancingly and ironically, the confidently rhetorical question in the sonnets: 'And when a woman woes, what womans sonne, / Will sourely leaue her till he haue preuailed?' (sonnet 41). It calls into question not only the predatory view of female sexuality in that sonnet, but also its assumption of the naturalness of male libidinous response, which in sonnet 41 at least, deftly converts female agency into male action: 'till *he* haue preuailed'.

Helen's sonnet comes closer to Petrarch than many in the 1609 Quarto. It gives up the physical beloved in favour of a spiritual pilgrimage, and its wish to save the beloved from death by renouncing all erotic claims on him recalls the player-poet's thought of his own death in order to 'set [the beloved] free' from the stigma of 'ambitious love'. It is simultaneously a declaration of achieved status through action and a form of action in itself, powerfully urging the addressee to reproduce in turn its own rhetorical activity. The sonnet is almost obsessively concerned with the performative in its transformation of human relationships and status. Written from a position that Austin would term 'unhappy', it attests to its writer's being a 'wife' in name only: 'the name and not the thing' (*All's Well That Ends Well*, 5.3.310). And yet, that is not quite true. For it presumes upon and draws its power from family relationships that have indeed been forged by the (unconsummated) marriage, especially those of daughter and mother-in-law. Helen derives her freedom to write in such a confident way to the Countess – to presume upon the good grace of her *as* mother-in-law – from the relationships that her sonnet invokes rather than merely reports or describes. The double appellation, 'my dearest master, your dear son', ties her to the older woman through a shared bond with Bertram. As descriptions, these phrases are redundant; but as invocations they serve to place addresser and addressee in a reciprocal relationship which combines ties of social subordination and familial love. The opening line is likewise a performative transformation of status rather than a description: it is the verbal action by which Helen transforms herself from disappointed wife to penitent pilgrim.

Helen is thus acutely aware of the power of the performative. Having achieved Bertram in name through the King's promise, she now engages in further illocutionary acts ('bless', 'sanctify' and 'forgive') through the sonnet:

> Bless him at home in peace, whilst I from far
> His name with zealous fervour sanctify.
> His taken labours bid him me forgive ...

Despite the self-recriminatory tone of the sonnet, Helen does not relinquish her own agency. Seeking to undo the consequences of her translation of Bertram into reticent husband, willing soldier and supposed stranger to his 'courtly friends', she imposes upon the Countess all the urgency of her own will. 'Write, write', she charges her socially superior addressee, in a command conveyed through the mouth of a mediating servant. The immediate success of that injunction is signalled in the Countess's reiteration of the command in all its urgency back to and through her subordinate: 'Write, write', she enjoins her steward, 'To this unworthy husband of his wife' (3.4.29–30). She thereby accepts and adopts Helen's performative agency.

The circuit of this sonnet is therefore circuitous. Beginning as a self-recriminating renunciation of 'ambitious love', it is reversed via the Countess, who re-imposes the obligation of that love upon a recalcitrant husband and wayward son. It is a rebuke that achieves the very contrary of what it appears to say. The words that it provokes from the Countess – 'Ah what sharp stings are in her mildest words!' (3.4.18) – suggest themselves as a motto of the player-poet's sonnets to his young man, similarly distant and desired as an object of 'ambitious love'. Such stings are, of course, not written on the plain face of the poem or the sonnets. Why does Helen direct her sonnet to her mother-in-law and not to her husband? Because its performative appeal would pass him by. He would not recognise or acknowledge the moral force, the stinging irony, of her self-abnegation. It takes social pressure – a public audience of some power – to get Bertram to acknowledge both his own unworthiness and what it means to be told, in the fullest sense of the word and the relationship, 'of his wife' (3.4.30). Helen is aware of that audience, and, like her creator, she plays to its gallery with all the theatrical power she can muster. That power (which is simultaneously a recognition of her lack of power) lies in the knowledge that the 'mildest words' can contain the 'sharpest stings', and in the canny way in which this sonnet understands the indirections by which such stinging words must achieve their ends.[7]

Like the player-poet's sonnets to a similarly untrustworthy, aloof and intensely desired young man, Helen's sonnet claims to 'sanctify' the beloved's 'name' while simultaneously recognising that her own name (as addresser) achieves, at least in the eyes of some, the contrary effect

---

[7] For an account of such indirections in the discourses of politeness, see Lynne Magnusson, *Shakespeare and Social Dialogue: Dramatic Language and Elizabethan Letters* (Cambridge: Cambridge University Press, 1999).

through its contaminating action. The difference between the sonnets and this sonnet lies in the broader society through which their performatives may or may not achieve their goals. In a perhaps deliberate act of creative wish-fulfilment, the dramatist-poet creates a social world that is generally sympathetic to the claims of Helen's peculiarly 'ambitious love'. The 1609 Quarto lacks both the miraculous cure of the monarch and a generally benevolent court that may be seduced into siding with the deserving underdog. That is not to say, however, that the Quarto sonnets can dispense with the engagement of an audience – similarly, through indirection – by which Helen's letter-sonnet finds its mark. Her task is to find a way of transforming the status she suffers in the limbo of an unconsummated marriage through a different kind of performative, one that becomes apparent only when she hears of her husband's desire for Diana. Only then can she use the force of that desire to transformative purposes, showing how in Bertram's lust and loathing 'very force entangles / Itself with strength' (*Antony and Cleopatra*, 4.15.48–9). Here the asymmetry of power between men and women is acutely noted: if it is in the power of men to transform the mere ceremony of marriage into the thing itself through the force of will, women notoriously lack such direct power. To them fall the indirections of the bed-trick, by which the force of illegitimate male desire may be deflected, performatively, to turn them from 'name' into 'thing'.

The second of the sonnets in *All's Well that Ends Well* is equally intriguing in terms of its situation of address. It has received even less attention than Helen's, perhaps because, having only nine lines, it does not appear to be a sonnet at all. The First Lord Dumaine, however, calls it a sonnet. The dramatically effective hiatus between the opening and subsequent lines indicates that a full sonnet is being suggested dramatically rather than replicated textually:[8]

INTERPRETER Here 'tis, here's a paper. Shall I read it to you?
PAROLES I do not know if it be it or no.
BERTRAM (*aside*) Our interpreter does it well.
FIRST LORD DUMAINE (*aside*) Excellently.
INTERPRETER (*reads the letter*)
    'Dian, the Count's a fool, and full of gold.'
PAROLES That is not the Duke's letter, sir. That is an advertisement to a proper
    maid in Florence, one Diana, to take heed of the allurement of one Count

---

[8] The first line, which rhymes with nothing that follows, suggests that the three lines that would make up the first quatrain with a traditional abab rhyme scheme are not read out aloud.

Roussillon, a foolish idle boy, but for all that very ruttish. I pray you, sir, put it up again.

INTERPRETER Nay, I'll read it first, by your favour.

PAROLES My meaning in 't, I protest, was very honest in the behalf of the maid, for I knew the young Count to be a dangerous and lascivious boy, who is a whale to virginity, and devours up all the fry it finds.

BERTRAM (*aside*) Damnable both-sides rogue.

INTERPRETER (*reads*)
'When he swears oaths, bid him drop gold, and take it.
After he scores he never pays the score.
Half-won is match well made; match, and well make it.
He ne'er pays after-debts, take it before.
And say a soldier, Dian, told thee this:
Men are to mell with, boys are not to kiss.
For count of this, the Count's a fool, I know it,
Who pays before, but not when he does owe it.
Thine, as he vowed to thee in thine ear,
Paroles.'

(4.3.211–37)

Like Helen's, Paroles's sonnet takes a circuitous route. Addressed on behalf of Bertram to Diana, it is read out publicly to a wider audience by someone other than its author. The usual directions of address are reversed in a comic splitting of authorship and the reintegration of the author into the audience: both Bertram as the supposed 'begetter' of the sonnet and Paroles as the proxy author are now members of the sonnet's audience. The sonnet, as it turns out, is neither a blazon of Diana's beauty nor the 'loyal cantons of contemnèd love' (*Twelfth Night*, 1.5.259) that Orsino's proxy promises to deliver on his behalf. It is a hard-headed piece of advice to Bertram's object of desire to insist on payment in advance. But it is also a piece of blunt wooing by Paroles 'for himself'.[9] Again, like Helen's sonnet, Paroles's is not merely descriptive. It warns about the dangers of involving oneself with 'boys', and follows that warning

---

[9] Cf. *Much Ado About Nothing*, 1.5.164–72:

> 'Tis certain so, the Prince woos for himself.
> Friendship is constant in all other things
> Save in the office and affairs of love.
> Therefore all hearts in love use their own tongues.
> Let every eye negotiate for itself,
> And trust no agent; for beauty is a witch
> Against whose charms faith melteth into blood.
> This is an accident of hourly proof,
> Which I mistrusted not. Farewell, therefore, Hero.

Orsino is quick to assume a similar degree of treachery in Cesario's proxy wooing.

with a frank insinuation of himself in his master's place. That Bertram should now be the primary audience of this supposed slander, written simultaneously upon and in his name, is both comically and morally appropriate. A by now eager witness to the undoing of his companion ('Our interpreter does it well'), he suddenly finds himself undone through the stinging representation of himself as a 'foolish idle boy' and 'whale to virginity'. This is possible only because the occasion is public. Bertram as spectator is uncomfortably positioned into looking at himself as the object of the pejorative gaze: the plotter hoist with his own petard.[10] Whereas the Lords Dumaine can laugh at the outlandishness of Paroles's slanders upon themselves – treating them as a series of entertaining fictions, laughable in their extravagance – Bertram can only squirm and sulk because the sonnet that reflects so badly on him does so in his own name. The Second Lord Dumanine pointedly asks Paroles for a copy of it. Like the sonnet found by Holofernes in *Love's Labour's Lost* and rerouted to another recipient, Paroles's sonnet will recirculate far from its original point of address as indelible testimony of its 'onlie begetter's' moral failure. This movement represents the recirculation of sonnets as alienable texts beyond the control of their authors. It suggests that the import of the sonnet as a form of essentially public discourse extended even beyond the 'private friends' to whom the poet might have wished to confine his or her work (see Marotti, *John Donne*).

There is no direct correlation between Shakespeare and Paroles. Wheeler, who has also noticed a structural similarity between them, remarks that 'the handling of Paroles . . . suggests a savage parody of the love expressed for the young friend in the *Sonnets*' (*Shakespeare's Development*, 70). As a man of fictive words and borrowed clothes, a member of a lowly profession who lives off a young aristocrat through friendship and flattery, Paroles suggests the profession and the position of the writer of the sonnets. He is disliked and resented by the young count's noble contemporaries, accused of dishonouring Bertram's name through his mere proximity to him and of actively leading him astray. But there is no evidence in the play itself of the latter vice. Even if Paroles does little to discourage Bertram from headstrong behaviour, the accusations are no more than a class-conscious projection of Bertram's lack of proper nobility on to a convenient scapegoat, and the plot that unmasks Paroles turns out to be more damaging to Bertram. If anything, Paroles's sonnet

---

[10] He is therefore hoodwinked twice: by the bed-trick and by the trick played upon Paroles.

to Diana suggests both his clear-headed awareness of the shallowness of
his aristocratic companion and his readiness to engage in sexual rivalry
with him. Paroles's response to his gulling is similar to those final sonnets
in which the player-poet affirms his independent integrity. 'Who cannot
be crushed with a plot?' (4.3.326), Paroles asks, a question that both uni-
versalises his condition and looks ironically forward to Bertram's own
undoing by the bed-trick. More significant, however, is his clear-headed
affirmation of identity and agency:

> Captain I'll be no more,
> But I will eat and drink and sleep as soft
> As captain shall. *Simply the thing I am*
> *Shall make me live.* Who knows himself a braggart,
> Let him fear this, for it will come to pass
> That every braggart shall be found an ass.
> Rust, sword; cool, blushes; and Paroles live
> Safest in shame; being fooled, by fool'ry thrive.
> There's place and means for every man alive.
> I'll after them.
> (*All's Well That Ends Well* 4.3.332–41; emphasis added)

Compare sonnet 121:

> T I S better to be vile then vile esteemed,
> When not to be,receiues reproach of being,
> And the iust pleasure lost,which is so deemed,
> Not by our feeling,but by others seeing.
> For why should others false adulterat eyes
> Giue salutation to my sportiue blood?
> Or on my frailties why are frailer spies;
> Which in their wils count bad what I think good?
> Noe,I am that I am,and they that leuell
> At my abuses,reckon vp their owne,
> I may be straight though they them-selues be beuel
> By their rancke thoughtes,my deedes must not be shown
>   Vnlesse this generall euill they maintaine,
>   All men are bad and in their badnesse raigne.

If, in sonnets such as 36 and 87, the player-poet suffers under the class-
directed gaze of public opinion, and in sonnet 96 he aligns himself with
that gaze for his own purposes, sonnet 121 marks a shift away from such
a public world altogether, through an affirmation of personal independence and integrity that is discernible in dramatic characters as different
as Paroles and Edmund, Bottom and Iago, Falstaff and Achilles. Insofar as

it is difficult to tell whether the 'sportiue blood' that features in sonnet 121 is an accepted quality of the player-poet or a projection of 'frailer spies', it is similar to the equivocating insinuations of sonnet 96. The point of the poem, however, lies not in whether or not the writer is guilty of the behaviour attributed to him by a world steeped in intrigue, conspiracy and vice. It lies in the clear-headed performative that informs the sonnet at every level: its declaration of independence, which, in the words of the Old Testament divinity, refuses judgement in the name of a resolutely egalitarian principle. How different sonnet 121 is from other sonnets, such as sonnet 112 below, in which the world of public opinion is abjured:

> Your loue and pittie doth th'impression fill,
> Which vulgar scandall stampt vpon my brow,
> For what care I who calles me well or ill,
> So you ore-greene my bad,my good alow?
> You are my All the world,and I must striue,
> To know my shames and praises from your tounge,
> None else to me,nor I to none aliue,
> That my steel'd sence or changes right or wrong,
> In so profound *Abisme* I throw all care
> Of others voyces,that my Adders sence,
> To cryttick and to flatterer stopped are:
> Marke how with my neglect I doe dispence.
>   You are so strongly in my purpose bred,
>   That all the world besides me thinkes y'are dead.

Here the young man displaces 'all the world' in a move that we recognise from sonnet 23: through a withdrawal into a 'private' world of mutual love in which the lovers live as reflections of each other's light. 'Lovers can see to do their amorous rites / By their own beauties' (*Romeo and Juliet*, 3.2.8–9), as Juliet puts it. Sonnet 112 neither declares the innocence of its speaker nor proclaims his transcendence of a social existence. 'Vulgar scandall', whether as his acknowledged bad behaviour or as a form of projection inscribed upon him by the ill thoughts of a prejudiced public, indubitably marks the player-poet's existence within a social world. Turning his back on that world in an affirmation of the beloved's opinion is neither a declaration of total, individual independence nor a denial of any 'shames' that may accrue to him. It merely shrinks that social world to a Donne-like couple, reaffirming the public existence of the individual through the other by turning the conventional lover's platitude that 'you are all the world to me' into an intensified recognition of dependency. By contrast, 121 appears to go further than merely declaring the world outside the relationship 'dead' as long as the beloved plays his role by 'ore-green[ing] [his] bad' and 'alow[ing] [his] good'. Its Jehovian tautology, eschewing the relativism by which one lover exists as a mirror to the other, rejects not only the 'others voyces' that make up a broader public of 'cryttick and ... flatterer' (sonnet 112), but also, crucially, the dependency upon the beloved that is so strongly affirmed in 112. For all its declarative force, 112 remains a plea for reciprocity. It affirms 'loue and pittie' in its opening line in order to bring it into being. Sonnet 121, on the other hand, refuses even that reduced world of fragile dependence and reciprocity. This is the refusal that we recognise in Paroles's remarkably clear-headed declaration of independence, evident in the *relief* with which he accepts a life lived 'safest in shame' and resolves that 'being fool'd, by foolery thrive'.

Paroles's fate after this declaration reminds us that no speech act, however resounding, can deny a person's existence as a social being. The failed social upstart finds a new, and at times humiliating, existence for himself serving the Lord Lafew. The declaration of independence that the player-poet makes through the implication of the common, ironically levelling 'badness' in which 'all men ... raigne' might dissolve the humiliating pressures of specific ties, but life must go on in its relation to a myriad of other constructive and trammelling social relationships. Sonnet 87, with its curiously falling, tenuous rhymes and its attempt to rationalise the moral turpitude of taking back a gift already given, is reminiscent of the nature of the world from which the player-poet derives his strength and scandal alike. It confirms the only power by which he, like Paroles, could be a 'king' in a world that conspires to unmask him: the world of flattering dreams:

> FArewell thou art too deare for my possessing,
> And like enough thou knowst thy estimate,
> The Charter of thy worth giues thee releasing:
> My bonds in thee are all determinate.
> For how do I hold thee but by thy granting,
> And for that ritches where is my deseruing?
> The cause of this faire guift in me is wanting,
> And so my pattent back againe is sweruing.
> Thy selfe thou gau'st,thy owne worth then not knowing,
> Or mee to whom thou gau'st it,else mistaking,
> So thy great guift vpon misprision growing,
> Comes home againe,on better iudgement making.
> > Thus haue I had thee as a dreame doth flatter,
> > In sleepe a King,but waking no such matter.

The two sonnets from *All's Well* suggest different thematic connections with Shakespeare's 1609 Quarto. They also illustrate the circuitous routes of circulation that the sonnet as a form of social action might take, especially with regard to the possibilities of multiple audiences and the capacity of such audiences to use the sonnet in a multiplicity of relations of address and direction. Paroles's sonnet is a kind of performative mirror. It shows Bertram to himself and the world at large via the words of his closest companion. Many of Shakespeare's sonnets do the same thing. Take sonnet 62:

> Sinne of selfe-loue possesseth al mine eie,
> And all my soule,and al my euery part;
> And for this sinne there is no remedie,
> It is so grounded inward in my heart.
> Me thinkes no face so gratious is as mine,
> No shape so true,no truth of such account,
> And for my selfe mine owne worth do define,
> As I all other in all worths surmount.
> But when my glasse shewes me my selfe indeed
> Beated and chopt with tand antiquitie,
> Mine owne selfe loue quite contrary I read
> Selfe,so selfe louing were iniquity,
> > T'is thee(my selfe)that for my selfe I praise,
> > Painting my age with beauty of thy daies,

The peculiarity of this sonnet lies in its unusual degree and type of self-accusation. If self-love is the fault of anyone in the sequence, it is that of the young man, whose persistent self-absorption lies at the centre of the first seventeen poems, is openly castigated in sonnet 84 ('You to your beautious blessings adde a curse, / Being fond on praise, which makes your praises worse') and is the occasion for the chilling valedictory admonition in sonnet 126. Self-absorption of the kind attributed to the young man and embodied by Bertram involves a perverse refusal to see oneself in the social glass by which others might 'modestly discover to yourself / That of yourself which you yet know not of' (*Julius Caesar*, 1.2.71–2). It betrays an incapacity for the kind of self-reflection via others that leads to a morally enriching form of shame.[11]

No reason is ever given for the young man's refusal to have a child, other than the enigmatic hint of an aversion to heterosexual relationships

---

[11] See Lars Engle, '"I am that I am": Shakespeare's Sonnets and the Economy of Shame', in *Shakespeare's Sonnets: Critical Essays*, ed. Schiffer, 185–97.

in sonnet 40, which castigates the noble youth for his 'wilfull taste of what thyself refusest', presumably in the form of the player-poet's mistress. In his thwarted reluctance to marry and his subsequent refusal to conceive a child with his wife, Bertram embodies the unreflecting, youthful, upper-class arrogance of such a refusal. Such arrogance is impervious to its own image as it is reflected in the pronounced judgements of the society at large. That is why Paroles's sonnet, reproduced and redistributed by the Lord Dumaine, is so significant. It reflects Bertram to himself and to others via the poetic writings of a character who is generally considered unworthy because of his inappropriate social ambition. The sonnet succeeds in shaming the young aristocrat in the eyes of the world, not because of the exorbitant behaviour of its composer, but because of the home truths that it reveals about the noble youth.

The player-poet of the sonnets admits, shortly before the end of the sequence to the young aristocrat, that his name 'receiues a brand' from his 'publick means which publick manners breeds' (sonnet 111). Further-more, he has 'made [himself] a motley to the view' and 'lookt on truth / Asconce and strangely' (sonnet 110). But why such a person should accuse himself of blind self-absorption is unclear. Unless the poem is another mirror, a response to the failure of an earlier injunction to the young man to 'Looke in thy glasse and tell the face thou vewest, / Now is the time that face should forme an other' (sonnet 3). In that poem it is not enough for the young man merely to look into his mirror. The poem itself mirrors that looking in order to reflect the young man's narcissism back upon himself. It turns mere reflection into a more urgent form of self-reflection through its performative injunctions to the beloved to see more than merely his mirrored image in his glass: to let 'all [his] eye' be 'possessed' (sonnet 62) with something more than 'self-love':

> Looke in thy glasse and tell the face thou vewest,
> Now is the time that face should forme an other,
> Whose fresh repaire if now thou not renewest,
> Thou doo'st beguile the world,vnblesse some mother.
> For where is she so faire whose vn-eard wombe
> Disdaines the tillage of thy husbandry?
> Or who is he so fond will be the tombe,
> Of his selfe loue to stop posterity?
> Thou art thy mothers glasse and she in thee
> Calls backe the louely Aprill of her prime,
> So thou through windowes of thine age shalt see,
> Dispight of wrinkles this thy goulden time.
>> But if thou liue remembred not to be,
>> Die single and thine Image dies with thee.

The young man is enjoined to address that image, to transform it from static reflection to living entity. Free indirect speech allows the poet to merge his voice with that of the young man, fusing the 'thou' of his poetic address with the speech of the youth talking to himself. An editor who followed this reading might place lines 2–14 in quotation marks, to mark them as an imagined, displaced, exteriorised voice of self-reflection, simultaneously enjoined and reflected by the poem itself. As such they would be read as the represented speech of the young man. But it is perhaps more useful to see the two voices diverging – the 'thous' split between two different referents – in the course of the second quatrain. Each of the two questions could then be read as being directed by two different personae, reflecting two different moral attitudes. The first, ('For where is she so fair whose vn-eard wombe / Disdaines the tillage of thy husbandry?') would be the self-satisfied complacency of adolescent arrogance addressing itself; the second, the interrupting, older voice of moral reprimand ('Or who is he so fond will be the tombe / Of his self loue to stop posterity?'). This differentiates the sexist assumption of women as the passive vehicle of male 'husbandry' in the first question from an implicit moral judgement on that very attitude in the second. It also gives unqualified weight to the admiration of the young man's mother as the origin of the beauty that he reflects: 'Thou art thy mothers glasse and she in thee / Calls back the louely Aprill of her prime'. Despite the passive image of young man as mirror, and the female passivity in the second quatrain, the young man's mother here 'calls back' her own prime, gazing at her son as he is directed to gaze at himself in the opening of the poem. (Taken in this sense, the notion that motherhood is a 'blessing' (line 4) need not be taken as patronising.) The mother's productive gaze is shared by the poet. He characteristically ungenders beauty, not in a single reflected image, but as a chain of relations of reflection and recall produced through the poem itself.

There is a crucial difference, then, between the sterile, narcissistic reflection of the young man in the image that his glass returns to him, and the capacity of his mother (and others such as the poet) to recall her pristine beauty through him. That difference is marked by the speech acts performed by the poem: by the fact that the young man is told not merely to view himself in the mirror, but also to enact before that reflected self the lesson against self-absorption that the poem performs. The poem thus differentiates between two kinds of reflection. One is the self-indulgent reflection of self-love. The other is a productive relationship in which the self, initially caught up in the confining mirror of self-love, is released by an awareness of the individual's debt to others, in the mode of 'shame' analysed by Engle.

Seen in this light, sonnet 62 may be read as an indirect way of mirroring the young man's self-absorption to himself and to a wider audience, as Paroles's sonnet does. It attempts, through the mimicry of the discourse of self-love, to inhabit the voice of the young man in the hope that he will recognise in it not only his own moral entrapment in his own image, but also a way out of that entrapment through reciprocity. The poem re-enacts the earlier moment in sonnet 3 by which the mirror becomes an escape from self-absorption through its mirroring of the self through others: 'Selfe, so self louing were iniquity, / 'Tis thee (my selfe) that for my self I praise, / Painting my age with beauty of thy daies'. Although the older player-poet here speaks in his own person, the poem attempts to induce in the young man the same sense of reciprocity – the mirroring of self through the other – in terms of which it renounces its own 'self-love'. It seeks to induce in the young man – through the very internalising of the poetic speech of which Vendler and Wright write – a recognition of his own 'iniquity' by mimicking his stance and voice.

'The name and not the thing'. There lies the rub for both Helen and Paroles. Each may be said to be the name rather than the thing for philosophically similar, though not identical, reasons. Paroles is a soldier in name only because he fails to embody the performative actions that the name implies. His loss of the drum, coupled with the cowardice and treachery with which he capitulates on being 'captured', prove him no soldier at all: thing and name are discrepant because the thing does not live up to the name. His behaviour under interrogation strips him of the 'name' of a soldier, so that he finally accepts his bare 'thingness', as it were: 'Simply the thing I am / Shall make me live'. This does not mean that Paroles ceases to be a social being, constituted by and subject to 'names' in a hierarchy of deference and difference reflected and kept in place through language. The brief scene that precedes the final act, in which Paroles is forced to endure the double humiliation of Lavatch's scatological humour and his own begging to Lafew for support, shows the social upstart finding his 'proper' place, which is in effect, finding his 'proper' name.

The disjunction between names and things, underscored so pointedly by Helen in the scene to come, is comically emphasised as Lavatch takes literally what Paroles intends to be a mere metaphor of his disgrace: 'I have ere now been better known to you, sir, when I have held familiarly with fresher clothes. But I am now, sir, muddied in Fortune's mood, and smell somewhat strong of her strong displeasure' (5.2.2–5). What Paroles means as mere words, Lavatch mischievously takes to be the things themselves: Paroles's misfortune turns him into 'Fortune's close-stool' (5.3.16), his social disgrace announcing itself in the stigma of pigsty. If Lavatch delights in treating words as things by taking Paroles's metaphor literally, he is smart enough to underscore in his parting remark the fact that words cannot substitute for deeds: 'I do pity his distress in my similes of comfort, and leave him to your worship' (5.2.24–5). Lafew finally offers Paroles not 'similes' of comfort, but real compassion: 'Though you are a fool and a knave, you shall eat' (5.2.52). What then, do we make of the 'similes of comfort' to be found in one of the most celebrated of Shakespeare's sonnets?

> v v Hen in disgrace with Fortune and mens eyes,
> I all alone beweepe my out-cast state,
> And trouble deafe heauen with my bootlesse cries,
> And looke vpon my selfe and curse my fate.
> Wishing me like to one more rich in hope,
> Featur'd like him, like him with friends possest,
> Desiring this mans art, and that mans skope,
> With what I most inioy contented least,
> Yet in these thoughts my selfe almost despising,
> Haplye I thinke on thee, and then my state,
> (Like to the Larke at breake of daye arising)
> From sullen earth sings himns at Heauens gate,
>   For thy sweet loue remembred such welth brings,
>   That then I skorne to change my state with Kings.
>
> (sonnet 29)

The remarkable thing about this sonnet is the way in which, in complete contrast to Paroles (and Helen, for that matter), it seems to find solace in the rejection of performative action as a response to a social situation. The first part of the poem consists of a catalogue of fruitless performatives that signal either privation or complaint: 'beweepe', 'trouble deafe heauen with my bootlesse cries', 'curse my fate', 'wishing', 'desiring', 'with what I most inioy contented least', 'my selfe almost despising'. These are abandoned, however, 'with a thought', as the poet-player's 'state' – a passive condition – replaces his former actions. 'Arising' from a condition as 'sullen' as his former state, it now 'sings himns at Heauens gate'. But far from transcending the social and political world that ostracises and condemns the player-poet in the early part of the poem, the memory of the beloved's affection merely enables him to scorn all that he formerly envied. The sonnet does not end on the transcendental, religious note sounded by the 'hymns' at heaven's gate. Rather, its final emphasis is on 'scorn': the performative boast of the successful parvenu, possibly as empty as those of the word-spinner of *All's Well that Ends Well.* The critical controversy that this poem has elicited concerns precisely the question whether its 'similes of comfort' are delusory or effective: the mere name, or the thing itself.[12] The answer to this question lies not in reducing or elevating one above the other, but in trying to register the differences that each sonnet or play brings to the question. One of the remarkable qualities of sonnet 29 is its capacity both to enact the genuine 'comfort' that can lie in 'thought' and to remind us (through the persistence of performatives such as 'scorn') that thought is not disconnected from the material forces of the world: 'But ah, thought kills me that I am not thought' (sonnet 44).

We may say the same thing about the vexed question of things and names. Shakespeare offers no theory that will settle this matter. He neither looks forward to a postmodern dogma which holds either that there is no connection between them or that names constitute things, nor is he caught in a supposed early modern view of the identity of language and the world. We need to remind ourselves, too, that while Shakespeare registers the way in which words are central to misunderstanding and deception, he does not subscribe to the general modernist doctrine of the essential unreliability of language. He plays language as it comes, registering its multiple uses in different contexts, forms of life, social organisations and times. The gibberish spoken by Paroles's 'captors' does not symbolise the emptiness of language, as many critics have supposed, but rather the capacity of human beings to transform sound into meaning through performance or use. There is a systematic quality to the French soldiers' use of nonsense that turns it into a kind of sense, demonstrating, not the gap between word and sense, but the power of action to convert sound to significance.

This brings us back to Helen. In what sense does she declare herself 'the name and not the thing' at the end of *All's Well that Ends Well?* We have seen ways in which names can be divorced from things in Paroles's failure to behave like a soldier. We have also seen instances in which names and things are inseparable, in the fact that Romeo can be reduced to neither 'hand, nor foot, / Nor arm, nor face, nor any other part / Belonging to

---

[12] See, for example, John Barrell, 'Editing Out: the Discourse of Patronage and Shakespeare's Twenty-ninth sonnet', in *Poetry, Language and Politics* (Manchester: Manchester University Press, 1988), 18–43.

a man' – that is to say, to a 'thing' without a 'name' – and in the sonnets' derivation of names from things as paradigmatic examples in sonnets 127 and 84. In each case, the relationship between name and thing is different, constituted by use rather than linguistic structure. It cannot be encompassed by any single theory of language or names. When Helen declares publicly that she is a mere name, she does so in a context in which 'riddle' is played off against 'meaning', 'shadow' against what is 'real', the 'letter' against the 'ring':

> DIANA ... And now behold the meaning.
> (*Enter Helen and the Widow*)
> KING   Is there no exorcist
>   Beguiles the truer office of mine eyes?
>   Is 't real that I see?
> HELEN   No, my good lord,
>   'Tis but the shadow of a wife you see,
>   The name and not the thing.
> BERTRAM   Both, both. O, pardon!
> HELEN O, my good lord, when I was like this maid
>   I found you wondrous kind. There is your ring.
>   And, look you, here's your letter. This it says:
>   'When from my finger you can get this ring,
>   And are by me with child,' et cetera. This is done.
>   Will you be mine now you are doubly won?
> BERTRAM (*to the King*)
>   If she, my liege, can make me know this clearly
>   I'll love her dearly, ever ever dearly.   (5.3.306–18)

To tease out these relationships is as difficult as to come to a decision about the quality of love that they appear to forge. I hope to show that names and love are not unrelated. Announced as the 'meaning' of Diana's riddle, Helen responds at first by underscoring her status as a mere 'shadow'. But it is not as a ghost (thus she appears to the King at first) that she lacks substance: it is as a wife. And the substance that distinguishes a real person from a ghost is very different from the substance that embodies a real wife. One can tell a ghost from a person by touching them; touching Helen will, however, reveal nothing about the critical difference that she insists upon, because the difference is conceptual and social rather than physical. That is not to say that touching and the physical are irrelevant: they are, in fact, germane, but not in the way in which they come into play in determining the putative difference between ghosts and people. Helen is a wife in name only because she has not engaged in the transformative act that will make her a wife. Or rather, she has done so, but in another name: in the name of Diana, of chastity. In her own name, therefore, she is in a kind of limbo: the name of a thing, but not the thing named. We should note that this appears to be a status (or a shadow-status) that is peculiarly gendered. We encounter it in *All's Well's* sister play, *Measure for Measure*, where Mariana, in an identical position, is reduced to less than a 'thing', to 'nothing': 'Why, you are nothing then; neither maid, widow, nor wife!' (5.1.176–7). And Bertram's own acknowledgement that he slept with Diana similarly induces him to declare that that performance has reduced her to 'nothing'. His supposed seduction of Diana does not, however, transform her status in the same way – to behave as he does, it appears, is simply to love 'as a gentleman loves a woman' (*All's Well that Ends Well*, 5.3.248).

The limbo in which Mariana and Helen find themselves arises from the fact that certain concepts pertaining to social – especially sexual – status require performatives extending beyond the mere saying of certain words; they require that one should *do* something non-linguistic as well. It is this (sexual) action that is decisively transformative, turning one from a mere name into the thing itself, or from name ('maid') into 'nothing'. An unconsummated marriage is still, in Austin's terms, an 'unhappy' event: the very concept 'consummation' turns the action into a symbolic, not a merely physical one – an unspoken illocutionary act, as it were. In this sense, wives and husbands are not things found in the world, like rocks and trees; they are made through social and personal action.

Helen is a study of the possibilities of making oneself through such action. The deferral of her status as 'proper' wife, through the unwillingness of one party to go through with the necessary performative action, focuses especially clearly on the tangle of the performative in its relation to intention. Within this tangle is embroiled the relationship of individual to institution, agency to structure, desire to convention and the personal to power. When she uses the King's promise to give her the young nobleman of her choice as a means of transforming her lowly status from hopeless lower-class lover to aristocratic wife, our attention is focused on the tension within a social institution that is both a vehicle through which political power is brokered and an illocutionary act by which people declare their gift of themselves to one another. Unusually in Shakespeare, it is the man who is for once forced to bear the burden of choosing love by another's eyes, and we miss the complexity of the play's exploration of the broader issues if we remain totally unsympathetic to Bertram's predicament, however much we may side with Helen in personal terms:

HELEN (*to Bertram*) I dare not say I take you, but I give
   Me and my service ever whilst I live
   Into your guiding power. – This is the man.
KING Why then, young Bertram, take her, she's thy wife.
BERTRAM My wife, my liege? I shall beseech your highness,
   In such a business give me leave to use
   The help of mine own eyes.
KING   Know'st thou not, Bertram,
   What she has done for me?
BERTRAM   Yes, my good lord,
   But never hope to know why I should marry her.
                         (2.3.103–11)

Bertram's objection to Helen on the politically appropriate grounds that marriage to her would be a form of disparagement – that he would be dishonoured by being forced, as a ward, to marry someone of a lower class – runs up against the declared power of the King to make up the lacking title or name: "Tis only title thou disdain'st in her, the which / I can build up' (2.3.118–19). But the King goes further. The relationship between things and names is raised once again in his pronouncement on the performative nature of 'virtue': the capacity for action to 'dignify' the 'place'. After musing on the 'mighty' distinction that names impose upon something that is otherwise indistinguishable in itself (as a 'thing'), namely, human blood, he disparagingly mocks Bertram's commitment to the ideological rather than the substantial:

   Strange is it that our bloods,
   Of colour, weight, and heat, poured all together,
   Would quite confound distinction, yet stands off
   In differences so mighty. If she be
   All that is virtuous, save what thou dislik'st –
   'A poor physician's daughter' – thou dislik'st
   Of virtue for the name.   (2.3.119–25)

What is it that Bertram dislikes? Merely the words – 'a poor physician's daughter' – or the woman herself? And can these be separated?

The King takes a surprisingly egalitarian view that honour and virtue are performative concepts. We show ourselves honourable or virtuous by what we do, rather than by the names we carry:

   From lowest place when virtuous things proceed,
   The place is dignified by th' doer's deed.
   Where great additions swell's, and virtue none,
   It is a dropsied honour. Good alone

> Is good without a name, vileness is so:
> The property by what it is should go,
> Not by the title.   (2.3.126–32)

This is not surprising, coming from the pen of the person who wrote sonnets 69 and 94, and we can certainly join other commentators in feeling that the player-dramatist speaks here in the appropriated name of the King, if not exactly to take his revenge on a young aristocrat who in his personal experience placed too much faith in the intrinsic worth of blood and names, then certainly to make a broader point about the asymmetrical relationship between goodness and nobility. In contrast to the player-poet's necessary indirections, the King can be made to speak with real authority by the player-dramatist, not only declaring that the 'mere word's a slave' (2.3.138), but also displaying his power to put such words to use in socially and politically transformative ways: 'If thou canst like this creature as a maid, / I can create the rest'(2.3.143–5).

A contradiction or conflict informs the attitude to names and things, then. On the one hand, things are declared to have an intrinsic quality quite apart from names, which tend to be misleadingly taken for things. On the other, the very power of royalty to 'create the rest' attests to the power of names to transform things. So too, it is not merely the name, title or epithet by which Helen is known, as 'a poor physician's daughter', that Bertram 'disdains'; it is Helen herself. Helen by any other name, he is saying, would still be as repulsive. In the face of Bertram's obstinacy, the King, who has just delivered a disquisition on the misleading character of the name 'honour', is forced to act in the name of his own honour – 'My honour's at the stake, which to defeat / I must produce my power' (2.3.150–1). He produces a withering display of such power, forcing from Bertram an acknowledgement of his authority to 'drive [dis]liking to the name of love' (*Much Ado*, 1.1.283):

> BERTRAM (*kneeling*) Pardon, my gracious lord, for I submit
>   My fancy to your eyes. When I consider
>   What great creation and what dole of honour
>   Flies where you bid it, I find that she, which late
>   Was in my nobler thoughts most base, is now
>   The praisèd of the King; who, so ennobled,
>   Is as 'twere born so.
> KING   Take her by the hand
>   And tell her she is thine; to whom I promise
>   A counterpoise, if not to thy estate
>   A balance more replete.
> BERTRAM (*rising*)   I take her hand.
>   (2.3.168–78)

Before we come down too hard on Bertram as an individual, we should note that none of the young noblemen who were potentially objects of Helen's choice would have accepted her. A philosopher of speech acts given to thinking too nicely upon this scene would be struck at once by difficulties that may have their origins in its historical distance from us. A king may well have the power to force someone into a marriage against their will, but does he have the power (logically speaking) to force someone to give themselves against their will: to 'tell her she is thine'? How 'happy', in other words, are each of the multiple performatives in this scene: the King's commanding threats, Bertram's submission and request for pardon, the transformation of Helen's status through the 'breath of kings' (*Richard II*, 1.3.208), the King's injunction that Bertram accept Helen by telling her that she is his and Bertram's subsequent taking of her hand? How happy is the performative towards which the whole scene moves, the marriage of Helen and Bertram? To what degree, finally, is this exchange successful in turning Helen into a wife, and, a very different question, to what degree does it satisfy her desires?

A full answer to this question would be impossibly long and complex. It would be complex in part at least because it is uncertain how the concept of 'love' that lies beneath its surface is to be taken. When the King declares, in his parting line, 'As thou lov'st her / Thy love's to me religious; else, does err' (2.3.184), the ominous discourse of imposed religious orthodoxy, immediately and pointedly taken up by Lafew's reference to Bertram's 'recantation' (2.3.188), renders the issue even more opaque to a modern sensibility. To what degree does it lie in the power of a King to enforce 'love', whether of a secular or religious kind? And how would such 'love' be registered, enacted, performed?

Bertram pointedly obeys only one of the King's commands. He takes Helen by the hand, but he does not (within our earshot anyway) tell her that she is his, as Hero tells Claudio in *Much Ado* (2.1.296). We subsequently know that although he (presumably) carries out all the performatives that constitute a marriage, he resolutely refuses to perform the final act that, conventionally, turns a man into a husband, a woman into a wife. What kind of 'love' does the King expect from a dutiful Bertram? And how does it differ from the 'love' that Helen expects? Presumably, love as the King understands it does not necessarily extend to actually liking Helen. It is enough that Bertram accepts the match as a social arrangement, beneficial in economic terms to each party, and certainly beneficial in social terms to the 'poor physician's daughter', just as the King is himself fulfilling an obligation incurred previously in arranging the marriage. Such a marriage, it seems, is indeed in the power of the King to command. But the King could hardly command Bertram to love Helen in a different sense: to fall in love with her, or find her attractive, or desire her or enjoy her companionship. Whereas it is in the King's power to command love in the sense of a secular and religious contract of lifelong partnership, it is not in the King's power to insist upon a *companionate* marriage. Wanting a 'companionate' marriage, or at least one by which she can lose her virginity 'to her own liking' (1.1.148), Helen suddenly comes up against the limits of the performative as an exercise of power, rather than as a gift. The King gives according to his bond, and although that is sufficient to validate his promise to her, it is not enough for her. She finds herself in the limbo between 'name' and 'thing', the unhappy object of an only partially exercised performative because, although Bertram performs all that is required within the strict limits of the marriage ceremony, he does not give himself to her; he takes her hand but refuses to tell her that she is his.

I think that we can see something of Helen's anguish in the sonnets. The parallels between Helen and the player-poet lie not merely in their self-sacrificial love, but in their struggles to transform their status and their relationships with those they love through performatives that are either not always within their control or do not extend far enough in performative force. It is one of the central insights of Austin's contextualism that social status and authority are intrinsic to the performability of speech acts: only an umpire may declare a ruling in a sports game, only a judge may pass sentence, only a priest or magistrate may officiate at a wedding. What has been less often noticed by philosophers of speech acts is that speech acts are marked by a gendered asymmetry. So, in *Much Ado About Nothing*, a significant part of Beatrice's outrage after the slander of her cousin arises from the fact that, as a woman, she is structurally precluded from engaging in the one performative that might rescue Hero's reputation: challenging Claudio to a duel. In Helen's case, it is impossible for her to complete the performative act that will consummate her marriage and turn her from name to thing without the consent of her partner. The opposite is not true. It is in the physical power of a man to force the consummation of a marriage against the wishes of his wife, and we must suppose that this happened all too often. The impersonal power, indeed, the violence in some cases, of the performative is conveyed especially starkly in such a case: the marriage would be considered consummated whether or not the wife consented. The question is, then, does the player-poet suffer from a similar kind of asymmetry? There is no doubt that his class position places considerable constraints upon what he may or may not say, but it is not merely a matter of class, it is the intensified vulnerability that arises from a lack of social power and the position of beseeching lover. Furthermore, is the love that the player-poet expresses for the young man gendered in any way? How close is he, not merely in class but in gender terms, to the openly desiring but similarly thwarted Helen?

> A womans face with natures owne hand painted,
> Haste thou the Master Mistris of my passion,
> A womans gentle hart but not acquainted
> With shifting change as is false womens fashion,
> An eye more bright then theirs, lesse false in rowling:
> Gilding the obiect where-vpon it gazeth,
> A man in hew all *Hews* in his controwling,
> Which steales mens eyes and womens soules amaseth.
> And for a woman wert thou first created,
> Till nature as she wrought thee fell a dotinge,
> And by addition me of thee defeated,
> By adding one thing to my purpose nothing.
>   But since she prickt thee out for womens pleasure,
>   Mine be thy loue and thy loues vse their treasure.

Sonnet 20 is one of the most controversial of the 1609 Quarto. It is one of the most puzzling in terms of gender identity and has been regarded as the key to the question of the homosexuality of, if not of Shakespeare, then certainly of the persona of the sonnets. It is often taken to be decisive proof of the platonic nature of the relationship between poet and fair friend, especially since it appears to close with a decisive separation of 'loue' and 'loues vse': the former belonging to the male poet; the latter to women more generally.[13] What is most unusual about the poem, however, is the way in which it tries to position the aesthetic appreciation that is part of sexual desire. Developing the suggestion in sonnet 3 that the young man is his 'mothers glasse', in which she 'calls back the louely Aprill of her prime', sonnet 20 is itself a kind of performative mirror. The (male) poet, looking at the young man, offers the sonnet as a mirror of his beauty, a glass that does not merely reflect his image back to him, but displaces it as the image that a woman sees of herself. In this relatively simple way, the man is the image of a woman who sees herself in him.

---

[13] But see Joseph Pequigny, *Such is My Love: A Study of Shakespeare's Sonnets* (Chicago: University of Chicago Press, 1985), for a forceful argument to the effect that the relationship between the poet and the young man is fully erotic.

More significantly, the vantage point of the poem moves undecidably between male and female perspectives. In the octave, the poem registers male admiration and desire through the metaphorical transformation of male beauty into female loveliness, thereby preserving the sexual difference between observer and observed that will allow for both 'loue' and 'loues vse'. (To say this is to import no extraneous prejudice about the appropriateness or not of homosexual desire; it is simply to move within the poem's own argument.) The male perspective is underscored by the misogynist tenor of the comparison, by which, paradoxically, the young man is seen as a perfect woman, without the moral blemishes that are said to mark females as such.

But by the sestet the admiring (male) perspective of the poet is confused. The poem suddenly looks with the eyes of a desiring woman. It now occupies the subject position that has been disparaged earlier in its gynophobic solidarity with the addressee: we realise that we have been looking all along at the youth through the female eyes of Nature. These eyes are, like Helen's, the medium of an intensely desiring female sexual subjectivity. The poem therefore oscillates between male and female desire and desirability, in both its position of representation and in the position being represented. The object of desire is both male and female; but so is the desiring subject. Only at the very end of the poem is the chiastic confusion of sex and gender 'naturalised' through the transformative power of 'doting' Nature. Same-sex desire in the form of (female) Nature's love for her (female) creature is occupied (in the sense of being appropriated, taken over), imagined and felt in the sonnet just as it is in plays such as *As You Like It* and *Twelfth Night*, which embody the possibilities of homosexual attraction. Just as the closures of those comedies, whereby Cesario is translated into Viola or Ganymede into Rosalind, normalise homosexual attraction, sonnet 20 invents a fiction whereby Nature can 'naturalise' her desire by a simple 'addition'. The 'thing' thus added transforms the 'name' of beauty. But this happens at the cost of excluding the desiring poet. It turns 'one thing' into 'no thing' for his erotic purposes. This leaves the mirroring poet in precisely the position occupied by Nature *before* her transformative intervention: if before that addition he could legitimately admire the youth as a woman, now he is like doting Nature before she was able to transform the object of her desire into a man. Furthermore, the triangular situation now anticipates the sexual rivalry among the player-poet, the young aristocrat and the dark woman, as Nature and the poet dote equally upon a shared 'Master Mistris'.

The difference between the poet and Nature does not lie in the legitimacy or otherwise of their desires or perspectives; it lies in the fact that,
unlike Nature, the poet lacks the capacity to transform the beloved into a
legitimate object of desire. The poem appears, on one reading, to resolve
the problem through the neat, implicitly misogynist and Platonic bifurcation of love into platonic and carnal forms. Stephen Orgel reminds
us, however, of Randall McLeod's and Peter Stallybrass's suggestions
that such a reading appears to be natural only in the modernised text.
Unmodernised, the couplet 'does in fact allow for an explicitly sexual
relationship between the poet and the young man' since 'vse' may then
be read as a verb rather than a noun and 'loues' as its plural subject.[14]
Moreover, like the plays in which we are drawn into the playful representation of desire that is neither wholly male nor female, neither hetero-
nor homosexual, neat closures cannot undo the represented experience
or take away that felt perspective. Having shared the delightful intensity
of the love-making between Ganymede and Orlando, or the lingering
signs of homosexual desire in Cesario's cross-dressed identity beyond
the end of the play, we cannot simply pretend that these things never
happened or that they are obliterated by orthodox comic closure. The
anti-theatrical pamphleteers understood only too well the dynamics of
imaginative representation and its libidinous force. They also understood
that language is not a mere substitute for erotic foreplay, but a major,
performative medium of sexual exchange.

The similarities that critics have noted between the player-poet and
Helen could thus be said to be prefigured in sonnet 20, where the subject
position of a desiring woman is inhabited alongside that of a libidinous
man. We see the young man through Nature's eyes before the full progress
of that perspective is blocked by the transformation wrought by the
woman herself. After this poem, one might say, the young man is always
seen through the eyes of a woman. The difference between Helen and the
player-poet, which is also what binds her to Nature, is that, like Nature,
she has the power to transform a blocked desire into a consummated
marriage: to turn 'loue' into 'loues vse'. Herein lies the significance of
the infamous 'bed-trick'. Before anything else, the bed-trick allows Helen
to put into effect her own final transformation in status from rejected
lover to confirmed wife. It is a crucial performative. That Bertram is
not a conscious party to this transformation merely speaks of the power
of convention to act impersonally through the performative despite the

[14] Stephen Orgel, *Impersonations: The Performance of Gender in Shakespeare's England* (Cambridge: Cambridge University Press, 1996), 57.

active intentions of the parties.[15] Helen transforms what to Bertram is a mute act into a signifying one: one in which he unwittingly fulfils the impossible condition that he imposed upon her and binds himself irrevocably to what we might call, paraphrasing Juliet, '[his] only love sprung from [his] only hate'. We should again note the asymmetry of the performative significance of this act. It is only accidentally transformative for Bertram; it is, however, necessarily transformative for both Helen and Diana. For the latter it would mean the reduction of her social and sexual status to that 'nothing' – that excluded fourth – embodied by the woman who occupies the riddle of being 'neither maid, widow, nor wife' (*Measure for Measure*, 5.1.176–7). That does not stop Diana from declaring him her husband, herself his wife, on the strength of his words and deeds:

> BERTRAM (*to the King*) She's none of mine, my lord.
> DIANA   If you shall marry
>   You give away this hand, and that is mine;
>   You give away heaven's vows, and those are mine;
>   You give away myself, which is known mine,
>   For I by vow am so embodied yours
>   That she which marries you must marry me,
>   Either both or none.   (5.3.171–7)

Diana's claim affirms the transformative power of the performative. By his thoughtless vows Bertram has not only turned what is 'his' into what is 'hers'; he has 'embodied' her as himself. In the end, Shakespeare's comedies tend to resolve the riddle by confirming the woman concerned as *one* of the tripartite possibilities in the equation: Diana and Hero are finally confirmed 'maids', Helen and Mariana are each proved 'wives'. Nowhere is the excluded fourth position as thoroughly explored as in the sonnets, where, if the dark woman occupies none of the legitimate positions, she is not 'nothing' either.

The sense of reciprocity forged through the performative exchange of vows, which is the spin that Romeo (disingenuously) puts on his request for 'satisfaction', is what the sonnets strive for but cannot achieve. In the case of the young aristocrat, despite the player-poet's repeated affirmations, no such binding vow is ever recorded by which lover and beloved

---

[15] This is an issue that has been much misunderstood in Austin. While Austin might posit a requisite intentionality for the success or happiness of certain speech acts, he is clear that the speech act, not any inward intention, 'puts on record my spiritual assumption of a spiritual shackle ... Accuracy and morality alike are on the side of the plain saying that *our word is our bond*' (*How To Do Things With Words* (Oxford and New York: Oxford University Press, 1975), 10).

become one. In the case of the dark woman, vows have always already been foresworn owing to the prior marital commitments of both parties:

> IN louing thee thou know'st I am forsworne,
> But thou art twice forsworne to me loue swearing,
> In act thy bed-vow broake and new faith torne,
> In vowing new hate after new loue bearing:
> But why of two othes breach doe I accuse thee,
> When I breake twenty:I am periur'd most,
> For all my vowes are othes but to misuse thee:
> And all my honest faith in thee is lost.
> For I haue sworne deepe othes of thy deepe kindnesse:
> Othes of thy loue,thy truth,thy constancie,
> And to inlighten thee gaue eyes to blindnesse,
> Or made them swere against the thing they see.
>   For I haue sworne thee faire:more periurde eye,
>   To swere against the truth fo foule a lie.
>
> (sonnet 152)

There are fourteen instances of 'swear' and its cognates or variant forms ('sworn', 'swearing', 'vow', 'vows', 'oaths', 'forsworn', 'bonds of love') in the dark-woman group of sonnets; only three in the group to or about the young man. Of those, one is used generally of a prevalent social practice (sonnet 66), one is used rather abstractly of the poet's promise to 'vow debate' against himself and only one refers obliquely to the young aristocrat's lack of truth: the player-poet offers to forswear his own truth for his beloved's sake, promising to 'proue thee virtuous, though thou art forsworne' (sonnet 88). It might be misleading to look only at such instances in which promises or vows are indicated directly through the word or its cognates rather than indirectly through other forms of the performative, but the sample nonetheless indicates a remarkable asymmetry between the two parts of the 1609 Quarto. This imbalance is even more remarkable if we note the fact that the first group (the young-man group) is almost five times larger than the second.

It is not coincidental that promises or vows are paradigm examples of illocutionary acts in Austin's analysis of the performative. They are the primary instance of human interaction in which exchange is genuinely transformative – in which to say something is not only to do something, but also to change social relations and individual status. Sonnet 138 predicates the possibility of human and sexual relations on a mutual lie (in a parody of the marriage vow); sonnet 152 struggles against this paradoxical state of affairs. But, rather than accept falsehood as a mutually enabling condition, one which marks a certain kind of reciprocity, the later sonnet makes use of the self-accusatory move, already encountered in the sonnets to the young man, including sonnet 88, to accuse the other of its own fault. Who is more to blame: the woman who is forsworn by breaking her marriage vows through the very vows by which she swears love to her lover, or the lover who swears her beautiful and true when both know that she is not? Like sonnet 138, this sonnet is predicated upon a shared knowledge of infidelity.

It is tempting to see this sonnet as a chiefly theoretical or philosophical analysis of the essential discrepancy between what is seen and what can be said. Its chief struggle, however, lies in its attempt to forge the possibility of a relationship under conditions in which promises have from the beginning been broken, avowals always already undermined. Merely to love, in this relationship, is to be 'forsworn'. How, then, given the prior condition of infidelity, can a relationship, rather than a one-night stand such as Bertram seeks, be forged? Bertram believes that he can use vows purely rhetorically: as perlocutionary acts without illocutionary effects. His disillusionment in the final act of *All's Well that Ends Well* arises from his being forced to face the illocutionary consequences of what he thought were merely perlocutionary acts. Like the sonneteering voice of his creator, Bertram is more than 'twice forsworne': he breaks his 'bed-vow' to Helen by seducing Diana; he vows 'new hate after new loue' by abandoning Diana when he thinks he has slept with her; he is 'periur'd most' when he denies having slept with her at all; and, faced by incontrovertible evidence of the latter, he uses his oaths to 'misuse' Diana by denouncing her as a conniving whore:

> She's impudent, my lord,
> And was a common gamester to the camp.
>   . . .
>   Certain it is I liked her
> And boarded her i' th' wanton way of youth.
> She knew her distance and did angle for me,
> Madding my eagerness with her restraint,
> As all impediments in fancy's course
> Are motives of more fancy; and in fine
> Her inf'nite cunning with her modern grace
> Subdued me to her rate. She got the ring,
> And I had that which my inferior might
> At market price have bought.
>   (5.3.190–91; 213–22)

The contempt expressed here for women as ensnaring sirens, and for sexual pleasure enjoyed fleetingly and then 'despised straight', echoes the sonnets. In Bertram's view of the night with Diana he is the loser in a bad bargain, the victim, not the perpetrator: 'Her inf'nite cunning with her modern grace / Subdued me to her rate'. This is the 'lasciuious grace' of sonnet 40 written in a differently gendered key, now the dark woman who, in the words of the player-poet, has a 'powrefull might, / With insufficiency my heart to sway' (sonnet 150). In the play it is possible to provide a distanced view of emotions, attitudes and postures that are internal to the sensibility of the writer of a sonnet such as 150. In the play the ardent vows with which Bertram attempts to sway Diana's heart are recognised as no more than an echo of the empty platitudes of a thousand young men:

> BERTRAM A heaven on earth I have won by wooing thee.
> DIANA For which live long to thank both heaven and me.
> You may so in the end.
> (*Exit Bertram*)
> My mother told me just how he would woo,
> As if she sat in 's heart. She says all men
> Have the like oaths. He had sworn to marry me
> When his wife's dead; therefore I'll lie with him
> When I am buried. Since Frenchmen are so braid,
> Marry that will; I live and die a maid.   (4.2.67–75)

'As if she sat in 's heart': there is something deliciously ironic in the thought that the place supposedly reserved by the Petrarchan lover for his beloved turns out to be already occupied by her mother, who knows well enough the emptiness of this heart and its discourse. Living up to her name, Diana in turn vows to avoid love if the possibility of being forsworn in love cannot be excluded entirely. Helen offers a different perspective, closer to that of the sonnets. Having set her trap for Bertram with the paradoxical notion that it 'Is wicked meaning in a lawful deed / And lawful meaning in a wicked act, / Where both not sin, and yet a sinful fact' (3.7.45–7), she entertains no illusions about the transcendental purity of absolute honesty. However much the bed-trick is a *reductio ad absurdum* of the closing couplet of sonnet 138, it allows Helen both to confirm her incomplete marital status through the performative dimensions of sexual intercourse, and to reflect on the peculiarity of human pleasure, which can be taken against the promptings of conscious desire and aversion. Bertram runs away to find his greatest pleasure – so valued before the act that he will exchange his family's ring for it, so despised afterwards, that he dismisses it as the meanest commodity – in the very thing from which he flees in disgust:

> But O, strange men,
> That can such sweet use make of what they hate,
> When saucy trusting of the cozened thoughts
> Defiles the pitchy night; so lust doth play
> With what it loathes, for that which is away.
>
> (4.4.21–5)

Shakespeare frequently dwells on the peculiarity of human psychology to see what it expects to see, especially at moments of special moral or tragic pressure. It is a mistake to take this as merely another variation on that tired old theme, 'appearance versus reality', as if these things are given. For, unlike his contemporaries who tended to condemn the imagination as a corrupting or misleading faculty, Shakespeare recognises projection for what it is: a constitutive part of human perception.[16] For every occasion on which projection has tragic consequences, it is also shown on another to make human relationships possible. For every Othello there is a Beatrice and Benedick, for every Demetrius there is a Lysander, for every Diana there is a Helen. Although Helen's language is strongly pejorative, ascribing to the delusions of an overheated fantasy the capacity to defile what in Shakespeare is a quintessentially defiling element ('pitchy night'), her own obsession with Bertram, seen in the light of his actions and others' judgements, is equally 'trusting' of 'cozened thoughts'.

The projection encountered so frequently in the sonnets is therefore not a necessarily pathological condition, even if some of the sonnets to the woman treat it as such. It is the condition of possibility of adult erotic consciousness, rendered problematic only when something in the relationship renders projective desire so patent as to draw attention to a total discrepancy between eye and object. When Mercutio thus assumes without enquiry that Romeo has fallen into the trap whereby all lovers denigrate even acknowledged paradigms of beauty in favour of their own object of desire, he is underlining the lover's psychological need to deny such projection through the mere *rhetoric* of objectivity:

Now is he for the numbers that Petrarch flowed in. Laura to his lady was a kitchen wench – marry, she had a better love to berhyme her – Dido a dowdy, Cleopatra a gypsy, Helen and Hero hildings and harlots, Thisbe a grey eye or so, but not to the purpose. (*Romeo and Juliet*, 2.3.36–41)

---

[16] See David Schalkwyk, 'The Role of Imagination in *A Midsummer Night's Dream*', *Theoria*, 66 (May 1986), 52–65.

That Mercutio mistakes Romeo's new beloved for the old underscores the point. The 'numbers that Petrarch flowed in' thus contain a virtually insoluble problem: how does one convey the felt uniqueness of the beloved, which is the very condition of romantic love, in a language that is not only always already belated, but also necessarily the vehicle of projection. Shakespeare overcomes this problem by uniquely focusing on what Petrarchan poetry often tries to forget: its irreducibly projective – that is to say, its performative, constitutive – nature. Performative projection is not confined to the 'periurde eye' of the last twenty-eight sonnets. It may be less overt, less emotionally charged, in the poems to the young man, but it remains deeply constitutive of the tensions in that relationship. In sonnet 61, for example, it is the player-poet's own love that keeps the projected image of the beloved before his mind's eye, even when he knows that the beloved himself 'dost wake elsewhere . . . with others all too neere'. Sonnet 93 – 'So shall I liue, supposing thou art true, / Like a deceiued husband' – is a conscious exercise in refusing to see what is palpably before one. But the issue is developed most thoroughly in a pair of sonnets, 113 and 114:

> s ince I left you, mine eye is in my minde,
> And that which gouernes me to goe about,
> Doth part his function, and is partly blind,
> Seemes seeing, but effectually is out:
> For it no forme deliuers to the heart
> Of bird, of flowre, or shape which it doth lack,
> Of his quick obiects hath the minde no part,
> Nor his owne vision houlds what it doth catch:
> For if it see the rud'st or gentlest sight,
> The most sweet-fauor or deformedst creature,
> The mountaine, or the sea, the day, or night:
> The Croe, or Doue, it shapes them to your feature.
>   Incapable of more repleat, with you,
>   My most true minde thus maketh mine vntrue.
>
>   (sonnet 113)

> or whether doth my minde being crown'd with you
> Drinke vp the monarks plague this flattery ?
> Or whether shall I say mine eie saith true,
> And that your loue taught it this *Alcumie*?
> To make of monsters, and things indigest,
> Such cherubines as your sweet selfe resemble,
> Creating euery bad a perfect best
> As fast as obiects to his beames assemble:
> Oh tis the first, tis flatry in my seeing,

And my great minde most kingly drinkes it vp,
Mine eie well knowes what with his gust is greeing,
And to his pallat doth prepare the cup.
   If it be poison'd,tis the lesser sinne,
   That mine eye loues it and doth first beginne.

                      (sonnet 114)

The second sonnet is a subtle, but telling, reconsideration of the first. The irrepressible capacity to see in everything, from the greatest to the meanest, the image of the beloved is recognised in 113 as the projective work of the 'mind'. Such a tendency is universal rather than selective, encompassing the 'rud'st or gentlest sight, / The most sweet-fauor or deformedst creature' without discrimination. Here imaginative projection is recognised as a positive process: the transformative perjury of the eye is a sign of the totality of the poet-player's love, an interiorised version of the young nobleman's own 'guilding' eye in sonnet 33. That sonnet, however, never loses sight of the fact that the gilding eye of nobility acts in a social context, a political structure of relationships rather than a merely psychological subjectivity. Sonnet 114 gestures towards that world by occupying the place of the monarch in a moment in which the pressing existence of hierarchy and difference may be forgotten. But, in a cunning twist, the poem claims that such a purposeful forgetting arises out of the occupational hazard of the ruler. It stems from his or her own desire to be the subject of the very flattering projection that in 113 is the prerogative of the all-consuming consciousness at the centre of the sonnet. How else can eye and mind's collusion in the making 'of monsters, and things indigest / Such cherubines as your sweet selfe resemble, / Creating euery bad a perfect best' flatter the *player-poet* (or as now, the player-king)? The projective tendency celebrated in 113 as the sign of true love becomes in 114 the mark of a wilful indulgence in the celebration of self through the social 'alchemy' wrought by the young man's transformative but tenuously imagined social and emotional proximity. The sonnet recognises, as 113 does not, that such indulgence may be a poisonous illusion, but it can find no way out of the trap that would not involve a rejection of the illusionary coronation that invites the 'monarks plague ... flattery' in the first place.

Although the terms are different, especially regarding the social and political contexts of the respective forms of projection, the problem is thus equally rooted in the first 126 poems. This fact may be grist to Dubrow's mill, insofar as she questions the narrative by which these two groups are usually kept apart. The parallels between the two groups might suggest a number of things: that the usual ascription of two distinct objects of address to them is mistaken; that the two figures are not as different as is usually supposed; or that the quality of the poet-player's infatuation does not differ fundamentally between the woman and the man. Nor are these possibilities mutually exclusive. The multiple subject positions in the sonnets that this reading of *All's Well that Ends Well* has suggested indicate a more complex fusing of gender, social and sexual roles than the absolute distinction usually drawn, in the name of 'Otherness', between male and female in the sonnets. A recent essay sees in Helen's reflection – 'But O, strange men, / That can such sweet use make of what they hate, / When saucy trusting of the cozened thoughts / Defiles the pitchy night; so lust doth play / With what it loathes, for that which is away' (4.4.21–5) – her alienation of 'Bertram as male Other, as personification of difference, as a creature from whom she is estranged'.[17] But this reading turns both the complex negotiation of relationships with others (lower case and plural), and the instability of the performance of gender in the interactive progress of the plays and the poems themselves, into the misleading monolith of (anachronistic) theory. Helen is talking to two other women, and in the momentary context of their solidarity she certainly reflects with them on the peculiarity of Bertram's behaviour as exemplary of his sex. But that does not mean that she alienates either Bertram or men in general as being totally different or estranged. There is a degree of sympathy – even love – in her tone, and her own active and pleasurable participation in the act is strongly conveyed by the sense that, no matter how perverse such 'use' might be, she too finds it 'sweet'.

Such complexity of tone and feeling is registered time after time in the sonnets, and careful attention to what connects the two sub-sequences shows that it is not confined to one gender. In the sonnets traditionally assumed to be about the dark mistress, for example, the central complication of the relationship arises from the fact that *both* of the protagonists make 'sweet use of what they hate'. This is most obvious in the case of the (male) poet, who struggles to come to terms not merely with the equal degrees of attraction and repulsion with which he seeks to 'vse' his mistress, but also with the more fundamentally 'strange' possibility that it is precisely her 'defiling' qualities that attract him. This situation can arise only because the woman is in the same position: she 'lies with' him despite her own 'hate' (sonnets 138, 142 and 149), her promiscuity repeatedly complicated by references to her 'tyranny' (sonnet 131), 'cruelty'

---

[17] David McCandless, 'Helen's Bed-trick: Gender and Performance in *All's Well that Ends Well*', *Shakespeare Quarterly*, 45.4 (Winter 1994), 449–68 (459).

(sonnets 131 and 132), 'reproouing' 'unkindnesse' (sonnets 141 and 139) and 'disdaine' (sonnets 132 and 140). It is possible to read some of the sonnets supposedly addressed to her as if they were in her voice: as if she were responding to the contradictory petitions and accusations of her lover. Why might 149, for example, not reflect her frustrated response to his tiresome and unfair hectoring; and if 148 may be recognised as an exemplification of Helen's position, why not that of the dark mistress as well? This argument may be extended to the sonnets to the young man. It is not only possible, as Dubrow points out, to 'cross-read' sonnets from the two groups as applying to the other beloved. It is also possible to recognise in some poems attitudes and feelings that might be those of the beloved himself. The series of admissions of neglect and apology from 109 to 112 may be in the voice of the young man, or the exculpatory poems from 117–19 that culminate in the reciprocity of shared unfaithfulness and mutual acceptance in 120:

> THat you were once vnkind be-friends mee now,
> And for that sorrow, which I then didde feele,
> Needes must I vnder my transgression bow,
> Vnlesse my Nerues were brasse or hammered steele.
> For if you were by my vnkindnesse shaken
> As I by yours,y'haue past a hell of Time,
> And I a tyrant haue no leasure taken
> To waigh how once I suffered in your crime.
> O that our night of wo might haue remembred
> My deepest sence,how hard true sorrow hits,
> And soone to you,as you to me then tendred
> The humble salue,which wounded bosomes fits!
>   But that your trespasse now becomes a fee,
>   Mine ransoms yours,and yours must ransome mee.

To see in this poem the possible expression of the different social and personal perspectives of *each* of the protagonists is to recognise the complex reciprocity that it enacts and to give full weight to the tension between social position and private love registered in the sonnets as a whole. The imagined role of unmoved 'tyrant' will differ considerably, depending on whether it is occupied by the abject player-poet or the injured man-of-rank. The very possibility of reciprocity is enacted in the switching of roles, whereby the poet may empathetically assume the position of tyrant and feel its attraction, and the well-born man can imaginatively reject his customary habit of careless power. To feel the obligation to 'bow' under a 'transgression' because not to do so would negate one's humanity means something subtly different, depending on whether one is socially accustomed or unused to such 'bowing'. That is not to say that the desired reciprocity will necessarily be achieved. Unlike sonnet 34, in which the demand for an apology is sentimentalised by the too-effusive couplet ('Ah, but those teares are pearl which thy loue sheeds, / And they are ritch, and ransome all ill deeds'), sonnet 120 leaves open the possibility that the required ransom might be withheld. The latter couplet opens up the possibility of diverging responses in the future by recalling the thoughtless 'tyranny' recounted as part of the sonnet's past. This sonnet is much more tough-minded than the mawkishness at the end of sonnet 34. For the acknowledgement of personal suffering – expressed in the deeply empathetic quality of 'y'haue past a hell of Time' and 'my deepest sence, how hard true sorrow hits' – maintains a firm sense of constraining mutual obligation through which, miraculously, the feudal and the personal aspects of the relationship, so much at war elsewhere in the group, are reconciled.

To suggest such 'cross-reading' of different possible personae in the sonnets does not necessarily involve the extravagant multiplication of actual speakers. It merely recognises that the interactive experiences and attitudes are shared. In contrast to the differences often ossified in Petrarchan discourse, Shakespeare's occupation of that convention is as wide-ranging as his skills as a dramatist, by which the self always contains and is contained by others (in lower case and in the plural), reduplicating itself through them as much as it defines itself against them in interactive dialogue. This is why, in her reflections on the 'strangeness' of the man who has just used her, Helen is not registering absolute estrangement, but reflecting on the possibility of a reciprocity that she has been attempting to engineer from the very beginning, in the form of a 'kindness' that is given and mutually enjoyed despite oneself: 'O, my good lord, when I was like this maid / I found you wondrous kind' (5.3.311–2). As in sonnets 120 and 138, transformative reciprocity is wrenched from a mutual fault, achieved through the conjoined infidelity of Bertram's desire and the untruth of Helen's trick.

The 1609 Quarto is unusual for joining the traditional Petrarchan language of female 'cruelty' with the fact of an explicitly carnal liaison. This may run contrary to conventional expectations, but it reflects the complex uncertainties and ambivalences of actual relationships. Diana, characterised by a witty critic as the 'girl-who-says-yes-but-means-no'

(McCandless, 'Helen's Bed-trick', 464), does not actually compromise her chastity through that 'yes'. Her counterpart in the sonnets, however, repeatedly enacts that contradiction: promiscuous yet cruel, faithless yet aloof. Her lover both connives in that contradiction and vilifies her for it. Urging her on the one hand to 'beare [her] eyes straight, though [her] proud heart goe[s] wide' (sonnet 140), he at other times blames her for 'mak[ing] [him] loue her more, / The more [he] heare[s] and see[s] iust cause of hate' (sonnet 150). Helen's lived experience of the way in which 'lust doth play/ With what it loathes, for that which is away' echoes sonnet 129; but it also touches on experiences that draw all the sonnets together.

All's Well that Ends Well is unusual for the place that it gives to an already, if darkly achieved, carnal union. This is perhaps, more than anything else, what ties it to the sonnets. *All's Well* looks like a comedy, not merely in its whimsical title, but also in the comic use of a transcendental signifier – the plain-speaking rings – which cannot be mis-taken. There are no such transcendental signifiers in the sonnets, despite the player-poet's desperate illusion, for a while, that he has found one in the infamous 'fair friend', and despite a whole critical tradition's wish to see one of a different complexion in the promiscuous 'ring' of the 'dark lady'. *All's Well that Ends Well* and the sonnets embody and explore carnal experience as the path and obstacle to others. This affinity marks their radical difference from other examples of their respective genres. They suspend their generic differences with each other through their remarkably similar treatment of gender difference and affinity. I have argued in chapter 1 that Shakespeare's sonnet 138 exemplifies his sonnets' distance from the Petrarchan through its recourse to the performative. The double accommodation of that sonnet, embodied in the mutuality of its 'lying', creates an erotic space that is quite different from the usual Petrarchan quests for truth and idealisation.

Returning to the argument with which this book began, I propose that we read the comic movement of *All's Well* as sonnet 138 writ large: the accommodations of contradictory erotic desire – lying 'with' each other – embody a shared falsehood – lying 'to' each other. Like the protagonists of that sonnet, Helen and Bertram's far from ideal accommodation rests upon the mutuality of lies that has made their fraught but consummated relationship possible. The asymmetry of the protagonists' genders in the play and sonnets attests furthermore to Shakespeare's remarkably undogmatic vision of gender. If what Susan Snyder calls 'Shakespeare's own experience' ('The King's Not Here') confronted him with an erotic life dominated by a duplicitous, commonplace woman and an enigmatic, well-placed young man, the comic fictions by which he lived allowed him to explore not merely the reversal of those roles, but also the radical complication of the performative genres by which gender is itself constituted and performed.

Conclusion

In this systematic reading of Shakespeare's sonnets in relation to his plays I have set out from the assumption that Shakespeare's involvement with the theatre informs his writing of sonnets in decisive ways. Such a reading has made possible the argument that the language of the sonnets is composed of a variety of essentially performative, rather than descriptive, speech acts. The player-poet of Shakespeare's sonnets engages in a discourse of self-authorisation by mobilising, not merely the perlocutionary (or rhetorical) force of language (this has been long recognised), but also its illocutionary force. In the latter, situations may be transformed *in* the saying of something, personal and social relations forged and reflected in ways not registered in formal rhetorical handbooks. The elaborate, embodied contexts of address and interaction in Shakespeare's theatrical art enable us to imagine situations of personal interaction and social pressure that their purely textual existence has tended to obscure.

Linking the contextualist linguistic philosophies of Ludwig Wittgenstein and John Austin to the sonnets and plays – especially the sonnets *in* the plays – has enabled me to focus more precisely on recent materialist, historicist and feminist concerns with the ways in which Shakespeare's sonnets worked in their historical and social world. The agency embodied in the sonnets is circumscribed by inequalities of social class, informed by the exigencies of personal desire and made possible by received literary conventions and socially given language games. But the sonnets' gradual removal from originally embodied situations of address has tended to attenuate the interaction of social pressure, subjective will and linguistic formation that continues to be staged within the dramatic texts through which their player-poet made his living. Under such circumstances it is vital to work with a philosophy of language that can register both the given speech genres that make individual expression possible and the rich nuances through which personal and social relationships are imposed and renegotiated.

The post-Saussurean theory of language that continues to inform the major critical movements that have recently wished to explore the consolidation or subversion of relations of power and desire, including the Foucauldian notion of discourse, has been far too blunt an instrument to probe the range and nuance of language at work in Shakespeare. The performative view of language emphasises language as utterance – as a form of action that responds to and anticipates a world of others while seeking to transform that world and the speaker's relationship to it. Such a view also replaces the insidious notion of language as system or code with the perspective that there are many languages within a single 'language system'. There are countless speech acts, language games or speech genres that act in dialogue or conflict, working in and through a world, repeating themselves in different contexts to different effects, always negotiating social relations through a process of interactive dialogue that is simultaneously personal and public.

Historical and materialist studies of early modern texts have scarcely begun to explore this richness of linguistic performance – the site where the interaction of politics, history and society is most fully registered – while traditional formalist criticism has tended to ignore such forms of social life through a myopic attention to language either as a purely formal system or the means of purely individual expression.[1] Far from acting as a mere parody of outdated literary convention and shallow feeling, the staged representations of interactive dialogue embody the lived reality of received discourses in all their performative richness.[2] Not confined to the stage, such performative dimensions attest to the imbrication of individual agency and socially given speech genres everywhere language is used.

Shakespeare's sonnets are deeply informed not only by the fact of the player-poet's lowly social status, but also by his peculiar self-consciousness about this simultaneously debilitating and empowering condition. Despite the sense of personal inadequacy and social taint with which such self-consciousness about his profession imbues the poet's Petrarchan moments, as player-dramatist he is able to bring to the poet's task an extraordinarily developed sense of language as a performative force, in

---

[1] For a classic critique of both these formalist positions, see V. N. Voloshinov, *Marxism and the Philosophy of Language*, trans. Ladislaw Matejka and I. R. Titunik (Cambridge, MA: Harvard University Press, 1986).

[2] See, for example, Katherine M. Wilson, *Shakespeare's Sugared Sonnets* (London: George Allen & Unwin, 1974) for the argument that both the sonnets and plays are no more than parodies of an empty literary tradition.

the Austinian and Wittgensteinian, rather than the merely theatrical, sense of the word. By examining the deliberate staging of the sonnet as a form of public discourse in the theatre, I have emphasised the situations of embodied address of the sonnet as performative and the modes by which even silence may be a form of power or resistance through its very embodiment. This has allowed a review of readings of the sonnet form as an essentially disempowering discourse for women. By exploring the relationships among a number of variously gendered characters in the plays and a variety of subject positions registered in the sonnets, I have also sought to complicate the traditional narrative regarding the fair young man, the unreliable dark lady and our devoted poet. The variety of characters and relations in the plays complicate the notion of stable personae in the poems. There are traces of the player-poet in the subject positions of Cordelia and Lear; Ophelia and Hamlet; Helen, Bertram *and* Paroles – and the now traditionally coded positions of 'fair' friend and 'dark' lady are equally complicated by reading them through the interactive discourses of the drama.

The question of the sonnets' autobiographical mode is posed especially forcefully via the logic of proper names and naming events. Arguing that it is precisely the peculiar absence of proper names in 'SHAKE-SPEARES SONNETS' that testifies to their autobiographical nature, I have explored the power of the proper name not only to tie individuals to ineluctable networks of social relations, but also to allow for the fictional exploration of alternative, counter-traditional connotations for historically given names, such as 'Cressida'. I have also looked at the ways in which naming events may act performatively, to transform social and personal relations, and have explored the unstable tension between 'proper' and 'common' name in discourses of racial and sexual stereotyping. By posing the question of biography as a matter of (Wittgensteinian) 'grammar' I have sought to give greater human substance to the sonnets' dark woman by asking, *pace* A. L. Rowse, whether we can indeed assume that Shakespeare has told us everything about her, and why we should believe what he does say about her. This is both a matter of the underdetermination of humanity in the sonnets as dislocated, disembodied texts and a question of tracing the implicit contours of interactive dialogue between two or more people in a sonnet that may be rendered more apparent on the stage. That is to say, the question of the (multiple) audiences of the sonnets is raised by the plays' double nature: as a site in which the sonnet as a form of public discourse may be displayed and as a place in which speech engages a variety of audiences.

The sense of the textual or 'inward' nature of the poems as lyrics has, I hope, been enriched and made more complex by reading them through the historical embodiment of sonnets in theatrical representations. Shakespeare's dramatic art made possible the extraordinary uses of language in the sonnets, but the plays themselves also render more palpable circumstances of address which the restricted body of the sonnet may suggest but not contain. By emphasising their concern with situations of dialogical interaction I demonstrate that the sonnets' performative language encompasses much more than the solitary mind of their lyric speaker or isolated reader. It arises out of the triangular relationship of addresser, addressee(s) and the context or event of such action, which is constantly informed and negotiated through publicly available language games.

The public or social nature of such language games does not, however, mean that interiority or the private is a mere illusion. I have revisited the vexed question of subjectivity in the sonnets via *Hamlet* in order to find a critical space between Helen Vendler's denial of the social, public nature of the poems, and the historicist claim that in the early modern period the private is entirely consumed by the public. I have argued that Shakespeare's dramatic work makes visible the contexts that render speech acts intelligible and make possible the language of interiority. Interiority is neither an ineffable inward state hidden from public view nor a mere ephiphenomenon of the social, but rather a condition made possible by the availability of certain socially sustained language games. Plays such as *King Lear* and *Hamlet* show us that such language games may be robbed of their conditions of possibility by particular social and political conditions, but that does not obliterate the personal as a concept. In fact, it may make it all the more indispensable.

Finally, my analysis of Shakespeare's sonnets as documents that negotiate a passage between private and public realms has consequences for their status as literary texts. Lynne Magnusson's analysis of sonnet 58 in the light of the rhetoric of politeness in contemporary letter-writing shows how Shakespeare's sonnets employ the very rhetorical strategies in their negotiations of hierarchical relationship and personal desire evident in the letters (Magnusson, *Shakespeare and Social Dialogue*, 50ff.). But she also cautions against the assumption that the sonnets are merely a more elaborate form of epistolary writing – that they play an identical set of language games. Their language games are related to those used in other areas of social discourse, both public and private, but they do not merely replicate them. Nor are they, as some philosophers suppose, merely *pretended* speech acts – fictions, 'non-serious', or 'etiolated' forms of 'serious' language.[3] In their original context, and in the contexts rehearsed by Shakespeare's plays, they were forms of real social action that attempted to affect and effect social relations in lived rather than merely imaginary ways.

But the imaginative pressures peculiar to their generic difference from other modes of public speech and writing allow a certain play in the given language games of social interaction that Magnusson analyses so perceptively. In both poem and play a distance is created between representer and represented so that circumscribed discourses may be staged and highlighted, thus allowing usually implicit tensions to be revealed, scrutinised and transformed. The literary convention that obliges the unrequited lover to see himself as a 'slave' to the beloved allows Shakespeare to explore the real, political implications of slavery in his 'literary' negotiations with a master's 'will and pleasure' over the relationship between love and duty. It allows him to push the otherwise circumscribed boundaries of politeness and duty to and beyond their limits in ways that are not merely imaginary, so that the speech act continues to do its pragmatic work in the poem itself as a form of real performative action.

I have sought to negotiate a passage between formal analysis and a concern with the social and historical conditions of Shakespeare's writing. Language is the site on which these two traditionally disparate enterprises meet, or should meet. This book is no more than an exploratory foray into a terrain that, as Magnusson, points out, has been largely unexplored (*Shakespeare and Social Dialogue*, 4–5). Her own work promises to revolutionise the way in which we see and respond to Shakespeare's uses of language as a form of immediate verbal action. What is required now is a combination of the philosophies of Wittgenstein and Austin with the insights of Bakhtin, Bourdieu and the theorists of social discourse that have come in their wake, so that the full range of Shakespeare's 'dialogic art' may be seen in more than 'broken glimpses' (*Shakespeare and Social Dialogue*, 182).

---

[3] See John R. Searle, 'The Logical Status of Fictional Discourse', *New Literary History*, 6 (1975), 319–32, and J. L. Austin, *How To Do Things with Words* (Oxford and New York: Oxford University Press, 1975), 21–2.

Bibliography

Adelman, Janet. *Suffocating Mothers: Fantasies of Maternal Origin in Shakespeare's Plays*. London and New York: Routledge, 1992.

Althusser, Louis. *Lenin and Philosophy and Other Essays*. Trans. D. Brewster. London: New Left Books, 1997.

Austin, J. L. *How To Do Things With Words*. Oxford and New York: Oxford University Press, 1975.

Bakhtin, Mikhail. *Rabelais and his World*. Trans. Helene Iswolksy. Bloomington: Indiana University Press, 1984.

Speech Genres and Other Late Essays. Trans. Vern W. McGee. Ed. Caryl Emerson and Michael Holquist. Austin: University of Texas Press, 1986.

Barber, C. L. 'An Essay on the Sonnets'. In *Elizabethan Poetry: Modern Essays in Criticism*. Ed. Paul J. Alpers, New York: Oxford University Press, 1967, 299–320.

Barish, Jonas. *The Anti-Theatrical Prejudice*. Berkeley and Los Angeles: University of California Press, 1991.

Barker, Deborah E. and Ivo Kamps (eds.). *Shakespeare and Gender: A History*. London and New York: Verso, 1995.

Barker, Francis. *The Tremulous Private Body: Essays in Subjection*. London and New York: Methuen, 1984.

Barrell, John. 'Editing Out: the Discourse of Patronage and Shakespeare's Twenty-ninth Sonnet'. In *Poetry, Language and Politics*. Manchester: Manchester University Press, 1988, 18–43.

Barthes, Roland. 'The Death of the Author'. In *The Rustle of Language*. Trans. Richard Howard. Oxford: Blackwell, 1986, 49–55.

Belsey, Catherine. *The Subject of Tragedy: Identity and Difference in Renaissance Drama*. London: Methuen, 1985.

Berger, Harry Jr. *Making Trifles of Errors: Redistributing Complicities in Shakespeare*. Ed. Peter Erickson. Stanford, CA: Stanford University Press, 1997.

Berthoud, Jacques. Introduction to *Titus Andronicus*. Ed. Sonja Massai. The New Penguin Shakespeare. Harmondsworth: Penguin, 2001, 7–58.

Booth, Stephen. *An Essay on Shakespeare's Sonnets*. New Haven, CT and London: Yale University Press, 1969.

Bourdieu, Pierre. 'The Economics of Linguistic Exchanges'. *Social Science Information*, 16 (1977), 645–68.

Language and Symbolic Power. Ed. John B. Thompson. Trans. Gino Raymond and Mathew Adamson. Cambridge, MA: Harvard University Press, 1991.

Bradbrook, Muriel. 'Virtue is the True Nobility: A Study of the Structure of *All's Well that Ends Well*'. *Review of English Studies*, 26 (1950), 289–301.

Bruster, Douglas. 'The Structural Transformation of Print in Late Elizabethan England.' In *Print, Manuscript, & Performance: The Changing Relations of the Media in Early Modern England*. Ed. Arthur F. Marotti and Michael D. Bristol. Columbus: Ohio State University Press, 2000, 49–89.

Cavell, Stanley. *Disowning Knowledge in Six Plays of Shakespeare*. Cambridge: Cambridge University Press, 1976.

The Claim of Reason: Wittgenstein, Skepticism, Morality, and Tragedy. Oxford: Oxford University Press, 1982.

Carroll, William C. *The Great Feast of Language in 'Love's Labor's Lost'*. Princeton, NJ: Princeton University Press, 1976.

Chartier, Roger. 'Leisure and Sociability: Reading Aloud in Modern Europe'. Trans. Carol Mossman. In *Urban Life in the Renaissance*. Ed. Susan Zimmerman and Robert E. Weissman. Newark: University of Delaware Press, 1989, 103–20.

Clarkson, Carrol. 'Naming and Personal Identity in the Novels of Charles Dickens: A Philosophical Approach'. Unpublished DPhil thesis. University of York, England (November 1998).

'Dickens and the *Cratylus*'. *British Journal of Aesthetics*, 30.1 (January 1999), 53–61.

Cloud, Random. ' "The very names of Persons": Editing and the Invention of Dramatic Character'. In *Staging the Renaissance: Reinterpretations of Elizabethan and Jacobean Drama*. Ed. David Scott Kastan and Peter Stallybrass. London and New York: Routledge, 1991, 88–96.

Colie, Rosalie. *Shakespeare's Living Art*. Princeton, NJ: Princeton University Press, 1974.

Crew, Jonathan. *Hidden Designs: The Critical Profession and Renaissance Literature*. New York and London: Methuen, 1986.

Day, Angel. *The English Secretorie*. London: 1592.

De Grazia, Margareta. 'The Motive for Interiority: Shakespeare's *Sonnets* and *Hamlet*'. *Style*, 23.3 (Fall 1989), 430–44.

Shakespeare Verbatim: The Reproduction of Authenticity and the 1790 Apparatus. Oxford: Clarendon Press, 1991.

'The Scandal of Shakespeare's Sonnets'. In *Shakespeare's Sonnets: Critical Essays*. Ed. James Schiffer. New York: Garland, 1999, 89–112.

Derrida, Jacques. *Speech and Phenomena*. Evanston, IL: Northwestern University Press, 1973.

Limited Inc. Ed. Gerald Graff. Evanston, IL: Northwestern University Press, 1988.

Acts of Literature. Ed. Derek Attridge. London: Routledge, 1992.

Doran, Madeleine. 'Good Name in *Othello*'. *Studies in English Literature, 1500–1900*, 7 (1967), 195–217.

Dubrow, Heather. *Captive Victors: Shakespeare's Narrative Poems and Sonnets*. Ithaca, NY and London: Cornell University Press, 1987.

Echoes of Desire: English Petrarchism and its Counterdiscourses. Ithaca, NY and London: Cornell University Press, 1995.

'"Incertainties now crown themselves assur'd": The Politics of Plotting Shakespeare's Sonnets'. *Shakespeare Quarterly*, 47 (1996), 291–305. Reprinted in *Shakespeare's Sonnets: Critical Essays*. Ed. James Schiffer. New York: Garland, 1999, 113–34.

'Criticism on the Sonnets: 1994–7.' *The Shakespearean International Yearbook Volume One: Where are We Now in Shakespearean Studies?*. Ed. W. R. Elton and John M. Mucciolo. Brookfield, VT: Ashgate, 1999, 302–10.

Duncan-Jones, Katherine. 'Was the 1609 *Shake-speares Sonnets* Really Unauthorized?'. *Review of English Studies*, 34 (1983), 151–71.

'Filling the Unforgiving Minute: Modernizing SHAKE-SPEARES SONNETS (1609).' *Essays in Criticism*, 45.3 (1995), 199–207.

Duncan-Jones, Katherine (ed.). *The Sonnets*. The New Arden Shakespeare. London: Routledge, 1997.

Elam, Keir. *Shakespeare's Universe of Discourse: Language Games in the Comedies*. Cambridge: Cambridge University Press, 1984.

Engle, Lars. *Shakespearean Pragmatism: Market of His Time*. Chicago and London: University of Chicago Press, 1993.

'"I am that I am": Shakespeare's Sonnets and the Economy of Shame.' In *Shakespeare's Sonnets: Critical Essays*. Ed. James Schiffer. New York: Garland, 1999, 185–97.

Everett, Barbara. 'Spanish Othello: The Making of Shakespeare's Moor'. *Shakespeare Survey*, 35 (1982), 101–12.

Feinberg, Nona. 'Erasing the Dark Lady: Sonnet 138 in the Sequence'. *Assays: Critical Approaches to Medieval and Renaissance Texts*, 4 (1987), 97–108.

Ferry, Anne. *The 'Inward' Language: Sonnets of Wyatt, Sidney, Shakespeare, and Donne*. Chicago: University of Chicago Press, 1983.

Fiedler, Leslie. *The Stranger in Shakespeare*. New York: Macmillan, 1960.

Fineman, Joel. *Shakespeare's Perjured Eye: The Invention of Poetic Subjectivity in the Sonnets*. Berkeley, Los Angeles and London: University of California Press, 1986.

'Shakespeare's Ear'. *Representations*, 28 (Fall 1989), 6–13.

Fish, Stanley. 'How to Do Things with Austin and Searle'. In *Is There a Text in this Class?* Cambridge, MA, Harvard University Press, 1980, 197–245.

Fleissner, Robert F. 'The Moor's Nomenclature'. *Notes and Queries*, 25 (1978), 143.

Foucault, Michel. 'What Is an Author?'. In *Language–Countermemory–Practice*. Ed. Donald F. Bouchard. Trans. Donald F. Bouchard and Sheery Simon. Oxford: Blackwell, 1977, 113–38.

Fumerton, Patricia. *Cultural Aesthetics: Renaissance Literature and the Practice of Social Ornament.* Chicago: University of Chicago Press, 1991.

Girouard, Robert. *Life in the English Country House: A Social and Architectural History.* New Haven, CT: Yale University Press, 1978.

Glock, Hans-Johann. *A Wittgenstein Dictionary.* Oxford: Blackwell, 1996.

Goldberg, Jonathan. *Sodometries: Renaissance Texts, Modern Sensibilities.* Stanford, CA: Stanford University Press, 1992.

Greenblatt, Stephen. 'Fiction and Friction.' In *Shakespearean Negotiations.* Berkeley and Los Angeles: University of California Press, 1988, 66–93.

Introduction to *Romeo and Juliet.* The Norton Shakespeare. Ed. Stephen Greenblatt, Walter Cohen, Jean E. Howard and Katherine Eisaman Maus. London and New York: W.W. Norton, 1997, 865.

Greene, Thomas M. 'Pitiful Thrivers: Failed Husbandry in the Sonnets'. In *Shakespeare and the Question of Theory.* Ed. Patricia Parker and Geoffrey Hartman. London and New York: Methuen, 1986, 230–44.

Griffin, Eric. 'Un-sainting James: Or, *Othello* and the "Spanish Spirits" of Shakespeare's Globe'. *Representations*, 62 (Spring 1998), 58–99.

Gross, Kenneth. 'Slander and Skepticism in *Othello*'. *ELH*, 56.4 (Winter 1989), 819–52.

Hamer, Mary. 'Cleopatra: Housewife'. *Textual Practice*, 2.2 (September 1988), 159–79.

Harvey, Elizabeth D. and Katherine Eisamen Maus (ed.). *Soliciting Interpretation: Literary Theory and Seventeenth-Century English Poetry.* Chicago and London: University of Chicago Press, 1990.

Howard, Jean. 'Renaissance Antitheatricality and the Politics of Gender and Rank in *Much Ado About Nothing*'. In *Shakespeare Reproduced.* Ed. Jean Howard and Marion F. O'Connor. New York: Routledge, 1987, 163–87.

'Cross-Dressing, the Theatre, and Gender Struggle in Early Modern England'. *Shakespeare Quarterly*, 39.4 (1988), 418–40.

Hulse, Clark. 'Stella's Wit: Penelope Rich as Reader of Sidney's Sonnets'. In *Rewriting the Renaissance: The Discourse of Sexual Difference in Early Modern Europe.* Ed. Margaret W. Ferguson *et al.* Chicago and London: University of Chicago Press, 1986, 272–86.

Hunter, G. K. 'The Dramatic Technique of Shakespeare's Sonnets'. *Essays in Criticism*, 3 (1953), 152–64.

Husserl, Edmund. *Ideas: An Introduction to Pure Phenomenology.* Trans. W. R. Boyce Gibson. London: George Allen and Unwin, 1931.

Hutson, Lorna. 'Why the Lady's Eyes are Nothing Like the Sun'. In *New Feminist Discourses: Critical Essays on Theories and Texts.* Ed. Isobel Armstrong. London and New York: Routledge, 1992, 154–75.

Innes, Paul. *Shakespeare and the English Renaissance Sonnet: Verses of Feigning Love.* New York, St Martin's Press and London: Macmillan, 1997.

Jardine, Lisa. ' "Why should he call her whore?": Defamation and Desdemona's Case.' In *Addressing Frank Kermode: Essays in Criticism and Interpretation.* Ed.

Margaret Tudeau Clayton and Martin Warner. London: Macmillan, 1991, 124–53.

Reading Shakespeare Historically. London and New York: Routledge, 1996.

Kahane, Henry and Renée. 'Desdemona: A Star-Crossed Name'. *Names*, 35.1–2 (1987), 232–5.

Kamps, Ivo (ed.). *Materialist Shakespeare*. London and New York: Verso, 1995.

Kernan, Alvin. *The Playwright as Magician: Shakespeare's Image of the Poet in the English Public Theatre*. New Haven, CT and London: Yale University Press, 1979.

Kesler, R. L. 'The Idealization of Women: Morphology and Change in Three Renaissance Texts'. *Mosaic*, 23.2 (Spring 1990), 107–25.

Knight, G. Wilson. *The Sovereign Flower: Shakespeare as the Poet of Royalism*. London: Methuen, 1958, 157–8.

Kripke, Saul. *Naming and Necessity*. Cambridge, MA: Harvard University Press, 1980.

Lamb, Mary Ellen. *Gender and Authorship in the Sidney Circle*. Madison: University of Wisconsin Press, 1990.

Latham, Agnes. Introduction. In *As You Like It*. The Arden Shakespeare. London: Methuen, 1975, 133–4.

Lees, F. N. 'Othello's Name'. *Notes and Queries*, 8 (1961), 139–41.

Levenson, Jill L. 'The Definition of Love: Shakespeare's Phrasing in *Romeo and Juliet*'. *Shakespeare Studies*, 15 (1982), 21–36.

'*Romeo and Juliet* before Shakespeare'. *Studies in Philology*, 81.3 (Summer 1984), 325–47.

'*Romeo and Juliet*: Tragical-Comical-Lyrical History'. *Proceedings of the PMR Conference*. Augustinian Historical Institute, Villanova University, PA, 12. 13 (1987–8), 31–46.

Lezra, Jacques. *Unspeakable Subjects: The Genealogy of the Event in Early Modern Europe*. Stanford, CA: Stanford University Press, 1997.

Lyotard, Jean-Francois. *The Differend: Phrases in Dispute*. Trans. Georges van Den Abbeele. Minneapolis: University of Minnesota Press, 1988.

Macey, Samuel L. 'The Naming of the Protagonist in Shakespeare's *Othello*'. *Notes and Queries*, 25 (1978), 143–5.

Magnusson, Lynne. 'Language and Symbolic Capital in *Othello*'. *Shakespeare Survey*, 50 (1997), 91–9.

Shakespeare and Social Dialogue: Dramatic Language and Elizabethan Letters, Cambridge: Cambridge University Press, 1999.

Marotti, Arthur F. ' "Love is Not Love": Elizabethan Sonnet Sequences and the Social Order'. *ELH*, 49 (1982), 396–428.

John Donne: Coterie Poet. Madison: University of Wisconsin Press, 1986.

'Shakespeare's Sonnets as Literary Property'. In *Soliciting Interpretation: Literary Theory and Seventeenth-Century English Poetry*. Ed. Elizabeth D. Harvey and Katherine Eisamen Maus. Chicago and London: University of Chicago Press, 1990, 143–73.

Manuscript, Print, and the English Renaissance Lyric. Ithaca, NY: Cornell University Press, 1995.

Masten, Jeffrey. 'Circulation, Gender, and Subjectivity in Wroth's Sonnets'. In *Reading Mary Wroth: Representing Alternatives in Early Modern England*. Ed. Naomi J. Miller and Gary Waller. Knoxville: University of Tennessee Press, 1991.

    Textual Intercourse: Collaboration, Authorship, and Sexualities in Renaissance Drama. Cambridge: Cambridge University Press, 1997.

Matz, Robert. 'Slander, Renaissance Discourses of Sodomy, and *Othello*'. *ELH*, 66 (1999), 261–76.

Maus, Katherine Eisaman. *Inwardness and the Theatre of the English Renaissance*. Chicago and London: University of Chicago Press, 1995.

    'Proof and Consequences: Inwardness and its Exposure in the English Renaissance'. In *Materialist Shakespeare*. Ed. Ivo Kamps. London and New York: Verso, 1995, 157–180.

May, Stephen. *The Elizabethan Courtier Poets: The Poems and their Contexts*. Columbia and London: University of Missouri Press, 1991.

McCandless, David. 'Helen's Bed-trick: Gender and Performance in *All's Well that Ends Well*'. *Shakespeare Quarterly*, 45.4 (Winter 1994), 449–68.

Melchiori, Giorgio. *Shakespeare's Dramatic Meditations: An Experiment in Criticism*. Oxford: Clarendon Press, 1976.

Miller, Naomi J. and Gary Waller (eds.). *Reading Mary Wroth: Representing Alternatives in Early Modern England*. Knoxville: University of Tennessee Press, 1991.

Miller, Naomi. 'Playing "the mother's part": Shakespeare's Sonnets and Early Modern Codes of Maternity'. In *Shakespeare's Sonnets: Critical Essays*. Ed. James Schiffer. New York: Garland, 1999, 347–68.

Montaigne, Michel. *The Essays of Michel de Montaigne*. Trans. and ed. M. A. Screech. Harmondsworth: Penguin, 1991.

Mullaney, Steven. *The Place of the Stage: Licence, Play, and Power in Renaissance England*. Chicago and London: Chicago University Press, 1988.

Neely, Carol Thomas. 'Women and Men in *Othello*'. *Shakespeare Studies*, 10 (1978), 133–58.

Neill, Michael. 'Changing Places in *Othello*'. *Shakespeare Survey*, 37 (1984), 115–31.

    ' "Mulattos', 'Blacks", and 'Indian Moors": *Othello* and Early Modern Constructions of Human Difference'. *Shakespeare Quarterly*, 49.4 (Winter 1998), 361–74.

Nelson, William. 'From "Listen Lordings" to "Dear Reader"'. *University of Toronto Quarterly*, 46 (1976–7), 110–24.

Orgel, Stephen. *Impersonations: The Performance of Gender in Shakespeare's England*. Cambridge: Cambridge University Press, 1996.

Parker, David. 'Verbal Moods in Shakespeare's Sonnets'. *Modern Language Quarterly*, 30.3 (September 1969), 331–9.

Patterson, Annabel. *Shakespeare and the Popular Voice*. Oxford: Blackwell, 1989.

Pequigney, Joseph. *Such Is My Love: A Study of Shakespeare's Sonnets*. Chicago: University of Chicago Press, 1985.

'Sonnets 71–74: Texts and Contexts'. In *Shakespeare's Sonnets: Critical Essays.* Ed. James Schiffer. New York: Garland, 1999, 284–301.

Pirkhoffer, Anton M. 'The Beauty of Truth: The Dramatic Character of Shakespeare's Sonnets'. In *New Essays on Shakespeare's Sonnets.* Ed. Hilton Landry. New York: AMS Press, 1976, 109–28.

Popper, Karl. *The Open Society and its Enemies. Volume I. The Spell of Plato.* Princeton, NJ: Princeton University Press, 1971.

Pratt, Mary Louise. *Towards a Speech-Act Theory of Literary Discourse.* Bloomington: Indiana University Press, 1977.

Puttenham, George. *The Arte of English Poesie.* Ed. G. D. Willcock and A. Walker. Cambridge: Cambridge University Press, 1936; reprinted 1970.

The Arte of English Poesie. London: 1589. Scholar Press Facsimile. Menston, England: The Scholar Press, 1968.

Ramsey, Paul. *The Fickle Glass: A Study of Shakespeare's Sonnets.* New York: AMS Press, 1979.

Rea, John. 'Iago'. *Names,* 34 (1986), 97–8.

Rose, Jacqueline. '*Hamlet* – the *Mona Lisa* of Literature'. *Critical Quarterly,* 28 (1986), 35–49.

Rowse, A. L. *Shakespeare's Sonnets: The Problems Solved.* London: Macmillan, 1973.

Discovering Shakespeare. London: Weidenfeld and Nicholson, 1989.

Ryle, Gilbert. 'Categories'. *Proceedings of the Aristotelian Society,* 38 (1937–8).

Schalkwyk, David. 'The Role of Imagination in *A Midsummer Night's Dream*'. *Theoria,* 66 (May 1986), 52–65.

' "What's in a name?", Derrida, Apartheid, and the Name of the Rose'. *Language Sciences,* 22.2 (April 2000), 167–92.

'Shakespeare's Talking Bodies'. *Textus: English Studies in Italy,* 13 (2000), 269–94.

'The Chronicles of Wasted Time'? Shakespeare's Sonnets Revisited'. *The English Academy Review,* 16 (2000), 121–44.

Literature and The Touch of the Real: Words in the World and Literary Theory. Newark: University of Delaware Press, forthcoming.

Schiffer, James, ed. *Shakespeare's Sonnets: Critical Essays.* New York: Garland, 1999.

Schoenbaum, Samuel. *Shakespeare and Others.* London: Scholar Press, 1985.

Shakespeare's Lives, new edition. Oxford: Clarendon Press, 1991.

Searle, John R. *Speech Acts: An Essay in the Philosophy of Language.* Cambridge: Cambridge University Press, 1969.

'The Logical Status of Fictional Discourse', *New Literary History,* 6 (1975), 319–32.

'Reiterating the Differences: A Reply to Derrida'. *Glyph,* 2 (1977), 198–208.

Seddgwick, Eve Kosovsky. *Between Men: English Literature and Male Homosocial Desire.* New York: Columbia University Press, 1985.

Shakespeare, William. *The Works of Shakespeare.* Ed. Alexander Pope and William Warburton. 8 vols. London: J. and R. Tonson, 1747.

The First Folio of Shakespeare. The Norton Facsimile. Ed. Charlton Hinman. New York: W.W. Norton, 1968.

Shakespeare's Sonnets. Ed. Stephen Booth. New Haven, CT: Yale University Press, 1978.

The Sonnets and *A Lover's Complaint*. The New Penguin Shakespeare. Ed. John Kerrigan. Harmondsworth: Penguin, 1986.

The Complete Works. The Oxford Shakespeare. Ed. Stanley Wells and Gary Taylor. Oxford: Oxford University Press, 1987.

The Sonnets. The New Cambridge Shakespeare. Ed. G. Blakemore Evans. Cambridge and New York: Cambridge University Press, 1996.

The Norton Shakespeare. Ed. Stephen Greenblatt, Walter Cohen, Jean E. Howard and Katherine Eisaman Maus. New York and London: W.W. Norton, 1997.

The Sonnets. The New Arden Shakespeare. Ed. Katherine Duncan-Jones. London and New York: Routledge, 1997.

Sidney, Sir Philip. *Astrophil and Stella*. In *The Poems of Sir Philip Sidney*. Ed. William A. Ringler Jr. Oxford: Clarendon, 1962, 163–237.

Sipahigli, T. 'Othello's Name. Once Again'. *Notes and Queries*, 18 (1971), 147–8.

Smith, Bruce R. *Homosexual Desire in Shakespeare's England: A Cultural Poetics*. Chicago and London: University of Chicago Press, 1991.

'I, You, He, She, and We: On the Sexual Politics of Shakespeare's Sonnets'. In *Shakespeare's Sonnets: Critical Essays*. Ed. James Schiffer. New York: Garland, 1999, 411–29.

Snow, Edward. A. 'Loves of Comfort and Despair: A Reading of Shakespeare's Sonnet 138'. *ELH*, 47 (1980), 462–83.

Snyder, Susan. 'Naming Names in *All's Well that Ends Well*'. *Shakespeare Quarterly*, 42.3 (Fall 1992), 265–79.

'The King's Not Here: Displacement and Deferral in *All's Well that Ends Well*'. *Shakespeare Quarterly*, 42.1 (Spring 1992), 20–32.

Spenser, Edmund. *The Poetical Works of Spenser*. Ed. J. C. Smith and E. de Selincourt. London: Oxford University Press, 1929.

Spencer, T. J. B. ' "Greeks" and "Merrygreeks": A Background to *Timon of Athens* and *Troilus and Cressida*'. In *Essays on Shakespeare and Elizabethan Drama in Honor of Hardin Craig*. Ed. Richard Hosley. Columbia: University of Missouri Press, 1962, 223–33.

Spiller, Michael. *The Development of the Sonnet: An Introduction*. London: Routledge, 1992.

Stallybrass, Peter. 'Editing as Cultural Formation: The Sexing of Shakespeare's Sonnets'. In *Shakespeare's Sonnets: Critical Essays*. Ed. James Schiffer. New York: Garland, 1999, 75–88.

Stevens, John. *Music and Poetry in the Early Tudor Court*. London: Methuen, 1961.

Stewart, Alan. 'The Early Modern Closet Discovered'. *Representations*, 50 (Spring 1995), 76–99.

Targoff, Ramie. 'The Performance of Prayer: Sincerity and Theatricality in Early Modern England'. *Representations*, 60 (Fall 1997), 49–69.

Tennenhouse, Leonard. *Power on Display: The Politics of Shakespeare's Genres*. London: Methuen, 1986.

Tilyard, E. M. W. *Shakespeare's Problem Plays*. Harmondsworth: Peregrine, 1951.

Thomson, Peter. *Shakespeare's Theatre*. 2nd edn. London and New York: Methuen, 1992.

Vendler, Helen. 'Reading, Stage by Stage: Shakespeare's Sonnets'. In *Shakespeare Reread: The Texts in New Contexts*. Ed. Russ McDonald. Ithaca, NY: Cornell University Press, 1994, 23–41.

   'Shakespeare's Sonnets: Reading for Difference'. *Bulletin for the American Academy of Arts and Sciences*, 47.6 (1994), 33–55.

   The Art of Shakespeare's Sonnets. Cambridge, MA: Harvard University Press, 1997.

Vickers, Nancy. 'Diana Described: Scattered Woman and Scattered Rhymes'. *Critical Inquiry*, 8 (1981–2), 265–79.

Voloshinov, V. N. *Marxism and the Philosophy of Language*. Trans. Ladislaw Matejka and I. R. Titunik. Cambridge, MA: Harvard University Press, 1986.

Warren, Roger. 'Why Does It End Well?: Helen, Bertram, and the Sonnets'. *Shakespeare Survey*, 22 (Spring 1969), 79–92.

Weimann, Robert. 'Bi-fold Authority in Shakespeare's Theatre'. *Shakespeare Quarterly*, 39.4 (Winter 1988), 401–17.

   'Shakespeare (De)Canonized: Conflicting Uses of "Authority" and "Representation".' *New Literary History*, 20.1 (Autumn 1988), 65–81.

   'Representation and Performance: Authority in Shakespeare's Theater'. *PMLA*, 107.3 (May 1992), 497–510.

   'Thresholds of Memory and Commodity in Shakespeare's Endings.' *Representations*, 53 (Winter 1996), 1–20.

   Authority and Representation in Early Modern Discourse, ed. David Hilman. Baltimore, MD: Johns Hopkins University Press, 1996.

   Author's Pen and Actor's Voice: Playing and Writing in Shakespeare's Theatre. Cambridge: Cambridge University Press, 2000.

Wheeler, Richard P. *Shakespeare's Development and the Problem Comedies: Turn and Counter-Turn*. Berkeley, Los Angeles and London: University of California Press, 1981.

Whittier, Gayle. 'The Sonnet's Body and the Body Sonnetized in *Romeo and Juliet*'. *Shakespeare Quarterly*, 40 (1989), 27–41. Reprinted in *Critical Essays on 'Romeo and Juliet*.' Ed. Joseph A. Porter. New York: G. K. Hall, 1997, 82–96.

Wilson, Katherine M. *Shakespeare's Sugared Sonnets*. London: George Allen & Unwin, 1974.

Wilson, Thomas. *The Art of Rhetoric 1560*. Ed. Peter E. Medine. University Park: Pennsylvania State University Press, 1994.

Wittgenstein, Ludwig. *Tractatus Logico-Philosophicus*. Trans. C. K. Ogden. London: Routledge and Kegan Paul, 1922.

   Philosophical Investigations. Trans. G. E. M. Anscombe. Oxford: Blackwell, 1953.

   On Certainty. Ed. G. E. M. Anscombe and G. H. Von Wright. Trans. Denis Paul and G. E. M. Anscombe. Cambridge: Blackwell, 1979.

   Last Writings, vol. 1. Ed. G. H. von Wright and Heikki Nyman. Trans. C. G. Luckhardt and Maximilian A. E. Aue. Chicago: University of Chicago Press, 1990.

Wofford, Susanne L. ' "To You I Give Myself, For I Am Yours": Erotic Performance and Theatrical Performatives in *As You Like It*'. In *Shakespeare Reread: The Texts in New Contexts*. Ed. Russ McDonald. Ithaca, NY: Cornell University Press, 1994, 147–69.

Wright, George T. 'The Silent Speech of Shakespeare's Sonnets'. In *Shakespeare's Sonnets: Critical Essays*. Ed. James Schiffer. New York: Garland, 1999, 136–58.

Wroth, Mary. *The Poems of Lady Mary Wroth*. Ed. Josephine A. Roberts. Baton Rouge and London: Louisiana State University Press, 1983.

Zandevoort, R. W. 'Putting Out the Light: Semantic Indeterminacy and the Deconstitution of Self in *Othello*'. *English Studies*, 75 (1994), 110–22.

Zitner, Sheldon P. *All's Well that Ends Well*. New York and London: Harvester Wheatsheaf, 1989.

Index

absence 139

accusation 136

action (*see also* speech acts) 69, 192; active female desire 74

address 61, 86, 99; circle of 62; circumstances of 61, 129, 199, 202, 205; directions of 206; embodied situations of 58; gap between addresser and addressee 65; proper address 79; theatrical 62

addressee 60, 143; embodiment of the 60, 86; gap between addresser an addressee 65

Adelman, Janet 127 n. 23

aesthetics: aesthetic appreciation 223

agency 73, 74, 75, 161, 173, 183, 188, 197, 204, 218, 239; female 203; of praise 173

agreement 44

Althusser, Louis 154 n. 5

Amoretti (*see* Spenser)

anachronism 104

androgyny 87, 97

anti-theatricality (*see* theatricality)

apology 133, 136

appropriation: dialogical 128

arbitrariness of signs 179

aristocratic patronage 12; and the player-poet 131; inequality 12, 33; negotiations between power and weakness 12; poetry as aristocratic pastime 64; transformation of terms of relationship 12; relationship between addressor and addressee 12; social relations of power 12

Astrophil and Stella 23, 26, 27, 38, 72, 74, 75, 76, 80; songs 75, *Song 4* 75, *Song 8* 75, *Song 11* 76; Sonnets, *sonnet 35* 80, *sonnet 45* 72, 178, *sonnet 47* 74, *sonnet 54* 75, *sonnet 63* 75, *sonnet 64* 75

audience 5, 7, 34, 47, 48, 55, 56, 60, 66, 69, 78, 81, 85, 132, 133, 135, 143, 144, 206, 207, 240; complexities of 129; dissemination 61; multiple 211; public audience 204

Austin, John 1, 2, 11, 15, 31 and n. 6, 32, 33, 50, 150, 203, 218, 222, 226 n. 15, 227, 238, 240, 242 and n. 3; *How To Do Things With Words* 2, 11, 31, 33; illocutionary force 11, 12; perlocutionary force 11, 12

authorisation 28, 45, 137; authorising power 44; politics of self-authorisation 33, 39, 42; self-authorising power 46, 50, 150, 238; self-authorising public show 48; self-proclaimed performative authority 40

autobiographical mode 4, 20, 21, 201, 240; deictic autobiographical references 25; internal logical evidence 21; sonnets as "pure" autobiography 25

Bakhtin 16 n. 27, 58, 72 n. 11, 76 and n. 15, 186 and n. 24, 242; 'event' of the utterance 76

Barber, C. L. 5, 30 and n. 2, 61 n. 6; 'An Essay on the Sonnets' 5

Barish, Jonas 118 and n. 15

Barker, Francis 102 and n. 3, 104, 118 n. 16

Barrell, John 216 n. 12

Barthes, Roland 17 and n. 31, 18, 27

beauty 46, 84, 213, 223; the ungendering of beauty 213

bed-trick 205, 225

being: inner 105; outer 105

beloved 120; aristocratic 131; beloved's proper name 156

Belsey, Catherine 102

Benson 25, 26, 27; 1640 edition 25

Berthould, Jacques 5, 146 n. 33; Introduction to *Titus Andronicus* 5, 6; dialogical interaction 5

betrayal 101

bi-fold authority 34, 35

biography 17, 87; biographical criticism 20, 28, 59; biographical scholarship 25; revulsion from 90

blackness 46

Blakemore Evans, G. 9, 184 and n. 21 and 22

blame 137

blazon 8, 47, 55, 74, 76, 79, 86, 95, 152, 172, 206
blood 86: noble 95
Boccaccio 198
body, the 171; emblazoned 36; idealised 178; materiality of 186; scattered 36; transcending the corporeality of the body 83
Booth, Stephen 4 and n. 9, 8 n. 16, 59 and n. 1, 80 n. 17
Bourdieu, Pierre 191 and n. 29, 242
Bradbrook, Muriel 198 n. 1
Bristol, Michael 16; *Print Manuscript and Performance* 16
Bruster, Douglas 3, 21 and n. 36; 'The Structural Transformation of Print in Late Elizabethan England' 3

carnivalesque, the 186
category mistake 44
Cavell, Stanley 193 n. 33, 195, 196, 197 n. 35
Chapman 1
chastity 186; female 186, 188
character 201; different possible personae 235
citation 42
Clarkson, Carrol 179 n. 18, 182, 183; *Naming and Personal Identity* 180; performative act of renaming 181
class 34, 121, 141, 158, 207, 212, 218, 219, 223; blood and class 84, 144, 186, 234; class aspirations of playwright 62, 133, 239; class rivalry 63; difference 135, 155, 198; inequalities 238; lowliness 134
closet: as most private, 'inward' room of aristocratic house 124
clothing 136
Cloud, Random 22 n. 37, 201 and n. 4
code 15; sings as coded entities 192
Colie, Rosalie 64 and n. 10
collage 26
comedy 236
common name 72, 151, 156, 179, 180, 183, 185, 186
common player 128, 156
communal speech 67
community 45, 61
concepts 110; concepts as signs 15; conceptual and ideal 161; conceptual distinction between inwardness and outwardness 109; of love 80; of private and public 107; performative concepts 219; pertaining to inwardness or interiority 108, 124; rule for concept 43, 169; the purely conceptual 109
constancy 141, 147, 163
constantive: acts 32; speech 52

contexts 89, 151; original context of address and reception 55, 238
corporeality of the referent 60
costume 133
courtly values 133
Cratylitic: desire 179; identity 29; match between word and object 30, 180
Crew, Jonathan 26 n. 43, 75 n. 14
critics: feminist 55; literary 61
criticism 137
Cultural Materialism 2
Cupid 135

Daniel 5
dark lady 7, 26, 54, 59, 87, 88, 89, 90, 167, 234, 236, 240; dark woman 46, 92, 140, 150, 176, 183, 224, 226, 229, 233
dark lord 26, 120, 123, 130, 138, 139, 167, 196
darkness 172, 188, 196; black 174, 188
Day, Angel 124 n. 20
death of the author 17, 27
declaration of love 127
definition 42, 175; definition poem 175; definitions rather than descriptions 44
de Grazia, Margareta 4 n. 9, 91 n. 27, 102 n. 1
deixis 152
Delia 23
Derrida, Jacques 2, 7, 42, 60, 116, 117, 141, 151, 152 and n. 3, 153, 154; *Acts of Literature* 151 n. 2; iterability 116; *Limited Inc* 2, 42 n. 11, 116 n. 13, 189 n. 25, 191 n. 30; presence 117; *Speech and Phenomena* 106 n. 8
description 10, 44
de Selincourt, E. 81 n. 20
desire 139, 170, 186, 221, 229; agency 73, 218; deferred 177; desire is death 99, 174; erotic 177, 199; female 74, 187, 222, 224; gendered 200; homosexual 225; in the sonnets 20; Lacanian 94; lust 174, 176; male 174, 205; object of 140, 185; sexual 223; thwarted 173
dialogue: dialogical appropriation 128; dialogical fusion of voices and desires 72; dialogue sonnets 162; interactive 53, 68, 147, 181, 235, 240
difference 83, 93, 95, 99, 116, 142, 158; between men and women 94, 236; between 'use' and 'mention' 189 n. 25; class and economic 65, 82, 84, 135, 138, 155, 195, 232; conceptual 217; generic 236; in the theatre 35; of rank, blood and social power 42, 83, 129, 157; of speech acts 51; represented by name 159, 160; sexual 94, 224
discourses 191; historical 15; indirect 75; Petrarchan 235; political 137; public 137; racist 182

discrepancy between language and sight 30
disembodiment 16, 85
disgrace 158
disillusionment 172, 176, 178; disparagement 219
dismemberment 74, 85
dissemination of poetry 91
display 133; public 133
distance: social and physical 138
distinction: between love and lust 187; between metaphysical and material anti-theatricality 115; between tragedy and farce 187
Donne, John 63, 73 n. 12
Doran, Madeleine 190 and n. 27
Drayton 5
dress 95
Dubrow, Heather 4 n. 9, 12 and n. 22, 25 and n. 42, 27, 30 n. 4, 38, 59, 60 n. 2, 167 n. 10, 232, 234; *Captive Victors* 38
Duncan-Jones, Katherine 17, 21, 23, 24 n. 40 and 41, 62, 133, 134 and n. 27; 'Shakespeares Sonnets' 21
duty 133, 134, 135, 137, 145; love-as-duty 137, 194, 242; public duty 141

Egyptian crocodile 36
Elam, Keir 1; *Shakespeare's Universe of Discourse: Language Games in the Comedies 1*
Elizabethan sonnet 65; as form of social action 65; public and embodied medium 65
eloquence: and impotence 83
emblazonment (*see also* blazon) 172
embodiment 60, 67, 74, 75, 78, 79, 80, 85, 86, 87, 88, 89, 91, 95, 96, 100, 102, 240; embodied action 77; embodied androgyny 97; embodied characters 2; embodied response 76; embodied texts 3, 166; embodiment and address 6, 91, 198, 238; embodiment inescapable in the theatre 17, 169, 170, 241; necessary embodiment 64; of sonnet's voice via the plays 105; theatrical 62, 98
energeia 121
Engle, Lars 30 and n. 3, 33, 150 and n. 1, 162 n. 7, 211 n. 11, 214
epideixis 7, 29, 36, 76, 80, 81
epistemological correspondence between word and object 29
epithet 179
essence 170, 171
erotic, the 137
eternal 'no' 76
Everett, Barbara 179 n. 17
example 171
exchange: erotic and economic 86

fair 174; fairness 188; whiteness 188
fair friend 8, 59, 139. 166–167, 176; identities 59
falsehood 70, 178
farce 185
female: agency 203; desire 74, 202, 224; sexuality 195, 200, 224; subjectivity 224
feminism 91
feminist critics 55, 103; feminist criticism 74, 238
Feinberg, Nona 54, 55 n. 22, 87
Ferry, Ann 4 n. 9, 60 and n. 2, 102 and n. 2, 104, 109, 110, 111, 116
fiction 49; fictional world 72; fictions 57, 91; transcendence of fact and fiction 49
Fineman, Joel 4 and n. 9, 29 and n. 1, 30, 60 and n. 3, 80, 87, 93, 94, 95, 141; *Shakespeare's Perjured Eye: The Invention of Poetic Subjectivity in The Sonnets* 7, 30
First Folio 200
Fish, Stanley 32 and n. 7, 39
Fleissner, Robert F. 179 n. 16
forgiveness 137
formalism 16, 20, 61; formalist criticism 62, 239; formalist disembodiment of poetry 16, 63; formalist ideas of lyric 130
forms of life 91
Foucault, Michel 17 and n. 31, 18, 19, 239
Fumerton, Patricia 124 n. 19

gay studies 91
gaze 213; perjorative 207; public 130
gender 155, 218, 223, 236, 237; gendered asymmetry of speech acts 222; gendered desire 200; gendered speech position 165; gendered subject positions 176; identity 223; performance of gender 233; ungendering of beauty 213
genre 14; normativity 14
Gerhard, John 9; *The Herbal* 9
Girouard, Robert 124 n. 19
Glock, Hans-Johann 91 n. 29
grammar: in the Wittgensteinian sense 91; the grammatical 59
Grazia, Margareta de 102
Greenblatt, Stephen 11 n. 21, 52 and n. 19
Greene, Thomas M. 40 n. 10, 44
Greville 6
Gross, Kenneth 191 and n. 28, 192

Hamer, Mary 54 n. 20
Helen 225
hierarchy (*see also* class) 232; hierarchical relationship 241
historicism 15, 107

historicist criticism 103, 130, 238, 241; historicising criticism 14, 239
history: of ideas 107; of subjectivity 107; of the representation of subjectivity 107
histrionics 126, 127. 148
Holofernes 62
homoerotic desire 19
homosexuality 99, 223; homosexual fantasies 194, 225
homosocial: fantasies 194; rivalry 99
honour 158, 219
Howard, Jean E. 92 n. 31, 136 n. 29
Hulse, Clark 80 n. 18
Hunter, G. K., 'The Dramatic Technique of Shakespeare's Sonnets' 4 n. 9
husband 204, 226
Husserl, Edmund 139 n. 30
Hutson, Lorna 88, 97

identity 180, 189, 200; confused 99; fair friend 59; gendered 223; names 189; of form 51; social 192
idealisation 74, 169, 170, 175, 236; counter-ideal 169, 170; idealised body 178; the conceptual and ideal 161, 169, 171, 173, 176, 196
ideological structures 15
illocutionary act 11, 12, 32, 38, 50, 52, 83, 203, 218, 227; discrepancy of illocutionary force 51; illocutionary effects 228; illocutionary force 11, 12, 13, 238; necessary logic of 12; unspoken 218
image of young man 139
imago 7, 9
imperative mood 11
inadequacy of words to their objects 80
inequality of social class and rank 95
indicative mood 11
indirect discourse 75; free indirect speech 213
independence 209; declaration of 210
inequality 12, 123; inequalities of power 123
infamia 190
the inexpressible 116; inexpressible inwardness 120; unknowable and inexpressible 'inside' 117
informer 144, 145
inner: feeling 108; speech 105; state 108
Innes 17 n. 30
instance 169, 171, 176
interactivity 13; interaction 68, 201; interaction and response 15; interactive dialogue 53, 60, 68, 147, 181, 239, 240
interiority 13, 17, 110, 114, 115, 118, 122, 124, 134, 138, 241; as inextricably imbricated in theatricality 110, 146; Elizabethan concept of interiority 13; material interiority 124; modern 109, 130; of love 135; properly female 103; unrepresentable interiority 123, 124
invention 163; fresh invention 165
inwardness 103, 105, 106, 108, 109, 112, 113, 119; and language games 117; as problem of other minds 105; being at odds with society 117; early modern inwardness 104; inexpressible inwardness 120
iterability 116; iteration 156, 163, 166, 170, 171

Jardine, Lisa 189, 190 n. 26
Jehovian tautology 210
Jonson 1

Kahane, Henry and Renée 179 n. 16
Kamps, Ivo 103 n. 6
Kernan, Alvin 128 n. 24, 146 n. 32
Kerrigan, John 9; *The Sonnets and A Lover's Complaint* 9 n. 17
Kesler, R. L. 84 n. 23, 85
Kripke, Saul 18, 23 and n. 38, 24, 153 and n. 4, 167, 168 n. 11; proper names as rigid designators 23

Lacan, Jacques 7, 60, 94
language 109, 118, 125, 175, 176; as a form of action 10; as a code 239; as performative medium of sexual exchange 225; as unreliable 216; consensual linguistic practice 150; early modern view of the identity of language and the world 216; games 91, 107, 113, 117, 124, 147, 148, 170, 239, 241; inadequacy of words to their objects 80; inward/of interiority 60, 106, 109; in use 31, 111; linguistic action 15; linguistic rule 169; of the self 60; Petrarchan 235
Lanyer, Emilia 88, 89, 90, 188
Latham, Agnes 51 and n. 17
Lees, F. N. 179 n. 16
Levenson, Jill 64 and n. 8, 66
literary critic 61
logical necessity 23
love 97, 101, 111, 114, 128, 137, 156, 164, 185, 203, 209, 217, 221, 222, 229, 232, 233, 234; ambitious 204, 205; and duty 113, 134, 135, 137, 145, 194, 242; and language games 113; as inexpressible and private 111; as war 162; concept of 80; constancy of 141; consuming and negating 100; cruel love 99, 196; declaration of 127, 133; familial 203; forced 221; Hamlet's for Ophelia 128; idealised 95; of the player-poet 96; romantic 231; self-love

211, 213; self-sacrificial 222; 'silent loue' 136;
 triangle 194, 195; unrequited 158
lying 57; falsehood 69
Lyotard, Jean-François 23 n. 39
lyric 13, 14, 16, 5, 110; formalist ideas of 130;
 sonnet as lyric 66; speaker 241; surrounding
 social circumstances 16

Macey, Samuel L. 179 n. 16
madness 174, 175
Magnusson, Lynne 2, 109 n. 12, 191 n. 31, 192,
 204 n. 7, 241; *Shakespeare and Social Dialogue:
 Dramatic Language and Elizabethan Letters* 1–2,
 241, 242
Maitland, F. W. 51 n. 18, 52
male: admiration 224; desire 95, 205,
 224
Malone 25, 27
Malone/Steevens debate 20
manuscript circulation 129
materialism 238, 239
Marotti, Arthur 16 and n. 28, 63 and n. 7, 76,
 129 and n. 25, 207; manuscript circulation
 129; *Print Manuscript and Performance* 16
Masten, Jeffrey 118 n. 16
Matz, Robert 194 n. 34
Maus, Katherine Eisaman 102, 103 n. 4, 104,
 105, 106, 107, 109 n. 11, 116; the problem of
 other minds 117
marriage 195, 203, 221, 222; ceremony 50, 54,
 193; companionate 222; consummation of
 222; *per verba de praesenti* 51; self-initiating,
 self-authorising performative 50, 221;
 unconsummated 218
Marston 1
materialist criticism 103, 130, 133; material
 anti-theatricality 115, 117; material privacy
 138
May, Stephen 16 and n. 29
McCandless 233 n. 17, 236
McLeod, Randall 225
meaning 175; and names 179, 180; projected
 188
Melchiori 4 n. 9, 5; *Shakespeare's Dramatic
 Meditations* 5
Meres, Francis 16, 62, 129
metaphysical: anti-theatricality 115, 117, 141;
 privacy 138
Miller, Naomi 201 n. 5
mimesis 107, 142
mimicry 85, 214
mirror (*see also* reflection) 213; mirroring 214;
 mirroring of self through others 214;
 performative mirror 223
misogyny 187, 193, 224, 225

modern: formalist disembodiment of poetry
 16; interiority 109, 115, 130
Montaigne, Michel 201, 202 n. 6
moral 137; right 135, 136
muteness 76; on stage 92
mutuality 73, 74, 132, 133, 138, 140; 'mutuall
 render' 128

names 157, 159, 161, 165, 170, 176, 179, 180,
 204, 216; as a network of relationships 72; as
 rigid designators 161, 168, 179, 181; as web of
 irreducible social relations 151, 154; bearer
 and name 153, 179; divided self 182; good
 name 192, 193; 'inhumanity' of name 153; in
 Othello 178; name of the father 71; names and
 love 217; names and things 214, 216, 217,
 218, 219, 220, 222; performative power of
 names and naming events 149, 180, 181,
 182, 189, 197, 198, 240; wife in name only
 203
Nature 45, 224, 225
Neill, Michael 180 n. 19, 181 n. 20
Nelson, William 13 n. 23
New Criticism 59
New Historicism 2, 133
noble blood 95

objects: ideal matching of word and object 148;
 in the world 43; of desire 140, 185
Ophelia: allowed no language for an interior
 self 125; denied privacy 124
Orgel, Stephen 92 n. 31, 225 and n. 14
ornament 29, 31, 35, 37, 44, 117
otherness 88
outwardness 109, 119; outward show 116

pain 108
Pamphilia to Amphilanthus 23
paradigm 42, 43, 45, 48, 49, 169, 170; new
 paradigms 45; of names 165, 168; of truth
 163; paradigmatic definition 44; paradigms
 and standards 43
parentage 95, 155
Parker, David 4 n. 9, 10, 11 n. 20
Paroles 200; as Shakespeare 207; Paroles's
 sonnet 206, 207
The Passionate Pilgrim 61, 62
patriarchal expectations of female chastity 188
patronage 40
patrons 34, 42, 82
Pequigny, Joseph 3 n. 7, 4 n. 9, 20 and n. 35,
 21, 223 n. 13; bisexual character of sonnets
 20; 'Shakespeares Sonnets' 21; *Such Is My
 Love: A Study of Shakespeare's Sonnets* 3, 20
performance 121, 123; public 103

performative language 1, 4, 10, 12, 26, 29, 31,
42, 45, 52, 60, 117, 179, 182, 198, 209, 218,
241; non-linguistic performatives 218;
performative agency 204; performative as
love 221; performative aspects of prayer 104;
performative concepts 219, 239;
performative discourse 169, 200;
performative effects of rhetoric 32, 35;
performative mirror 223; performative
power 38, 44, 48, 149, 197, 239;
performatives 49, 50, 51, 54, 57, 70, 83, 106,
111, 112, 128, 137, 148, 150, 161, 166, 189,
194, 195, 203, 205, 214, 215, 221, 222, 225,
236; performative vs. constative 10;
philosophy of speech acts 7; politics of
self-authorisation 12; publicly available logic
of the performative 12, 145; quasi-fictitious
performatives 52; quasi-performatives 33,
37, 38, 41, 57, 132; self-authorising
performative 38, 45
perlocution 11, 12, 32; contingent force of 12;
perlocutionary acts 228; perlocutionary
effects of a statement or description 32,
172; perlocutionary force 11, 12, 37, 57
personal (*see also* privacy) 218
personal relations 147, 148
Petrarchan 155, 158, 159, 162, 164, 170, 172,
176, 183, 203, 231, 236; anti-Petrarchan
thought 176; beloved 84, 157, 177; blazon 8,
47; comparison 163; deigesis 142; discourse
160, 186, 235; love 77, 81; poet 165; Petrarch
69, 231; mode 65, 79, 81, 129; oxymoron 64;
sonnets (*Sonnets 127–52*) 185; stereotypes 73;
theatricality 127; tradition 7, 12, 46, 57, 64,
66, 67, 68, 73, 74, 76, 85, 86, 99, 135; verse
92
phenomenological reduction 14, 139
Pirkhoffer, Anton M. 4 n. 9
Plato: platonic readings 45, 141, 142, 169, 223,
225
player 118, 121, 122; common 128, 156;
precarious social position of 34; the players
118, 120
player-poet 5, 22, 33, 87, 96, 112, 113, 120, 126,
128, 131, 134, 137, 156, 165, 183, 188, 196,
199, 203, 204, 209, 212, 222, 224, 225, 227,
234, 238; anti-theatricality of 127; distance
between player-poet and aristocratic
beloved 131, 239; Helen as player-poet 222;
Iago as a fantasy image of player-poet 193;
man of the theatre 128; resembling Bertram
200; subjectivity of 195
poem as mirror 212
poet: Petrarchan 162, 165
poetics: of blame 136; of 'true vision' 29

poetic: speech 214; subject 59; subjectivity 4, 7,
60, 91, 110
poetry 30, 31; and theatre 130; as force and
action 30; as form of social action 31; private
space of 141; theatricality of 142
political, the 12, 137; political inscriptions of
love 135; political agency 131; politics 120;
politics of gender and class 198; politics of
self-authorisation 33; political structure 232;
world 147; vicissitudes 131
Pollock, F. 51 and n. 18
Pope, Alexander 22, 68
Popper, Karl 141 n. 31
popular songs and ballads 125
portraiture 8
possible worlds 153, 166, 167, 168
poststructuralism 59
power 137, 218, 221; asymmetry of power
between men and women 205; of a King to
enforce 'love' 221; of language 11; of the
spectator 56, 81; of the women to break
sonnet against their bodies 77; silence as
source of power 35; social 81
power relations 29, 91, 135, 142, 179, 181, 204;
authorising power 44; re-negotiation of 84;
unequal power relations 37, 123–124
praise 30, 35, 42, 43, 47, 77, 84, 114, 140, 170;
agency of 173; the exorbitant power of 47
Pratt, Mary Louise, *Towards a Speech-Act Theory
of Literary Discourse* 1
presence 117, 139
primary model of language 11, 124
privacy 13, 102, 103, 114, 126, 126, 132, 142,
148, 151, 161, 187, 190, 191, 241; is not
reducible, as a concept, to the public 118; of
the written page 14; division of private from
public 66, 130, 147; metaphysical and
material privacy 138; personal space of
'mutuall render' 144; private and public
distinguished by differences in language
games 113; private language 106, 117; private
modern interiority 130; private muteness 35;
private or interior discourses 16, 42, 48;
private sphere 83, 107, 115, 141, 159, 209; the
value of the personal 147; solitary reading
14, 129, 141
profit 144
projections 230, 231, 232; imaginative
projection as a positive process 232
promises 52, 53, 227, 228
pronouns 72; in the sonnets 19, 27
proper address 79
proper names 1, 4, 8, 18, 19, 20, 21, 22, 23, 24,
72, 82, 86, 151, 152, 154–6, 158, 160, 161,
167, 169, 179–81, 183–6, 188, 198, 214, 240;

absence of names in sonnets 21, 24, 25, 201; author's name 21; description theory of proper names 18; fictional texts 23; grammatical and logical roles of 18; indispensability of 23; in Shakespeare's sonnets 19, 20, 21–5; of an author 18, 19; 'Othello' 181; persona's name 21; presence of names in sonnets 21; rigidity of 153, 154, 167, 168, 179, 185, 187; 'Shakespeare' as a proper name 18, 19, 21; the nature of the name 22

public 12, 13, 14, 67, 107, 110, 112, 114, 126, 142, 151, 161, 190, 191, 241; affiliations 159; and private distinguished by differences in language games 113; attention 145; audience 204; declarations of love 42, 133, 202; discourses 125, 137; display 133, 134; division of private from public 66, 118, 145, 147; duty 141; eloquence 132; gaze 130; life 103, 143; occasion 114, 207; performance 103; performatives 111, 145; pressures 132, 209; publicly accessible standards of behaviour 54, 133; space 42, 115, 144; space of aristocratic audience 35; speech 14, 66; staging 48

pure deixis 24

Puttenham, George 10, 30 and n. 5, 31, 121; *The Arte of English Poesie* 10

Quarto, 1609 20

quasi-performative, the (*see* performative)

racism 182

rank 132

Ramsey, Paul 6 n. 13

Rea, John 179 n. 17

reciprocity 35, 65, 66, 67, 68, 72, 73, 74, 143, 144, 145, 146, 147, 156, 158, 159, 160, 183, 186, 187, 210, 214, 226, 235; of lies 226; of shared unfaithfulness and mutual acceptance 234; reciprocated love 136, 203; reciprocating sonnets 69; reciprocity of kisses 71

reception 99

referent 80, 153; corporeality of the 60; embodied 100

reflection 213; reflected self 213

reiteration 172; reiterated scattering 76

repetition 156, 158, 163, 184; of the proper name 184

representation 116, 126; anxiety of 34; authority of 34; limits and precariousness of 34; re-representation 118

restitutio 190

revulsion 170; from representation 116

rhetoric 10, 30, 32, 37, 112; of erotic persuasion 155; performative rhetoric 35; persuasive rhetoric 11

right: to love and be loved 137; to accuse 137

rivalry 128; homosocial 99; rival poetry 114; with unknown poet 35, 141

romance: romantic and companionate union 80

Rose, Jacqueline 127 n. 23

routes of circulation 211

Rowse, A. L. 88 and n. 25, 89, 90 and n. 26, 166 and n. 9, 188, 240

rules for the use of words 43, 45; defining rules 170

Ryle, Gilbert 44 and n. 14

sample 169, 170; Saussure 7, 192; post-Saussurean theory of language 239; semiotics 192

scepticism: the sceptical disposition (Wittgenstein) 123

Schalkwyk, David 15 n. 26, 43 n. 13, 50 n. 16, 92 n. 30, 230 n. 16

Schiffer 4 n. 8, 7

Schoenbaum, Samuel 88 and n. 24

Searle, John R. 2, 18 and n. 32, 150, 168 n. 11, 189 and n. 25, 242 n. 3; 'Reiterating the Differences: A Reply to Derrida' 2

self 149, 182, 213, 235; authentic or real 102, 110, 111; dispersal of 201; divided 182; interior 102; love 211, 213; reflected 213, 214

self-authorisation (*see* authorisation)

semiotics 192; Saussurean 192

sense 153

sexuality 200; female 195, 200, 224; sexual desire 223; sexual difference 224

Shakespeare, William: plays: *All's Well that Ends Well* 3, 87, 92, 197, 198, 199, 200, 201, 202, 205, 228, 233, 236, *A Midsummer Night's Dream* 8, 83, 119, 186, *Antony and Cleopatra* 2, 33, 35, 38, 47, 49, 54, 58, 89, 150, 170, 205, *As You Like It* 2, 33, 50, 52, 58, 150, 224, *Coriolanus* 39, *Hamlet* 2, 102, 104, 108, 109, 114, 115, 117, 118, 125, 127, 129, 130, 134, 136, 146, 148, 151, 241, *Henry V* 83, 92, *Henry VI* 123, *Julius Caesar* 211, *King Lear* 2–3, 51, 111, 124, 146, 147, 148, 151, 241, *Love's Labour's Lost* 2, 8, 41, 53, 58, 60, 61, 62, 76, 77–9, 84, 86, 87, 89, 92, 94, 97, 99, 115, 130, 207, *Measure for Measure* 175 n. 15, 218, 226, *Much Ado About Nothing* 8, 69, 135, 136, 206 n. 9, 220, 221, 222, *Othello* 3, 52, 89, 151, 160, 169, 178, 179, 180, 181, 183, 185, 188, 189, 191, 193, 198, *Richard II* 221, *Romeo and Juliet* 3, 22, 23, 24, 58, 60, 64, 67, 71–3, 151, 152,

Shakespeare, William: (*cont.*)
153, 159, 160, 161, 167, 174, 177, 185 and n.
23, 196, 198, 209, *The Taming of the Shrew* 136,
The Two Gentlemen of Verona 8, *The Winter's Tale*
200, *Troilus and Cressida* 3, 8, 22, 23, 24, 53,
60, 69, 79, 151, 161, 165, 166, 168, 169, 170,
173, 174, 175, 180, 198, *Twelfth Night* 2, 58,
84–5, 92, 93, 94, 96, 98–101, 130, 139, 155,
173 and n. 14, 196, 206, 224; Shakespearean
comedy 99; 'SHAKE-SPEARES SONNETS'
22, 23, 24, title as proper name or
description? 24, lack of proper names 24;
sonnets: 130, *sonnet 1* 187, *sonnet 2* 187, *sonnet
3* 187, 212, 214, 223, *sonnet 4* 187, *sonnet 5*
187, *sonnet 6* 187, *sonnet 7* 187, *sonnet 8* 187,
sonnet 9 187, *sonnet 10* 187, *sonnet 11* 187, *sonnet
12* 187, *sonnet 13* 187, *sonnet 14* 187, *sonnet 15*
165, 166, 187, *sonnet 16* 5, 134, 187, *sonnet 17*
10, 187, *sonnet 18* 10, *sonnet 19* 41, *sonnet 20* 44,
92, 94, 98, 99, 223, 224, 225, *sonnet 21* 10,
36, 37, 40, 41, *sonnet 23* 14, 34, 35, 36, 42,
55, 56, 81–82, 84, 101, 112, 114, 128, 129,
130, 133, 134, 136, 141, 142, 143, 209, *sonnet
24* 9, 138, 139, 142, *sonnet 25* 131, 132, 133,
136, 138, *sonnet 26* 132, 133, 134, 136, 139,
144, *sonnet 27* 9, 139, *sonnet 29* 158, 216, *sonnet
30* 139, *sonnet 31* 139, *sonnet 32* 141, *sonnet 33*
97, 232, *sonnet 34* 129, 235, *sonnet 36* 152, 157
and n. 6, 208, *sonnet 37* 9, 98, 99, 139, 146,
sonnet 39 140, *sonnet 40* 212, 229, *sonnet 41*
203, *sonnet 42* 9, *sonnet 43* 139, *sonnet 44* 139,
140, 145, 216, *sonnet 46* 138, *sonnet 47* 9, 139,
sonnet 53 9, 139, *sonnet 55* 167, *sonnet 57* 99,
134, *sonnet 58* 99, 134, 135, 136, 137, 241,
sonnet 61 9, 120, 231, *sonnet 62* 211, 212 *sonnet
63* 41, 213 *sonnet 66* 227, *sonnet 67* 120, *sonnet
68* 45, *sonnet 69* 137, 220 *sonnet 71* 99, 157,
sonnet 72 22, 99, 146, 152, 157, 158, *sonnet 73*
98, *sonnet 76* 21, 22, 44, 86, 97, 141, 163,
sonnet 79 10, 41, 44, *sonnet 81* 41, *sonnet 82* 10,
sonnet 83 10, 26, 152, *sonnet 84* 10, 36, 41, 42,
211, 217, *sonnet 85* 10, 42, 113 *sonnet 86* 47,
sonnet 87 99, 208, 210, *sonnet 88* 99, 227, 228,
sonnet 89 83, 99, 158, *sonnet 90* 99, *sonnet 91*
99, *sonnet 92* 99, 142, *sonnet 93* 55, 56, 57,
142, 231, *sonnet 94* 56, 142, 220, *sonnet 96*
208, 209, *sonnet 98* 9, *sonnet 99* 8, *sonnet 105*
44, 95, 120, 141, 156, 158, 163, *sonnet 108* 68,
155, 200, *sonnet 109* 26, 234, *sonnet 110* 212,
234, *sonnet 111* 152, 158, 160, 212, 234, *sonnet
112* 209, 210, 234, *sonnet 113* 231, 232, *sonnet
114* 96, 231, 232, *sonnet 115* 163, 165, 166,
168, *sonnet 116* 33, 57, *sonnet 117* 234, *sonnet
118* 234, *sonnet 119* 234, *sonnet 120* 96, 234,
235, *sonnet 121* 45, 208, 209, 210, *sonnet 123*
165, *sonnet 124* 95, *sonnet 125* 45, 46, 120, 129,
141, 146, 193, *sonnet 126* 177, 200, 211, *sonnet
127* 45, 97, 217, *sonnet 128* 67, *sonnet 129* 47,
87, 171, 174, 175, 187, 236, *sonnet 130* 8, 9,
78, 85, *sonnet 131* 46, 185, 233, 234, *sonnet
132* 46, 234, *sonnet 135* 183, 185, 186, 187,
sonnet 136 183, 185, 186, 187, *sonnet 137* 56,
186, 195, *sonnet 138* 38, 54, 55, 56, 57, 166,
226, 228, 229, 233, 235, 236, *sonnet 139* 234,
sonnet 140 234, 236, *sonnet 141* 234, *sonnet 142*
233, *sonnet 144* 8, 101, 165, 176, 195, *sonnet
147* 47, 99, 171, 173, 196, *sonnet 148* 196, 234,
sonnet 149 233, 234, *sonnet 150* 229, 236,
sonnet 152 165, 227, as extended apology 133,
136, as public documents 143, 207, 240,
audience of sonnets 240, autobiography in
sonnets 25, 201, 240, bisexual character of
sonnets 20, desire in the sonnets 20,
dialogue sonnet 162, contexts of sonnets 63,
embodiment of sonnets 241, epistolary
sonnets 132, 202, multiple subject positions
in sonnets 233, non-fictional nature of
sonnets 24, performative language of
sonnets (*see* performatives) 241, proper
names in sonnets (*see* proper names) 24, 25,
recirculation of sonnets 207, representations
of the sonnets in Shakespeare's plays 16,
scandalous problem 28, social action in
sonnet form 199, 211, situation of address 5,
sonnets in plays 202, 205, sonnets in printed
anthologies 16, sonnets on absence 138, title
of sonnets 21, 24; the man 20, 24; the man
of the theatre 22; the writer 24
shame 157, 211, 214; shaming 212
shifters 24
Sidney, Philip 5, 6, 45, 68, 72, 74, 75, 76, 80,
87, 102, 109, 120 n. 17, 121 and n. 18, 129,
135
signifier: transcendental 236
signs: coded entities 192; arbitrariness of 179
silence (*see also* muteness) 42, 57, 74, 75, 82, 87,
91, 92, 96, 100, 112, 117, 118, 128, 136, 240;
enforced 97; female 73; of the beloved 56; of
the spectator and the written word 82;
silencing of the woman 54, 91, 170; silencing
of the young man 55; silent interiority 114;
silent love 136; silent speech or words 17, 96,
129, 140; silent thoughts 114; wonder and be
silent – Antonio 101
similitude 29, 31, 36, 40, 57; as a match
between a word and object 31; denigration
of 37; similarities 225
Sipahigli, T. 179 n. 16
situation of address 5, 77, 78
slander 191

slavery 134
Smith, Bruce R. 19 and n. 33, 27; homoerotic desire 19
Smith, J. C. 81 n. 20
Snow, Edward A. 54, 55 n. 21, 57
Snyder, Susan 198, 199 and n. 2, 201 n. 4, 236
social: action 28, 29, 60, 62, 64, 78, 85, 89, 130, 199, 242; ambition 212; context 14; class and rank 95, 134, 135, 137, 155, 193, 200, 222; contamination 158; criticism 62; difference 157, 186, 195; distance 120, 138; force 42; inadequacy 83, 203; identity 192; love as liminal social condition 135; network 160, 185, 240; practices 91, 189; private as social 130; private discourses informed by social world 16; relations of power 12, 81, 156, 158, 185; relationships and conflicts 76, 180, 188, 198, 210; self as social product 104; specification and circumstance 15
sodomy 20
solitary: mind 60, 241; speech 65, 130
songs 75; from *Astroplil and Stella* 75
spacing 42; intimate space of writing 134
speech: communal speech 67; indirect 189, 213; inner speech 106, 109, 110; poetic 214; position 165; solitary speech 105, 130; sounded, public or theatrical (outer) 106, 109
speech acts 15, 107, 111, 151, 191, 192, 213, 221, 222, 239; descriptive 238; modalities of different speech acts 176; performative 238; pretend 242; speech as action 53; unsounded 105; vow 70
speech genres 239
Spenser 5, 81, 82; *Amoretti* 81; *sonnet 54* 81
Spencer, T. J. B. 170 n. 12
Spiller, Michael 91 n. 28
Stallybrass, Peter 4 n. 9, 20, 225
standard 169
Stevens, John 78 n. 16
Stewart, Alan 124 n. 19
style 141
structuralism 15
subject: female subject of poetic description 36; poetic 59; positions 97, 198, 200, 240
subjectivity 59, 103, 107, 185, 195, 241; effect 95; poetic 60, 110; the availability of human subjectivity 108
substitution 79, 80, 85, 100, 152, 178, 181, 189; of names 183
Sumptuary Laws 133; sumptuary exhibition 134
Surrey 6
swearing 71
syntax 15

Targoff, Ramie 103 and n. 5, 104, 123, 124
tautology 10, 36, 40, 42, 43, 45, 167, 185; Jehovian 210; 'you are you' 41
Tennenhouse, Leonard 95 n. 32
textuality 91
the textual 79
theatre 89, 99, 110, 168, 171; audience 69, 78 (*see also* 'audience'); material space of the 60, 199; necessary embodiment in theatre 63–4, 96; poetry and theatre 130; situation of address and reception 77
theatricality 83, 102, 103, 110, 115, 119, 121, 127, 140, 141, 146, 168; anti-theatricality 115, 117, 118, 127, 128, 132, 141, 145; as a set of social conditions, actions and techniques 119; of poetry 142; theatrical condition to writing 141; theatrical display of costume 133; theatrical embodiment 169, 170; theatrical mode of the sonnets 60; theatrical power 204; theatrical practice 119; theatrical representation 116
theory 15, 107, 111, 124, 216, 233; of inwardness and theatricality 119; post-Saussurean 239
thought 157, 216
Tilyard, E. M. W. 198 n. 1
time 163, 164, 165; analysis of 165; necessity of change over time 166
tragedy 6, 180
transcendence 49, 133; of classical oppositions 49; of corporeality of the body 83; transcendental signifier 236
transformation 54, 198, 205, 218, 220, 221, 224, 225; by a performative speech act 31, 48, 49, 51, 226; of the terms of relationship 12, 203; of a situation 12; of status 222
transformative: act 217; magic of speech 52, 53; power 12, 52, 203
triangular situations 224
truth 42, 49, 54, 88, 118, 134, 142, 150, 162, 164, 165, 168, 173, 175, 227, 236; claim to truthfulness 166; dilemma between flattery and truth 45; of history 47; Troilus as paradigm of truth 163, 176

unequal political and social relationship 12
union: romantic and companionate 80
the unknowable 107, 112; unknowable and inexpressible 'inside' 117
utterance 2, 15, 239

values 163; courtly 133; value 175
vassalage 134
Vendler, Helen 4 n. 9, 13 and n. 24, 14 and n. 25, 15, 59, 60 and n. 4, 66, 130, 133, 134, 136, 139, 174, 214, 241; *The Art of Shakespeare's*

Vendler, Helen (cont.)
  Sonnets 130 n. 26, 135 n. 28, 174; epistolary sonnets 132; generic difference between lyric and other genres 13; novel and drama 13; phenomenological reduction 14; social matrix 13; solitary reading consciousness 14; socially shaped consciousness 14
Vickers, Nancy 74 and n. 13, 76
violence 222
virtue 219
voice 14, 69
Voloshinov, V. N. 106 n. 8, 239 n. 1
vow 226, 227; as speech act 70; swearing 71, 227
vulnerability: and inadequacy 82; of Petrarchan lover 81; of the player 81

Warren, Roger 198 n. 1
Weimann, Robert 3, 34 and n. 9, 81 and n. 19, 116 n. 14, 168; *Authority and Representation in Early Modern Discourse* 3
Wheeler, Richard 199 and n. 3, 207
whiteness 188
Whittier, Gayle 64 n. 9, 65, 68, 69
whore 188, 189, 228
wife 204, 217, 221, 226; confirmed 225; in name only 203
Will 158, 167, 183, 185, 186
will 184
Wilson, Katherine M. 239 n. 2

Wilson, Thomas 10; *Art of Rhetoric* 10 116;
Wilson Knight, G. 198 and n. 1
Wittgenstein, Ludwig 1, 2, 11, 15, 17, 43, 108 and n. 9 and 10, 110, 117, 121, 123, 124, 151, 238, 240, 242; beetle in the box 108, 109, 116; explanation of a meaning of a word is its use in a sentence in a play 109; forms of life 107; grammar 91, 240; language games 11; *On Certainty* 170 n. 13; *Philosophical Investigations* 2, 43 n. 12, 123; the meaning of words lies in their use 15; *Tractatus Logico-Philosophicus* 101 n. 33
Wofford, Susanne 50 and n. 15, 84 n. 22
words: as essentially inner things 121; ideal matching of word and object 148
Wright, George T. 105 and n. 7, 106, 214
writing 83, 114, 140; the intimate space of 134
Wroth, Mary 126; *The Poems of Lady Mary Wroth* 126 n. 22
Wyatt, Thomas 102, 129

young man 26, 43, 55, 56, 87, 92, 121, 150, 166, 211, 234, 240; as mirror 213; described as standard 43; young aristocrat 224; young man's social position 137, 138; self-absorption in the first seventeen sonnets 211

Zandevoort, R. W. 192 and n. 32

Printed in the United Kingdom
by Lightning Source UK Ltd.
124836UK00001BA/209/A